There's a business school for everyone—meet yours!

The world's top business schools are coming to a free GMAC Tours event in a city near you. Connect in-person with admissions decision-makers or through virtual 1:1 meetings. Meeting representatives is crucial to your application; don't miss out!

Find an event near you

mba.com/gmactours

Your best GMAT score is still ahead

Think your score can't improve? Think again.

Data shows retaking the GMAT exam can increase your score by **20-30 points**. Don't settle for your first attempt and give yourself the best chance at business school success — the second time's a charm!

Take the GMAT again

mba.com/gmat

Learn the skills you need to succeed in your program

GMAC Business Fundamentals is designed to give you the confidence and fundamental quantitative knowledge you need to start business school.

Learn at Your Own Pace

Access a variety of resources including videos, quizzes, and practical exercises.

Showcase Your Learning

Earn digital badges that highlight your skills and achievements.

Master Core Concepts

Gain a solid foundation in Statistics, Accounting, and Finance, ensuring you're ready to excel from day one.

> "I am very grateful that I took the Business Fundamentals courses. My classmates who didn't are struggling in classes where **I feel confident.**"
>
> — **MBA Candidate, Portland State University**

> "The courses provided exactly what I was looking for. The instructors were great, the content was well delivered, and I now **feel back-to-school ready.**"
>
> — **MBA Candidate, Emory University**

Start business school off right

mba.com/businessfundamentals

Power up your prep with Official Practice Exams!

Research shows that first-time GMAT test takers can **increase their scores by up to 75 points** after taking all Official Practice Exams!

Full-length, adaptive GMAT practice exams that simulate the real test-taking experience

Scaled section scores and a total score that aligns to the actual test

Detailed score performance report, including time management

Get started with GMAT Official Practice Exams

mba.com/gmatprep

Want to get noticed by top business schools?

GradSelect is your connection to more than 500 global business and management programs that are looking for the best candidate — YOU. Plus, receive exclusive information on school programs, financial aid, and scholarships.

Why connect with schools through GradSelect?

GradSelect is part of the Graduate Management Admission Council (GMAC), a global mission-driven organization of top business schools.

Through GradSelect, you can receive exclusive information on school programs, financial aid, and scholarships.

You can quickly connect with the world's leading schools and discover new opportunities you may not have been familiar with.

It's free to use!

Join GradSelect

mba.com/gradselect

GMAC GMAT Exam

GMAT Exam
Official Guide Verbal Review 2026-2027

From the makers of the GMAT Exam

The only Verbal Reasoning guide with real GMAT Exam questions

More than 275 practice questions with detailed answer explanations

Sharpen reading and reasoning skills with digital flashcards, games, and a customizable question bank

Get exclusive strategies and insights straight from the exam creators

INCLUDES newly released GMAT Exam questions

GMAT™ Official Guide Verbal Review 2026–2027

Library of Congress Cataloging-in-Publication Data:
ISBN 978-1-394-41267-9 (pbk); ISBN 978-1-394-41268-6 (ePub)

Cover Design: GMAC
Cover Icons: Phosphor Icons

SKY10137934_040726

Table of Contents

Dear GMAT™ Test Taker,

Thank you for taking this important step toward your graduate management education. The GMAT exam remains one of the most trusted indicators of readiness for rigorous business study, relied on by more than 7,700 MBA, business master's, and other graduate-level degree programs worldwide to help identify candidates who are prepared to excel.

By choosing the GMAT™ Official Guide, you are preparing with the only study resource developed by the makers of the exam. Together with the tools available at **mba.com**, this guide is designed to build the skills and confidence you need for your best performance on test day.

The GMAT exam, which has been available to business aspirants like you for more than seven decades, provides schools with meaningful insight into your potential, complementing your academic record and offering a reliable way to demonstrate readiness. It helps signal that you can successfully engage with analytical coursework and thrive in a demanding academic environment.

But the value of the GMAT extends well beyond the classroom. Today's employers continue to prioritize problem-solving, strategic thinking, and data literacy. GMAC's own industry-leading **survey** of the world's top corporate recruiters—the majority of them with Fortune Global 500 companies—has perennially shown these abilities remain among the most sought-after skills for hiring and long-term career growth. Preparing for the GMAT strengthens precisely these capabilities. The exam's emphasis on higher-order reasoning—particularly in the Data Insights section—develops analytical fluency and evidence-based decision-making, competencies that leaders use daily in modern organizations.

In this way, the GMAT serves not only as a trusted admissions tool but also as an early investment in your professional future. By preparing for and taking the exam, you are building the mindset and skill set that drive success in business school, enhance employability upon graduation, and support lasting career advancement.

We applaud your commitment and wish you every success on your exam and in the opportunities that lie ahead.

Warm regards,

Joy J. Jones
CEO, GMAC

GMAT™ Official Guide Verbal Review 2026–2027

1.0 What Is the GMAT™ Exam?

1.1 What Is the GMAT™ Exam?

The Graduate Management Admission Test™ (GMAT™) is used in admissions decisions by more than 7,700 graduate management programs at over 2,400 business schools worldwide. Unlike undergraduate grades and courses, whose meanings vary across regions and institutions, your GMAT scores are a standardized, statistically valid, and reliable measure for both you and these schools to predict your future performance and success in core courses of graduate-level management programs.

Hundreds of studies across hundreds of schools have demonstrated the validity of GMAT scores as being an accurate indicator of business school success. Together, these studies have shown that performance on the GMAT predicts success in business school even better than undergraduate grades.

The exam tests you on skills expected by management faculty and admission professionals for incoming graduate students. These skills include problem-solving, data analysis, and critical thinking, which all require complex judgments and are tested in the three sections of the GMAT exam: Quantitative Reasoning, Data Insights, and Verbal Reasoning. These three sections feature content relevant to today's business challenges and opportunities, ensuring you are prepared for graduate business school and beyond.

Your GMAT Official Score is meant to be an objective, numeric measure of your ability and potential for success. Business schools will use it as part of their holistic admissions processes, which may also consider recommendation letters, essays, interviews, work experiences, and other signs of social and emotional intelligence, as well as leadership. Even if your program does not require a GMAT score, you can stand out from the crowd by doing well on the exam to show you are serious about business school and have the skills to succeed.

The exam is always delivered in English on a computer, either online (such as at home) or at a test center. The exam tests your ability to apply foundational knowledge in the following areas: algebra and arithmetic, analyzing and interpreting data, reading and comprehending written material, and reasoning and evaluating arguments.

Myth -vs- **FACT**

M – My GMAT score does not predict my success in business school.

F – The GMAT exam measures your critical thinking skills, which you will need in business school and your career.

1.2 Why Take the GMAT™ Exam?

Taking the exam helps you stand out as an applicant and shows you're ready for and committed to a graduate management education. Schools use GMAT scores in choosing the most qualified applicants. They know an applicant who has taken the exam is serious about earning a graduate business degree, and they know the exam scores reliably predict how well applicants can do in graduate business programs.

No matter how you do on the exam, you should contact schools that interest you to learn more about them, and to ask how they use GMAT scores and other criteria in admissions decisions. School admissions offices, websites, and publications are key sources of information when you are researching business schools. Note that schools' published GMAT scores are *averages* of the scores of their admitted students, not minimum scores needed for admission.

While you might aim to get a high or perfect score, such a score is not required to get into top business school programs around the world. You should try your best to achieve a competitive score that aligns with the ranges provided by the schools of your choice. Admissions officers will use GMAT scores as one factor in admissions decisions along with undergraduate records, application essays, interviews, letters of recommendation, and other information.

To learn more about the exam, test preparation materials, registration, and how to use your GMAT Official Score in applying to business schools, please visit **www.mba.com/gmat.**

Myth -vs- **FACT**

M – If I don't get a high GMAT score, I won't get into my top-choice schools.

F – Schools use your GMAT score as a part of their holistic evaluation process.

1.3 GMAT™ Exam Format

The GMAT exam has three separately timed sections (see the table on the following page). The Quantitative Reasoning section and the Verbal Reasoning section consist of only multiple-choice questions. The Data Insights section includes multiple-choice questions along with other kinds of graphical and data analysis questions. Before you start the exam, you can choose any order in which you will take the three sections. For example, you can choose to start with Verbal Reasoning, then do Quantitative Reasoning, and end with Data Insights. Or you can choose to do Data Insights first, followed by Verbal Reasoning, and then Quantitative Reasoning. You can take one optional ten-minute break after either the first or second section.

All three GMAT sections are computer adaptive. This means the test chooses from a large bank of questions to adjust itself to your ability level, so you will not get many questions that are too hard or too easy for you. The first question will be of medium difficulty. As you answer each question, the computer uses your answer, along with your responses to earlier questions, to choose the next question with the right level of difficulty. Because the computer uses your answers to choose your next question, you cannot skip questions.

Computer adaptive tests get harder as you answer more questions correctly. But getting a question that seems easier than the last one doesn't always mean your last answer was wrong. At the end of each section, you can review any question(s) and edit up to three answers within the allotted section time.

Though each test taker gets different questions, the mix of question types is always consistent. Your score depends on the difficulty and statistical traits of the questions you answer, as well as on which of your answers are correct. If you don't know how to answer a question, try to rule out as many wrong answer choices as possible. Then pick the answer choice you think is best. By adapting to each test taker, the exam can accurately and efficiently gauge a full range of skill levels, from very high to very low. Many factors may make the questions easier or harder, so don't waste time worrying if some questions seem easy.

To make sure every test taker gets equivalent content, the test gives specific numbers of questions of each type. While the test covers the same kinds of questions for everyone, some questions may seem harder or easier for you because you may be stronger in some questions than in others.

At the end of the exam, you will see your unofficial score displayed on the screen. A few days after your exam, you will receive your Official Score Report, which includes detailed performance insights. Once you receive your report, you can select to send your Official Score to schools of your choice.

Format of the GMAT™ Exam

	Questions	Timing
Quantitative Reasoning Problem-Solving	21	45 min.
Data Insights Data Sufficiency Multi-Source Reasoning Table Analysis Graphics Interpretation Two-Part Analysis	20	45 min.
Verbal Reasoning Reading Comprehension Critical Reasoning	23	45 min.
	Total Time	135 min.

A ten-minute optional break can be taken after the first or the second section.

Each section of the GMAT exam contains the following features:

- **Bookmarking:** Mark any questions you are unsure about so you can easily get back to them after you complete the section. Bookmarking can make the Question Review & Edit process more efficient.

- **Question Review & Edit:** Review as many questions as you would like (whether or not they're bookmarked) and change or edit up to three answers per section, within the section's allotted time.

> **Myth -vs- FACT**
>
> **M – Getting an easier question means I answered the previous one wrong.**
>
> **F – Many factors may make the questions easier or harder, so don't waste time worrying if some questions seem easy.**

1.4 What Is the Testing Experience Like?

You can take the exam either online (such as at home) or at a test center—whichever you prefer. You may feel more comfortable at home with the online delivery format. Or you may prefer the uninterrupted, structured environment of a test center. It is your choice. Both options have the same content, structure, features, optional ten-minute break, scores, and score scales.

At the Test Center: Over 700 test centers worldwide administer the GMAT exam under standardized conditions. Each test center has proctored testing rooms with individual computer workstations that allow you to take the exam in a peaceful, quiet setting, with some privacy. To learn more about exam day, visit **www.mba.com/gmat**.

Online: In available regions, the GMAT exam is delivered online and is proctored remotely, so you can take it in the comfort of your home or office. You will need a quiet workspace with a desktop or laptop computer that meets minimum system requirements, a webcam, microphone, and a reliable internet connection. For more information about taking the exam online, visit **www.mba.com/gmat**.

Whether you're taking the GMAT exam online or at a test center, there are several accommodations available. To learn more about available accommodations for the exam, visit **www.mba.com/accommodations**.

1.5 What Is the Exam Content Like?

The GMAT exam measures several types of analytical reasoning skills. The Quantitative Reasoning section gives you basic arithmetic and algebra problems. The questions present you with a mix of word or pure math problems. The Data Insights section asks you to use diverse reasoning skills to solve real-world problems involving data. It also asks you to interpret and combine data from different sources and in different formats to reach conclusions. The Verbal Reasoning section tests your ability to read and comprehend written material and to reason through and evaluate arguments.

The test questions are contextualized in various subject areas, but each question provides you everything you need to know to answer it correctly. In other words, you do not need detailed outside knowledge of the subject areas.

1.6 Verbal Reasoning Section

The GMAT Verbal Reasoning section measures how well you reason, understand what you read, and evaluate arguments. The Verbal Reasoning section includes passages about many topics. Verbal Reasoning questions do not assume you have any background knowledge on the topic. Therefore, all of the information you need to answer the questions correctly is contained in the passages.

The Verbal Reasoning section has two types of questions:

- **Reading Comprehension:** These questions measure your ability to read and understand written statements, understand logical relationships between significant points, and draw inferences and conclusions. More specifically, you'll be asked to identify main and supporting ideas, draw inferences from information presented in the passage, apply knowledge learned from the passage to unrelated contexts, and recognize the logical structures and style of the passage.

- **Critical Reasoning:** These questions measure your ability to make valid arguments, evaluate different lines of reasoning, and formulate or assess a plan of action. Critical Reasoning questions are based on a short reading passage, usually fewer than 100 words. Typically, the short text is followed by a question that asks you which of the five answer options strengthens or weakens the argument, tells why the argument is flawed, or strongly supports or damages the argument. You will not need specialized knowledge of the subject matter to answer the questions.

Chapter 3 of this book, "Verbal Review," reviews the basic verbal analysis and reasoning skills you need for the Verbal Reasoning section. Chapter 4, "Verbal Reasoning," explains the Verbal Reasoning question subtypes. It also provides test-taking tips for each subtype, as well as practice questions and answer explanations both in this book and in the Online Question Bank.

1.7 How Are Scores Calculated?

The Quantitative Reasoning, Data Insights, and Verbal Reasoning sections are each scored on a scale from 60 to 90, in 1-point increments. You will get four scores: a Section Score each for Quantitative Reasoning, Data Insights, and Verbal Reasoning, along with a Total Score based on your three section scores. The Total Score ranges from 205 to 805. Your scores depend on:

- Which questions you answered correctly.

- How many questions you answered.

- Each question's difficulty and other statistical characteristics.

There is a penalty for not completing each section of the exam. If you do not finish in the allotted time, your score will be penalized, reflecting the number of unanswered questions. Your GMAT exam score will be the best reflection of your performance when all questions are answered within the time limit.

Immediately after completing the exam, your unofficial scores and percentile for the Quantitative Reasoning, Data Insights, and Verbal Reasoning, as well as your Total Score, are displayed on-screen. You are **not** allowed to record, save, screenshot, or print your unofficial score. You will receive an email notification when your Official Score Report is available in your **www.mba.com** account.

The following table summarizes the different types of scores and their scale properties.

Score Type	Scale	Increment
Quantitative Reasoning	60–90	1
Data Insights	60–90	1
Verbal Reasoning	60–90	1
Total	205–805	10

Your GMAT Official Scores are valid for five years from your exam date. Your Total GMAT Score includes a percentile ranking, which shows the percentage of tests taken with scores lower than your score.

In addition to reviewing your Total and Section Scores, it's important to pay attention to your percentile ranking. Percentile rankings indicate what percentage of test takers you performed better than. For example, a percentile ranking of 75% means that you performed better than 75% of other test takers, and 25% of test takers performed better than you. Percentile ranks are calculated using scores from the most recent five years. Visit **www.mba.com/scores** to view the most recent predicted percentile rankings tables.

To better understand the exam experience and view score reports before exam day, we recommend taking at least one GMAT official practice exam to simulate the test-taking experience and gauge your potential score. The more practice exams you take, the better prepared you will be on your actual testing day. Visit **www.mba.com/examprep** to learn more about the practice exams offered by GMAC.

2.0 How to Prepare

2.1 How Should I Prepare for the GMAT™ Exam?

The GMAT™ exam has several unique question formats. We recommend that you familiarize yourself with the test format and the different question types before you take the test. The key to prepping for any exam is setting a pace that works for you and your lifestyle. That might be easier said than done, but the *GMAT™ Official 6-Week Study Planner* does the planning for you! Our step-by-step planner will help you stick to a schedule, inform your activities, and track your progress. Go to **www.mba.com/examprep** to download the planner.

Here are our recommended steps to starting your prep journey with your best foot forward.

1. **Study the structure.** Use the study plan in our **free GMAT™ Official Starter Kit** to become familiar with the exam format and structure. The study plan will guide you through each question type and give you sample questions. This will boost your confidence come test day when you know what to expect.

2. **Understand the question types.** Beyond knowing how to answer questions correctly, learn what each type of question is asking of you. GMAT questions rely on logic and analytical skills, not underlying subject matter mastery, as detailed in the *GMAT™ Official Guide 2026–2027* **and Online Question Bank**.

3. **Establish your baseline.** Take the **GMAT™ Official Practice Exam 1 (FREE)** to establish your baseline. It uses the same format and scoring algorithm as the real test, so you can use the Official Score Report to accurately assess your strengths and growth areas.

4. **Study the answer explanations.** Take advantage of each question you get wrong by studying the correct answers, so you know how to get it right the next time. **GMAT™ Official Practice Questions** provide detailed answer explanations for hundreds of real GMAT questions. This will help you understand why you got a question right or wrong.

5. **Simulate the test-taking experience.** Take the **GMAT™ Official Practice Exams**. All GMAT™ Official Practice Exams use the same algorithm, scoring, and timing as the real exam, so take them with test-day-like conditions (e.g., quiet space, use the tools allowed on test day) for the truest prep experience.

Remember, the exam is timed, so learning to pace yourself and understanding the question formats and the skills you need can be a stepping stone to achieving your desired score. The timed practice in the **Online Question Bank** can help you prepare for this. The time management performance chart provided in practice exam score reports can also help you practice your pacing.

Because the exam assesses reasoning rather than knowledge, memorizing facts probably won't help you. You don't need to study advanced math, but you should know basic arithmetic and algebra. Likewise, you don't need to study advanced vocabulary words, but you should know English well enough to understand writing at an undergraduate level.

> **"In Reading Comprehension and Critical Reasoning, carefully review the question and pay attention to its specific perspective."**
>
> —**A test instructor from New Oriental Educational and Technological Group**

2.2 Getting Ready for Exam Day

Whether you take the exam online or in a test center, knowing what to expect will help you feel confident and succeed. To understand which exam delivery is right for you, visit **www.mba.com/plan-for-exam-day**.

Our Top Exam Day Strategies:

1. Get a good night's sleep the night before.

2. Pacing is key. Consult your on-screen timer periodically to avoid having to rush through sections.

3. Read each question carefully to fully understand what is being asked.

4. Don't waste time trying to solve a problem you recognize as too difficult or time-consuming. Instead, eliminate answers you know are wrong and select the best from the remaining choices.

5. Leverage the bookmarking tool to make your question review and edit process more efficient.

> "During the test, you should avoid making mistakes on relatively simple questions. Do not waste too much time on questions that you do not know how to answer. Your mastery of assumptions determines your success in critical reasoning. Grasping the types of information in articles that are often used for exam questions can improve your reading efficiency."
>
> —A test instructor from Merica Group

> "Don't take a 'brute force' approach to GMAT questions—think strategically instead."
>
> —A test instructor from GMAT Genius

> "Compile summarized notes that can be reviewed on the morning of the test. Awareness of the key points and types of mistakes will boost your scores."
>
> —A test instructor from LeadersMBA

2.3 How to Use the *GMAT™ Official Guide Verbal Review 2026–2027*

The GMAT™ Official Guide series is the largest official source of actual GMAT questions. You can use this series of books and the included Online Question Bank to practice answering the different types of questions. The *GMAT™ Official Guide Verbal Review* is designed for those who have completed the Verbal Reasoning questions in the *GMAT™ Official Guide 2026–2027* and are looking for additional practice questions, as well as those who are interested in practicing only Verbal Reasoning questions. Questions of each type are organized by difficulty level of easy, medium, and hard. Your rate of accuracy in each level might differ from what you expect. You might be able to answer the "hard" questions easily, while the "easy" ones are challenging. This is common and is not an indicator of exam performance. The questions in this book are not adaptive based on your performance but are meant to serve as exposure to the range of question types and formats you might encounter on the exam. Also, the proportions of questions about different content areas in this book don't reflect the proportions in the actual exam. To find questions of a specific type and difficulty level (for example, easy reading comprehension questions), use the index of questions in Chapter 5.

We recommend the steps below for how to best use this book:

1. Start with the review chapter to gain an overview of the required concepts.

   > **Building a strong foundation is crucial to achieve a high score. If you struggle with fundamental questions, your progress on more advanced questions will be hindered.**
   >
   > —A test instructor from XY Education

2. Go through the practice questions in this book. Once you've familiarized yourself with the concepts and question types, use the Online Question Bank to further customize your practice by choosing your preferred level of difficulty, category of concepts, or question types.

   > **The Official Guide offers in-depth answer explanations. After completing a question, reviewing it alongside the explanation helps you gain a deeper understanding of the question's key concepts and solution strategies. On the result interface of the online question bank, it serves a dual purpose: on one hand, it encourages us to review incorrect answers; on the other hand, it provides detailed insights into the time spent on each question, aiding in optimizing our pace during exercises.**
   >
   > —A test instructor from Jiangjiang GMAT

3. Use the **Online Question Bank** to continue practicing based on your progress. To better customize and enhance your practice, use the Online Question Bank to:

   a. Review and retry practice questions to improve performance by using the untimed or timed features along with a study mode or an exam mode.

   b. Analyze key performance metrics to help assess focus area and track improvement.

   c. Use flashcards to master key concepts.

   > **The biggest mistake students make is completing too many new problems. Completing problems doesn't move your score! Learning from problems does. Keep a list of questions you want to go back to and redo. Redo at least three of these questions every time you study. This book is one of the most important resources you can use to create the future you want. Make sure you understand every question you complete extremely well. You should be able to explain every problem you complete to someone who is new to the exam. Don't focus on simply 'getting through' the book. That mindset will work against you and your dreams.**
   >
   > —A test instructor from The GMAT Strategy

 **TIP**

Since the exam is given on a computer, we suggest you practice the questions in this book using the **Online Question Bank** accessed via **www.mba.com/my-account**. It includes all the questions in this book, and it lets you create practice sets—both timed and untimed—and track your progress more easily. The Online Question Bank is also available on your mobile device through the GMAT™ Official Practice mobile app. To access the Online Question Bank on your mobile device, first create an account at **www.mba.com**, and then sign into your account on the mobile app.

2.4 How to Use Other GMAT™ Official Prep Products

We recommend using our other GMAT™ Official Prep products along with this guidebook.

- **For a realistic simulation of the exam:** GMAT™ Official Practice Exams 1–6 are the only practice exams that use real exam questions along with the scoring algorithm and user interface from the actual exam. The first two practice exams are free to all test takers at **www.mba.com/ gmatprep.**

- **For more practice questions:** *GMAT™ Official Guide Data Insights Review 2026–2027* and *GMAT™ Official Guide Quantitative Review 2026–2027* offer over 400 additional practice questions not included in this book.

- **For focused practice:** GMAT™ Official Practice Questions for Quantitative, Data Insights, and Verbal products offer 100+ questions that are not included in the Official Guide series.

> **"Build teaching-level depth; don't just finish content mindlessly. Even if you solve thousands of questions on a shaky foundation, you will remain stuck on a really low accuracy."**
>
> —A test instructor from Top One Percent

2.5 Tips for Taking the Exam

Tips for answering questions of the different types are given later in this book. Here are some general tips to help you do your best on the test.

1. **Before the actual exam, decide in what order to take the sections.**
   The exam lets you choose in which order you'll take the sections. Use the GMAT™ Official Practice Exams to practice and find your preferred order. No order is "wrong." Some test takers prefer to complete the section that challenges them the most first, while others prefer to ease into the exam by starting with a section that they're stronger in. Practice each order and see which one works best for you.

2. **Try the practice questions and practice exams.**
   Timing yourself as you answer the practice questions and taking the practice exams can give you a sense of how long you will have for each question on the actual test, and whether you are answering them fast enough to finish in time.

 **TIP**

After you've learned about all the question types, use the practice questions in this book and practice them online at **www.mba.com/my-account** to prepare for the actual test.

3. **Review all test directions ahead of time.**
   The directions explain exactly what you need to do to answer questions of each type. You can review the directions in the GMAT™ Official Practice Exams ahead of time so that you don't miss anything you need to know to answer properly. To review directions during the test, you can click on the Help icon. But note that your time spent reviewing directions counts against your available time for that section of the test.

4. **Study each question carefully.**
   Before you answer a question, understand exactly what it is asking, then pick the best answer choice. Never skim a question. Skimming may make you miss important details or nuances.

5. **Use your time wisely.**
   Although the exam stresses accuracy over speed, you should use your time wisely. On average, you have just about 2 minutes and 9 seconds per Quantitative Reasoning question; 2 minutes and 15 seconds per Data Insights question; and under 2 minutes per Verbal Reasoning question. Once you start the test, an on-screen clock shows how much time you have left. You can hide this display if you want, but by checking the clock periodically, you can make sure to finish in time.

6. **Do not spend too much time on any one question.**
   If finding the right answer is taking too long, try to rule out answer choices you know are wrong. Then pick the best of the remaining choices and move on to the next question.

   Not finishing sections or randomly guessing answers can lower your score significantly. As long as you've worked on each section, you will get a score even if you didn't finish one or more sections in time. You don't earn points for questions you never get to see.

   Pacing is important. If a question stumps you, pick the answer choice that seems best and move on. If you guess wrong, the computer will likely give you an easier question, which you're more likely to answer correctly. Soon the computer will return to giving you questions matched to your ability. You can bookmark questions you get stuck on, then return to change up to three of your answers if you still have time left at the end of the section. But if you don't finish the section, your score will be reduced.

7. **Confirm your answers ONLY when you are ready to move on.**
   In the Quantitative Reasoning, Data Insights, and Verbal Reasoning sections, once you choose your answer to a question, you are asked to confirm it. As soon as you confirm your response, the next question appears. You can't skip questions. In the Data Insights and Verbal Reasoning sections, several questions based on the same prompt may appear at once. When more than one question is on a single screen, you can change your answers to any questions on that screen before moving on to the next screen. But until you've reached the end of the section, you can't navigate back to a previous screen to change any answers.

Myth -vs- **FACT**

M – **Avoiding wrong answers is more important than finishing the test.**

F – **Not finishing can lower your score a lot.**

Myth -vs- **FACT**

M – **The first ten questions are critical, so you should spend the most time on them.**

F – **All questions impact your score.**

2.6 Verbal Reasoning Section Strategies

Utilize the strategies below to better prepare for the exam. Creating a solid study plan and selecting the right prep materials are two key elements of getting accepted into your top business schools. But knowing how to strategically approach the exam is another crucial factor that can increase your confidence going into test day and help you perform your best.

> "Don't just read explanations. Review your notes and learn from your mistakes."
>
> —A test instructor from Admit Master

Reading Comprehension Questions

- Do not expect to be completely familiar with the material presented in passages. Your understanding of the subject matter is not required to answer the question.

- Read and analyze the passage carefully before reading the questions.

- Focus on key words and phrases to maintain an overall sense about the context of the passage.

- Select the answer that fits based on the information given in the passage.

- Don't rush through the passages. This section is about comprehension, not speed.

Critical Reasoning Questions

- Determine exactly what the question is asking. For this section, read the question first and then the material on which it is based.

- Keep the following in mind as you read through the passage:

  - What is put forward as factual information?

  - What is not said but necessarily follows from what is said?

  - What is claimed to follow from facts that have been put forward?

  - How well are those claims substantiated?

- When reading arguments, determine how sound the reasoning is. It is not necessary to pass judgment on the actual truth of anything put forward as fact.

- If a question is based on an argument, identify what part of the argument is its conclusion.

3.0 Verbal Review

3.0 Verbal Review

To prepare for the GMAT™ exam's Verbal Reasoning section and Data Insights section, and to succeed in graduate business programs, you need basic skills in analyzing and evaluating texts and the ideas they express. This chapter explains concepts to help you develop these skills. This is only a brief overview. So, if you find unfamiliar terms or concepts, consult outside resources to learn more.

The sections below can help you develop skills you need for the Verbal Reasoning and Data Insights sections of the GMAT exam.

Section 3.1, "Analyzing Passages," includes:

1. Arguments
2. Explanations and Plans
3. Narratives and Descriptions

Section 3.2, "Inductive Reasoning," includes:

1. Inductive Arguments
2. Generalizations and Predictions
3. Causal Reasoning
4. Analogies

Section 3.3, "Deductive Reasoning," includes:

1. Deductive Arguments
2. Logical Operators
3. Reasoning with Logical Operators
4. Necessity, Probability, and Possibility
5. Quantifiers
6. Reasoning with Quantifiers

3.1 Analyzing Passages

1. Arguments

A. An *argument* gives one or more ideas as reasons to accept one or more other ideas. Often some of these ideas are implied but not stated.

> *Example:*
>
> The sidewalk is dry, so it must not have rained last night.
>
> This argument gives the observation that the sidewalk is dry as a reason to accept that it didn't rain last night. The argument implies but doesn't say that rain typically leaves sidewalks wet.

B. A *premise* is an idea that an argument gives as a reason to accept another idea. An argument can have any number of premises.

The words and phrases below often mark premises:

after all	*for one thing*	*moreover*
because	*furthermore*	*seeing that*
for	*given that*	*since*
for the reason that	*in light of the fact that*	*whereas*

Example:

Our mayor shouldn't support the proposal to expand the freeway **because** the expansion's benefits wouldn't justify the costs. **Furthermore**, most voters oppose the expansion.

This is an argument with two stated premises. The word *because* marks the first premise, that the expansion's benefits wouldn't justify the costs. The word *furthermore* marks the second premise, that most voters oppose the expansion. These premises are given as reasons the mayor shouldn't support the proposal.

C. A *conclusion* is an idea an argument supports with one or more premises. An *intermediate conclusion* is a conclusion the argument uses to support another conclusion. A *main conclusion* is a conclusion the argument doesn't use to support any other conclusion.

The words and phrases below often mark conclusions:

clearly	*it follows that*	*suggests that*
entails that	*proves*	*surely*
hence	*shows that*	*therefore*
implies that	*so*	*thus*

Example:

Julia just hiked fifteen kilometers, **so** she must have burned a lot of calories. **Surely**, she's hungry now.

This argument has a premise, an intermediate conclusion, and a main conclusion. The word *so* marks the intermediate conclusion: that Julia must have burned a lot of calories. The word *surely* marks the main conclusion: that Julia is hungry now. The premise that Julia just hiked fifteen kilometers supports the intermediate conclusion, which in turn supports the main conclusion.

Conclusions may be stated before, between, or after premises. Sometimes no marker words show which statements are premises and which are conclusions. To find premises and conclusions without marker words, consider which statements the author gives as reasons to accept which other statements. The reasons given are the premises. The ideas the author tries to persuade readers to accept are the conclusions.

Example:

For healthy eating, Healthful Brand Donuts are the best donuts you can buy. Unlike any other donuts on the market, Healthful Brand Donuts have plenty of fiber and natural ingredients.

In this argument, the author tries to persuade the reader that Healthful Brand Donuts are the best donuts to buy for healthy eating. So, the first sentence is the conclusion. The statement about Healthful Brand Donuts' ingredients is a premise because it's given as a reason to accept the conclusion. Since the author's intent is clear, no marker words are needed.

D. A *valid* argument is one whose conclusions follow from its premises. A valid argument can have false premises and conclusions. In a valid argument with false premises, the conclusion **would** follow if the premises **were** true.

A *sound* argument is a valid argument with true premises. Since a sound argument's premises are true, and its conclusions follow from those premises, its conclusions must also be true.

> *Examples:*
>
> (i) Everyone who tries fried eggplant is guaranteed to love the taste. So, if you try it, you'll love the taste too.
>
> In example (i), the premise is false: not everyone who tries fried eggplant is guaranteed to love the taste. So, example (i) is not a sound argument. But it is a valid argument because if everyone who tried fried eggplant **were** guaranteed to love the taste, it would follow that you, too, would love the taste if **you** tried it.
>
> (ii) Some people who try fried eggplant dislike the taste. So, if you try it, you'll probably dislike the taste too.
>
> In example (ii), the premise is true: some people who try fried eggplant do dislike the taste. However, example (ii) is an invalid argument, so it's not sound. **Some** people dislike the taste of fried eggplant, but that does not mean **you personally** will **probably** dislike the taste.

E. An *assumption* is an idea taken for granted. An assumption may be a premise in an argument, a claim about a cause or effect in a causal explanation, a condition a plan relies on, or any other type of idea taken for granted. A conclusion is never an assumption—an argument doesn't take a conclusion for granted, but rather gives reasons to accept it.

A passage may also have ***implicit assumptions*** the author considers too obvious to state. These unstated ideas fill logical gaps between the passage's statements.

An argument, plan, or explanation with implausible assumptions is weak and vulnerable to criticism.

F. A *necessary assumption* of an argument is an idea that must be true for the argument's stated premises to be good enough reasons to accept its conclusions. That is, a necessary assumption is one the argument needs in order to work.

> *Example:*
>
> Mario has booked a flight scheduled to arrive at 5:00 p.m.—which should let him get here by around 6:30 p.m. So, by 7:00 p.m. we'll be going out to dinner with Mario.
>
> In this argument, one necessary assumption is that the flight Mario booked will arrive not much later than scheduled. A second necessary assumption is that Mario caught his flight. Unless these and all the argument's other necessary assumptions are true, the argument's stated premises aren't good enough reasons to accept the conclusion.

G. A *sufficient assumption* of an argument is an idea whose truth would make the argument's main conclusion follow from the stated premises. That is, adding a sufficient assumption to an argument makes the argument valid.

> *Example:*
>
> The study of poetry is entirely without value since poetry has no practical use.
>
> In this argument, one sufficient assumption is that studying anything with no practical use is entirely without value. This assumption, together with the argument's stated premise, is enough to make the conclusion follow. If both the premise and the assumption are true, the conclusion must also be true. But this sufficient assumption is not a necessary assumption.

H. Arguments are often classified based on what kinds of conclusions they have.

> i. A *prescriptive* argument has a conclusion about what should or shouldn't be done. Prescriptive arguments may advocate for or against policies, procedures, strategies, goals, laws, or ethical norms.

> *Example:*
>
> Our company's staff is too small to handle our upcoming project. So, to make sure the project succeeds, the company **should** hire more employees.
>
> Another example of a prescriptive argument is shown above in Section 3.1.1.B. That argument is prescriptive because it concludes that the mayor ***should not*** support the proposed freeway expansion.

> ii. An *evaluative* argument concludes that something is good or bad, desirable or undesirable, without advocating any particular policy or actions.

> *Example:*
>
> This early novel is clearly one of the greatest of all time. Not only did it pioneer brilliantly innovative narrative techniques, but it did so with exceptional grace, subtlety, and sophistication.

> iii. An *interpretive* argument has a conclusion about something's underlying significance. An interpretive argument may be about the meaning, importance, or implications of observations, a theory, an artistic or literary work, or a historical event.

> *Example:*
>
> Many famous authors have commented emphatically on this early novel, either praising or condemning it. This suggests the novel has had an enormous influence on later fiction.

iv. A *causal* argument concludes that one or more factors did or did not contribute to one or more effects. A causal argument may be about the causes, reasons, or motivations for an event, condition, decision, or outcome. For example, a causal argument may support or oppose an account of the influences behind a literary or artistic style or movement.

> *Example:*
>
> Our houseplant started to thrive only when we moved it to a sunny window. So, probably the reason it was sickly before then was that it wasn't getting enough sunlight.
>
> Another causal argument can be found in the example in Section 3.1.1.C above, which concludes that Julia must be hungry now.

v. A basic *factual* argument has a factual conclusion that doesn't fit in any other category explained above.

> *Example:*
>
> All dogs are mammals. Rover is a dog. Therefore, Rover is a mammal.

2. Explanations and Plans

A. A *causal explanation* claims that one or more factors contribute to one or more effects. A causal explanation might not be an argument. It might have no premises or conclusions. But a causal explanation can be a premise or conclusion in an argument.

The words and phrases below often mark a causal explanation:

as a result	*due to*	*results in*
because	*leads to*	*that's why*
causes	*produces*	*thereby*
contributes to	*responsible for*	*thus*

Some of these words can also mark premises or conclusions in arguments. To tell what the words mark, you may have to judge whether the author is giving reasons to accept a conclusion or only saying what causes an effect. If the author is only saying what causes an effect, without trying to persuade the reader that the effect is real, then the passage is a causal explanation but not an argument.

Just as an argument may have premises, intermediate conclusions, and main conclusions, a causal explanation may claim that one or more factors cause one or more intermediate effects that, in turn, cause further effects.

> *Example:*
>
> Julia just hiked fifteen kilometers, **thereby** burning a lot of calories. **That's why** she's hungry now.
>
> This is a causal explanation claiming that a factor (Julia's fifteen-kilometer hike) caused an intermediate effect (Julia burning a lot of calories) that, in turn, caused another effect (Julia being hungry now). The word *thereby* marks the intermediate effect, and the phrase *that's why* marks the final effect. This explanation doesn't try to convince the reader that Julia's hungry. It just explains what made her hungry. So, it's not an argument.

B. An *observation* is a claim that something was observed or is otherwise directly known. In the example of a causal explanation above, the claims that Julia just hiked fifteen kilometers and that she's hungry are observations. But if her burning of calories was not directly known or observed, the claim that she burned a lot of calories is not an observation.

C. A *hypothesis* is a tentative idea neither known nor assumed to be true. A hypothesis can be an argument's conclusion. Causal explanations are often hypotheses. A passage may discuss *alternative hypotheses*, such as competing explanations for the same observation. Sometimes a passage gives pros and cons of alternative hypotheses without arguing for any particular hypothesis as a conclusion.

> *Example:*
>
> A bush in our yard just died. The invasive insects we've seen around the yard lately might be the cause. Or the bush might not have gotten enough water. It's been a dry summer.
>
> This example presents two alternative hypotheses. The first hypothesis gives the observation that invasive insects have been in the yard as a possible causal explanation for the bush's observed death. This hypothesis assumes the insects can hurt bushes like the one in the yard. The second hypothesis provides the observation that it's been a dry summer as an alternative causal explanation for the bush's observed death. This hypothesis assumes dry weather can result in bushes getting too little water. The passage presents observations to tentatively support each hypothesis. But it doesn't argue for either hypothesis as a conclusion.

D. A *plan* describes an imagined set of actions meant to work together to achieve one or more goals. A plan is not itself an argument. Its actions aren't proposed as reasons to accept a goal, but rather as ways to reach the goal. However, a prescriptive argument may recommend or oppose a plan. A plan may also be among an argument's premises.

Just as an argument may have premises, intermediate conclusions, and main conclusions, a plan may suggest actions to reach intermediate goals that, in turn, are meant to help achieve main goals. And like an argument, a plan may have assumptions, including necessary and sufficient assumptions. A necessary assumption of a plan is one that must be true for the plan to achieve its goals. And a sufficient assumption of a plan is one whose truth guarantees the plan would achieve its goals if followed.

A plan is not a causal explanation. The actions a plan suggests haven't been done yet, so they can't have caused anything. However, any plan does assume possible future causal links between its proposed actions and its goals.

> *Example:*
>
> To repaint our house, we'll need to buy gallons of paint. To do that, we could go to the hardware store.
>
> In this plan, going to the hardware store is an action imagined to help reach the intermediate goal of getting gallons of paint. The intermediate goal is imagined to help reach the main goal of repainting the house. This plan isn't itself an argument. But, combined with the premise that we ***should*** repaint the house, the plan could be part of a prescriptive argument that we ***should*** go to the hardware store.

3. Narratives and Descriptions

A. A ***narrative*** describes a sequence of related events. A narrative is not an argument, an explanation, or a plan. But it may contain one or more arguments, causal explanations, or plans—or be contained in them.

The words and phrases below often show narrative sequence:

after	*earlier*	*then*
afterwards	*later*	*thereafter*
before	*previously*	*until*
beforehand	*since*	*while*
during	*subsequently*	*when*

> *Example:*
>
> **While** Julia was hiking fifteen kilometers, she burned a lot of calories. **Afterwards**, she felt hungry.
>
> This narrative describes a sequence of three events. The word ***while*** shows that Julia's hike and her burning of calories happened at the same time. The word ***afterwards*** shows that her hunger arose soon after the first two events. Although you can reasonably assume these events were causally linked, the narrative doesn't say they were. So, it's not an explicit causal explanation. And since the narrative doesn't report the events as reasons to accept a particular conclusion, it's not an argument either.

B. Not all passages are arguments, causal explanations, plans, or narratives. Some passages report on views, findings, innovations, places, societies, artistic works, devices, organisms, etc., without arguing for a conclusion, explaining what caused what, suggesting actions to reach a goal, or narrating what happened.

C. Likewise, not all statements in passages are premises, conclusions, observations to be explained, hypotheses, or reports of events. Statements in passages can also:

- Give background information to help the reader understand the rest of the passage
- Describe details of something that the passage is discussing
- Express the author's attitude toward material in the passage
- Provide examples to illustrate general statements
- Summarize ideas that the passage is arguing against

3.2 Inductive Reasoning

1. Inductive Arguments

A. In an ***inductive argument***, the premises are meant to support a conclusion but not to fully prove it. For example, the premises may just be meant to give evidence that the conclusion is **probably** true, leaving a chance that the conclusion is false despite that evidence.

B. An inductive argument may be ***strengthened*** by adding reasons that directly support the conclusion or that help the argument's premises better support the conclusion. Conversely, an inductive argument may be ***weakened*** by adding reasons that directly cast doubt on the argument's conclusion, or that make the argument's premises less effective at supporting the conclusion. Below, we discuss how various types of inductive arguments are evaluated, strengthened, and weakened.

2. Generalizations and Predictions

A. An argument by ***generalization*** often uses premises about a sample of a population to support a conclusion about the whole population.

> *Example:*
>
> Six of the eight apartments available for lease in this building are studio apartments. So, probably about $\frac{3}{4}$ of all the apartments in the building are studio apartments.
>
> In this example, the whole set of apartments in the building is a population. The apartments available for lease are a ***sample*** of that population. Since six of the eight apartments available for lease are studio apartments, $\frac{3}{4}$ of the apartments in the sample are studio apartments. The argument generalizes from this by assuming the whole population is probably like the sample. It concludes that as in the sample, probably about $\frac{3}{4}$ of the apartments in the population are studio apartments.

B. A similar type of argument by generalization uses premises about a whole population to support a conclusion about part of that population.

> *Example:*
>
> About $\frac{3}{4}$ of all the apartments in the building are studio apartments. So, probably about $\frac{3}{4}$ of the apartments on the building's second floor are studio apartments.
>
> This example uses a premise about the proportion of studio apartments in the population of all the apartments in the building to support the conclusion that there's a similar proportion of studio apartments in just a part of the population—the apartments on the second floor.

C. A ***predictive*** argument by generalization uses a premise about the sample observed so far in a population to support a conclusion about another part of the population.

Example:

Of the eight apartments I've visited in this building so far, six have been studio apartments. So, probably about six out of the next eight apartments I visit in the building will also be studio apartments.

In this example, the apartments the author has visited so far are a sample of the total population of apartments in the building. The observation about the proportion of studio apartments in the sample supports a prediction that roughly the same proportion of studio apartments will be found in another part of the population—the next eight apartments the author will visit in the building.

D. The strength of an argument by generalization partly depends on how similar the sample is to the overall population, or to the unobserved part of the population a prediction is about. A sample chosen in a way likely to make it relevantly different than the population is a ***biased sample***. An argument using a biased sample is flawed.

Example:

In a telephone survey of our city's residents, about four out of every five respondents said they usually answer the phone when it rings. So, about four out of every five residents of our city usually answer the phone when it rings.

In this example, the sample is the respondents to the telephone survey. People who usually answer the phone when it rings are more likely than other people to respond to telephone surveys. Because the sample was selected through a telephone survey, probably a greater proportion of the sample than of all city residents usually answer the phone when it rings. So, the argument is flawed because the sample is biased.

E. The strength of an argument generalizing from a sample also partly depends on the sample's size. The smaller the sample, the weaker the argument. This is because a smaller sample is statistically likely to differ more from the population in its average traits. An argument by generalization that uses too small a sample to justify its conclusion is flawed by ***hasty generalization***.

Example:

A coin came up heads five of the eight times Beth flipped it. This suggests the coin she flipped is weighted to make it come up heads more often than tails.

In this argument, the sample is the eight flips of the coin, and the population is all the potential flips of the same coin. The sample is probably not biased because Beth's flips of the coin are probably no more likely than anyone else's flips of the same coin to come up heads or tails. However, the sample is too small to justify the conclusion that the coin is weighted to favor heads. A fair, unweighted coin flipped eight times usually comes up heads more or fewer than exactly four times—just by chance. So, this argument is flawed by hasty generalization. If Beth and other people flipped the coin thousands or millions of times, and still saw it come up heads in five out of every eight flips, that would strengthen the argument. But no matter how many times the coin was flipped to confirm this pattern, a tiny chance would be left that the coin was not weighted to favor heads and that the results had been purely random.

F. An argument by generalization is weaker when its conclusion is more precise, and stronger when its conclusion is vaguer, given the same premises. That's because a sample usually doesn't precisely match the population it's extracted from. A less precise conclusion allows a larger range of potential mismatches between sample and population. So, it's more likely to be true, given the same evidence. An argument whose conclusion is too precise for its premises to justify is flawed by the ***fallacy of specificity***.

Example:

Biologists carefully caught, weighed, and released fifty frogs out of the hundreds in a local lake. These fifty frogs weighed an average of 32.86 grams apiece. So, the frogs in the lake must also weigh an average of 32.86 grams apiece.

In this example, the sample might be biased because frogs of certain types might have been easier for the biologists to catch. But even if the biologists avoided any sampling bias, the average weight of the fifty sampled frogs probably wouldn't exactly match the average weight of the hundreds of frogs in the lake. The conclusion is too precise, so the argument suffers from the fallacy of specificity. A stronger argument might use the same evidence to conclude less precisely that the frogs in the lake weigh on average between 25 and 40 grams apiece. This less precise conclusion would still be true even if the average weight of the sampled frogs didn't exactly match the average weight of all the frogs in the lake. Since the less precise conclusion is more likely to be true given the same evidence, that evidence justifies it better. That means the argument for the less precise conclusion is stronger.

3. Causal Reasoning

A. Causal arguments use premises about correlations or causal links to support conclusions about causes and effects. Causal reasoning is hard because causal links can't be directly observed. And there's no scientific or philosophical consensus about what causality is. But saying that one type of situation causally contributes to another usually implies that after a situation of the first type, situations of the second type are more likely. It also implies that situations of the first type help to explain situations of the second type.

Example:

Bushes of the species in our yard tend to die after several weeks without water. So, they must need water at least every few weeks to survive.

In this example, the premise is that after situations of one type (bushes of a certain species getting no water for several weeks), situations of another type become more likely (the bushes dying). The conclusion implies that the first type of situation causes the second: getting no water for several weeks causes bushes of that species to die.

B. A causal argument may use a general correlation to support the conclusion that a situation of one type caused a situation of another type.

> *Example:*
>
> A bush in our yard just died. There's been no rain this summer, and no one has been watering the yard. Bushes of the species in our yard tend to die after several weeks without water. So, probably, the bush died because it didn't get enough water.
>
> In this example, the first premises say that a *specific* situation of one type (a bush of a specific species dying) followed a specific situation of another type (the bush going without water for weeks). The final premise says that *in general*, situations of the first type (bushes of that species dying) follow situations of the second type (bushes of that species getting no water for weeks). These premises together support the conclusion that the lack of water caused the bush to die.

C. Causal arguments can be weakened by observations that suggest alternative causal explanations. A way to check which of two competing explanations is stronger is to look at situations with the possible cause from one explanation but not the possible cause from the other.

> *Example:*
>
> **Explanation 1**: Bushes of this species tend to die after several weeks without water. Maybe the lack of water kills the bushes.
>
> **Explanation 2**: Bushes of this species grow only in a region where long dry spells are always very hot. Maybe the heat alone kills these bushes during weeks without water.
>
> To check which of these two hypothetical explanations is stronger, we can run two experiments. Each experiment creates a situation with one of the two proposed causes but not the other.
>
> **Experiment 1**: Water some of the bushes often during weeks of extreme heat and see how well they survive.
>
> **Experiment 2**: Keep some of the bushes dry in cooler weather and see how well they survive.
>
> Finding that the bushes survive well in Experiment 1 but not in Experiment 2 would support Explanation 1 and cast doubt on Explanation 2.
>
> Finding that the bushes survive well in Experiment 2 but not in Experiment 1 would support Explanation 2 and cast doubt on Explanation 1.
>
> Finding that the bushes always die in both experiments would support both explanations, suggesting either heat or drought alone can kill the bushes.
>
> Finding that the bushes survive well in both experiments would cast doubt on both explanations. It would suggest that something other than drought or heat is killing the bushes—or that drought and heat must occur together to kill the bushes.

D. Experiments to test causal hypotheses shouldn't add or remove possible causal factors other than those tested for.

> *Examples:*
>
> (i) To run Experiment 1 above, a scientist planted some of the bushes in a tropical rainforest where very hot days are usually rainy.
>
> (ii) To run Experiment 2 above, a scientist planted some of the bushes under an awning where rain couldn't reach them in cooler weather.
>
> These versions of the two experiments are problematic because they add other possible causal factors. In example (i), the rainforest's soil type, insects, or humidity might make it harder or easier for the bushes to survive, regardless of the heat and rainfall. In example (ii), putting the bushes under an awning would likely help keep them shaded. That, too, might make it easier or harder for the bushes to survive, regardless of the heat and rainfall. These experimental design flaws cast doubt on any argument that cites these versions of the experiments as evidence to support Explanation 1 or Explanation 2.

Testing a hypothesis through experiments usually means reasoning by generalization: a conclusion about a whole population is reached by observing a sample in the experiment. Causal arguments based on experiments can have the flaws discussed above in Section 3.2.2, "Generalizations and Predictions." A causal argument is weak if it generalizes from a sample that's too small or chosen in a biased way. In small or biased samples, correlations between factors that aren't causally linked often appear just by chance or because of outside factors.

E. Even when two factors clearly are causally linked, it can be hard to tell which causes which, or whether a third, underlying factor causes them both.

> *Example:*
>
> One type of earthworm is far more often found in soil under healthy bushes of a certain species than in soil under sickly bushes of that same species.
>
> Even if the earthworms' presence is causally linked to the bushes' health, the causal link could be that:
>
> (i) the earthworms improve the bushes' health, or
>
> (ii) healthier bushes attract the earthworms, or
>
> (iii) certain soil conditions both improve the bushes' health and attract the earthworms.
>
> More than one of these causal links, and others, may hold at once. A way to untangle the causal links is to find out:
>
> (i) how healthy the bushes are in the same soil conditions without earthworms,
>
> (ii) how attracted the earthworms are to those soil conditions without the bushes, and
>
> (iii) whether the earthworms tend to appear around healthier bushes even in different soil conditions.

F. Even reliable correlations sometimes arise just by chance. One way to check whether a correlation between two types of situations is just a coincidence is to test whether stopping situations of the first type also stops situations of the other type. Even when no test is possible, you can consider whether there's any plausible way either type of situation could cause the other.

Example:

For years, Juan has arrived at work at a hair salon every weekday at exactly 8:00 a.m. Five hundred miles to the north, over the same years, Ashley has arrived at work at a car dealership every weekday at exactly 8:01 a.m. So, Juan's daily arrival at his work must make Ashley arrive at her work a minute later.

In this example, even though for years Ashley has always arrived at work a minute after Juan has, the argument is absurdly weak. That's because Juan's arrival at his work has no apparent way to affect when Ashley arrives at her work. But we could still test the hypothesis in the argument's conclusion. For example, we could persuade Juan to vary his arrival times, then see whether Ashley's arrival times change to match. With no plausible link between the two workers' arrival times, we'd need a lot of evidence like this to reasonably overcome the suspicion that the correlation is pure coincidence. However, finding out that Juan and Ashley know each other and have reasons to coordinate their work schedules could give us a plausible causal link between their arrival times. That would greatly strengthen the argument that their arrival times are indeed causally linked.

4. Analogies

A. An argument by ***analogy*** starts by saying two or more things are alike in certain ways. The argument then gives a claim about one of those two things as a reason to accept a similar claim about the other.

Example:

Laotian cuisine and Thai cuisine use many of the same ingredients and cooking techniques. Ahmed enjoys Thai cuisine. So, if he tried Laotian cuisine, he'd probably enjoy it.

This example starts by saying how Laotian cuisine and Thai cuisine are alike: they use similar ingredients and cooking techniques. The argument then makes a claim about Thai cuisine: that Ahmed enjoys it. By analogy, these premises support a similar claim about Laotian cuisine: Ahmed would enjoy it if he tried it.

B. For an argument by analogy to work well, the noted similarities must be ***relevant*** to whether the two things are also similar in the way the conclusion claims. The argument in the example above meets this standard. A cuisine's ingredients and cooking techniques usually affect how much a specific person would enjoy it. Noting that Laotian cuisine and Thai cuisine have similar ingredients and cooking techniques is relevant to whether Ahmed is likely to similarly enjoy the two cuisines.

An argument by analogy is weaker if its premises only note similarities that are less relevant to its conclusion.

> *Example:*
>
> Laotian cuisine and Latvian cuisine both come from nations whose English names start with the letter *L*. Ahmed enjoys Latvian cuisine. So, if he tried Laotian cuisine, he'd probably enjoy it too.
>
> This example notes that Laotian cuisine and Latvian cuisine are similar with respect to the English names of the nations they're from. Since the spelling of a nation's name almost never affects how much anyone enjoys that nation's cuisine, this similarity is irrelevant to whether Ahmed would similarly enjoy the two cuisines. The analogy is absurd, so the argument is flawed. To save the argument, we'd need a good reason why the noted similarity is relevant after all—for example, evidence that Ahmed is an unusual person whose enjoyment of different cuisines depends on English spellings.

C. A reasonable argument by analogy can be strengthened by noting other relevant similarities between the things compared, or weakened by noting relevant dissimilarities.

> *Example:*
>
> Beth and Alan are children living on the same block in the Hazelfern School District. Beth attends Tubman Primary School. Therefore, Alan probably does as well.
>
> Noting that Beth and Alan are both in the same grade would strengthen this moderately reasonable argument, because that similarity increases the odds that they attend the same school. However, noting that Beth is eight years older than Alan would weaken the argument, because that dissimilarity suggests Alan may be too young to attend the school Beth attends.

3.3 Deductive Reasoning

1. Deductive Arguments

A. The premises of a *deductive argument* are given to fully prove its conclusion. A valid deductive argument with only true premises **must** have a true conclusion. An argument presented as deductive is flawed if its premises can all be true while its conclusion is false. However, a flawed deductive argument might still work well as an inductive argument if the author doesn't wrongly present the premises as **proving** the conclusion. Deductive arguments often use *logical operators* or *quantifiers* or both, as explained below.

2. Logical Operators

A. A *logical operator* shows how the truth or falsehood of one or more statements affects the truth or falsehood of a larger statement made from those statements and the operator. The basic logical operators are *negations*, *logical conjunctions*, *disjunctions*, and *implications*.

B. A statement's *negation* is true just when the statement is false. Words and phrases like *not, it is false that*, and *it is not the case that* often mark negation.

Statements are often vague, ambiguous, context-sensitive, or subjective. They may be true in one sense and false in another, they may be only partly true, or their truth may be indefinite. If a statement is true only in one way or to a limited degree, its negation is false in the same way and to the same degree.

Example:

"The cat is on the mat" can have the negation "The cat is not on the mat." Either of these statements is true if the other is false—but only when both are about the same cat and the same mat, in the same sense and the same context. If you make the first statement while the cat is sleeping on the mat, but then the cat wakes up and leaves before you make the second statement, the context has changed. Then your second statement isn't the negation of your first. If the cat is only partly on the mat when both statements are made, then the second statement is *partly* false just as much as the first is partly true, and in just the same way.

C. A *logical conjunction* of two statements is true just when both are true. The words and phrases below can mark a logical conjunction of statements *A* and *B*:

A and B	*A even though B*	*not only A but also B*
Although A, B	*A. Furthermore, B.*	*A, whereas B*
A but B	*A, however, B*	

The conjunction markers ***and, furthermore***, and ***not only . . . but also*** usually imply that *A* and *B* are relevant to each other or mentioned for similar reasons—for example, that both are premises supporting the same conclusion. On the other hand, the conjunction markers ***although, but, even though, however***, and ***whereas*** suggest tension between *A* and *B*—for example, that it's surprising *A* and *B* are both true, or that *A* and *B* support conflicting conclusions, or that *A* and *B* differ in some other unexpected way.

Examples:

(i) Raul has worked for this company a long time, **and** he's searching for another job.

(ii) **Although** Raul has worked for this company a long time, he's searching for another job.

Both these examples say that Raul has worked for the company a long time, and that he's searching for another job. But in example (ii), *although* suggests Raul's search for another job is **surprising**, given that he's worked for the company a long time. In contrast, the *and* in example (i) suggests Raul's search for another job is **unsurprising** now that he's worked for the company a long time.

D. A *disjunction* of two statements is true only when one of them is true. The words and phrases *A or B*, *either A or B*, and *A unless B* often mark a disjunction of *A* and *B*.

There are two kinds of disjunction. An *inclusive disjunction* of two statements is true when **at least** one of them is true, and **also** when both are. An *exclusive disjunction* of two statements is true just when **exactly** one of them is true—**not** when both are. English disjunctions often aren't clearly inclusive or clearly exclusive. But *A or B or both* clearly means inclusive disjunction. And *A or B but not both* clearly means exclusive disjunction.

Examples:

(i) It will **either** rain **or** snow tomorrow.

(ii) It will rain tomorrow **unless** it snows.

These examples both say that at least one of the statements "It will rain tomorrow" and "It will snow tomorrow" is true. But neither example clearly says whether or not it might *both* rain *and* snow tomorrow. To clarify, we can say:

(iii) Tomorrow, it will rain or snow—or both. (*inclusive disjunction*)

or

(iv) Tomorrow, it will either rain or snow, but not both. (*exclusive disjunction*)

E. A *conditional* says that for one statement to be true, another must be true. In other words, a conditional means the first statement entails the second. The words and phrases below all mark the same conditional link between statements *A* and *B*:

A would mean that B	*B if A*	*A only if B*
If A, then B	*Not A unless B*	*B provided that A*

Conditionals of these forms do not mean that *A* is true, nor that *B* is. They do not give *A* as a reason to accept *B*. So, in a conditional, *A* isn't a premise and *B* isn't a conclusion. That is, a conditional is not an argument. However, the conditional *if A, then B* does mean that correctly assuming *A* as a premise lets you correctly reach *B* as a conclusion.

Examples:

(i) It will snow tonight **only if** the temperature falls below 5 degrees Celsius.

(ii) It **won't** snow tonight **unless** the temperature falls below 5 degrees Celsius.

(iii) **If** it snows tonight, it'll mean the temperature has fallen below 5 degrees Celsius.

These three conditionals all mean the same thing. Each says that snow tonight would require a temperature below 5 degrees Celsius. They do not say that it **will** snow tonight, nor that the temperature **will** be below 5 degrees Celsius. But they do suggest, for example, that seeing it snow tonight would tell you the temperature must be below 5 degrees Celsius.

Although conditionals often make or suggest causal claims, their meaning isn't always causal. The examples above do not mean that snow tonight would **cause** the temperature to fall below 5 degrees Celsius, nor vice versa.

None of these examples imply that it **must** snow if the temperature falls below 5 degrees Celsius tonight. A conditional *if A, then B* does not imply that *if B, then A*.

F. Two ***logically equivalent*** statements ***A and B*** are always both true or both false under the same conditions. Each implies the other. That is, ***if A, then B***, and ***if B, then A***. These two conditionals can be combined as ***A if and only if B***.

3. Reasoning with Logical Operators

A. Here's a list of some types of logically equivalent statements made with logical operators. In this list, ***not*** means negation, ***and*** means logical conjunction, ***or*** means inclusive disjunction, and ***if … then*** means conditional implication.

<table>
<tr><td colspan="3" align="center">Logical Equivalences with Logical Operators</td></tr>
<tr><td>A and B</td><td>is logically equivalent to</td><td>B and A</td></tr>
<tr><td>not (A and B)</td><td>is logically equivalent to</td><td>not-A or not-B</td></tr>
<tr><td>A or B</td><td>is logically equivalent to</td><td>B or A</td></tr>
<tr><td>not (A or B)</td><td>is logically equivalent to</td><td>not-A and not-B (in other words, neither A nor B)</td></tr>
<tr><td>if A, then B</td><td>is logically equivalent to</td><td>if not-B, then not-A</td></tr>
<tr><td>if A, then (B and C)</td><td>is logically equivalent to</td><td>(if A, then B) and (if A, then C)</td></tr>
<tr><td>if A, then (B or C)</td><td>is logically equivalent to</td><td>(if A, then B) or (if A, then C)</td></tr>
<tr><td>if (A or B), then C</td><td>is logically equivalent to</td><td>(if A, then C) and (if B, then C)</td></tr>
</table>

B. Of any two logically equivalent statements, either can be a premise supporting the other as a conclusion in a valid deductive argument. For any line in the list above, a valid deductive argument has a premise of the form on one side and a logically equivalent conclusion of the form on the other side.

Examples:

The second line in the list above says that for any statements ***A*** and ***B***, the statement ***not (A and B)*** is logically equivalent to ***not-A or not-B***. This gives us two valid deductive arguments:

(i) ***not (A and B), therefore not-A or not-B***

and

(ii) ***not-A or not-B, therefore not (A and B)***

For example, the statement ***Ashley and Tim don't both live in this neighborhood*** is logically equivalent to ***Either Ashley doesn't live in this neighborhood or Tim doesn't***. This lets us make two valid deductive arguments:

(iii) Ashley and Tim don't both live in this neighborhood. Therefore, either Ashley doesn't live in this neighborhood or Tim doesn't.

and

(iv) Either Ashley doesn't live in this neighborhood or Tim doesn't. Therefore, Ashley and Tim don't both live in this neighborhood.

C. Here's a list of some other valid deductive argument forms with logical operators, and of invalid forms often confused with them.

<table>
<tr><td colspan="2" align="center">Valid and Invalid Inferences with Logical Operators</td></tr>
<tr><td>Valid: A and B, therefore A</td><td>Invalid: A, therefore A and B</td></tr>
<tr><td>Valid: A, therefore A or B</td><td>Invalid: A or B, therefore A</td></tr>
<tr><td>Valid: not-A and not-B, therefore not (A and B)</td><td>Invalid: not (A and B), therefore not-A and not-B</td></tr>
<tr><td>Valid: not (A or B), therefore not-A or not-B</td><td>Invalid: not-A or not-B, therefore not (A or B)</td></tr>
<tr><td>Valid: if A, then B; and A; therefore B</td><td>Invalid: if A, then B; and B; therefore A</td></tr>
<tr><td>Valid: if A, then B; and not-B; therefore not-A</td><td>Invalid: if A, then B; and not-A; therefore not-B</td></tr>
</table>

Examples:

The third line in the table above says that ***not-A and not-B, therefore not (A and B)*** is valid, but ***not (A and B), therefore not-A and not-B*** is invalid. A simple example of a **valid** argument is:

(i) Ashley doesn't live in this neighborhood, and Tim doesn't either. Therefore, Ashley and Tim don't both live in this neighborhood.

But swapping argument (i)'s premise with its conclusion makes this **invalid** argument:

(ii) Ashley and Tim don't both live in this neighborhood. Therefore, Ashley doesn't live in this neighborhood and Tim doesn't either.

As another example, the table's fifth line says that ***if A, then B; and A; therefore B*** is valid, but ***if A, then B; and B; therefore A*** is invalid. So, another **valid** argument is:

(iii) If Ashley lives in this neighborhood, so does Tim. Ashley does live in this neighborhood. Therefore, Tim also lives in this neighborhood.

However, swapping argument (iii)'s second premise with its conclusion makes this **invalid** argument:

(iv) If Ashley lives in this neighborhood, so does Tim. Tim does live in this neighborhood. Therefore, Ashley lives in this neighborhood.

4. Necessity, Probability, and Possibility

A. Some words and phrases mark how likely a statement is to be true. For example, they may mean that:

- The statement is *necessarily* true; that is, there's a 100 percent chance the statement is true; or

- The statement is *probably* true; that is, there's a good chance the statement is true;

- The statement is *possibly* true; that is, the odds are greater than 0 percent that the statement is true.

Saying a claim is possibly true or probably true usually implies it's not necessarily true.

B. The table below shows three categories of words and phrases that can stand for degrees of probability:

Words Standing for Necessity, Probability, and Possibility		
Necessity	**Probability**	**Possibility**
certainly	*probably*	*can*
clearly	*likely*	*could*
definitely	*more likely than not*	*may*
must		*maybe*
necessarily		*might*
surely		*perhaps*
		possibly

The words **probably** and **likely** sometimes mean high probability, like a 95 percent chance. Other times they mean a medium chance, even one below 50 percent. Don't give these terms any exact meanings when you find them on the GMAT exam.

C. The table below lists some valid deductive argument forms with necessity, probability, and possibility, as well as invalid forms often confused with them.

Valid and Invalid Inferences with Necessity, Probability, and Possibility	
Valid: *Probably A, therefore possibly A*	**Invalid:** *Possibly A, therefore probably A*
Valid: *Possibly (A and B), therefore possibly A and possibly B*	**Invalid:** *Possibly A and possibly B, therefore possibly (A and B)*
Valid: *Probably (A and B), therefore probably A and probably B*	**Invalid:** *Probably A and probably B, therefore probably (A and B)*
Valid: *Probably A or probably B, therefore probably (A or B)*	**Invalid:** *Probably (A or B), therefore probably A or probably B*
Valid: *Necessarily A or necessarily B, therefore necessarily (A or B)*	**Invalid:** *Necessarily (A or B), therefore necessarily A or necessarily B*

Examples:

The table's second line says that **possibly (A and B), therefore possibly A and possibly B** is valid, while **possibly A and possibly B, therefore possibly (A and B)** is invalid. A simple **valid** argument is:

(i) Possibly Tim and Ashley both live in this house. So, possibly Tim lives in this house, and possibly Ashley does.

Swapping argument (i)'s premise with its conclusion gives us this **invalid** argument:

(ii) Possibly Tim lives in this house, and possibly Ashley does. So, possibly both Tim and Ashley live in this house.

To see that argument (ii) is invalid, suppose you know only one person lives in the house, but you don't know whether that person is Tim, Ashley, or someone else. Then argument (ii)'s premise would be true, but its conclusion would be false.

5. Quantifiers

A. A *quantifier* is a word or phrase for a proportion, number, or amount. Some basic quantifiers are ***all***, ***most***, ***some***, and ***none***.

   i. A quantifier like ***all*** means 100 percent of the individuals in a category, or the whole of an amount.

   ii. A quantifier like ***most*** usually means more than half the individuals in a category, or more than half of a whole. ***Most*** usually implies ***not all***, but not always. Writing ***most but not all***, or else ***most or all***, can clarify the meaning.

   iii. A quantifier like ***some*** often means one or more individuals in a category, or part of a whole. ***Some*** usually but not always implies ***not all***. However, ***only some*** clearly does imply ***not all***, while ***at least some*** clearly doesn't. ***Some*** with a plural usually means ***more than one***. In contrast, ***some*** with a singular usually means ***exactly one***. For example, "some dogs" usually means "more than one dog," while "some dog" usually means "exactly one dog." But "some dog or dogs" means "at least one dog."

   iv. A quantifier like ***no*** or ***none of*** means something is being denied about all the individuals in a category, or about all of some whole.

   v. Other common quantifiers have more nuanced meanings. For example, ***a few*** vaguely means a small number more than two. The upper limit of what counts as ***a few*** depends on context. For example, "a few Europeans" might mean thousands of people (still a tiny part of Europe's population). But "a few residents in our building" might mean only three or four people if the building has only fifteen residents.

B. The table below classifies some quantifier words by their meanings.

<table>
<thead>
<tr><th colspan="4" align="center">Basic Quantifier Words</th></tr>
<tr><th>"All" and similar quantifier words</th><th>"Most" and similar quantifier words</th><th>"Some" and similar quantifier words</th><th>"No" and similar quantifier words</th></tr>
</thead>
<tbody>
<tr><td>all</td><td>generally</td><td>a number</td><td>never</td></tr>
<tr><td>always</td><td>a majority</td><td>a portion</td><td>no</td></tr>
<tr><td>any</td><td>most</td><td>any</td><td>none</td></tr>
<tr><td>both</td><td>more than half</td><td>at least one</td><td>not any</td></tr>
<tr><td>each</td><td>usually</td><td>occasionally</td><td>not one</td></tr>
<tr><td>every</td><td></td><td>one or more</td><td>nowhere</td></tr>
<tr><td>everywhere</td><td></td><td>some</td><td></td></tr>
<tr><td>whenever</td><td></td><td>sometimes</td><td></td></tr>
<tr><td>wherever</td><td></td><td>somewhere</td><td></td></tr>
</tbody>
</table>

Notice the table shows ***any*** both as a quantifier like ***all*** and as a quantifier like ***some***. That's because ***any*** can have either meaning. For example, ***Any of the students would prefer chocolate ice cream*** means ***Each of the students would prefer chocolate ice cream***. However, ***I don't know if any of the students would prefer chocolate ice cream*** means ***I don't know if even one of the students would prefer chocolate ice cream***.

C. A quantifier used with a category usually implies the category isn't empty. But this doesn't always hold in hypothetical statements, in conditionals, or with the quantifier ***any***.

> *Examples:*
>
> (i) **All** life forms native to planets other than Earth **are** carbon-based.
>
> (ii) **Any** life forms native to planets other than Earth **would be** carbon-based.
>
> In (i), the words *all* and *are* show the author is claiming there really are life forms native to planets other than Earth. But in (ii), the words *any* and *would be* show the author is carefully avoiding that claim.

D. Statements with two or more quantifiers sometimes look alike but differ in meaning because of word order and phrasing.

> *Example:*
>
> (i) Some beverage must be the favorite of every student in the class.
>
> (ii) Each student in the class must have some favorite beverage.
>
> Statement (i) suggests that every student in the class must have **the same** favorite beverage. In contrast, statement (ii) can be true even if each student has a **different** favorite beverage.

6. Reasoning with Quantifiers

A. Here's a list of some logically equivalent statement forms with quantifiers. In this list, *some* means **one or more**. The forms in the list use plurals, but similar equivalences can hold without plurals. For example, *No water is fire* is logically equivalent to *No fire is water*, even though those two statements don't have plurals like the forms in the list do.

<table>
<tr><td colspan="3" align="center">Logical Equivalences with Quantifiers</td></tr>
<tr><td>All As are Bs</td><td>is logically equivalent to</td><td>No As are not Bs.</td></tr>
<tr><td>Some As are Bs</td><td>is logically equivalent to</td><td>Some Bs are As.</td></tr>
<tr><td>No As are Bs</td><td>is logically equivalent to</td><td>No Bs are As.</td></tr>
<tr><td>Some As are not Bs</td><td>is logically equivalent to</td><td>Not all As are Bs.</td></tr>
</table>

However, *All As are Bs* is **not** equivalent to *All Bs are As*. And *Some As are not Bs* is **not** equivalent to *Some Bs are not As*.

> *Examples:*
>
> (i) The true statement *All ostriches are birds* is not equivalent to the false statement *All birds are ostriches*.
>
> (ii) The true statement *Some birds are not ostriches* is not equivalent to the false statement *Some ostriches are not birds*.

B. As explained above, either of two logically equivalent statements can be a premise supporting the other as a conclusion in a valid deductive argument. This works for equivalences with quantifiers just like it does for equivalences with logical operators.

C. A *syllogism* is a type of simple deductive argument whose two premises have one quantifier apiece, and whose conclusion also has one quantifier.

Here's a list of some valid syllogism forms along with invalid forms sometimes confused with them. As above, in this list, *some* means *one or more*.

<table>
<tr><td colspan="2" align="center">**Valid and Invalid Syllogisms**</td></tr>
<tr><td>**Valid:** *All As are Bs. All Bs are Cs. So, all As are Cs.*</td><td>**Invalid:** *All As are Bs. All Bs are Cs. So, all Cs are As.*
Invalid: *All As are Bs. All Cs are Bs. So, all As are Cs.*
Invalid: *All Bs are As. All Bs are Cs. So, all As are Cs.*</td></tr>
<tr><td>**Valid:** *Some As are Bs. All Bs are Cs. So, some As are Cs.*</td><td>**Invalid:** *All As are Bs. Some Bs are Cs. So, some As are Cs.*
Invalid: *Some As are Bs. Some Bs are Cs. So, some As are Cs.*</td></tr>
<tr><td>**Valid:** *All As are Bs. No Bs are Cs. So, no As are Cs.*</td><td>**Invalid:** *No As are Bs. All Bs are Cs. So, no As are Cs.*
Invalid: *No As are Bs. No Bs are Cs. So, all As are Cs.*
Invalid: *No As are Bs. All Bs are Cs. So, some As are not Cs.*</td></tr>
</table>

Examples:

The list's first line says that ***All As are Bs. All Bs are Cs. So, all As are Cs*** is valid. And here's a **valid** syllogism of that form:

(i) All the trees in the local park were planted by the town arborist. All the trees the arborist planted have been labeled by her. So, all the trees in the park must have been labeled by the arborist.

A similar-looking but **invalid** syllogism has the form ***All As are Bs. All Bs are Cs. So, all Cs are As*** from the list's second line:

(ii) All the trees in the local park were planted by the town arborist. All the trees the arborist planted have been labeled by her. So, all the trees the arborist has labeled must be in the park.

To see that argument (ii) is invalid, notice that even if both premises are true, the arborist might also have labeled trees outside the park—maybe even trees she didn't plant.

Another **invalid** syllogism has the form ***All As are Bs. All Cs are Bs. So, all As are Cs*** from the list's third line:

(iii) All the trees in the local park were planted by the town arborist. All the trees the arborist has labeled are trees she planted. So, all the trees in the park must have been labeled by the arborist.

To see that argument (iii) is invalid, notice that even if both premises are true, the arborist might not have labeled every tree she planted, nor even every tree she planted in the park.

The form in the list's fourth line (***All Bs are As. All Bs are Cs. So, all As are Cs***) gives us yet another **invalid** syllogism:

(iv) All the trees the town arborist has planted are in the local park. All the trees the arborist planted have been labeled by her. So, all the trees in the park must have been labeled by the arborist.

To see that argument (iv) is invalid, notice that even if both premises are true, the park might have many trees that the arborist neither planted nor labeled.

D. Some quantifier words in the table "Basic Quantifier Words" in Section 3.3.5.B above refer to time or place. For example, *whenever* means ***every time***, *usually* means ***most times***, and *never* means ***at no time***. Understanding these meanings can help you rewrite deductive arguments using these words into standard syllogisms to check their validity.

> *Example:*
>
> Max never goes running when the sidewalks are icy. The sidewalks are usually icy on January mornings, so Max must not go running on most January mornings.
>
> We can rewrite this argument in the valid syllogism form ***No As are Bs. Most Cs are Bs. So, most Cs are not As***:
>
> No occasions when Max goes running are occasions when the sidewalks are icy. Most January mornings are occasions when the sidewalks are icy. So, most January mornings are not occasions when Max goes running.
>
> Since arguments in this syllogism form are valid, we can tell that the argument in this example is valid.

To register for the GMAT™ exam, go to www.mba.com/register

4.0 Verbal Reasoning

4.0 Verbal Reasoning

The Verbal Reasoning section of the GMAT™ exam uses multiple-choice questions to measure your skill in reasoning, understanding what you read, and evaluating arguments. This section has passages about many topics, but it doesn't assume you already know about the topics. Mingled throughout the section are questions of two main types: Reading Comprehension and Critical Reasoning.

Reading Comprehension questions are based on passages of around 200 to 350 words. With each passage are several questions asking you to understand, analyze, apply, and evaluate that passage's information and concepts. On the left side of your screen, the passage stays visible as you answer the questions about it. On the right side of your screen, one question appears at a time, along with its answer choices. Different passages may have different numbers of questions.

Critical Reasoning questions are based on passages usually of fewer than 100 words. Unlike Reading Comprehension passages, each Critical Reasoning passage has just one question. This question asks you to logically analyze, evaluate, or reason about an argument, situation, or plan the passage presents. Only one passage and its single question appear at a time.

You have 45 minutes to answer the 23 questions in the Verbal Reasoning section, an average of just under two minutes per question.

To prepare for the Verbal Reasoning section, first review basic concepts of text analysis and logical reasoning. Read Chapter 3, "Verbal Review," which briefly covers these concepts. After reviewing, practice on questions from past GMAT exams.

4.1 What Is Measured

The Verbal Reasoning section measures how well you understand, analyze, apply, evaluate, and reason about information and ideas in texts. Specifically, it tests the following skills:

Skill Category	Details	Examples
Recognize stated ideas	Understand, restate, and summarize information and ideas	• Find a passage's overall theme or point • Find a specific detail • Summarize a set of statements • Tell if an idea is stated or implied • Tell what a word or phrase means in context
Analyze reasoning structure	Identify premises, conclusions, explanations, argument techniques, reasons for plans, and background information	• Tell what argument technique someone uses • Tell a statement's role in a passage
Apply ideas in new contexts	Use general ideas in new situations the passage doesn't discuss	• Decide which new situation is most like one in the passage • Tell which new action would follow or break a rule in the passage • Decide which new example would best illustrate an idea in the passage

Skill Category	Details	Examples
Infer	Draw an unstated conclusion from a passage	• Decide which conclusion a passage most strongly supports • Tell what follows logically from information given • Decide what a stated opinion implies • Recognize an author's attitude from word choices
Identify unstated assumptions	Find an assumption that fills a logical gap in an argument, explanation, or plan	• Find an assumption an argument depends on • Find an assumption that makes an argument's conclusion follow logically • Tell what must happen for a plan to succeed
Evaluate hypotheses	Judge explanations for a situation	• Decide what would most help explain why a plan failed • Decide what most likely caused an observed effect
Resolve discrepancies	Explain or justify an apparent conflict between two statements or situations	• Explain why a factor didn't cause its usual effect • Decide which principle resolves a conflict between two opinions
Strengthen or weaken reasoning	Identify new information that either supports or undermines an argument, explanation, plan, or claim	• Tell which discovery would cast the most doubt on an argument's reasoning • Tell what added evidence would best support a causal explanation
Identify reasoning flaws	Identify mistakes such as confusing correlation with causation or confusing a sufficient assumption with a necessary one	• Decide which observation points to a reasoning flaw • Tell which criticism an argument is most vulnerable to
Identify points of disagreement	Tell what two parties disagree about, based on their statements	• Find the main implied point of disagreement in a dialogue
Solve a practical problem	Recognize a good strategy for solving a problem	• Find a way of sampling a population accurately despite an obstacle

4.2 Question Types

Reading Comprehension and Critical Reasoning are the two main Verbal Reasoning question types. Each has several subtypes. During the test, the subtypes aren't labeled. Each question tells you what you need to do.

1. Reading Comprehension

The five Reading Comprehension question subtypes are Main Idea, Supporting Idea, Inference, Application, and Evaluation. Each tests a different main skill, but sometimes the skills overlap. For example, to find a passage's main idea, you must understand the passage's logical and rhetorical structure. To make inferences or apply ideas from a passage, you often must find its main and supporting ideas.

Below, we discuss the Reading Comprehension question subtypes.

A. Main Idea

- In each passage, all the sentences and paragraphs develop one central point or share one overall purpose. A Main Idea question asks you to find this central point or purpose. Sometimes the passage tells you its central point. Other times you must infer it from the passage's structure and content.

- A Main Idea question may ask which answer option best restates the central point, best explains the author's main goal for the passage, or works best as a title for the passage.

- Main Idea questions use phrases like these:

  . . . most accurately expresses the main idea . . .,

  The primary purpose of the passage as a whole is to . . ., or

  In the passage, the author seeks primarily to. . . .

- The right answer to a Main Idea question about an argumentative passage often restates or describes the main conclusion of the main argument. To find the main conclusion, you must notice which statements in the passage are given as reasons to accept which other statements. The main conclusion is an idea that the whole passage gives reasons to accept, but that isn't in turn given as a reason to accept some further conclusion.

- When the passage isn't argumentative, the right answer to a Main Idea question usually gives the passage's overall theme or purpose. The overall theme is often an idea repeated in different paragraphs. The overall purpose is usually a goal toward which all the paragraphs work. If the passage has no overall theme or purpose, the right answer may just summarize the passage. For example, the right answer to a Main Idea question about a narrative passage might summarize the events described or state their overall outcome.

- Wrong answer choices often repeat passage details that aren't the main point, make claims that look like the main point but are different, or state ideas not mentioned in the passage but related to it.

B. Supporting Idea

- Supporting Idea questions may ask you about anything the passage states except for the main point. To answer a Supporting Idea question, you must understand individual statements and their roles in the passage.

- Answers to Supporting Idea questions almost never directly quote the passage. They usually rephrase statements from the passage or describe them abstractly. A Supporting Idea question may ask which statement plays a specific role in the passage. For example, it may ask you to find a premise, an intermediate conclusion, a described viewpoint, an objection, an example or counterexample, a causal claim, background information, a descriptive detail, or part of an explanation or narrative. Or it may also ask what a word or phrase in the passage means in context.

- Supporting Idea questions often use phrases like these:

  According to the passage . . .,

  Which of the following does the author cite as . . .,

  Which of the following does the author offer as an objection to . . .,

  The passage compares . . .,

  The passage mentions . . ., or

  Which of the following does the author propose. . . .

C. Inference

- Inference questions ask about ideas the passage suggests or supports but doesn't state. Some of these questions ask about ideas the author clearly meant the passage to imply. Others ask about logical implications, which the author may not have noticed.

- An Inference question may ask you to find:

  a likely cause or effect of a situation the passage describes,

  a specific implication of a generalization in the passage, or

  a statement that someone discussed in the passage would likely accept or reject.

- Sometimes the inference follows from one small part of the passage. Other times it depends on several statements scattered through different paragraphs. Sometimes the question says where to look in the passage, but not always.

- Inference questions often use phrases like these:

  Which of the following statements about . . . is most strongly supported by . . .,

  It can be inferred from the passage that . . .,

  If the claims about . . . are true, which of the following is most likely also true?

  The passage implies that . . ., or

  The information in the passage suggests that. . . .

- Wrong answer choices may be true, and related to the passage, but not supported by it. Conversely, the right answer choice may be false but follow logically from false statements in the passage. For example, even if the passage rightly says a theory is mistaken, a question might ask what would follow if the theory were true.

D. Application

- Application questions ask how situations or ideas the passage discusses relate to other situations or ideas the passage doesn't mention.

- Application questions may use words like *would, could, might,* or *should,* or phrases like *most clearly exemplifies, most similar to,* or *most likely ruled out by.*

- Some Application questions ask you to reason by analogy. They may ask which of several roles, methods, goals, or relationships is most like one the passage mentions. Review Section 3.2.4, "Analogies," which explains reasoning by analogy.

- Other Application questions ask you to apply general rules. For example, they may ask:

  which rule's enforcement would help achieve a goal the passage mentions, which principle a judgment in the passage relies on,

which action would break or follow a rule the passage states,

which generalization the evidence in the passage best fits, or

which general strategy could solve a problem the passage describes.

- The third type of Application question asks you to extend the passage. Questions of this type may ask for:

the best topic for a new paragraph added to the end of the passage,

a good example of a point the author makes, or

the author's most likely response to a possible objection.

- The fourth type of Application question asks about "what-if" scenarios. These questions may ask:

how different experimental results might affect a researcher's conclusions,

how a trend the passage mentions might be disrupted, or

how events might have gone differently if a situation had never occurred.

- Don't rule out answer choices just because they're not about the passage. Because Application questions relate the passage to new topics, the right answers are often about topics the passage never mentions. For instance, the right answer to an analogy question about a water-treatment process the passage explains might be about book publishing.

E. Evaluation

- Evaluation questions ask you to assess the passage's organization and logic.

- They often use phrases like these:

The purpose of . . .,

. . . most accurately describes the structure of . . .,

. . . most strengthens . . .,

. . . would most justify . . .,

. . . is most vulnerable to the objection that . . ., or

Which . . . additional information would most help. . . .

- An Evaluation question's answer choices are often abstract. They may not use specific words or ideas from the passage. For example, a question about a paragraph's function might have this answer choice: *It rejects a theory presented in the preceding paragraph and offers some criteria that an alternative theory would need to meet.*

- Some Evaluation questions ask about the roles of different parts of the passage. They may ask:

how the whole passage or part of it is structured,

why the author put a specific detail in the passage,

what purpose a statement in the passage serves,

how the author tries to persuade readers to accept a claim, or

what attitude most likely motivated an opinion the passage mentions.

- Other Evaluation questions ask about:

  the strengths, weaknesses, relevance, or effectiveness of parts of the passage,

  implicit assumptions in the passage,

  what would best resolve apparent conflicts between parts of the passage, or

  potential objections, justifications, supporting evidence, or counterexamples.

These questions are often similar to Critical Reasoning questions, discussed below.

2. Critical Reasoning

The four subtypes of Critical Reasoning question are Analysis, Construction, Critique, and Plan. We discuss each below.

A. Analysis

- Analysis questions ask about a passage's logical structure and the roles that statements play in it.
- Analysis questions often use phrases like these:

  *. . . the two portions in **boldface** play which of the following roles?*

  The argument proceeds by . . .,

  A technique used in the argument is to . . .,

  . . . responds to . . . by . . .,

  The statements above can best serve as part of an argument against . . ., or

  Which of the following is the main point of disagreement between. . . .

- Some Analysis questions ask about the roles of one or two statements in the passage. Often the passage shows these statements in **boldface**.
- Other Analysis questions ask about an argumentative method in the passage. Sometimes the passage itself is an argument, and the question asks how it works. Other times, the passage is a dialogue, and the question asks what argumentative technique one speaker uses in replying to the other.
- Another type of Analysis question asks about an unstated point in the passage. This point may be a conclusion the passage is meant to support. Or it may be a point of agreement or disagreement between the two speakers in a dialogue.

B. Construction

- Construction questions ask how to best complete partial arguments or explanations.
- Construction questions often use phrases like these:

  . . . most logically completes . . .,

  If the statements above are true . . .,

  . . . most strongly support . . .,

  . . . best explains the discrepancy . . .,

  . . . depends on the assumption that . . .,

  . . . enables the conclusion to be properly drawn? or

  . . . provides the strongest justification for. . . .

- Some Construction questions ask what conclusion a set of premises best supports. These questions may ask for a conclusion that logically follows from the premises, or for a conclusion that the premises merely give evidence for.

- Other Construction questions ask for a missing premise to support a given conclusion. A question like this usually says whether the premise must be a necessary assumption, a sufficient assumption, a relevant observation, or a justification for a position. The passage may state only the conclusion, or it may also give other premises to combine with the missing premise.

- Another type of Construction question asks what would best explain either an observation or a puzzling discrepancy between observations.

C. Critique

- Critique questions ask you to judge reasoning in passages, find its strengths or weaknesses, and decide how it could be improved.

- Critique questions often use phrases like these:

  . . . most vulnerable to the criticism that . . . ,

  . . . logically flawed in that . . . ,

  . . . most seriously weakens . . . ,

  . . . casts the most serious doubt on . . . ,

  . . . most strengthens . . . ,

  . . . most strongly supports . . . , or

  . . . would be most useful to know in order to evaluate. . . .

- Some Critique questions ask how an argument is flawed or weak. These questions are often about arguments with standard reasoning flaws, like the flaws discussed in Sections 3.2, "Inductive Reasoning," and 3.3, "Deductive Reasoning." In other cases, the arguments have no standard flaw but don't work because they rely on some obviously implausible assumption.

- Other Critique questions ask what new evidence would most strengthen or weaken an argument. These arguments are always inductive because evidence can't strengthen or weaken a deductive argument. Section 3.2, "Inductive Reasoning," explains how evidence can strengthen and weaken arguments.

- Finally, some Critique questions ask you what would be most helpful to know in order to assess a hypothesis or argument in the passage. The answer choices for these questions start with the word *Whether*, followed by an idea whose truth is unknown. The right answer choice gives the idea whose truth or falsehood would be most helpful to know in order to decide whether the hypothesis in the passage is true. The wrong answer choices give ideas that, whether true or false, are less relevant to the hypothesis.

D. Plan

- Plan questions ask you to construct or judge reasoning about actual or proposed courses of action, or plans. Section 3.1.2.D briefly explains this type of reasoning.

- Plan questions use many of the same phrases found in Construction and Critique questions, but the questions are always about plans, strategies, or courses of action.

- Plan questions may ask:

  what must be true for a plan to succeed,

what conditions would make a plan more or less likely to succeed,

what would be most helpful to know in order to judge a plan,

what evidence would best support an opinion about a plan,

how a plan is flawed,

what strategy would most help overcome a problem,

what policy would most help reach a goal under certain conditions, or

why a plan succeeded, failed, or had some unexpected effect.

4.3 Tips for Answering Verbal Reasoning Questions

1. Answer using only the information given and common knowledge.

The passages and common knowledge tell you everything you need to answer correctly. If you already know about the passage topic, don't use that knowledge to answer. Answer based on what the passage states or implies, and on common knowledge. For example, if the passage says something happened during a snowstorm, you can use common knowledge about snowstorms to infer that the weather wasn't hot.

2. Look for cue words marking statements' roles.

Section 3.1, "Analyzing Passages," explains how certain cue words often mark premises, conclusions, causal explanations, and narrative sequences. These cue words tell you what roles statements near them play. Also notice transition words marking a shift from one topic to another, and how those words suggest the topics are related. Usually, you can tell a statement's role even without a cue word. For example, if the passage clearly gives one statement as a reason to accept another, you don't need cue words to tell that the first statement is a premise and the second a conclusion.

3. Analyze the passage's structure and purpose.

Once you know the roles individual statements play, you can find the passage's overall structure and purpose. Does the passage mainly report facts and events? Does it argue for a conclusion? Does it discuss competing causal explanations? Does it comment on situations or other writers' views? Notice which premises are given to support which conclusions, and which causes are said to produce which effects. Notice also if the passage uses intermediate conclusions to support a main conclusion. Finally, notice any clear but unstated implications of the passage.

4. Use basic principles of good reasoning to judge the passage's reasoning.

Sections 3.2, "Inductive Reasoning," and 3.3, "Deductive Reasoning," review some principles of good reasoning. When a question asks you to judge the reasoning in the passage, use these basic principles. You don't need advanced knowledge of logic or any other subject to answer correctly.

5. Notice exactly what the question asks.

Often the wrong answer to one question would be the right answer to another question that looks similar. You need to pick the right answer to the specific question asked. To do that, focus on the question. For example, if the question asks about one part of the passage, don't pick an answer choice about some other part of the passage. As another example, these two questions could easily be confused:

i) Which of the following crops is grown by *the most farms* in Nation X?

ii) Farms in Nation X grow *the most of* which of the following crops?

The nation's farms may grow the most of a crop that's not grown by the most farms. If many small farms grow potatoes while a few huge farms grow wheat, the right answer to (i) could be *potatoes* even if the right answer to (ii) is *wheat*.

6. Read all the answer choices before picking one.

Verbal Reasoning questions often ask you to pick the best answer choice of those given. To tell which answer choice is best, read them all.

7. If you're not sure which answer choice is right, try ruling out some that are clearly wrong.

Ruling out some clearly wrong answer choices can help you find the right answer choice. If you're still undecided between two answer choices, study the passage again for clues you may have missed.

8. Pace yourself.

You have less than two minutes per question. You need to spend much of that time reading the passages. To avoid running out of time, don't spend too long on any one question. If you get stuck on a question for a couple of minutes after you've ruled out some of the answer choices, just pick the remaining choice that seems best. Then go to the next question.

To register for the GMAT™ exam, go to www.mba.com/register

4.4 Practice Questions: Reading Comprehension

Each of the Reading Comprehension questions is based on the content of a passage. After reading the passage, answer all questions pertaining to it on the basis of what is stated or implied in the passage. For each question, select the best answer of the choices given. On the actual GMAT exam, you will see no more than four questions per passage.

Questions 1 to 35 — Difficulty: Easy

Line   Human beings, born with a drive to explore
and experiment, thrive on learning. Unfortunately,
corporations are oriented predominantly toward
controlling employees, not fostering their learning.
(5)   Ironically, this orientation creates the very
conditions that predestine employees to mediocre
performances. Over time, superior performance
requires superior learning, because long-term
corporate survival depends on continually exploring
(10) new business and organizational opportunities that
can create new sources of growth.
   To survive in the future, corporations must
become "learning organizations," enterprises that
are constantly able to adapt and expand their
(15) capabilities. To accomplish this, corporations must
change how they view employees. The traditional
view that a single charismatic leader should set the
corporation's direction and make key decisions is
rooted in an individualistic worldview. In an
(20) increasingly interdependent world, such a view is
no longer viable. In learning organizations, thinking
and acting are integrated at all job levels. Corporate
leadership is shared, and leaders become
designers, teachers, and stewards, roles requiring
(25) new skills: the ability to build shared vision, to
reveal and challenge prevailing mental models, and
to foster broader, more integrated patterns of
thinking. In short, leaders in learning organizations
are responsible for building organizations in which
(30) employees are continually learning new skills and
expanding their capabilities to shape their future.

Questions 1–4 refer to the passage.

1.   According to the passage, traditional corporate leaders differ from leaders in learning organizations in that the former

  (A) encourage employees to concentrate on developing a wide range of skills

  (B) enable employees to recognize and confront dominant corporate models and to develop alternative models

  (C) make important policy decisions alone and then require employees in the corporation to abide by those decisions

  (D) instill confidence in employees because of their willingness to make risky decisions and accept their consequences

  (E) are concerned with offering employees frequent advice and career guidance

2.   Which of the following best describes employee behavior encouraged within learning organizations, as such organizations are described in the passage?

  (A) Carefully defining one's job description and taking care to avoid deviations from it

  (B) Designing mentoring programs that train new employees to follow procedures that have been used for many years

  (C) Concentrating one's efforts on mastering one aspect of a complicated task

  (D) Studying an organizational problem, preparing a report, and submitting it to a corporate leader for approval

  (E) Analyzing a problem related to productivity, making a decision about a solution, and implementing that solution

3. According to the author of the passage, corporate leaders of the future should do which of the following?

    (A) They should encourage employees to put long-term goals ahead of short-term profits.

    (B) They should exercise more control over employees in order to constrain production costs.

    (C) They should redefine incentives for employees' performance improvement.

    (D) They should provide employees with opportunities to gain new skills and expand their capabilities.

    (E) They should promote individual managers who are committed to established company policies.

4. The primary purpose of the passage is to

    (A) endorse a traditional corporate structure

    (B) introduce a new approach to corporate leadership and evaluate criticisms of it

    (C) explain competing theories about management practices and reconcile them

    (D) contrast two typical corporate organizational structures

    (E) propose an alternative to a common corporate approach

Line   Ecoefficiency (measures to minimize environmental
impact through the reduction or elimination of waste
from production processes) has become a goal for
companies worldwide, with many realizing significant
(5)   cost savings from such innovations. Peter Senge and
Goran Carstedt see this development as laudable but
suggest that simply adopting ecoefficiency innovations
could actually worsen environmental stresses in the
future. Such innovations reduce production waste but
(10)   do not alter the number of products manufactured
nor the waste generated from their use and discard;
indeed, most companies invest in ecoefficiency
improvements in order to increase profits and growth.
Moreover, there is no guarantee that increased
(15)   economic growth from ecoefficiency will come in
similarly ecoefficient ways, since in today's global
markets, greater profits may be turned into investment
capital that could easily be reinvested in traditionally
eco-inefficient industries. Even a vastly more
(20)   ecoefficient industrial system could, were it to grow
much larger, generate more total waste and destroy
more habitat and species than would a smaller, less
ecoefficient economy. Senge and Carstedt argue
that to preserve the global environment and sustain
(25)   economic growth, businesses must develop a new
systemic approach that reduces total material use
and total accumulated waste. Focusing exclusively
on ecoefficiency, which offers a compelling business
case according to established thinking, may distract
(30)   companies from pursuing radically different products
and business models.

Questions 5–7 refer to the passage.

5.   The primary purpose of the passage is to

(A)   explain why a particular business strategy has
been less successful than was once anticipated

(B)   propose an alternative to a particular business
strategy that has inadvertently caused ecological
damage

(C)   present a concern about the possible
consequences of pursuing a particular business
strategy

(D)   make a case for applying a particular business
strategy on a larger scale than is currently practiced

(E)   suggest several possible outcomes of
companies' failure to understand the economic
impact of a particular business strategy

6.   The passage mentions which of the following as a
possible consequence of a company's realization of
greater profits through ecoefficiency?

(A)   The companies may be able to sell a greater
number of products by lowering prices.

(B)   The companies may be better able to attract
investment capital in the global market.

(C)   The profits may be reinvested to increase
economic growth through ecoefficiency.

(D)   The profits may be used as investment capital
for industries that are not ecoefficient.

(E)   The profits may encourage companies to make
further innovations in reducing production waste.

7. The passage implies that which of the following is a possible consequence of a company's adoption of innovations that increase its ecoefficiency?

    (A) Company profits resulting from such innovations may be reinvested in that company with no guarantee that the company will continue to make further improvements in ecoefficiency.

    (B) Company growth fostered by cost savings from such innovations may allow that company to manufacture a greater number of products that will be used and discarded, thus worsening environmental stress.

    (C) A company that fails to realize significant cost savings from such innovations may have little incentive to continue to minimize the environmental impact of its production processes.

    (D) A company that comes to depend on such innovations to increase its profits and growth may be vulnerable in the global market to competition from traditionally eco-inefficient industries.

    (E) A company that meets its ecoefficiency goals is unlikely to invest its increased profits in the development of new and innovative ecoefficiency measures.

Line   A key decision required of advertising managers is whether a "hard-sell" or "soft-sell" strategy is appropriate for a specific target market. The hard-sell approach involves the use of direct, forceful

(5)   claims regarding the benefits of the advertised brand over competitors' offerings. In contrast, the soft-sell approach involves the use of advertising claims that imply superiority more subtly.

    One positive aspect of the hard-sell approach is

(10)   its use of very simple and straightforward product claims presented as explicit conclusions, with little room for confusion regarding the advertiser's message. However, some consumers may resent being told what to believe, and some may distrust

(15)   the message. Resentment and distrust often lead to counterargumentation and to boomerang effects where consumers come to believe conclusions diametrically opposed to conclusions endorsed in advertising claims. By contrast, the risk of

(20)   boomerang effects is greatly reduced with soft-sell approaches. One way to implement the soft-sell approach is to provide information that implies the main conclusions the advertiser wants the consumer to draw but leave the conclusions

(25)   themselves unstated. Because consumers are invited to make up their own minds, implicit conclusions reduce the risk of resentment, distrust, and counterargumentation.

    Recent research on consumer memory and

(30)   judgment suggests another advantage of implicit conclusions. Beliefs or conclusions that are self-generated are more accessible from memory than beliefs from conclusions provided explicitly by other individuals and thus have a greater impact on

(35)   judgment and decision making. Moreover, self-generated beliefs are often perceived as more accurate and valid than the beliefs of others, because other individuals may be perceived as less knowledgeable or may be perceived as

(40)   manipulative or deliberately misleading.

    Despite these advantages, implicit conclusions may not always be more effective than explicit conclusions. One risk is that some consumers may fail to draw their own conclusions and thus miss the

(45)   point of the message. Inferential activity is likely only when consumers are motivated and able to engage in effortful cognitive processes. Another risk is that some consumers may draw conclusions other than the one intended. Even if inferential

(50)   activity is likely, there is no guarantee that consumers will follow the path provided by the advertiser. Finally, a third risk is that consumers may infer the intended conclusion but question the validity of their inference.

Questions 8–14 refer to the passage.

8.   It can be inferred from the passage that one reason an advertiser might prefer a hard-sell approach to a soft-sell approach is that

(A)   the risks of boomerang effects are minimized when the conclusions an advertiser wants the consumer to draw are themselves left unstated

(B)   counterargumentation is likely from consumers who fail to draw their own conclusions regarding an advertising claim

(C)   inferential activity is likely to occur even if consumers perceive themselves to be more knowledgeable than the individuals presenting product claims

(D)   research on consumer memory suggests that the explicit conclusions provided by an advertiser using the hard-sell approach have a significant impact on decision making

(E)   the information presented by an advertiser using the soft-sell approach may imply different conclusions to different consumers

9.   Each of the following is mentioned in the passage as a characteristic of the hard-sell approach EXCEPT:

(A)   Its overall message is readily grasped.

(B)   It appeals to consumers' knowledge about the product.

(C)   It makes explicit claims that the advertised brand is superior to other brands.

(D)   It uses statements that are expressed very clearly.

(E)   It makes claims in the form of direct conclusions.

10. It can be inferred from the passage that advertisers could reduce one of the risks discussed in the last paragraph if they were able to provide

    (A) motivation for consumers to think about the advertisement's message

    (B) information that implies the advertiser's intended conclusion but leaves that conclusion unstated

    (C) subtle evidence that the advertised product is superior to that of competitors

    (D) information comparing the advertised product with its competitors

    (E) opportunity for consumers to generate their own beliefs or conclusions

11. The primary purpose of the passage is to

    (A) point out the risks involved in the use of a particular advertising strategy

    (B) make a case for the superiority of one advertising strategy over another

    (C) illustrate the ways in which two advertising strategies may be implemented

    (D) present the advantages and disadvantages of two advertising strategies

    (E) contrast the types of target markets for which two advertising strategies are appropriate

12. Which of the following best describes the function of the sentence in lines 25–28 in the context of the passage as a whole?

    (A) It reiterates a distinction between two advertising strategies that is made in the first paragraph.

    (B) It explains how a particular strategy avoids a drawback described earlier in the paragraph.

    (C) It suggests that a risk described earlier in the paragraph is less serious than some researchers believe it to be.

    (D) It outlines why the strategy described in the previous sentence involves certain risks for an advertiser.

    (E) It introduces an argument that will be refuted in the following paragraph.

13. It can be inferred from the passage that one situation in which the boomerang effect often occurs is when consumers

    (A) have been exposed to forceful claims that are diametrically opposed to those in an advertiser's message

    (B) have previous self-generated beliefs or conclusions that are readily accessible from memory

    (C) are subjected to advertising messages that are targeted at specific markets to which those consumers do not belong

    (D) are confused regarding the point of the advertiser's message

    (E) come to view the advertiser's message with suspicion

14. It can be inferred from the passage that the research mentioned in line 29 supports which of the following statements?

    (A) Implicit conclusions are more likely to capture accurately the point of the advertiser's message than are explicit conclusions.

    (B) Counterargumentation is less likely to occur if an individual's beliefs or conclusions are readily accessible from memory.

    (C) The hard-sell approach results in conclusions that are more difficult for the consumer to recall than are conclusions resulting from the soft-sell approach.

    (D) When the beliefs of others are presented as definite and forceful claims, they are perceived to be as accurate as self-generated beliefs.

    (E) Despite the advantages of implicit conclusions, the hard-sell approach involves fewer risks for the advertiser than does the soft-sell approach.

Line   Suppose we were in a spaceship in free fall, where
objects are weightless, and wanted to know a small
solid object's mass. We could not simply balance
that object against another of known weight, as we
(5)   would on Earth. The unknown mass could be
determined, however, by placing the object on a
spring scale and swinging the scale in a circle at
the end of a string. The scale would measure the
tension in the string, which would depend on both
(10)   the speed of revolution and the mass of the object.
The tension would be greater, the greater the mass
or the greater the speed of revolution. From the
measured tension and speed of whirling, we could
determine the object's mass.
(15)   Astronomers use an analogous procedure to
"weigh" double-star systems. The speed with which
the two stars in a double-star system circle one
another depends on the gravitational force between
them, which holds the system together. This
(20)   attractive force, analogous to the tension in the
string, is proportional to the stars' combined mass,
according to Newton's law of gravitation. By
observing the time required for the stars to circle
each other (the period) and measuring the distance
(25)   between them, we can deduce the restraining
force and hence the masses.

Questions 15–19 refer to the passage.

15. It can be inferred from the passage that the two
procedures described in the passage have which of
the following in common?

(A)   They have been applied in practice.

(B)   They rely on the use of a device that measures
tension.

(C)   Their purpose is to determine an unknown mass.

(D)   They can only be applied to small solid objects.

(E)   They involve attraction between objects of
similar mass.

16. According to the passage, the tension in the string
mentioned in lines 8–9 is analogous to which of the
following aspects of a double-star system?

(A)   The speed with which one star orbits the other

(B)   The gravitational attraction between the stars

(C)   The amount of time it takes for the stars to circle
one another

(D)   The distance between the two stars

(E)   The combined mass of the two stars

17. Which of the following best describes the relationship
between the first and the second paragraph of the
passage?

(A)   The first paragraph provides an illustration useful
for understanding a procedure described in the
second paragraph.

(B)   The first paragraph describes a hypothetical
situation whose plausibility is tested in the
second paragraph.

(C)   The first paragraph evaluates the usefulness of a
procedure whose application is described further
in the second paragraph.

(D)   The second paragraph provides evidence to
support a claim made in the first paragraph.

(E)   The second paragraph analyzes the practical
implications of a methodology proposed in the
first paragraph.

18. The author of the passage mentions observations regarding the period of a double-star system as being useful for determining

    (A) the distance between the two stars in the system

    (B) the time it takes for each star to rotate on its axis

    (C) the size of the orbit the system's two stars occupy

    (D) the degree of gravitational attraction between the system's stars

    (E) the speed at which the star system moves through space

19. The primary purpose of the passage is to

    (A) analyze a natural phenomenon in terms of its behavior under special conditions

    (B) describe the steps by which a scientific measurement is carried out

    (C) point out the conditions under which a scientific procedure is most useful

    (D) contrast two different uses of a methodological approach in science

    (E) explain a method by which scientists determine an unknown quantity

Line   Most pre-1990 literature on businesses' use of
information technology (IT)—defined as any form of
computer-based information system—focused on
spectacular IT successes and reflected a general
(5)   optimism concerning IT's potential as a resource
for creating competitive advantage. But toward the
end of the 1980s, some economists spoke of a
"productivity paradox": despite huge IT investments,
most notably in the service sectors, productivity
(10)   stagnated. In the retail industry, for example, in
which IT had been widely adopted during the 1980s,
productivity (average output per hour) rose at an
average annual rate of 1.1 percent between 1973 and
1989, compared with 2.4 percent in the preceding
(15)   25-year period. Proponents of IT argued that it takes
both time and a critical mass of investment for IT
to yield benefits, and some suggested that growth
figures for the 1990s proved these benefits were
finally being realized. They also argued that measures
(20)   of productivity ignore what would have happened
without investments in IT—productivity gains might
have been even lower. There were even claims that IT
had improved the performance of the service sector
significantly, although macroeconomic measures of
(25)   productivity did not reflect the improvement.
    But some observers questioned why, if IT had
conferred economic value, it did not produce
direct competitive advantages for individual firms.
Resource-based theory offers an answer, asserting
(30)   that, in general, firms gain competitive advantages
by accumulating resources that are economically
valuable, relatively scarce, and not easily replicated.
According to a recent study of retail firms, which
confirmed that IT has become pervasive and
(35)   relatively easy to acquire, IT by itself appeared to
have conferred little advantage. In fact, though little
evidence of any direct effect was found, the frequent
negative correlations between IT and performance
suggested that IT had probably weakened some
(40)   firms' competitive positions. However, firms' human
resources, in and of themselves, did explain improved
performance, and some firms gained IT-related
advantages by merging IT with complementary
resources, particularly human resources. The findings
(45)   support the notion, founded in resource-based theory,
that competitive advantages do not arise from easily
replicated resources, no matter how impressive or
economically valuable they may be, but from complex,
intangible resources.

Questions 20–27 refer to the passage.

20.   The passage is primarily concerned with

(A)   describing a resource and indicating various
methods used to study it

(B)   presenting a theory and offering an opposing
point of view

(C)   providing an explanation for unexpected findings

(D)   demonstrating why a particular theory is
unfounded

(E)   resolving a disagreement regarding the uses of a
technology

21.   The author of the passage discusses productivity in
the retail industry in the first paragraph primarily in
order to

(A)   suggest a way in which IT can be used to create
a competitive advantage

(B)   provide an illustration of the "productivity
paradox"

(C)   emphasize the practical value of the introduction
of IT

(D)   cite an industry in which productivity did not
stagnate during the 1980s

(E)   counter the argument that IT could potentially
create competitive advantage

22.   The passage suggests that proponents of resource-
based theory would be likely to explain IT's inability to
produce direct competitive advantages for individual
firms by pointing out that

(A)   IT is not a resource that is difficult to obtain

(B)   IT is not an economically valuable resource

(C)   IT is a complex, intangible resource

(D)   economic progress has resulted from IT only in
the service sector

(E)   changes brought about by IT cannot be detected
by macroeconomic measures

23. Which of the following best describes the content of the first paragraph?

    (A) It presents two explanations for the success of IT.

    (B) It provides evidence that decreases in productivity will continue.

    (C) It presents reasons for a decline in productivity.

    (D) It demonstrates the effect IT has had on productivity.

    (E) It contrasts views concerning the degree of IT's success.

24. The passage suggests that the recent study of retail firms discussed in the second paragraph supports which of the following conclusions regarding a firm's competitive advantage?

    (A) Human resources alone are more likely to contribute to competitive advantage than is IT alone.

    (B) Human resources combined with IT are more likely than human resources alone to have a negative effect on competitive advantage.

    (C) Human resources combined with IT often have a negative effect on competitive advantage.

    (D) IT by itself is much more likely to have a positive effect than a negative effect on competitive advantage.

    (E) The positive effect of IT on competitive advantage increases with time.

25. According to the passage, most pre-1990 literature on businesses' use of IT included which of the following?

    (A) Recommendations regarding effective ways to use IT to gain competitive advantage

    (B) Explanations of the advantages and disadvantages of adopting IT

    (C) Information about ways in which IT combined with human resources could be used to increase competitive advantage

    (D) A warning regarding the negative effect on competitive advantage that would occur if IT were not adopted

    (E) A belief in the likelihood of increased competitive advantage for firms using IT

26. The author of the passage implies that toward the end of the 1980s, some economists described which of the following as a "productivity paradox" (line 8)?

    (A) Investments in IT would not result in increases in productivity until the 1990s.

    (B) Investments in IT did not lead to expected gains in productivity.

    (C) Productivity in the retail industry rose less rapidly than did productivity in other industries.

    (D) The gains in productivity due to the introduction of IT were not reflected in macroeconomic measures of productivity.

    (E) Most gains in productivity occurred in the service sector and were therefore particularly difficult to measure.

27. According to the passage, the recent study of retail firms discussed in the second paragraph (lines 33–36) best supports which of the following assessments of IT's potential?

   (A)   Even when IT gives a firm a temporary competitive advantage, that firm is unlikely to continue to achieve productivity gains.

   (B)   The competitive advantages conferred by a firm's introduction of IT are outweighed by IT's development costs.

   (C)   A firm's introduction of IT is less likely to limit its ability to achieve productivity gains than to enhance that ability.

   (D)   Although IT by itself is unlikely to give a firm a competitive advantage, IT combined with other resources may do so.

   (E)   Although IT by itself is unlikely to give a firm a competitive advantage, a firm that does not employ IT cannot achieve a competitive advantage.

Line   The Black Death, a severe epidemic that ravaged fourteenth-century Europe, has intrigued scholars ever since Francis Gasquet's 1893 study contending that this epidemic greatly intensified the political
(5)   and religious upheaval that ended the Middle Ages. Thirty-six years later, historian George Coulton agreed but, paradoxically, attributed a silver lining to the Black Death: prosperity engendered by diminished competition for food, shelter, and work led survivors
(10) of the epidemic into the Renaissance and subsequent rise of modern Europe.

     In the 1930s, however, Evgeny Kosminsky and other Marxist historians claimed the epidemic was merely an ancillary factor contributing to a general
(15) agrarian crisis stemming primarily from the inevitable decay of European feudalism. In arguing that this decline of feudalism was economically determined, the Marxist asserted that the Black Death was a relatively insignificant factor. This became the prevailing view
(20) until after the Second World War, when studies of specific regions and towns revealed astonishing mortality rates ascribed to the epidemic, thus restoring the central role of the Black Death in history.

     This central role of the Black Death (traditionally
(25) attributed to bubonic plague brought from Asia) has been recently challenged from another direction. Building on bacteriologist John Shrewsbury's speculations about mislabeled epidemics, zoologist Graham Twigg employs urban case studies suggesting
(30) that the rat population in Europe was both too sparse and insufficiently migratory to have spread plague. Moreover, Twigg disputes the traditional trade-ship explanation for plague transmissions by extrapolating from data on the number of dead rats aboard Nile
(35) sailing vessels in 1912. The Black Death, which he conjectures was anthrax instead of bubonic plague, therefore caused far less havoc and fewer deaths than historians typically claim.

     Although correctly citing the exacting conditions
(40) needed to start or spread bubonic plague, Twigg ignores virtually a century of scholarship contradictory to his findings and employs faulty logic in his single-minded approach to the Black Death. His speculative generalizations about the numbers of rats in medieval
(45) Europe are based on isolated studies unrepresentative of medieval conditions, while his unconvincing trade-ship argument overlooks land-based caravans, the overland migration of infected rodents, and the many other animals that carry plague.

Questions 28–31 refer to the passage.

28.   The passage suggests that Twigg believes that rats could not have spread the Black Death unless which of the following were true?

    (A)   The rats escaped from ships that had been in Asia.

    (B)   The rats were immune to the diseases that they carried.

    (C)   The rat population was larger in medieval Europe than Twigg believes it actually was.

    (D)   The rat population primarily infested densely populated areas.

    (E)   The rats interacted with other animals that Twigg believes could have carried plague.

29.   According to the passage, the post–Second World War studies that altered the prevailing view of the Black Death involved which of the following?

    (A)   Determining the death rates caused by the Black Death in specific regions and towns

    (B)   Demonstrating how the Black Death intensified the political and religious upheaval that ended the Middle Ages

    (C)   Presenting evidence to prove that many medieval epidemics were mislabeled

    (D)   Arguing that the consequences of the Black Death led to the Renaissance and the rise of modern Europe

    (E)   Employing urban case studies to determine the number of rats in medieval Europe

30. The "silver lining to the Black Death" (lines 7–8) refers
to which of the following?

   (A) The decay of European feudalism precipitated by
the Black Death

   (B) Greater availability of employment, sustenance,
and housing for survivors of the epidemic

   (C) Strengthening of the human species through
natural selection

   (D) Better understanding of how to limit the spread
of contagious diseases

   (E) Immunities and resistance to the Black Death
gained by later generations

31. The author's attitude toward Twigg's work is best
characterized as which of the following?

   (A) Dismissive
   (B) Indifferent
   (C) Vindictive
   (D) Cautious
   (E) Ambivalent

Line *This passage is based on an article written in 2000.*

The traditional model of employer-employee relations in the United States was a "psychological contract" in which employees made long-term

(5) commitments to organizations in exchange for long-term job security, training and development, and internal opportunities for promotion. Beginning mainly with the recession in the early 1970s, this paradigm began to unravel. Organizations began

(10) using extensive downsizing and outsourcing to decrease the number of permanent employees in the workforce. Among employees, this situation has resulted in a decided shift in desire: instead of working their way up in an organization, many now

(15) prefer to work their way out. Entrepreneurship and small business administration are now the fastest-growing majors in business schools.

Several factors have generated movement from the old paradigm to the new one. Organizations have

(20) had legitimate and pressing reasons to shift to a new paradigm of employer-employee relations. Large numbers of permanent employees make it difficult for organizations to respond quickly to downturns in demand by decreasing payroll costs. The enormous

(25) rise in wrongful discharge suits has created incentives for organizations to use temporary, contract, and leased employees in order to distance themselves from potential litigation problems. Moreover, top management is under increased pressure from

(30) shareholders to generate higher and higher levels of return on investment in the short run, resulting in declines in hiring, increases in layoffs, and shortage of funds for employee development.

At the same time, a lack of forthrightness on the

(35) part of organizations has led to increased cynicism among employees about management's motivation and competence. Employees are now working 15 percent more hours per week than they were 20 years ago, but organizations acknowledge this fact only

(40) by running stress-management workshops to help employees to cope. Salespeople are being asked to increase sales at the same time organizations have cut travel, phone, and advertising budgets. Employees could probably cope effectively with changes in the

(45) psychological contract if organizations were more forthright about how they were changing it. But the euphemistic jargon used by executives to justify the changes they are implementing frequently backfires; rather than engendering sympathy for management's

(50) position, it sparks employees' desire to be free of the organization altogether. In a recent study of employees' attitudes about management, 49 percent of the sample strongly agreed that "management will take advantage of you if given the chance."

Questions 32–35 refer to the passage.

32. Which of the following is NOT mentioned in the passage as a characteristic of the traditional model of employer-employee relations in the United States?

(A) Attractive compensation packages for employees

(B) Opportunities for employees to receive training

(C) Long-term job security for employees

(D) Opportunities for employee advancement within a company

(E) Long-term commitment toward a company by employees

33. According to the passage, managers' motivation for engaging in measures such as increased layoffs is often a result of

(A) the hope that a smaller workforce will decrease the managers' own workloads

(B) shareholder pressure to generate increased short-term financial gains

(C) a desire to eradicate the idea of a "psychological contract"

(D) dissatisfaction with the performance of disgruntled employees

(E) a desire to appear to be following modern organizational trends

34. The passage suggests that which of the following is a legitimate reason for organizations' shift to the new model of employer-employee relations?

    (A) Organizations tend to operate more effectively when they have a high manager-to-employee ratio.

    (B) Organizations can move their operations to less-expensive locations more easily when they have fewer permanent employees.

    (C) Organizations have found that they often receive higher-quality work when they engage in outsourcing.

    (D) Organizations with large pools of permanent workers risk significant financial losses if the demand for their product or service decreases.

    (E) Organizations are under increasing pressure to adopt new technologies that often obviate the need for certain workers.

35. Which of the following best characterizes the function of the final sentence of the passage?

    (A) It suggests an alternative explanation for a phenomenon discussed earlier in the passage.

    (B) It provides data intended to correct a common misconception.

    (C) It further weakens an argument that is being challenged by the author.

    (D) It introduces a specific piece of evidence in support of a claim made at the beginning of the final paragraph.

    (E) It answers a question that is implicit in the preceding sentence.

Questions 36 to 81 — Difficulty: **Medium**

Line   The dry mountain ranges of the western United States contain rocks dating back 440 to 510 million years, to the Ordovician period, and teeming with evidence of tropical marine life. This rock record

(5)   provides clues about one of the most significant radiations (periods when existing life-forms gave rise to variations that would eventually evolve into entirely new species) in the history of marine invertebrates. During this radiation the number of marine biological

(10)   families increased greatly, and these families included species that would dominate the marine ecosystems of the area for the next 215 million years. Although the radiation spanned tens of millions of years, major changes in many species occurred during a

(15)   geologically short time span within the radiation and, furthermore, appear to have occurred worldwide, suggesting that external events were major factors in the radiation. In fact, there is evidence of major ecological and geological changes during this period:

(20)   the sea level dropped drastically and mountain ranges were formed. In this instance, rather than leading to large-scale extinctions, these kinds of environmental changes may have resulted in an enriched pattern of habitats and nutrients, which in turn gave rise to the

(25)   Ordovician radiation. However, the actual relationship between these environmental factors and the diversification of life-forms is not yet fully understood.

Questions 36–38 refer to the passage.

36. The passage is primarily concerned with

(A) evaluating the evidence of a major geologic period and determining its duration

(B) describing an evolutionary phenomenon and speculating about its cause

(C) explaining the mechanisms through which marine life-forms evolved during a particular period

(D) analyzing the impact on later life-forms of an important evolutionary development

(E) contrasting a period of evolutionary change with other such periods

37. Which of the following can be inferred from the passage regarding the geologic changes that occurred during the Ordovician period?

(A) They were more drastic than those associated with other radiations.

(B) They may have created conditions favorable to the evolution of many new life-forms.

(C) They may have caused the extinction of many of the marine species living in shallow waters.

(D) They may have been a factor in the development of new species adapted to living both on land and in water.

(E) They hastened the formation of the extensive dry regions found in the western United States.

38. Which of the following best describes the function of the last sentence of the passage?

    (A) It points out that the events described in the passage may be atypical.

    (B) It alludes to the fact that there is disagreement in the scientific community over the importance of the Ordovician radiation.

    (C) It concludes that the evidence presented in the passage is insufficient to support the proposed hypothesis because it comes from a limited geographic area.

    (D) It warns the reader against seeing a connection between the biological and geologic changes described in the passage.

    (E) It alerts the reader that current knowledge cannot completely explain the relationship suggested by the evidence presented in the passage.

Line   Exactly when in the early modern era Native
Americans began exchanging animal furs with
Europeans for European-made goods is uncertain.
What is fairly certain, even though they left
(5)   no written evidence of having done so, is that
the first Europeans to conduct such trade during
the modern period were fishing crews working the
waters around Newfoundland. Archaeologists had
noticed that sixteenth-century Native American
(10)   sites were strewn with iron bolts and metal
pins. Only later, upon reading Nicolas Denys's
1672 account of seventeenth-century European
settlements in North America, did archaeologists
realize that sixteenth-century European fishing
(15)   crews had dismantled and exchanged parts of their
ships for furs.

   By the time Europeans sailing the Atlantic coast
of North America first documented the fur trade, it
was apparently well underway. The first to record
(20)   such trade—the captain of a Portuguese vessel
sailing from Newfoundland in 1501—observed that a
Native American aboard the ship wore Venetian silver
earrings. Another early chronicler noted in 1524 that
Native Americans living along the coast of what is now
(25)   New England had become selective about European
trade goods: they accepted only knives, fishhooks,
and sharp metal. By the time Cartier sailed the Saint
Lawrence River ten years later, Native Americans had
traded with Europeans for more than thirty years,
(30)   perhaps half a century.

Questions 39–47 refer to the passage.

39.   The author of the passage draws conclusions about
the fur trade in North America from all of the following
sources EXCEPT

(A)   Cartier's accounts of trading with Native
Americans

(B)   a seventeenth-century account of European
settlements

(C)   a sixteenth-century account written by a sailing
vessel captain

(D)   archaeological observations of sixteenth-century
Native American sites

(E)   a sixteenth-century account of Native Americans
in what is now New England

40.   The passage suggests that which of the following is
partially responsible for the difficulty in establishing
the precise date when the fur trade in North America
began?

(A)   A lack of written accounts before that of Nicolas
Denys in 1672

(B)   A lack of written documentation before 1501

(C)   Ambiguities in the evidence from Native
American sources

(D)   Uncertainty about Native American trade
networks

(E)   Uncertainty about the origin of artifacts
supposedly traded by European fishing crews for
furs

41. Which of the following, if true, most strengthens the author's assertion in the first sentence of the second paragraph?

    (A) When Europeans retraced Cartier's voyage in the first years of the seventeenth century, they frequently traded with Native Americans.

    (B) Furs from beavers, which were plentiful in North America but nearly extinct in Europe, became extremely fashionable in Europe in the final decades of the sixteenth century.

    (C) Firing arms were rarely found on sixteenth-century Native American sites or on European lists of trading goods since such arms required frequent maintenance and repair.

    (D) Europeans and Native Americans had established trade protocols, such as body language assuring one another of their peaceful intentions, that antedate the earliest records of trade.

    (E) During the first quarter of the sixteenth century, an Italian explorer recorded seeing many Native Americans with what appeared to be copper beads, though they may have been made of indigenous copper.

42. Which of the following best describes the primary function of lines 11–16?

    (A) It offers a reconsideration of a claim made in the preceding sentence.

    (B) It reveals how archaeologists arrived at an interpretation of the evidence mentioned in the preceding sentence.

    (C) It shows how scholars misinterpreted the significance of certain evidence mentioned in the preceding sentence.

    (D) It identifies one of the first significant accounts of seventeenth-century European settlements in North America.

    (E) It explains why Denys's account of seventeenth-century European settlements is thought to be significant.

43. It can be inferred from the passage that the author would agree with which of the following statements about the fur trade between Native Americans and Europeans in the early modern era?

    (A) This trade may have begun as early as the 1480s.

    (B) This trade probably did not continue much beyond the 1530s.

    (C) This trade was most likely at its peak in the mid-1520s.

    (D) This trade probably did not begin prior to 1500.

    (E) There is no written evidence of this trade prior to the seventeenth century.

44. Which of the following can be inferred from the passage about the Native Americans mentioned in line 24?

    (A) They had little use for decorative objects such as earrings.

    (B) They became increasingly dependent on fishing between 1501 and 1524.

    (C) By 1524, only certain groups of Europeans were willing to trade with them.

    (D) The selectivity of their trading choices made it difficult for them to engage in widespread trade with Europeans.

    (E) The selectivity of their trading choices indicates that they had been trading with Europeans for a significant period of time prior to 1524.

45. The passage supports which of the following statements about sixteenth-century European fishing crews working the waters off Newfoundland?

    (A) They wrote no accounts of their fishing voyages.

    (B) They primarily sailed under the flag of Portugal.

    (C) They exchanged ship parts with Native Americans for furs.

    (D) They commonly traded jewelry with Native Americans for furs.

    (E) They carried surplus metal implements to trade with Native Americans for furs.

46. Which of the following can be inferred from the passage about evidence pertaining to the fur trade between Native Americans and Europeans in the early modern era?

(A)   A lack of written evidence has made it difficult to establish which Europeans first participated in this trade.

(B)   In general, the physical evidence pertaining to this trade has been more useful than the written evidence has been.

(C)   There is more written evidence pertaining to this trade from the early part of the sixteenth century than from later in that century.

(D)   The earliest written evidence pertaining to this trade dates from a time when the trade was already well established.

(E)   Some important pieces of evidence pertaining to this trade, such as Denys's 1672 account, were long overlooked by archaeologists.

47. The passage suggests which of the following about the sixteenth-century Native Americans who traded with Europeans on the coast of what is now called New England?

(A)   By 1524, they had become accustomed to exchanging goods with Europeans.

(B)   They were unfamiliar with metals before encountering Europeans.

(C)   They had no practical uses for European goods other than metals and metal implements.

(D)   By 1524, they had become disdainful of European traders because such traders had treated them unfairly in the past.

(E)   By 1524, they demanded only the most prized European goods because they had come to realize how valuable furs were on European markets.

Line   Researchers studying how genes control animal behavior have had to deal with many uncertainties. In the first place, most behaviors are governed by more than one gene, and until recently geneticists

(5)   had no method for identifying the multiple genes involved. In addition, even when a single gene is found to control a behavior, researchers in different fields do not necessarily agree that it is a "behavioral gene." Neuroscientists, whose interest

(10)   in genetic research is to understand the nervous system (which generates behavior), define the term broadly. But ethologists—specialists in animal behavior—are interested in evolution, so they define the term narrowly. They insist that mutations

(15)   in a behavioral gene must alter a specific normal behavior and not merely make the organism ill, so that the genetically induced behavioral change will provide variation that natural selection can act upon, possibly leading to the evolution of a new species.

(20)   For example, in the fruit fly, researchers have identified the gene *Shaker*, mutations in which cause flies to shake violently under anesthesia. Since shaking is not healthy, ethologists do not consider *Shaker* a behavioral gene. In contrast, ethologists

(25)   do consider the gene *Period* (per), which controls the fruit fly's circadian (24-hour) rhythm, a behavioral gene because flies with mutated per genes are healthy; they simply have different rhythms.

Questions 48–50 refer to the passage.

48. The primary purpose of the passage is to

  (A) summarize findings in an area of research

  (B) discuss different perspectives on a scientific question

  (C) outline the major questions in a scientific discipline

  (D) illustrate the usefulness of investigating a research topic

  (E) reconcile differences between two definitions of a term

49. The passage suggests that neuroscientists would most likely consider *Shaker* to be which of the following?

  (A) An example of a behavioral gene

  (B) One of multiple genes that control a single behavior

  (C) A gene that, when mutated, causes an alteration in a specific normal behavior without making the organism ill

  (D) A gene of interest to ethologists but of no interest to neuroscientists

  (E) A poor source of information about the nervous system

50. It can be inferred from the passage that which of the following, if true, would be most likely to influence ethologists' opinions about whether a particular gene in a species is a behavioral gene?

  (A) The gene is found only in that species.

  (B) The gene is extremely difficult to identify.

  (C) The only effect of mutations in the gene is to make the organism ill.

  (D) Neuroscientists consider the gene to be a behavioral gene.

  (E) Geneticists consider the gene to be a behavioral gene.

Line   For most species of animals, the number of individuals in the species is inversely proportional to the average body size for members of the species: the smaller the body size, the larger the number of individual animals.
(5)   The tamarin, a small South American monkey, breaks this rule. Of the ten primate species studied in Peru's Manu National Park, for example, the two species of tamarins, saddle-backed and emperor, are the eighth and ninth least abundant, respectively. Only the pygmy
(10)   marmoset, which is even smaller, is less abundant. The tamarin's scarcity is not easily explained; it cannot be dismissed as a consequence of diet, because tamarins feed on the same mixture of fruit, nectar, and small prey as do several of their more numerous larger
(15)   counterparts, including the two capuchins known as the squirrel monkey and the night monkey. Although the relative proportions of fruits consumed varies somewhat among species, it is hard to imagine that such subtle differences are crucial to understanding
(20)   the relative rarity of tamarins.

    To emphasize just how anomalously rare tamarins are, we can compare them to the other omnivorous primates in the community. In terms of numbers of individuals per square kilometer, they rank well below
(25)   the two capuchins, the squirrel monkey and the night monkey. And in terms of biomass, or the total weight of the individuals that occupy a unit area of habitat, each tamarin species is present at only one-twentieth the mass of brown capuchins or one-tenth that of
(30)   squirrel monkeys. To gain another perspective, consider the spatial requirements of tamarins. Tamarins are rigidly territorial, vigorously expelling any intruders that may stray within the sharply defined boundaries of their domains. Groups invest an
(35)   appreciable part of their time and energy in patrolling their territorial boundaries, announcing their presence to their neighbors with shrill, sweeping cries. Such concerted territoriality is rather exceptional among primates, though the gibbons and siamangs of Asia
(40)   show it, as do a few other New World species such as the titi and night monkeys. What is most surprising about tamarin territories is their size.

Titi monkeys routinely live within territories of 6 to 8 hectares, and night monkeys seldom defend more
(45)   than 10 hectares, but tamarin groups routinely occupy areas of 30 to 120 hectares. Contrast this with the 1 to 2 hectares needed by the common North American gray squirrel, a nonterritorial mammal of about the same size. A group of tamarins uses about as much
(50)   space as a troop of brown capuchins, though the latter weighs 15 times as much. Thus, in addition to being rare, tamarins require an amount of space that seems completely out of proportion to their size.

Questions 51–57 refer to the passage.

51. The author indicates that tamarin territories are

(A)   surprisingly large

(B)   poorly situated

(C)   unusually abundant in food resources

(D)   incapable of supporting large troops of tamarins

(E)   larger in Peru than in other parts of South America

52. The author mentions the spatial requirements of the gray squirrel in order to

(A)   explain why they are so common

(B)   demonstrate the consequences of their nonterritoriality

(C)   emphasize the unusual territorial requirements of the tamarin

(D)   provide an example of a major difference between squirrels and monkeys

(E)   provide an example of an animal with requirements similar to those of the tamarin

53. The author regards the differences between the diets of the tamarins and several larger species as

(A)   generally explicable in terms of territory size

(B)   apparently too small to explain the rarity of tamarins

(C)   wholly predictable on the basis of differences in body size

(D)   a result of the rigid territoriality of tamarins

(E)   a significant factor in determining behavioral differences

54. Which of the following would most probably be regarded by the author as anomalous?

    (A) A large primate species that eats mostly plants

    (B) A species of small mammals that is fiercely territorial

    (C) Two species of small primates that share the same territories

    (D) A species of small birds that is more abundant than many species of larger birds

    (E) A species of small rodents that requires more living space per individual than most species of larger rodents

55. The author most probably regards the tamarins studied in Manu National Park as

    (A) an endangered species

    (B) typical tamarins

    (C) unusually docile

    (D) the most unusual primates anywhere

    (E) too small a sample to be significant

56. Which of the following is NOT mentioned in the passage as a species whose groups display territoriality?

    (A) Gibbons

    (B) Siamangs

    (C) Titi monkeys

    (D) Squirrel monkeys

    (E) Night monkeys

57. The primary concern of the passage is to

    (A) recommend a policy

    (B) evaluate a theory

    (C) describe an unusual condition

    (D) explain the development of a hypothesis

    (E) support one of several competing hypotheses

Line   According to many analysts, labor-management
relations in the United States are undergoing a
fundamental change: traditional adversarialism is giving
way to a new cooperative relationship between the
(5)   two sides and even to concessions from labor. These
analysts say the twin shocks of nonunion competition
in this country and low-cost, high-quality imports from
abroad are forcing unions to look more favorably
at a variety of management demands: the need for
(10)   wage restraint and reduced benefits as well as the
abolition of "rigid" work rules, seniority rights, and job
classifications.
    Sophisticated proponents of these new
developments cast their observations in a prolabor
(15)   light. In return for their concessions, they point
out, some unions have bargained for profit sharing,
retraining rights, and job-security guarantees. Unions
can also trade concessions for more say on the shop
floor, where techniques such as quality circles and
(20)   quality-of-work-life programs promise workers greater
control over their own jobs. Unions may even win a
voice in investment and pricing strategy, plant location,
and other major corporate policy decisions previously
reserved to management.
(25)   Opponents of these concessions from labor argue
that such concessions do not save jobs, but either
prolong the agony of dying plants or finance the plant
relocations that employers had intended anyway.
Companies make investment decisions to fit their
(30)   strategic plans and their profit objectives, opponents
point out, and labor costs are usually just a small
factor in the equation. Moreover, unrestrained by either
loyalty to their work force or political or legislative
constraints on their mobility, the companies eventually
(35)   cut and run, concessions or no concessions.
    Wage-related concessions have come under
particular attack, since opponents believe that high
union wages underlay much of the success of United
States industry in this century. They point out that a
(40)   long-standing principle, shared by both management
and labor, has been that workers should earn wages
that give them the income they need to buy what they
make. Moreover, high wages have given workers the
buying power to propel the economy forward.

(45)   If proposals for pay cuts, two-tier wage systems,
and subminimum wages for young workers continue
to gain credence, opponents believe the U.S. social
structure will move toward that of a less-developed
nation: a small group of wealthy investors, a sizable
(50)   but still minority bloc of elite professionals and highly
skilled employees, and a huge mass of marginal
workers and unskilled laborers. Further, they argue
that if unions willingly engage in concession bargaining
on the false grounds that labor costs are the source
(55)   of a company's problems, unions will find themselves
competing with Third World pay levels—a competition
they cannot win.

Questions 58–64 refer to the passage.

58.   It can be inferred from the passage that opponents of
labor concessions would most likely describe many
plant-relocation decisions made by United States
companies as

(A)   capricious

(B)   self-serving

(C)   naive

(D)   impulsive

(E)   illogical

59.   It can be inferred from the passage that, until recently,
which of the following has been true of United States
industry in the twentieth century?

(A)   Unions have consistently participated in major
corporate policy decisions.

(B)   Maintaining adequate quality control in
manufacturing processes has been a principal
problem.

(C)   Union workers have been paid relatively high
wages.

(D)   Two-tier wage systems have been the norm.

(E)   Goods produced have been priced beyond the
means of most workers.

60. The passage provides information to answer which of
the following questions?

    (A)   What has caused unions to consider wage
          restraints and reduced benefits?

    (B)   Why do analysts study United States labor-
          management relations?

    (C)   How do job-security guarantees operate?

    (D)   Are investment and pricing strategies effective in
          combating imports?

    (E)   Do quality circles improve product performance
          and value?

61. The passage is primarily concerned with the

    (A)   reasons for adversarialism between labor and
          management

    (B)   importance of cooperative labor-management
          relations

    (C)   consequences of labor concessions to
          management

    (D)   effects of foreign competition on the United
          States economy

    (E)   effects of nonunion competition on union
          bargaining strategies

62. The sentence "If proposals for pay cuts . . . unskilled
laborers" (lines 45–52) serves primarily to

    (A)   disprove a theory

    (B)   clarify an ambiguity

    (C)   reconcile opposing views

    (D)   present a hypothesis

    (E)   contradict accepted data

63. It can be inferred from the passage that opponents of
labor concessions believe that if concession bargaining
continues, then

    (A)   plants will close instead of relocating

    (B)   young workers will need continued job retraining

    (C)   professional workers will outnumber marginal
          workers

    (D)   wealthy investors will invest in Third World
          countries instead of the United States

    (E)   the social structure of the United States will be
          negatively affected

64. According to the author, "Sophisticated proponents"
(line 13) of concessions do which of the following?

    (A)   Support the traditional adversarialism
          characteristic of labor-management relations.

    (B)   Emphasize the benefits unions can gain by
          granting concessions.

    (C)   Focus on thorough analyses of current economic
          conditions.

    (D)   Present management's reasons for demanding
          concessions.

    (E)   Explain domestic economic developments in
          terms of worldwide trends.

Line   Historians who study European women of the
Renaissance try to measure "independence,"
"options," and other indicators of the degree to which
the expression of women's individuality was either
(5)   permitted or suppressed. Influenced by Western
individualism, these historians define a peculiar form
of personhood: an innately bounded unit, autonomous
and standing apart from both nature and society. An
anthropologist, however, would contend that a person
(10)   can be conceived in ways other than as an "individual."
In many societies a person's identity is not intrinsically
unique and self-contained but instead is defined within
a complex web of social relationships.
     In her study of the fifteenth-century Florentine
(15)   widow Alessandra Strozzi, a historian who specializes
in European women of the Renaissance attributes
individual intention and authorship of actions to her
subject. This historian assumes that Alessandra had
goals and interests different from those of her sons,
(20)   yet much of the historian's own research reveals
that Alessandra acted primarily as a champion of
her sons' interests, taking their goals as her own.
Thus Alessandra conforms more closely to the
anthropologist's notion that personal motivation is
(25)   embedded in a social context. Indeed, one could argue
that Alessandra did not distinguish her personhood
from that of her sons. In Renaissance Europe the
boundaries of the conceptual self were not always firm
and closed and did not necessarily coincide with the
(30)   boundaries of the bodily self.

Questions 65–69 refer to the passage.

65. According to the passage, much of the research on
Alessandra Strozzi done by the historian mentioned in
the second paragraph supports which of the following
conclusions?

(A)   Alessandra used her position as her sons' sole
guardian to further interests different from those
of her sons.

(B)   Alessandra unwillingly sacrificed her own
interests in favor of those of her sons.

(C)   Alessandra's actions indicate that her motivations
and intentions were those of an independent
individual.

(D)   Alessandra's social context encouraged her to
take independent action.

(E)   Alessandra regarded her sons' goals and
interests as her own.

66. In the first paragraph, the author of the passage
mentions a contention that would be made by an
anthropologist most likely in order to

(A)   present a theory that will be undermined in the
discussion of a historian's study later in the
passage

(B)   offer a perspective on the concept of
personhood that can usefully be applied to the
study of women in Renaissance Europe

(C)   undermine the view that the individuality of
European women of the Renaissance was largely
suppressed

(D)   argue that anthropologists have applied the
Western concept of individualism in their
research

(E)   lay the groundwork for the conclusion that
Alessandra's is a unique case among European
women of the Renaissance whose lives have
been studied by historians

67. The passage suggests that the historians referred to in line 1 make which of the following assumptions about Renaissance Europe?

    (A) That anthropologists overestimate the importance of the individual in Renaissance European society

    (B) That in Renaissance Europe, women were typically allowed to express their individuality

    (C) That European women of the Renaissance had the possibility of acting independently of the social context in which they lived

    (D) That studying an individual such as Alessandra is the best way to draw general conclusions about the lives of women in Renaissance Europe

    (E) That people in Renaissance Europe had greater personal autonomy than people do currently

68. It can be inferred that the author of the passage believes which of the following about the study of Alessandra Strozzi done by the historian mentioned in the second paragraph?

    (A) Alessandra was atypical of her time and was therefore an inappropriate choice for the subject of the historian's research.

    (B) In order to bolster her thesis, the historian adopted the anthropological perspective on personhood.

    (C) The historian argues that the boundaries of the conceptual self were not always firm and closed in Renaissance Europe.

    (D) In her study, the historian reverts to a traditional approach that is out of step with the work of other historians of Renaissance Europe.

    (E) The interpretation of Alessandra's actions that the historian puts forward is not supported by much of the historian's research.

69. The passage suggests that the historian mentioned in the second paragraph would be most likely to agree with which of the following assertions regarding Alessandra Strozzi?

    (A) Alessandra was able to act more independently than most women of her time because she was a widow.

    (B) Alessandra was aware that her personal motivation was embedded in a social context.

    (C) Alessandra had goals and interests similar to those of many other widows in her society.

    (D) Alessandra is an example of a Renaissance woman who expressed her individuality through independent action.

    (E) Alessandra was exceptional because she was able to effect changes in the social constraints placed upon women in her society.

Line   In its 1903 decision in the case of *Lone Wolf v. Hitchcock*, the United States Supreme Court rejected the efforts of three Native American tribes to prevent the opening of tribal lands to non-Indian settlement without
(5)   tribal consent. In his study of the *Lone Wolf* case, Blue Clark properly emphasizes the Court's assertion of a virtually unlimited unilateral power of Congress (the House of Representatives and the Senate) over Native American affairs. But he fails to note the decision's
(10)   more far-reaching impact: shortly after *Lone Wolf*, the federal government totally abandoned negotiation and execution of formal written agreements with Indian tribes as a prerequisite for the implementation of federal Indian policy. Many commentators believe that this change had
(15)   already occurred in 1871 when—following a dispute between the House and the Senate over which chamber should enjoy primacy in Indian affairs—Congress abolished the making of treaties with Native American tribes. But in reality, the federal government continued to
(20)   negotiate formal tribal agreements past the turn of the century, treating these documents not as treaties with sovereign nations requiring ratification by the Senate but simply as legislation to be passed by both houses of Congress. The *Lone Wolf* decision ended this era of
(25)   formal negotiation and finally did away with what had increasingly become the empty formality of obtaining tribal consent.

Questions 70–72 refer to the passage.

70.   According to the passage, which of the following was true of relations between the federal government and Native American tribes?

(A)   Some Native American tribes approved of the congressional action of 1871 because it simplified their dealings with the federal government.

(B)   Some Native American tribes were more eager to negotiate treaties with the United States after the *Lone Wolf* decision.

(C)   Prior to the *Lone Wolf* decision, the Supreme Court was reluctant to hear cases involving agreements negotiated between Congress and Native American tribes.

(D)   Prior to 1871, the federal government sometimes negotiated treaties with Native American tribes.

(E)   Following 1871, the House exercised more power than did the Senate in the government's dealings with Native American tribes.

71.   According to the passage, in the case of *Lone Wolf v. Hitchcock*, the Supreme Court decided that

(A)   disputes among Native American tribes over the ownership of tribal lands were beyond the jurisdiction of the Court

(B)   Congress had the power to allow outsiders to settle on lands occupied by a Native American tribe without obtaining permission from that tribe

(C)   Congress had exceeded its authority in attempting to exercise sole power over Native American affairs

(D)   the United States was not legally bound by the provisions of treaties previously concluded with Native American tribes

(E)   formal agreements between the federal government and Native American tribes should be treated as ordinary legislation rather than as treaties

72. The author of the passage is primarily concerned
    with

    (A) identifying similarities in two different theories
    (B) evaluating a work of scholarship
    (C) analyzing the significance of a historical event
    (D) debunking a revisionist interpretation
    (E) exploring the relationship between law and social
         reality

Line   *This passage was excerpted from material published in 1993.*

Like many other industries, the travel industry is under increasing pressure to expand globally in order
(5)   to keep pace with its corporate customers, who have globalized their operations in response to market pressure, competitor actions, and changing supplier relations. But it is difficult for service organizations to globalize. Global expansion through acquisition
(10)   is usually expensive, and expansion through internal growth is time-consuming and sometimes impossible in markets that are not actively growing. Some service industry companies, in fact, regard these traditional routes to global expansion as inappropriate for
(15)   service industries because of their special need to preserve local responsiveness through local presence and expertise. One travel agency has eschewed the traditional route altogether. A survivor of the changes that swept the travel industry as a result of the
(20)   deregulation of the airlines in 1978—changes that included dramatic growth in the corporate demand for travel services, as well as extensive restructuring and consolidation within the travel industry—this agency adopted a unique structure for globalization. Rather
(25)   than expand by attempting to develop its own offices abroad, which would require the development of local travel management expertise sufficient to capture foreign markets, the company solved its globalization dilemma effectively by forging alliances with the best
(30)   foreign partners it could find. The resulting cooperative alliance of independent agencies now comprises 32 partners spanning 37 countries.

Questions 73–75 refer to the passage.

73.   According to the passage, which of the following is true of the traditional routes to global expansion?

(A)   They have been supplanted in most service industries by alternative routes.

(B)   They are less attractive to travel agencies since deregulation of the airlines.

(C)   They may represent the most cost-effective means for a travel agency to globalize.

(D)   They may be unsuitable for service agencies that are attempting to globalize.

(E)   They are most likely to succeed in markets that are not actively growing.

74.   The passage suggests that one of the effects of the deregulation of the airlines was

(A)   a decline in the services available to noncommercial travelers

(B)   a decrease in the size of the corporate travel market

(C)   a sharp increase in the number of cooperative alliances among travel agencies

(D)   increased competition in a number of different service industries

(E)   the merging of some companies within the travel industry

75.   The author discusses a particular travel agency in the passage most likely in order to

(A)   provide evidence of the pressures on the travel industry to globalize

(B)   demonstrate the limitations of the traditional routes to global expansion

(C)   illustrate an unusual approach to globalizing a service organization

(D)   highlight the difficulties confronting travel agencies that attempt to globalize

(E)   underscore the differences between the service industry and other industries

Line   Many economists believe that a high rate
of business savings in the United States is a
necessary precursor to investment, because
business savings, as opposed to personal savings,
(5)   comprise almost three-quarters of the national
savings rate. The national savings rate heavily
influences the overall rate of business investment.
These economists further postulate that real
interest rates—the difference between the rates
(10) charged by lenders and the inflation rate—will
be low when national savings exceed business
investment (creating a savings surplus), and
high when national savings fall below the level of
business investment (creating a savings deficit).
(15) However, during the 1960s real interest rates were
often higher when the national savings surplus was
large. Counterintuitive behavior also occurred when
real interest rates skyrocketed from 2 percent in
1980 to 7 percent in 1982, even though national
(20) savings and investments were roughly equal
throughout the period. Clearly, real interest rates
respond to influences other than the savings/
investment nexus. Indeed, real interest rates
may themselves influence swings in the savings
(25) and investment rates. As real interest rates shot
up after 1979, foreign investors poured capital
into the United States, the price of domestic
goods increased prohibitively abroad, and the
price of foreign-made goods became lower in the
(30) United States. As a result, domestic economic
activity and the ability of businesses to save and
invest were restrained.

Questions 76–78 refer to the passage.

76.   The passage suggests that the economists mentioned
in line 1 would have expected which of the following to
occur during the 1960s in the United States?

(A)   Savings and investment rates to be equal in spite
of high real interest rates

(B)   Real interest rates to remain low when the
national savings surplus was large

(C)   Investment rates to remain constant while the
national savings rate changed

(D)   The national economy to suffer a decline as a
result of high national savings rates

(E)   Businesses to be encouraged to save due to
high real interest rates

77.   The author of the passage would be most likely to
agree with which of the following statements regarding
the economists mentioned in line 1?

(A)   Their beliefs are contradicted by certain
economic phenomena that occurred in the United
States during the 1960s and the 1980s.

(B)   Their theory fails to predict under what
circumstances the prices of foreign and
domestic goods are likely to increase.

(C)   They incorrectly identify the factors other than
savings and investment rates that affect real
interest rates.

(D)   Their belief is valid only for the United States
economy and not necessarily for other national
economies.

(E)   They overestimate the impact of the real interest
rate on the national savings and investment
rates.

78.   The passage is primarily concerned with

(A)   contrasting trends in two historical periods

(B)   presenting evidence that calls into question
certain beliefs

(C)   explaining the reasons for a common
phenomenon

(D)   criticizing evidence offered in support of a well-
respected belief

(E)   comparing conflicting interpretations of a theory

Line Traditional social science models of class groups
in the United States are based on economic status
and assume that women's economic status derives
from association with men, typically fathers or
(5) husbands, and that women therefore have more
compelling common interests with men of their
own economic class than with women outside
it. Some feminist social scientists, by contrast,
have argued that the basic division in American
(10) society is instead based on gender, and that the
total female population, regardless of economic
status, constitutes a distinct class. Social historian
Mary Ryan, for example, has argued that in early-
nineteenth-century America, the identical legal
(15) status of working-class and middle-class free women
outweighed the differences between women of
these two classes: Married women, regardless of
their family's wealth, did essentially the same unpaid
domestic work, and none could own property or
(20) vote. Recently, though, other feminist analysts have
questioned this model, examining ways in which
the condition of working-class women differs from
that of middle-class women as well as from that of
working-class men. Ann Oakley notes, for example,
(25) that the gap between women of different economic
classes widened in the late nineteenth century: Most
working-class women, who performed wage labor
outside the home, were excluded from the emerging
middle-class ideal of femininity centered around
(30) domesticity and volunteerism.

Questions 79–81 refer to the passage.

79. The primary purpose of the passage is to

(A) offer sociohistorical explanations for the cultural
     differences between men and women in the
     United States

(B) examine how the economic roles of women in
     the United States changed during the nineteenth
     century

(C) consider differing views held by social scientists
     concerning women's class status in the United
     States

(D) propose a feminist interpretation of class
     structure in the United States

(E) outline specific distinctions between working-
     class women and women of the upper and
     middle classes

80. It can be inferred from the passage that the most
recent feminist social science research on women and
class seeks to do which of the following?

(A) Introduce a divergent new theory about the
     relationship between legal status and gender

(B) Illustrate an implicit middle-class bias in earlier
     feminist models of class and gender

(C) Provide evidence for the position that gender
     matters more than wealth in determining class
     status

(D) Remedy perceived inadequacies of both
     traditional social science models and earlier
     feminist analyses of class and gender

(E) Challenge the economic definitions of class used
     by traditional social scientists

81. Which of the following statements best characterizes
     the relationship between traditional social science
     models of class and Ryan's model, as described in the
     passage?

     (A) Ryan's model differs from the traditional model
          by making gender, rather than economic status,
          the determinant of women's class status.

     (B) The traditional social science model of class
          differs from Ryan's in its assumption that women
          are financially dependent on men.

     (C) Ryan's model of class and the traditional social
          science model both assume that women work,
          either within the home or for pay.

     (D) The traditional social science model of class
          differs from Ryan's in that each model focuses
          on a different period of American history.

     (E) Both Ryan's model of class and the traditional
          model consider multiple factors, including
          wealth, marital status, and enfranchisement, in
          determining women's status.

Questions 82 to 110 — Difficulty: **Hard**

Line   In addition to conventional galaxies, the universe
contains very dim galaxies that until recently went
unnoticed by astronomers. Possibly as numerous
as conventional galaxies, these galaxies have the
(5)   same general shape and even the same
approximate number of stars as a common type of
conventional galaxy, the spiral, but tend to be much
larger. Because these galaxies' mass is spread out
over larger areas, they have far fewer stars per unit
(10)   volume than do conventional galaxies. Apparently
these low-surface-brightness galaxies, as they are
called, take much longer than conventional galaxies
to condense their primordial gas and convert it to
stars—that is, they evolve much more slowly.
(15)   These galaxies may constitute an answer to the
long-standing puzzle of the missing baryonic mass
in the universe. Baryons—subatomic particles that
are generally protons or neutrons—are the source
of stellar, and therefore galactic, luminosity, and so
(20)   their numbers can be estimated based on how
luminous galaxies are. However, the amount of
helium in the universe, as measured by
spectroscopy, suggests that there are far more
baryons in the universe than estimates based on
(25)   galactic luminosity indicate. Astronomers have long
speculated that the missing baryonic mass might
eventually be discovered in intergalactic space or as
some large population of galaxies that are difficult
to detect.

Questions 82–88 refer to the passage.

82. According to the passage, conventional spiral galaxies
differ from low-surface-brightness galaxies in which of
the following ways?

(A)   They have fewer stars than do low-surface-
brightness galaxies.

(B)   They evolve more quickly than low-surface-
brightness galaxies.

(C)   They are more diffuse than low-surface-
brightness galaxies.

(D)   They contain less helium than do low-surface-
brightness galaxies.

(E)   They are larger than low-surface-brightness
galaxies.

83. It can be inferred from the passage that which of the
following is an accurate physical description of typical
low-surface-brightness galaxies?

(A)   They are large spiral galaxies containing fewer
stars than conventional galaxies.

(B)   They are compact but very dim spiral galaxies.

(c)   They are diffuse spiral galaxies that occupy a
large volume of space.

(D)   They are small, young spiral galaxies that contain
a high proportion of primordial gas.

(E)   They are large, dense spirals with low luminosity.

84. It can be inferred from the passage that the
"longstanding puzzle" refers to which of the following?

(A)   The difference between the rate at which
conventional galaxies evolve and the rate at
which low-surface-brightness galaxies evolve

(B)   The discrepancy between estimates of total
baryonic mass derived from measuring helium
and estimates based on measuring galactic
luminosity

(C)   The inconsistency between the observed amount
of helium in the universe and the number of stars
in typical low-surface-brightness galaxies

(D)   Uncertainties regarding what proportion of
baryonic mass is contained in intergalactic space
and what proportion in conventional galaxies

(E)   Difficulties involved in detecting very distant
galaxies and in investigating their luminosity

85. The author implies that low-surface-brightness galaxies could constitute an answer to the puzzle discussed in the second paragraph primarily because

   (A) they contain baryonic mass that was not taken into account by researchers using galactic luminosity to estimate the number of baryons in the universe

   (B) they, like conventional galaxies that contain many baryons, have evolved from massive, primordial gas clouds

   (C) they may contain relatively more helium, and hence more baryons, than do galaxies whose helium content has been studied using spectroscopy

   (D) they have recently been discovered to contain more baryonic mass than scientists had thought when low-surface-brightness galaxies were first observed

   (E) they contain stars that are significantly more luminous than would have been predicted on the basis of initial studies of luminosity in low-surface-brightness galaxies

86. The author mentions the fact that baryons are the source of stars' luminosity primarily in order to explain

   (A) how astronomers determine that some galaxies contain fewer stars per unit volume than do others

   (B) how astronomers are able to calculate the total luminosity of a galaxy

   (C) why astronomers can use galactic luminosity to estimate baryonic mass

   (D) why astronomers' estimates of baryonic mass based on galactic luminosity are more reliable than those based on spectroscopic studies of helium

   (E) how astronomers know bright galaxies contain more baryons than do dim galaxies

87. The author of the passage would be most likely to disagree with which of the following statements?

   (A) Low-surface-brightness galaxies are more difficult to detect than are conventional galaxies.

   (B) Low-surface-brightness galaxies are often spiral in shape.

   (C) Astronomers have advanced plausible ideas about where missing baryonic mass might be found.

   (D) Astronomers have devised a useful way of estimating the total baryonic mass in the universe.

   (E) Astronomers have discovered a substantial amount of baryonic mass in intergalactic space.

88. The primary purpose of the passage is to

   (A) describe a phenomenon and consider its scientific significance

   (B) contrast two phenomena and discuss a puzzling difference between them

   (C) identify a newly discovered phenomenon and explain its origins

   (D) compare two classes of objects and discuss the physical properties of each

   (E) discuss a discovery and point out its inconsistency with existing theory

Line   *This passage is excerpted from material published in 1997.*

    Scientists have been puzzled by the seeming disparity between models of global warming based on
(5) greenhouse gas emissions and actual climatological data. In short, the world is not warming up as much as these models have predicted. In the early 1990s, Pat Michaels sought to explain this disparity, suggesting that sulfate emissions in industrial areas had a cooling
(10) effect, thus temporarily retarding global warming. Michaels later came to doubt this idea, however, pointing out that since most sulfate is emitted in the Northern Hemisphere, its cooling influence should be largely limited to that hemisphere. Yet, since 1987,
(15) warming in the Southern Hemisphere, which had been relatively intense, has virtually ceased, while warming in the north has accelerated. Thus, Michaels not only doubted the idea of sulfate cooling, but came to feel that global warming models themselves may be
(20) flawed.

    Ben Santer disagrees. Santer contends that, in general, global warming occurs more slowly in the south because this hemisphere is dominated by oceans, which warm more slowly than the landmasses
(25) that dominate the Northern Hemisphere. But, according to Santer, the situation remains complicated by sulfate cooling, which peaked in the north in the mid-twentieth century. It drastically slowed warming in the Northern Hemisphere, and warming in the
(30) Southern Hemisphere raced ahead. Since 1987, Santer argues, the greenhouse effect has reasserted itself, and the north has taken the lead. Thus, Santer disputes Michaels's claim that model predictions and observed data differ fundamentally.

Questions 89–91 refer to the passage.

89.   The passage suggests that, in the early 1990s, Michaels would have been most likely to agree with which of the following statements about the disparity mentioned in lines 3–4?

(A)   This disparity is relatively less extreme in the Northern Hemisphere because of sulfate cooling.

(B)   This disparity is only a short-term phenomenon brought about by sulfate cooling.

(C)   This disparity is most significant in those parts of the world dominated by oceans.

(D)   The extent of this disparity is being masked by the temporary effect of sulfate cooling.

(E)   The disparity confirms that current models of global warming are correct.

90.   According to the passage, Santer asserts which of the following about global warming?

(A)   It will become a more serious problem in the Southern Hemisphere than in the Northern Hemisphere in spite of the cooling influence of oceans in the south.

(B)   It is unlikely to be a serious problem in the future because of the pervasive effect of sulfate cooling.

(C)   It will proceed at the same general rate in the Northern and Southern Hemispheres once the temporary influence of sulfate cooling comes to an end.

(D)   Until the late 1980s, it was moderated in the Northern Hemisphere by the effect of sulfate cooling.

(E)   Largely because of the cooling influence of oceans, it has had no discernible impact on the Southern Hemisphere.

91. The passage suggests that Santer and Michaels would be most likely to DISAGREE over which of the following issues?

(A) Whether climatological data invalidates global warming models

(B) Whether warming in the Northern Hemisphere has intensified since 1987

(C) Whether disparities between global warming models and climatological data can be detected

(D) Whether landmasses warm more rapidly than oceans

(E) Whether oceans have a significant effect on global climate patterns

Line   Micro-wear patterns found on the teeth of long-
extinct specimens of the primate species
australopithecine may provide evidence about their
diets. For example, on the basis of tooth micro-wear
(5)   patterns, Walker dismisses Jolly's hypothesis that
australopithecines ate hard seeds. He also disputes
Szalay's suggestion that the heavy enamel of
australopithecine teeth is an adaptation to bone
crunching, since both seed cracking and bone
(10)   crunching produce distinctive micro-wear
characteristics on teeth. His conclusion that
australopithecines were frugivores (fruit eaters) is
based upon his observation that the tooth micro-
wear characteristics of east African
(15)   australopithecine specimens are indistinguishable
from those of chimpanzees and orangutans, which
are commonly assumed to be frugivorous primates.
    However, research on the diets of
contemporary primates suggests that micro-wear
(20)   studies may have limited utility in determining the
foods that are actually eaten. For example, insect
eating, which can cause distinct micro-wear
patterns, would not cause much tooth abrasion in
modern baboons, who eat only soft-bodied insects
(25)   rather than hard-bodied insects. In addition, the
diets of current omnivorous primates vary
considerably depending on the environments that
different groups within a primate species inhabit; if
australopithecines were omnivores too, we might
(30)   expect to find considerable population variation
in their tooth micro-wear patterns. Thus, Walker's
description of possible australopithecine diets
may need to be expanded to include a much more
diverse diet.

Questions 92–99 refer to the passage.

92.   According to the passage, Walker and Szalay disagree
on which of the following points?

(A)   The structure and composition of
australopithecine teeth

(B)   The kinds of conclusions that can be drawn from
the micro-wear patterns on australopithecine
teeth

(C)   The idea that fruit was a part of the
australopithecine diet

(D)   The extent to which seed cracking and bone
crunching produce similar micro-wear patterns
on teeth

(E)   The function of the heavy enamel on
australopithecine teeth

93.   The passage suggests that Walker's research indicated
which of the following about australopithecine teeth?

(A)   They had micro-wear characteristics indicating
that fruit constituted only a small part of their
diet.

(B)   They lacked micro-wear characteristics
associated with seed eating and bone crunching.

(C)   They had micro-wear characteristics that differed
in certain ways from the micro-wear patterns of
chimpanzees and orangutans.

(D)   They had micro-wear characteristics suggesting
that the diet of australopithecines varied from
one region to another.

(E)   They lacked the micro-wear characteristics
distinctive of modern frugivores.

94. The passage suggests that which of the following would be true of studies of tooth micro-wear patterns conducted on modern baboons?

(A) They would inaccurately suggest that some baboons eat more soft-bodied than hard-bodied insects.

(B) They would suggest that insects constitute the largest part of some baboons' diets.

(C) They would reveal that there are no significant differences in tooth micro-wear patterns among baboon populations.

(D) They would inadequately reflect the extent to which some baboons consume certain types of insects.

(E) They would indicate that baboons in certain regions eat only soft-bodied insects, whereas baboons in other regions eat hard-bodied insects.

95. The passage suggests which of the following about the micro-wear patterns found on the teeth of omnivorous primates?

(A) The patterns provide information about what kinds of foods are not eaten by the particular species of primate, but not about the foods actually eaten.

(B) The patterns of various primate species living in the same environment resemble one another.

(C) The patterns may not provide information about the extent to which a particular species' diet includes seeds.

(D) The patterns provide more information about these primates' diet than do the tooth micro-wear patterns of primates who are frugivores.

(E) The patterns may differ among groups within a species depending on the environment within which a particular group lives.

96. It can be inferred from the passage that if studies of tooth micro-wear patterns were conducted on modern baboons, which of the following would most likely be true of the results obtained?

(A) There would be enough abrasion to allow a determination of whether baboons are frugivorous or insectivorous.

(B) The results would suggest that insects constitute the largest part of the baboons' diet.

(C) The results would reveal that there are no significant differences in tooth micro-wear patterns from one regional baboon population to another.

(D) The results would provide an accurate indication of the absence of some kinds of insects from the baboons' diet.

(E) The results would be unlikely to provide any indication of what inferences about the australopithecine diet can or cannot be drawn from micro-wear studies.

97. It can be inferred from the passage that Walker's conclusion about the australopithecine diet would be called into question under which of the following circumstances?

(A) The tooth enamel of australopithecines is found to be much heavier than that of modern frugivorous primates.

(B) The micro-wear patterns of australopithecine teeth from regions other than east Africa are analyzed.

(C) Orangutans are found to have a much broader diet than is currently recognized.

(D) The environment of east Africa at the time australopithecines lived there is found to have been far more varied than is currently thought.

(E) The area in which the australopithecine specimens were found is discovered to have been very rich in soft-bodied insects during the period when australopithecines lived there.

98.   The passage is primarily concerned with

   (A)   comparing two research methods for
         determining a species' dietary habits

   (B)   describing and evaluating conjectures about a
         species' diet

   (C)   contrasting several explanations for a species'
         dietary habits

   (D)   discussing a new approach and advocating its
         use in particular situations

   (E)   arguing that a particular research methodology
         does not contribute useful data

99.   The author of the passage mentions the diets of
      baboons and other living primates most likely in
      order to

   (A)   provide evidence that refutes Walker's
         conclusions about the foods making up the diets
         of australopithecines

   (B)   suggest that studies of tooth micro-wear
         patterns are primarily useful for determining the
         diets of living primates

   (C)   suggest that australopithecines were probably
         omnivores rather than frugivores

   (D)   illustrate some of the limitations of using
         tooth micro-wear patterns to draw definitive
         conclusions about a group's diet

   (E)   suggest that tooth micro-wear patterns are
         caused by persistent, as opposed to occasional,
         consumption of particular foods

Line   The ultimate pendulum clock, indeed the ultimate
mechanical clock of any kind, was invented by a British
engineer, William Shortt. The first was installed in the
Royal Observatory in Edinburgh in 1921. The Shortt
(5)   clock had two pendulums, primary and secondary. The
primary pendulum swung freely in a vacuum chamber. Its
only job was to synchronize the swing of the secondary
pendulum, which was housed in a neighboring cabinet
and drove the time-indicating mechanism. Every 30
(10) seconds, the secondary pendulum sent an electrical
signal to give a nudge to the primary pendulum. In
return, via an elaborate electromechanical linkage, the
primary pendulum ensured that the secondary pendulum
never got out of step.
(15)   Shortt clocks were standard provision in
astronomical observatories of the 1920s and 1930s
and are credited with keeping time to better than two
milliseconds in a day. Many were on record as losing
or gaining no more than one second in a year—a
(20) stability of one part in 30 million. The first indications
of seasonal variations in the earth's rotation were
gleaned by the use of Shortt clocks.
    In 1984, Pierre Boucheron carried out a study of
a Shortt clock which had survived in the basement
(25) of the United States Naval Observatory since 1932.
After replacing the electromechanical linkage with
modern optical sensing equipment, he measured the
Shortt clock's rate against the observatory's atomic
clocks for a month. He found that it was stable to 200
(30) microseconds a day over this period, equivalent to two
to three parts in a billion. What is more, the data also
revealed that the clock was responding to the slight
tidal distortion of the earth due to the gravitational pull
of the moon and sun.
(35)   In addition to causing the familiar ocean tides,
both the sun and the moon raise tides in the solid
body of the earth. The effect is to raise and lower the
surface of the earth by about 30 centimeters. Since
the acceleration due to gravity depends on distance
(40) from the center of the earth, this slight tidal movement
affects the period of swing of a pendulum. In each
case, the cycle of the tides caused the clock to gain
or lose up to 140 microseconds.

Questions 100–103 refer to the passage.

100. According to the passage, the use of Shortt clocks led
to the discovery that

    (A)   optical sensing equipment can be used
effectively in timekeeping systems

    (B)   atomic clocks can be used in place of pendulum
clocks in observatories

    (C)   tides occur in solid ground as well as in oceans

    (D)   the earth's rotation varies from one time of year
to another

    (E)   pendulums can be synchronized with one another
electronically

101. The passage most strongly suggests that which of
the following is true of the chamber in which a Shortt
clock's primary pendulum was housed?

    (A)   It contained elaborate mechanisms that were
attached to, and moved by, the pendulum.

    (B)   It was firmly sealed during normal operation of
the clock.

    (C)   It was at least partly transparent so as to allow
for certain types of visual data output.

    (D)   It housed both the primary pendulum and another
pendulum.

    (E)   It contained a transmitter that was activated
at irregular intervals to send a signal to the
secondary pendulum.

102. The passage most strongly suggests that its author would agree with which of the following statements about clocks?

    (A)   Before 1921, no one had designed a clock that used electricity to aid in its timekeeping functions.

    (B)   Atomic clocks depend on the operation of mechanisms that were invented by William Shortt and first used in the Shortt clock.

    (C)   No type of clock that keeps time more stably and accurately than a Shortt clock relies fundamentally on the operation of a pendulum.

    (D)   Subtle changes in the earth's rotation slightly reduce the accuracy of all clocks used in observatories after 1921.

    (E)   At least some mechanical clocks that do not have pendulums are almost identical to Shortt clocks in their mode of operation.

103. The passage most strongly suggests that the study described in the third paragraph would not have been possible in the absence of

    (A)   accurate information regarding the times at which high and low ocean tides occurred at various locations during 1984

    (B)   comparative data regarding the use of Shortt clocks in observatories between 1921 and 1932

    (C)   a non-Shortt clock that was known to keep time extremely precisely and reliably

    (D)   an innovative electric-power source that was not available in the 1920s and 1930s

    (E)   optical data-transmission devices to communicate between the U.S. Naval Observatory and other research facilities

Line   Comparable worth, as a standard applied to eliminate
inequities in pay, insists that the values of certain tasks
performed in dissimilar jobs can be compared. In
the last decade, this approach has become a critical
(5)   social policy issue, as large numbers of private-sector
firms and industries as well as federal, state, and local
governmental entities have adopted comparable worth
policies or begun to consider doing so.

    This widespread institutional awareness of comparable
(10)   worth indicates increased public awareness that pay
inequities—that is, situations in which pay is not "fair"
because it does not reflect the true value of a job—
exist in the labor market. However, the question still
remains: have the gains already made in pay equity
(15)   under comparable worth principles been of a precedent-
setting nature, or are they mostly transitory, a function
of concessions made by employers to mislead female
employees into believing that they have made long-term
pay equity gains?

(20)   Comparable worth pay adjustments are indeed
precedent-setting. Because of the principles driving
them, other mandates that can be applied to reduce
or eliminate unjustified pay gaps between male and
female workers have not remedied perceived pay
(25)   inequities satisfactorily for the litigants in cases
in which men and women hold different jobs. But
whenever comparable worth principles are applied to
pay schedules, perceived unjustified pay differences
are eliminated. In this sense, then, comparable worth
(30)   is more comprehensive than other mandates, such
as the Equal Pay Act of 1963 and Title VII of the
Civil Rights Act of 1964. Neither compares tasks
in dissimilar jobs (that is, jobs across occupational
categories) in an effort to determine whether or not
(35)   what is necessary to perform these tasks—know-how,
problem-solving, and accountability—can be
quantified in terms of its dollar value to the employer.
Comparable worth, on the other hand, takes as its
premise that certain tasks in dissimilar jobs may
(40)   require a similar amount of training, effort, and skill;
may carry similar responsibility; may be carried on
in an environment having a similar impact upon the
worker; and may have a similar dollar value to the
employer.

Questions 104–107 refer to the passage.

104. According to the passage, comparable worth
principles are different in which of the following ways
from other mandates intended to reduce or eliminate
pay inequities?

    (A)   Comparable worth principles address changes
in the pay schedules of male as well as female
workers.

    (B)   Comparable worth principles can be applied to
employees in both the public and the private
sector.

    (C)   Comparable worth principles emphasize the
training and skill of workers.

    (D)   Comparable worth principles require changes in
the employer's resource allocation.

    (E)   Comparable worth principles can be used to
quantify the value of elements of dissimilar jobs.

105. According to the passage, which of the following is
true of comparable worth as a policy?

    (A)   Comparable worth policy decisions in pay-
inequity cases have often failed to satisfy the
complainants.

    (B)   Comparable worth policies have been applied to
both public-sector and private-sector employee
pay schedules.

    (C)   Comparable worth as a policy has come to be
widely criticized in the past decade.

    (D)   Many employers have considered comparable
worth as a policy, but very few have actually
adopted it.

    (E)   Early implementations of comparable worth
policies resulted in only transitory gains in pay
equity.

106. It can be inferred from the passage that application of "other mandates" (line 22) would be unlikely to result in an outcome satisfactory to the female employees in which of the following situations?

   I.   Males employed as long-distance truck drivers for a furniture company make $3.50 more per hour than do females with comparable job experience employed in the same capacity.

   II.   Women working in the office of a cement company contend that their jobs are as demanding and valuable as those of the men working outside in the cement factory, but the women are paid much less per hour.

   III.   A law firm employs both male and female paralegals with the same educational and career backgrounds, but the starting salary for male paralegals is $5,000 more than for female paralegals.

   (A)   I only

   (B)   II only

   (C)   III only

   (D)   I and II only

   (E)   I and III only

107. Which of the following best describes an application of the principles of comparable worth as they are described in the passage?

   (A)   The current pay, rates of increase, and rates of promotion for female mechanics are compared with those of male mechanics.

   (B)   The training, skills, and job experience of computer programmers in one division of a corporation are compared to those of programmers making more money in another division.

   (C)   The number of women holding top executive positions in a corporation is compared to the number of women available for promotion to those positions, and both tallies are matched to the tallies for men in the same corporation.

   (D)   The skills, training, and job responsibilities of the clerks in the township tax assessor's office are compared to those of the much better paid township engineers.

   (E)   The working conditions of female workers in a hazardous-materials environment are reviewed and their pay schedules compared to those of all workers in similar environments across the nation.

Line   Most business historians give the impression that Marseilles, a French Mediterranean city, was in dire economic straits from 1700 to 1715, when France was at war in the Mediterranean area. Their
(5)   conclusions are based partly on a documented 30 percent decline in revenue generated by the *cottimo*, an import tax collected on the cargo of ships returning to Marseilles from various Middle Eastern ports. The decline in revenue from this particular tax
(10)   could hypothetically have been caused by a massive drop in levels of commercial activity in Marseilles. However, during the war years Marseilles' role as a grain importer grew, and most foodstuffs had always been—and remained—exempt from the tax. Also,
(15)   due to a shift in trading patterns caused by the war, the city's merchants did more business with those Middle Eastern cities on whose trade the *cottimo* had always been collected at a lower rate. Moreover, during this period, a change occurred in the thinking
(20)   of Marseilles merchants, who, in response to the war's challenges, displayed a new sense of daring. They sent some ships outside the Mediterranean and began to engage in trade in the Atlantic and Pacific. This was significant, since the *cottimo* was collected only on
(25)   goods entering the city from Mediterranean ports in the Middle East.

Questions 108–110 refer to the passage.

108. In lines 14–18, the author implies which of the following about Marseilles trade during the period 1700–1715?

   (A)   Reluctance on the part of merchants to import goods taxable at high rates of the *cottimo* probably explains the drop in *cottimo* revenues.

   (B)   Even if imports subject to the *cottimo* decreased in volume, the city's total business activity in the Mediterranean was increasing.

   (C)   Shifts in trading patterns occurred primarily because ports whose goods were taxed at high rates of the *cottimo* were no longer accessible.

   (D)   The total volume of imports increased dramatically, even though imports subject to the *cottimo* generated less revenue.

   (E)   The total volume of imports subject to the *cottimo* need not have decreased in order for *cottimo* revenues to decline.

109. The passage suggests that, in comparison with the period before 1700, which of the following was true of imports to Marseilles in the period 1700–1715?

   (A)   Imports declined in volume throughout the period.

   (B)   Imports increased in volume throughout the period.

   (C)   The percentage of imports that was subject to the *cottimo* increased.

   (D)   A larger percentage of imports were food imports.

   (E)   A larger percentage of imports came from Mediterranean areas.

110. The author mentions all of the following as factors that could possibly account for the 30 percent decline in revenues in Marseilles during the period 1700–1715 EXCEPT:

   (A)   a decline in the city's commercial activity

   (B)   increased trade with cities subject to lower rates of the tax

   (C)   larger role for the city as an importer of food

   (D)   increased focus on trade with non-Mediterranean ports

   (E)   a decrease in exports to Middle Eastern ports in the Mediterranean

4.5 Answer Key: Reading Comprehension

1.	C	23.	E	45.	C	67.	C	89.	B
2.	E	24.	A	46.	D	68.	E	90.	D
3.	D	25.	E	47.	A	69.	D	91.	A
4.	E	26.	B	48.	B	70.	D	92.	E
5.	C	27.	D	49.	A	71.	B	93.	B
6.	D	28.	C	50.	C	72.	C	94.	D
7.	B	29.	A	51.	A	73.	D	95.	E
8.	E	30.	B	52.	C	74.	E	96.	D
9.	B	31.	A	53.	B	75.	C	97.	C
10.	A	32.	A	54.	E	76.	B	98.	B
11.	D	33.	B	55.	B	77.	A	99.	D
12.	B	34.	D	56.	D	78.	B	100.	D
13.	E	35.	D	57.	C	79.	C	101.	B
14.	C	36.	B	58.	B	80.	D	102.	C
15.	C	37.	B	59.	C	81.	A	103.	C
16.	B	38.	E	60.	A	82.	B	104.	E
17.	A	39.	A	61.	C	83.	C	105.	B
18.	D	40.	B	62.	D	84.	B	106.	B
19.	E	41.	D	63.	E	85.	A	107.	D
20.	C	42.	B	64.	B	86.	C	108.	E
21.	B	43.	A	65.	E	87.	E	109.	D
22.	A	44.	E	66.	B	88.	A	110.	E

4.6 Answer Explanations: Reading Comprehension

The following discussion of Reading Comprehension is intended to familiarize you with the most efficient and effective approaches to the kinds of problems common to Reading Comprehension. The particular questions in this chapter are generally representative of the kinds of Reading Comprehension questions you will encounter on the GMAT exam. Remember that it is the problem-solving strategy that is important, not the specific details of a particular question.

Questions 1 to 35 — Difficulty: **Easy**

Questions 1–4 refer to the passage on page 52.

1. According to the passage, traditional corporate leaders differ from leaders in learning organizations in that the former

    (A) encourage employees to concentrate on developing a wide range of skills

    (B) enable employees to recognize and confront dominant corporate models and to develop alternative models

    (C) make important policy decisions alone and then require employees in the corporation to abide by those decisions

    (D) instill confidence in employees because of their willingness to make risky decisions and accept their consequences

    (E) are concerned with offering employees frequent advice and career guidance

Supporting Idea

This question requires understanding of the contrast the passage draws between leaders of traditional corporations and leaders of learning organizations. According to the second paragraph, the former are traditionally charismatic leaders who set policy and make decisions, while the latter foster integrated thinking at all levels of the organization.

A   According to the passage, it is leaders in learning organizations, not traditional corporate leaders, who encourage the development of a wide range of skills.

B   Leaders in learning organizations are those who want their employees to challenge dominant models.

C   **Correct.** The second paragraph states that traditional corporate leaders are individualistic; they alone *set the corporation's direction and make key decisions*.

D   The passage does not address the question of whether traditional corporate leaders instill confidence in employees. In fact, the first paragraph suggests that they may not; rather, they might come across as objectionably controlling.

E   The passage suggests that advice and guidance are more likely to be offered by leaders of learning organizations than by leaders of traditional corporations.

The correct answer is C.

2. Which of the following best describes employee behavior encouraged within learning organizations, as such organizations are described in the passage?

    (A) Carefully defining one's job description and taking care to avoid deviations from it

    (B) Designing mentoring programs that train new employees to follow procedures that have been used for many years

    (C) Concentrating one's efforts on mastering one aspect of a complicated task

    (D) Studying an organizational problem, preparing a report, and submitting it to a corporate leader for approval

    (E) Analyzing a problem related to productivity, making a decision about a solution, and implementing that solution

Application

The second paragraph of the passage indicates that employees of learning organizations are encouraged to think and act for themselves; they learn new skills and expand their capabilities.

A   Avoiding deviations from one's carefully defined job description would more likely be encouraged in a traditional corporation, as described in the first paragraph, than in a learning organization.

B   Any employee training that involves following long-standing procedures would more likely be encouraged in a traditional corporation than a learning organization.

C   According to the passage, mastering only one aspect of a task, no matter how complicated, would be insufficient in a learning organization, in which broad patterns of thinking are encouraged.

D   As described in the passage, the role of corporate leaders in learning organizations is not, characteristically, to approve employees' solutions to problems, but rather to enable and empower employees to implement solutions on their own.

E   **Correct.** Employees in learning organizations are expected to act on their own initiative; thus, they would be encouraged to analyze and solve problems on their own, implementing whatever solutions they devised.

The correct answer is E.

3. According to the author of the passage, corporate leaders of the future should do which of the following?

(A)   They should encourage employees to put long-term goals ahead of short-term profits.

(B)   They should exercise more control over employees in order to constrain production costs.

(C)   They should redefine incentives for employees' performance improvement.

(D)   They should provide employees with opportunities to gain new skills and expand their capabilities.

(E)   They should promote individual managers who are committed to established company policies.

Supporting Idea

This question focuses on what the author recommends in the passage for future corporate leaders. In the second paragraph, the author states that, among other things, corporate leaders need to be teachers to provide challenges to their employees and create an atmosphere where *employees are continually learning new skills and expanding their capabilities to shape their future.*

A   The passage does not directly discuss the issue of corporate goals and profitability in the long or short term.

B   The passage does not address the topic of production costs, and it suggests that its author would favor reducing, rather than increasing, corporate leaders' control over employees. The first paragraph states that leaders who attempt to control employees lead those employees to perform in mediocre fashion.

C   The passage does not discuss incentivizing employees' performance; rather, employees' performance will improve, the passage suggests, under different corporate leadership.

D   **Correct.** The final sentence of the passage states directly that leaders must build organizations in which employees can learn new skills and expand their capabilities.

E   The first paragraph indicates that clinging to established company policies is a strategy for the future that is likely to be unproductive.

The correct answer is D.

4. The primary purpose of the passage is to

(A)   endorse a traditional corporate structure

(B)   introduce a new approach to corporate leadership and evaluate criticisms of it

(C)   explain competing theories about management practices and reconcile them

(D)   contrast two typical corporate organizational structures

(E)   propose an alternative to a common corporate approach

Main Idea

This question depends on understanding the passage as a whole. The first paragraph explains the way in which corporations fail to facilitate how humans learn. The second paragraph suggests that corporations should change the way they view employees in order to promote learning, and it explains the positive outcomes that would result from that shift in thinking.

A   The first paragraph explains that the traditional corporate structure leads to mediocre performance; it does not endorse that structure.

B   The second paragraph introduces the concept of a *learning organization* and its attendant approach to corporate leadership. Rather than identifying any criticisms of that approach, the passage endorses it wholeheartedly.

C   The passage discusses the difference between the idea of a single charismatic leader and that of a shared corporate leadership, but it does not attempt to reconcile these two ideas.

D   The passage's main focus is on advocating a particular approach, not on merely contrasting it with another. Furthermore, it portrays only one of the approaches as typical. It suggests that the organizational structure that relies on a single charismatic leader is typical but that another approach, that in which leadership is shared, should instead become typical.

E   **Correct.** The passage identifies a common corporate approach, one based on controlling employees, and proposes that corporations should instead become *learning organizations*.

The correct answer is E.

Questions 5–7 refer to the passage on page 54.

5.   The primary purpose of the passage is to

(A)   explain why a particular business strategy has been less successful than was once anticipated

(B)   propose an alternative to a particular business strategy that has inadvertently caused ecological damage

(C)   present a concern about the possible consequences of pursuing a particular business strategy

(D)   make a case for applying a particular business strategy on a larger scale than is currently practiced

(E)   suggest several possible outcomes of companies' failure to understand the economic impact of a particular business strategy

Main Idea

Ecoefficient processes involve reducing waste from industrial production to minimize environmental impact, and they have resulted in cost savings for companies. However, the passage cites the views of Senge and Carstedt, who argue that such a strategy, if not prudently pursued, can worsen environmental outcomes.

A   The passage does not indicate that implementing ecoefficient processes has been less successful than anticipated in reducing environmental impact. Rather, the primary focus of the passage is to present ways that, according to Senge and Carstedt, ecoefficient strategies can go wrong.

B   The passage does not suggest that implementing ecoefficient processes has caused ecological damage. In describing recommendations made by Senge and Carstedt, the passage indicates ways that ecoefficiency approaches can be moderated to improve environmental outcomes.

C   **Correct.** The passage, drawing on the views of Senge and Carstedt, argues that use of ecoefficient processes in industrial production, however commendable, can have bad environmental effects if exclusively pursued.

D   The passage cautions against more extensive use of an ecoefficiency approach than currently exists in industrial production.

E   The passage is not focused on exploring the economic impact of pursuing ecoefficiency in industrial production. The focus is on possible environmental outcomes.

The correct answer is C.

6.   The passage mentions which of the following as a possible consequence of a company's realization of greater profits through ecoefficiency?

(A)   The companies may be able to sell a greater number of products by lowering prices.

(B)   The companies may be better able to attract investment capital in the global market.

(C)   The profits may be reinvested to increase economic growth through ecoefficiency.

(D)   The profits may be used as investment capital for industries that are not ecoefficient.

(E)   The profits may encourage companies to make further innovations in reducing production waste.

Supporting Idea

The passage tells us that ecoefficient practices by industrial companies can result in higher profits. But according to the views of Senge and Carstedt cited by the passage, higher profits are a mixed blessing with respect to possible environmental impact. Note that the question concerns something that the passage *mentions* (as opposed to suggests or implies).

A   Although this could result from higher profits, the passage does not mention it.

B   No doubt higher profits could make this more likely, but it is not mentioned in the passage.

C   The company could reinvest some of its higher profits to grow in an ecoefficient manner, but this is not mentioned in the passage.

D   Correct. The passage states: *greater profits may be turned into investment capital that could easily be reinvested in traditionally eco-inefficient industries.*

E   This possibility is consistent with what is conveyed in the passage, but it is not mentioned in the passage.

The correct answer is D.

7.   The passage implies that which of the following is a possible consequence of a company's adoption of innovations that increase its ecoefficiency?

(A)   Company profits resulting from such innovations may be reinvested in that company with no guarantee that the company will continue to make further improvements in ecoefficiency.

(B)   Company growth fostered by cost savings from such innovations may allow that company to manufacture a greater number of products that will be used and discarded, thus worsening environmental stress.

(C)   A company that fails to realize significant cost savings from such innovations may have little incentive to continue to minimize the environmental impact of its production processes.

(D)   A company that comes to depend on such innovations to increase its profits and growth may be vulnerable in the global market to competition from traditionally eco-inefficient industries.

(E)   A company that meets its ecoefficiency goals is unlikely to invest its increased profits in the development of new and innovative ecoefficiency measures.

Inference

The question concerns something implied but not stated in the passage. The passage states that ecoefficient innovations, no matter how effective in reducing production waste, do not *alter the number of products manufactured nor the waste generated from their use and discard*. In fact, as the passage says, growth in profits allow a company *to generate more total waste*, with increased damage to the environment.

A   The passage contains no implication as to whether a company's profits from ecoefficient innovation, if reinvested in the company, would necessarily lead to further ecoefficiency gains.

B **Correct.** The passage implies that cost savings from ecoefficient production can enable a company to expand production, thus generating more total waste, not just from production itself, but also from the greater number of products eventually discarded after use.

C Although such a failure to achieve cost saving through ecoefficiency in production might well be a disincentive for further efforts to improve ecoefficiency, such an effect is not addressed in the passage either explicitly or by implication.

D The information in the passage suggests that ecoefficient production would improve a company's competitive edge over companies that did not enjoy gains from ecoefficient approaches.

E The passage suggests that some companies may not reinvest profits from ecoefficient production in further boosting their ecoefficiency, but the passage does not imply that such reinvestment is unlikely.

The correct answer is B.

Questions 8–14 refer to the passage on page 56.

8. It can be inferred from the passage that one reason an advertiser might prefer a hard-sell approach to a soft-sell approach is that

(A) the risks of boomerang effects are minimized when the conclusions an advertiser wants the consumer to draw are themselves left unstated

(B) counterargumentation is likely from consumers who fail to draw their own conclusions regarding an advertising claim

(C) inferential activity is likely to occur even if consumers perceive themselves to be more knowledgeable than the individuals presenting product claims

(D) research on consumer memory suggests that the explicit conclusions provided by an advertiser using the hard-sell approach have a significant impact on decision making

(E) the information presented by an advertiser using the soft-sell approach may imply different conclusions to different consumers

Inference

This question relies on what the passage suggests about the difference between the hard-sell and soft-sell approaches—and why the hard-sell approach might be preferred. The hard-sell approach, according to the second paragraph, presents explicit conclusions. The soft-sell approach, on the other hand, does not explicitly state conclusions about products; instead, consumers make up their own minds.

A While the passage makes clear that boomerang effects are minimized when conclusions are left unstated, this is an advantage of the soft-sell approach over the hard-sell approach.

B According to the second paragraph, counterargumentation is a disadvantage, not an advantage, of the hard-sell approach. This is a reason not to prefer the hard sell.

C The third paragraph suggests that in cases in which consumers may perceive themselves as more knowledgeable than individuals presenting product claims, the soft-sell approach offers an advantage over the hard-sell approach.

D According to the third paragraph, self-generated conclusions that are associated with the soft-sell approach have a greater impact on decision making than explicit conclusions. The passage does not allude to any research on memory that would favor the hard-sell approach.

E **Correct.** The fourth paragraph suggests that one problem with the soft-sell approach is that consumers could miss the point; they may not come to the conclusions that the advertiser would prefer. Thus an advertiser might prefer a hard-sell approach.

The correct answer is E.

9. Each of the following is mentioned in the passage as a characteristic of the hard-sell approach EXCEPT:

    (A) Its overall message is readily grasped.

    (B) It appeals to consumers' knowledge about the product.

    (C) It makes explicit claims that the advertised brand is superior to other brands.

    (D) It uses statements that are expressed very clearly.

    (E) It makes claims in the form of direct conclusions.

Supporting Idea

This question asks about what is directly stated in the passage about the hard-sell approach. The first and second paragraphs provide the details about this approach, including that it uses *direct, forceful claims* about benefits of a brand over competitors' brands; its claims are simple and straightforward, in the form of explicit conclusions; and consumers are generally left with little room for confusion about the message.

A   The second paragraph states that there is little room for confusion about the message.

B   Correct. The extent of consumers' knowledge about the product is not mentioned in the passage.

C   The first paragraph indicates that in the hard-sell approach advertisers make direct claims regarding the benefits of the advertised brand over other offerings.

D   The first and second paragraphs say that hard-sell claims are direct, simple, and straightforward.

E   The second paragraph emphasizes that the hard-sell approach presents it claims in the form of explicit conclusions.

The correct answer is B.

10. It can be inferred from the passage that advertisers could reduce one of the risks discussed in the last paragraph if they were able to provide

    (A) motivation for consumers to think about the advertisement's message

    (B) information that implies the advertiser's intended conclusion but leaves that conclusion unstated

    (C) subtle evidence that the advertised product is superior to that of competitors

    (D) information comparing the advertised product with its competitors

    (E) opportunity for consumers to generate their own beliefs or conclusions

Inference

This question requires understanding the risks discussed in the last paragraph of the passage. Those risks are, first, that consumers would not be motivated to think about the advertisement and thus would miss the message's point; second, that consumers may draw conclusions that the advertiser did not intend; and finally, that consumers could question the validity of the conclusions they reach, even if those are what advertisers intend.

A   Correct. Providing motivation for consumers to think about an advertisement's message would reduce the first risk discussed in the last paragraph: that consumers would fail to draw any conclusions because they would lack motivation to engage with advertisements.

B   Providing *information that implies a conclusion but leaves it unstated* is the very definition of the soft-sell approach, and it is this approach that gives rise to the risks discussed in the last paragraph.

C   Providing subtle evidence that a product is superior is most likely to give rise to all three of the risks identified in the last paragraph, in that its subtlety would leave consumers free to draw their own conclusions, to fail to draw those conclusions, or to question the validity of their own conclusions.

D   A direct comparison of the advertised product with its competitors would run all the risks identified in the last paragraph: consumers might not find the comparison motivating; they could draw conclusions that the advertiser did not intend (e.g., that the competing products are superior); or they could question whatever conclusions they do draw.

E   Giving consumers the opportunity *to generate their own beliefs or conclusions* is an intrinsic part of the soft-sell approach, which produces the risks discussed in the last paragraph.

The correct answer is A.

11.   The primary purpose of the passage is to

   (A)   point out the risks involved in the use of a particular advertising strategy

   (B)   make a case for the superiority of one advertising strategy over another

   (C)   illustrate the ways in which two advertising strategies may be implemented

   (D)   present the advantages and disadvantages of two advertising strategies

   (E)   contrast the types of target markets for which two advertising strategies are appropriate

Inference

Overall, the passage is concerned with two advertising strategies. The first paragraph introduces the strategies. The second paragraph explains how a particular aspect of one approach may be both positive and negative and how the second approach mitigates these problems. The third paragraph continues this discussion of mitigation, while the fourth paragraph points out that there are drawbacks to this approach, too. Thus, according to the passage, both strategies have positive and negative aspects.

A   The passage is concerned not with one particular advertising strategy but with two, and it discusses benefits, as well as risks, involved with both strategies.

B   The passage does not suggest that one strategy is superior to the other but rather that each has positive and negative aspects.

C   The passage does not discuss how to implement either of the strategies it is concerned with; instead, it deals with how consumers are likely to respond once the implementation has already taken place.

D   Correct. The passage is primarily concerned with showing that both of the strategies described have advantages and disadvantages.

E   The passage provides some indirect grounds for inferring the target markets for which each advertising strategy might be appropriate, but it is not primarily concerned with contrasting those markets.

The correct answer is D.

12.   Which of the following best describes the function of the sentence in lines 25–28 in the context of the passage as a whole?

   (A)   It reiterates a distinction between two advertising strategies that is made in the first paragraph.

   (B)   It explains how a particular strategy avoids a drawback described earlier in the paragraph.

   (C)   It suggests that a risk described earlier in the paragraph is less serious than some researchers believe it to be.

   (D)   It outlines why the strategy described in the previous sentence involves certain risks for an advertiser.

   (E)   It introduces an argument that will be refuted in the following paragraph.

Evaluation

The sentence in lines 25–28 explains how the kinds of conclusions consumers are invited to draw based on the soft-sell approach reduce the risk that consumers will respond with *resentment, distrust, and counterargumentation*—that is, the possible *boomerang effect* identified earlier in the paragraph as a drawback of the hard-sell approach.

A   The sentence does not reiterate the distinction between the hard- and soft-sell approaches; rather, it explains an advantage of the soft-sell approach.

B   Correct. The sentence explains how the soft-sell approach avoids the problems that can arise from the hard-sell approach's explicitly stated conclusions.

C   The sentence suggests that the risk of boomerang effects described earlier in the paragraph is serious but that a different approach can mitigate it.

D   The sentence outlines why the strategy described in the previous sentence reduces advertisers' risks, not why it involves risks.

E   At no point does the passage refute the idea that implicit conclusions reduce the risk of boomerang effects. It does say that there could be drawbacks to the soft-sell approach, but those drawbacks are related to the problem with implicit conclusions themselves and how people reach them. In addition, the *following paragraph* does not mention the drawbacks, only the advantages of implicit conclusions.

The correct answer is B.

13. It can be inferred from the passage that one situation in which the boomerang effect often occurs is when consumers

(A)   have been exposed to forceful claims that are diametrically opposed to those in an advertiser's message

(B)   have previous self-generated beliefs or conclusions that are readily accessible from memory

(C)   are subjected to advertising messages that are targeted at specific markets to which those consumers do not belong

(D)   are confused regarding the point of the advertiser's message

(E)   come to view the advertiser's message with suspicion

Inference

The passage discusses the boomerang effect in the second paragraph. This effect is defined as consumers deriving conclusions from advertising that are the opposite of those that advertisers intended to present, and it occurs when consumers resent and/or distrust what they are being told.

A   The passage provides no grounds for inferring that consumers need to be exposed to opposing claims in order to believe such claims; they may reach opposing claims on their own.

B   The passage indicates that the boomerang effect can be reduced by using a soft-sell approach, which can result in self-generated conclusions, but it provides no evidence about any possible effects of preexisting self-generated beliefs or conclusions on the boomerang effect.

C   The passage does not address how consumers who are subjected to advertising messages not intended for them might respond.

D   Confusion regarding the point of the advertiser's message is more likely to occur, the passage suggests, when advertisers use a soft-sell approach—but it is the hard-sell approach, not the soft-sell, that is likely to result in the boomerang effect.

E   **Correct.** The second paragraph indicates that consumers who resent being told what to believe and come to distrust the advertiser's message—that is, those who view the message with suspicion—may experience a boomerang effect, believing the opposite of the conclusions offered.

The correct answer is E.

14. It can be inferred from the passage that the research mentioned in line 29 supports which of the following statements?

(A)   Implicit conclusions are more likely to capture accurately the point of the advertiser's message than are explicit conclusions.

(B)   Counterargumentation is less likely to occur if an individual's beliefs or conclusions are readily accessible from memory.

(C)   The hard-sell approach results in conclusions that are more difficult for the consumer to recall than are conclusions resulting from the soft-sell approach.

(D)   When the beliefs of others are presented as definite and forceful claims, they are perceived to be as accurate as self-generated beliefs.

(E)   Despite the advantages of implicit conclusions, the hard-sell approach involves fewer risks for the advertiser than does the soft-sell approach.

Inference

The research this item refers to—research on consumer memory and judgment—indicates that beliefs are more memorable when they are self-generated and so matter when making judgments and decisions. Further, self-generated beliefs seem more believable to those who have them than beliefs that come from elsewhere.

A   The fourth paragraph indicates that implicit conclusions are more likely to fail to replicate the advertiser's message than explicit conclusions are.

B   The research discussed in the passage does not address when counterargumentation is more or less likely to occur. Even though counterargumentation is a risk when consumers distrust the advertiser's message—as they may do when harder-to-recall explicit conclusions are given—it may be as much of a risk when consumers reach an implicit conclusion that is readily accessible from memory.

C   **Correct.** The research indicates that it is easier for consumers to recall conclusions they have reached on their own—that is, the sorts of conclusions that are encouraged by the soft-sell approach—than conclusions that have been provided explicitly, as happens in the hard-sell approach.

D   The research does not show that the forcefulness with which claims are presented increases perceptions of the accuracy of those claims. Indeed, it is most likely the opposite, as the forcefulness of others' claims may make them seem even less related to any conclusions the consumer might generate for him- or herself.

E   The research suggests that it is the soft-sell, not the hard-sell, approach that has fewer risks. The fourth paragraph indicates that there could be some risks to the implicit conclusions that consumers draw, but this is not part of the research in question.

The correct answer is C.

Questions 15–19 refer to the passage on page 58.

15.   It can be inferred from the passage that the two procedures described in the passage have which of the following in common?

(A)   They have been applied in practice.

(B)   They rely on the use of a device that measures tension.

(C)   Their purpose is to determine an unknown mass.

(D)   They can only be applied to small solid objects.

(E)   They involve attraction between objects of similar mass.

Inference

The procedures described in the passage are introduced by the suggestion in the first paragraph that someone in a spaceship who wanted to determine a solid object's mass could do so in a particular way. The second paragraph uses the word *weigh* in quotes to refer to a similar procedure for determining the mass of a double-star system.

A   The language of the first paragraph is hypothetical: we *could* do particular things. Thus, there is no way to determine from the passage whether that procedure has been applied in practice.

B   The first procedure relies on a spring scale, which measures tension, but the second procedure measures time and distance to determine restraining force.

C   **Correct.** Both procedures determine mass: the first procedure can determine the mass of a small solid object on a spaceship in free fall, and the second can determine the mass of a double-star system.

D   The first procedure would, according to the passage, be applied to a small solid object, but the second *weighs* double-star systems, which are clearly not small objects.

E   The second procedure involves attraction between two stars, which could be of similar mass, in the same system, but the first procedure involves measuring tension in a string and speed of whirling, not attraction between objects.

The correct answer is C.

16. According to the passage, the tension in the string mentioned in lines 8–9 is analogous to which of the following aspects of a double-star system?

    (A) The speed with which one star orbits the other
    (B) The gravitational attraction between the stars
    (C) The amount of time it takes for the stars to circle one another
    (D) The distance between the two stars
    (E) The combined mass of the two stars

Supporting Idea

The second paragraph states that an *attractive force* is analogous to the tension in the string. This attractive force is identified in the previous sentence as the gravitational force between the two stars in a double-star system.

A   The second paragraph states that the speed with which the stars circle each other depends on the gravitational force between them, but it is that force that is analogous to the tension in the string.

B   Correct. The second paragraph clearly identifies the gravitational force between the two stars as the attractive force that is analogous to the tension in the spring scale's string.

C   The amount of time it takes for the stars to circle one another is necessary for calculating the force that holds them together, but it is the force itself that is analogous to the string's tension.

D   The distance between the stars must be measured if the attraction between them is to be determined, but the attraction, not the distance, is analogous to the string's tension.

E   The combined mass of the two stars is what the procedure is designed to determine; it is analogous to the mass of the small solid object, as described in the first paragraph.

The correct answer is B.

17. Which of the following best describes the relationship between the first and the second paragraph of the passage?

    (A) The first paragraph provides an illustration useful for understanding a procedure described in the second paragraph.
    (B) The first paragraph describes a hypothetical situation whose plausibility is tested in the second paragraph.
    (C) The first paragraph evaluates the usefulness of a procedure whose application is described further in the second paragraph.
    (D) The second paragraph provides evidence to support a claim made in the first paragraph.
    (E) The second paragraph analyzes the practical implications of a methodology proposed in the first paragraph.

Evaluation

This question requires understanding that the second paragraph describes a somewhat difficult-to-understand procedure that the first paragraph illustrates in smaller, and simpler, terms.

A   Correct. The first paragraph illustrates, hypothetically, a simple procedure for determining mass, and this illustration provides the grounds on which the passage explains the procedure of the second paragraph.

B   The first paragraph describes a situation in hypothetical terms, but the second paragraph does not test that situation's plausibility. Instead, the second paragraph draws an analogy between the initial situation and another procedure.

C   The first paragraph does not evaluate the usefulness of the procedure for determining a small solid object's mass while in a spaceship in freefall; it simply describes how that procedure would work.

D   The second paragraph provides no evidence; it describes a procedure analogous to what is described in the first paragraph.

E The second paragraph does not discuss the practical implications of the first paragraph's methodology but rather a procedure that is analogous to the hypothetical situation of the first paragraph.

The correct answer is A.

18. The author of the passage mentions observations regarding the period of a double-star system as being useful for determining

(A) the distance between the two stars in the system

(B) the time it takes for each star to rotate on its axis

(C) the size of the orbit the system's two stars occupy

(D) the degree of gravitational attraction between the system's stars

(E) the speed at which the star system moves through space

Supporting Idea

The author mentions the period of a double-star system in the final sentence of the second paragraph, defining it as the time required for stars to circle each other. Knowing this time, in combination with the distance between the stars, enables the determination of the restraining force between the stars.

A The final sentence of the second paragraph indicates that the period of a double-star system is measured independently of the distance between the two stars in the system.

B The passage is not concerned with how long it takes each star to rotate on its axis.

C The passage does not mention anyone's trying to determine the size of the orbit of a system's two stars. It does mention the related topic of distance between the stars but indicates that knowing such distance is required for measuring the stars' mass, not that it can be inferred from the period of the system.

D **Correct.** According to the passage, the restraining force, or gravitational attraction, between the two stars can be deduced based on the period and the distance between them.

E The passage does not mention the speed at which the star system moves through space.

The correct answer is D.

19. The primary purpose of the passage is to

(A) analyze a natural phenomenon in terms of its behavior under special conditions

(B) describe the steps by which a scientific measurement is carried out

(C) point out the conditions under which a scientific procedure is most useful

(D) contrast two different uses of a methodological approach in science

(E) explain a method by which scientists determine an unknown quantity

Evaluation

What is the primary purpose of the passage? What we call the weight of an object is its weight as measured in Earth's gravitational field; that weight is a function of gravity and the mass of the object. How is the mass of an object determined in a weightless, zero-gravity environment? The first paragraph of the passage explains a method to determine this. The second paragraph explains an analogous method that astronomers use to measure the masses of stars in a double-star system.

A Although the passage has portions containing analysis and references to characteristics of natural phenomena, these portions are merely subsidiary to explanations of measurement methods.

B A description of steps in a measurement procedure occurs in the first paragraph, but this is merely preliminary to an explanation of how masses of stars in double-star systems can be measured. The passage mentions two aspects of the method used to measure the masses of double stars—measuring the period and measuring the distance—but it does not tell whether these are separate steps of the process, and it does not primarily focus on these as a main topic.

C   The passage describes some conditions under which a particular measurement method is valid, but that description is merely subsidiary to an explanation meant to show why the method is valid.

D   The structure of the passage is based on analogy rather than contrast.

E   **Correct.** The primary purpose of the passage is to explain, using analogy, methods for determining mass independently of Earth's gravity.

The correct answer is E.

Questions 20–27 refer to the passage on page 60.

20.   The passage is primarily concerned with

(A)   describing a resource and indicating various methods used to study it

(B)   presenting a theory and offering an opposing point of view

(C)   providing an explanation for unexpected findings

(D)   demonstrating why a particular theory is unfounded

(E)   resolving a disagreement regarding the uses of a technology

Main Idea

What issue, problem, or puzzle is the passage primarily meant to address? The passage discusses whether—and if so why or under what conditions—adoption of information technology (IT) benefits businesses. The first paragraph provides background information by summarizing opinions and data concerning the extent to which businesses can benefit by adopting IT. It details pre-1990 findings showing that, contrary to some experts' expectations, overall productivity in business sectors that adopted IT did not improve. It summarizes contrasting attempts by proponents of IT to explain how, by different performance measures, IT may have actually yielded business benefits other than competitive advantage. The second paragraph discusses the puzzle that the passage primarily addresses: why, if IT had *conferred economic value*, the pre-1990 findings indicated that, contrary to expectations,

IT failed to *produce direct competitive advantage for individual firms.* The passage invokes *resource-based theory* to help resolve this puzzle.

A   IT is accurately described as *a resource,* but the passage is not concerned at all with *describing* IT, except in its very brief parenthetical definition of IT. Neither is it directly concerned with methods used to study IT.

B   Opinions are presented in the passage. But the only perspective or point of view that is referred to and characterized as a *theory* is *resource-based theory.* A possible application of that theory is described, but neither that theory nor any other theory is *presented.*

C   **Correct.** As explained above, the passage is primarily concerned with explaining why findings based on pre-1990 data suggested that, contrary to expectations, adoption of IT failed to produce direct competitive advantage for many businesses.

D   The only *theory* referred to in the passage is *resource-based theory,* but the passage neither opposes nor attempts to refute that theory.

E   The first paragraph indicates that there was some disagreement as to the magnitude or nature of any business benefits possibly produced by IT. But the passage is not aimed at resolving any such disagreements; it is aimed, rather, at explaining why expectations regarding certain business benefits of IT were not fulfilled.

The correct answer is C.

21.   The author of the passage discusses productivity in the retail industry in the first paragraph primarily in order to

(A)   suggest a way in which IT can be used to create a competitive advantage

(B)   provide an illustration of the "productivity paradox"

(C)   emphasize the practical value of the introduction of IT

(D) cite an industry in which productivity did not stagnate during the 1980s

(E) counter the argument that IT could potentially create competitive advantage

Evaluation

Why does the author, in the first paragraph of the passage, discuss productivity in the retail industry? In the first paragraph, the information concerning *productivity in the retail industry* is presented as an example that seemed to provide support for what some economists termed *the "productivity paradox."* The passage describes the paradox as follows: *despite huge IT investments, . . . productivity stagnated.* As an example of this, pre-1990 data is cited for the retail industry, which had widely adopted IT; the data indicated that productivity increases had significantly slowed relative to the average for the 25 years preceding 1973.

A The data in the first paragraph regarding productivity in the retail industry does not suggest that IT can be used to create a competitive advantage. In fact, the data presented could provide reason to doubt whether, in the retail sector, IT would fulfill expectations regarding its potential for creating competitive advantage.

B Correct. As explained above, the primary purpose of the author's first paragraph of productivity in the retail industry is to illustrate the "productivity paradox."

C This could not be the author's purpose in the discussion of productivity in the retail industry in the first paragraph, since that discussion casts doubt on whether IT would fulfill expectations regarding its potential for creating competitive advantage.

D This cannot be the primary purpose of the discussion of productivity in the retail industry in the first paragraph. The data concerning the retail industry is cited as an instance supporting and illustrating the general point that when there were huge IT investments, especially *in the service sectors, productivity stagnated.*

E The author's purpose in the discussion of productivity in the retail sector is not to *counter the argument that IT could potentially create competitive advantage.* In the first paragraph, the author neither argues for nor endorses the view that IT lacked potential to create competitive advantage.

The correct answer is B.

22. The passage suggests that proponents of resource-based theory would be likely to explain IT's inability to produce direct competitive advantages for individual firms by pointing out that

(A) IT is not a resource that is difficult to obtain

(B) IT is not an economically valuable resource

(C) IT is a complex, intangible resource

(D) economic progress has resulted from IT only in the service sector

(E) changes brought about by IT cannot be detected by macroeconomic measures

Inference

How would a proponent of resource-based theory be likely to explain the pre–1990 failure of IT to produce direct competitive advantage for firms that adopted it? According to the passage, resource-based theory implies that *in general, firms gain competitive advantages by accumulating resources that are economically valuable, relatively scarce, and not easily replicated.* However, the passage cites a study indicating that IT had become *pervasive and relatively easy to acquire* but did not seem sufficient by itself to confer competitive advantage. Based on this information, a proponent of resource-based theory would likely claim that since IT proved to be *easily replicated,* one of the conditions stipulated by resource-based theory for gaining competitive advantage was violated.

A   **Correct.** According to the study mentioned in the second paragraph, IT was *relatively easy to acquire.* According to the conditions for gaining competitive advantage as attributed in the passage to resource-based theory, a proponent of resource-based theory would likely claim that the ease of acquiring IT could help explain why adoption of IT was not by itself sufficient for gaining competitive advantage.

B   The passage suggests neither that IT lacks economic value nor that resource-based theory assumes or implies that it does. Rather, resource-based theory suggests that the economic value of IT during the period discussed in the passage typically did not provide competitive advantages to any company that adopted it over others that did so.

C   Although IT may in some respects be both complex and intangible, the passage does not suggest that resource-based theory entails that resources need to be simple or tangible in order to confer competitive advantage.

D   This is not a view that the passage attributes, even by implication, to proponents of resource-based theory.

E   The first paragraph of the passage indicates that some IT advocates claimed that macroeconomic measures of productivity failed to reflect the economic benefits of IT. But the passage neither endorses this viewpoint nor attributes it to proponents of resource-based theory.

The correct answer is A.

23.   Which of the following best describes the content of the first paragraph?

(A)   It presents two explanations for the success of IT.

(B)   It provides evidence that decreases in productivity will continue.

(C)   It presents reasons for a decline in productivity.

(D)   It demonstrates the effect IT has had on productivity.

(E)   It contrasts views concerning the degree of IT's success.

Evaluation

Among the choices given, which one best describes the content of the first paragraph of the passage? The first paragraph provides background information by summarizing opinions and data concerning the extent to which businesses benefited by adopting IT. It details pre-1990 findings showing that, contrary to some experts' expectations, overall productivity in business sectors that adopted IT did not significantly improve. It summarizes contrasting attempts by proponents of IT to explain how, judged by different performance measures, IT may have actually yielded business benefits other than competitive advantage.

A   The first paragraph provides information suggesting that IT did not provide the expected benefits. In other words, it casts doubt on whether IT succeeded.

B   The first paragraph considers neither past nor future decreases in productivity. (It does, however, describe past decreases in the rate of increase in productivity).

C   The first paragraph discusses certain pre-1990 decreases in the average rate of productivity growth, but it does not discuss declines in productivity.

D   The first paragraph suggests that IT may have had little or no effect in producing productivity growth. The passage does not claim that IT actually had an effect on productivity and does not demonstrate any way in which IT had such an effect.

E   **Correct.** The first paragraph describes differing views concerning whether IT may have met expectations in enhancing competitiveness or providing other economic benefits for business.

The correct answer is E.

24. The passage suggests that the recent study of retail firms discussed in the second paragraph supports which of the following conclusions regarding a firm's competitive advantage?

(A) Human resources alone are more likely to contribute to competitive advantage than is IT alone.

(B) Human resources combined with IT are more likely than human resources alone to have a negative effect on competitive advantage.

(C) Human resources combined with IT often have a negative effect on competitive advantage.

(D) IT by itself is much more likely to have a positive effect than a negative effect on competitive advantage.

(E) The positive effect of IT on competitive advantage increases with time.

Inference

The second paragraph describes a study of retail firms. The study confirmed that IT, having become relatively easy to acquire, by itself conferred little advantage. Negative correlations between IT and performance suggest that IT likely weakened some retail firms' competitive positions. Firms' human resources, however, did explain improved performance, both in and of themselves and when merged with IT.

A **Correct.** As explained above, the study indicated that human resources in and of themselves led to improved performance, whereas there were negative correlations between IT and performance.

B The passage indicates that some firms gained IT-related advantages when IT was merged with human resources. The passage gives no indication whether this—or human resources alone—ever has negative effects on performance.

C The passage indicates that some firms gained IT-related advantages when IT was merged with human resources. The passage gives no indication whether this ever has negative effects on performance.

D The passage states that the study found that IT by itself conferred little advantage, but the study found frequent negative correlations between IT and performance.

E The first paragraph states that some people have argued that it takes time for IT to yield results, but the study discussed in the second paragraph provides no evidence to support this. The finding of the study that indicates that IT can yield results when merged with human resources says nothing about whether all the effects are immediate or whether they instead increase with time.

The correct answer is A.

25. According to the passage, most pre-1990 literature on businesses' use of IT included which of the following?

(A) Recommendations regarding effective ways to use IT to gain competitive advantage

(B) Explanations of the advantages and disadvantages of adopting IT

(C) Information about ways in which IT combined with human resources could be used to increase competitive advantage

(D) A warning regarding the negative effect on competitive advantage that would occur if IT were not adopted

(E) A belief in the likelihood of increased competitive advantage for firms using IT

Supporting Idea

The passage begins by stating that most pre-1990 literature on businesses' use of IT was optimistic about IT's ability to create competitive advantage and focused on dramatic success stories.

A The passage does not state that pre-1990 literature on businesses' use of IT made recommendations regarding ways IT could be used to gain competitive advantage.

B	The passage indicates that most pre-1990 literature on businesses' use of IT focused on the advantages IT was believed to confer. The passage does indicate that some literature at the end of the 1980s discussed some disadvantages of adopting IT; but the passage suggests that most of the literature of this period did not discuss any disadvantages.

C	The passage does not clearly indicate whether any pre-1990 literature discussed the results of combining human resources and IT. The study described as "recent" in the second paragraph does discuss such results, but the study was not pre-1990 and does not discuss any specific ways IT combined with human resources could be used to increase competitive advantage.

D	Pre-1990 literature on businesses' use of IT expressed optimism that IT could confer competitive advantage, but the passage does not mention whether this literature presented a warning about negative effects on performance if IT was not adopted.

E	**Correct.** The first paragraph of the passage states that most pre-1990 literature on businesses' use of IT was optimistic about IT's ability to create competitive advantage.

The correct answer is E.

26.	The author of the passage implies that toward the end of the 1980s, some economists described which of the following as a "productivity paradox" (line 8)?

(A)	Investments in IT would not result in increases in productivity until the 1990s.

(B)	Investments in IT did not lead to expected gains in productivity.

(C)	Productivity in the retail industry rose less rapidly than did productivity in other industries.

(D)	The gains in productivity due to the introduction of IT were not reflected in macroeconomic measures of productivity.

(E)	Most gains in productivity occurred in the service sector and were therefore particularly difficult to measure.

Inference

The passage indicates in the first paragraph that toward the end of the 1980s, economists noticed that productivity was not increasing, as it had been expected to do as a result of significant investments in IT. The economists referred to this as a *productivity paradox*.

A	Although the first paragraph does indicate that productivity growth did occur in the 1990s, this is not what is referred to by the term *productivity paradox*.

B	**Correct.** The passage begins by indicating that before 1990 there was general optimism that investments in IT would lead to competitive advantages. However, by the late 1980s some economists had identified a *productivity paradox*, noting that *despite huge IT investments . . . productivity stagnated*; that is, the IT investments had not resulted in the expected gains in productivity.

C	The passage does not indicate that productivity rose less rapidly in the retail industry than in other industries. It merely indicates that it rose less rapidly than had been expected and less rapidly than it did prior to large IT investments.

D	The *productivity paradox* refers to a lack of gains in productivity due to IT, not to a failure of macroeconomic measures to capture actual productivity gains.

E	The passage indicates that the service sector failed to show significant gains, and it makes no mention of any difficulty related to measuring productivity gains in the service sector.

The correct answer is B.

27. According to the passage, the recent study of retail firms discussed in the second paragraph (lines 33–36) best supports which of the following assessments of IT's potential?

(A) Even when IT gives a firm a temporary competitive advantage, that firm is unlikely to continue to achieve productivity gains.

(B) The competitive advantages conferred by a firm's introduction of IT are outweighed by IT's development costs.

(C) A firm's introduction of IT is less likely to limit its ability to achieve productivity gains than to enhance that ability.

(D) Although IT by itself is unlikely to give a firm a competitive advantage, IT combined with other resources may do so.

(E) Although IT by itself is unlikely to give a firm a competitive advantage, a firm that does not employ IT cannot achieve a competitive advantage.

Supporting Idea

Answering this question correctly involves an understanding of what the second paragraph says about a particular study of retail firms, specifically, what that study has to say about IT's potential. The study confirmed that IT, having become relatively easy to acquire, by itself conferred little advantage. Negative correlations between IT and performance suggest that IT likely weakened some retail firms' competitive positions. On the other hand, the second paragraph states that *some firms gained IT-related advantages by merging IT with complementary resources.*

A   The study reveals that IT by itself does not give firms a competitive advantage, but that it does give some firms such an advantage when IT is merged with complementary resources. The study does not indicate that any productivity gains that are achieved in this way are short lived.

B   The passage does not indicate whether any competitive advantages conferred by a firm's introduction of IT (for instance, those that arise when merged with other resources) are outweighed by IT's development costs.

C   The study indicates that a firm's introduction of IT is likely to limit its ability to achieve productivity when it is not merged with complementary resources, but that it can enhance that ability when it is merged with such resources. The passage does not indicate the relative likelihood of those outcomes.

D   Correct. The study as described in the passage's second paragraph states that IT by *itself conferred little advantage* but that *some firms gained IT-related advantages by merging IT with complementary resources.*

E   This statement correctly indicates that the study states that IT by itself is unlikely to give a firm a competitive advantage. However, the passage does not indicate that the study states that firms that do not employ IT are unable to achieve a competitive advantage.

The correct answer is D.

Questions 28–31 refer to the passage on page 63.

28. The passage suggests that Twigg believes that rats could not have spread the Black Death unless which of the following were true?

(A) The rats escaped from ships that had been in Asia.

(B) The rats were immune to the diseases that they carried.

(C) The rat population was larger in medieval Europe than Twigg believes it actually was.

(D) The rat population primarily infested densely populated areas.

(E) The rats interacted with other animals that Twigg believes could have carried plague.

Inference

The question requires recognizing information that is strongly implied, but not directly stated, in the passage. The passage states that Graham Twigg claims the rat population in medieval Europe was too sparse to spread plague; therefore, it follows that he believes a larger rat population would have been required for rats to have spread the Black Death.

A   The passage states that Twigg disputes the idea that plague-carrying rats came on ships from Asia, but it does not suggest that Twigg believes either an Asian provenance or transport on ships was a necessary condition for rats to bring plague.

B   The passage states that Twigg believes there weren't enough rats, but it suggests nothing regarding the immunity to disease of those rats.

C   **Correct.** The passage states that Twigg believes there weren't enough rats to spread plague in medieval Europe; it would follow that he believes a larger rat population would have been necessary to spread plague.

D   The passage makes no mention of population density in relation to Twigg's ideas.

E   The passage states that Twigg overlooks the possibility that animals other than rats carried plague; it does not suggest that he believes rat interactions with other species would have been necessary for those other species to spread plague.

The correct answer is C.

29.   According to the passage, the post–Second World War studies that altered the prevailing view of the Black Death involved which of the following?

(A)   Determining the death rates caused by the Black Death in specific regions and towns

(B)   Demonstrating how the Black Death intensified the political and religious upheaval that ended the Middle Ages

(C)   Presenting evidence to prove that many medieval epidemics were mislabeled

(D)   Arguing that the consequences of the Black Death led to the Renaissance and the rise of modern Europe

(E)   Employing urban case studies to determine the number of rats in medieval Europe

Supporting Idea

The question requires recognizing specific information mentioned in the passage. The passage states that studies conducted after World War II changed then-common ideas regarding the Black Death, when examination of data from specific regions and towns revealed extremely high mortality rates at the time of the epidemic; this revelation of the plague's toll restored ideas of its historical significance.

A   **Correct.** The passage states that the post–WWII discovery of exceptionally high death rates in specific regions and towns during the time of the plague restored ideas of the plague's historical importance.

B   The passage states that a study in 1893—not the studies after WWII—made an argument for the plague's contribution to religious and political upheaval.

C   The passage refers to speculations regarding mislabeled epidemics, but not in connection with the post–WWII studies.

D   The passage attributes this argument regarding the rise of the Renaissance to George Coulton, not to the post–WWII studies.

E   The passage states that Graham Twigg employed such case studies to determine rat populations, not that the post–WWII studies did so.

The correct answer is A.

30. The "silver lining to the Black Death" (lines 7–8) refers to which of the following?

(A)   The decay of European feudalism precipitated by the Black Death

(B)   Greater availability of employment, sustenance, and housing for survivors of the epidemic

(C)   Strengthening of the human species through natural selection

(D)   Better understanding of how to limit the spread of contagious diseases

(E)   Immunities and resistance to the Black Death gained by later generations

Supporting Idea

The question requires recognizing the specific significance of the text: a "silver lining to the Black Death" in lines 7–8. The passage attributes the idea that there was such a silver lining to historian George Coulton, then expands on the idea by stating that Coulton believed reduced competition for resources and work—that is, increased sustenance, employment, and housing becoming available to survivors—led to prosperity and cultural development.

A   The passage discusses the plague's relationship with the decline of feudalism, but it does not do so in connection with lines 7–8.

B   Correct. The passage attributes the idea of a "silver lining to the Black Death" to historian George Coulton, then states that he believed that the silver lining consisted of reduced competition for resources among epidemic survivors, leading to prosperity and cultural blossoming.

C   The passage makes no mention of strengthening the human species through natural selection.

D   The passage discusses various possible mechanisms for the spread of the plague but never mentions ideas for how to limit the spread of disease.

E   The passage makes no mention of immunity gained by the generations following the Black Death.

The correct answer is B.

31. The author's attitude toward Twigg's work is best characterized as which of the following?

(A)   Dismissive

(B)   Indifferent

(C)   Vindictive

(D)   Cautious

(E)   Ambivalent

Evaluation

The question requires assessing the overall attitude the author holds toward the work of Graham Twigg. That attitude can be inferred through specific phrases the author uses to characterize Twigg's work, such as "faulty logic," "speculative generalizations," "isolated studies," and "unconvincing . . . argument." Taken together, these phrases suggest an attitude of irritated disdain and the belief that Twigg's work is insufficiently rigorous to be worthy of serious consideration by scholars of the Black Death.

A   Correct. The author describes Twigg's work in terms including "faulty logic," "speculative generalizations," and "unconvincing . . . argument," strongly suggesting that the author believes Twigg's work deserves dismissal.

B   The author's attitude toward Twigg's work is strongly negative, not indifferent.

C   While the author's attitude toward Twigg's work verges on disrespect, there is no suggestion in the passage that it is motivated by revenge.

D   The author's tone in regard to Twigg's work is confidently negative rather than cautious.

E   While the author acknowledges a single merit in Twigg's work—that it "correctly cites the exacting conditions" necessary for an epidemic of plague—the preponderance of the author's remarks on Twigg are so negative that an overall attitude of ambivalence is unlikely.

The correct answer is A.

Questions 32–35 refer to the passage on page 65.

32. Which of the following is NOT mentioned in the passage as a characteristic of the traditional model of employer-employee relations in the United States?

(A) Attractive compensation packages for employees

(B) Opportunities for employees to receive training

(C) Long-term job security for employees

(D) Opportunities for employee advancement within a company

(E) Long-term commitment toward a company by employees

Supporting Idea

The question requires recognizing specific details included in the passage. The passage specifies several benefits workers received from the traditional model of employer-employee relations, including long-term job security, training, and opportunities for promotion, and also states that these benefits led workers to form a corresponding long-term commitment to their companies. However, the passage does not mention good compensation packages among the listed benefits.

A   **Correct.** The passage does not mention attractive compensation packages for employees as one of the characteristics of traditional employee-employer relations.

B   The passage specifies training for employees as one characteristic of traditional employment models.

C   The passage includes long-term job security in its list of the characteristics of traditional employment models.

D   The passage mentions opportunities for promotion, or advancement, as a characteristic feature of traditional employment models.

E   The passage states that the benefits of traditional employment models generally led employees to make long-term commitments to their companies.

The correct answer is A.

33. According to the passage, managers' motivation for engaging in measures such as increased layoffs is often a result of

(A) the hope that a smaller workforce will decrease the managers' own workloads

(B) shareholder pressure to generate increased short-term financial gains

(C) a desire to eradicate the idea of a "psychological contract"

(D) dissatisfaction with the performance of disgruntled employees

(E) a desire to appear to be following modern organizational trends

Supporting Idea

The item requires recognizing specific information presented in the passage. In the second paragraph, the passage states that top management is under pressure from shareholders to generate high short-term returns on investment, and that this pressure drives measures such as layoffs and decreased hiring.

A   The passage makes no mention of managers seeking to decrease their workloads through layoffs.

B   **Correct.** The passage states that pressure from shareholders to generate high short-term returns on investment drives cost-cutting measures such as layoffs.

C   The passage makes no mention of a desire to eradicate the "psychological contract" but rather suggests that such eradication is the result of decreasing job security, training, and promotions.

D   The passage makes no mention of the performance of disgruntled employees.

E   The passage does not cite a desire to appear to be modern as a motive for layoffs.

The correct answer is B.

34.   The passage suggests that which of the following is a legitimate reason for organizations' shift to the new model of employer-employee relations?

(A)   Organizations tend to operate more effectively when they have a high manager-to-employee ratio.

(B)   Organizations can move their operations to less-expensive locations more easily when they have fewer permanent employees.

(C)   Organizations have found that they often receive higher-quality work when they engage in outsourcing.

(D)   Organizations with large pools of permanent workers risk significant financial losses if the demand for their product or service decreases.

(E)   Organizations are under increasing pressure to adopt new technologies that often obviate the need for certain workers.

Supporting Idea

The question requires recognizing specific information presented in the passage. The second paragraph describes as "legitimate and pressing" three reasons that employers have shifted to a paradigm of decreased commitment to their workers: that large numbers of permanent employees make it difficult for companies to avoid losses in downturns, that there has been an increase in wrongful discharge suits, and that there is shareholder pressure for short-term gains.

A   The passage does not include manager-to-employee ratio in its list of legitimate reasons for employers to decrease their commitment to employees.

B   The passage does not mention ease of relocating companies as a legitimate reason for decreasing employer commitment to employees.

C   The passage does not state that companies receive better work through outsourcing.

D   **Correct.** The passage states that companies with large numbers of permanent employees are susceptible to losses in downturns when demand decreases, and it characterizes this susceptibility as a legitimate reason for adopting the new model of lower employer commitment to employees.

E   The passage does not mention pressure to adopt new technologies as a reason for the new model of employer-employee relations.

The correct answer is D.

35.   Which of the following best characterizes the function of the final sentence of the passage?

(A)   It suggests an alternative explanation for a phenomenon discussed earlier in the passage.

(B)   It provides data intended to correct a common misconception.

(C)   It further weakens an argument that is being challenged by the author.

(D)   It introduces a specific piece of evidence in support of a claim made at the beginning of the final paragraph.

(E)   It answers a question that is implicit in the preceding sentence.

Evaluation

The question requires assessing the function of a specific detail included in the passage. The final sentence discusses a study of employee attitudes toward management and includes the fact that nearly half of those surveyed agreed that management is eager to take advantage of workers. The survey result provides evidence for the earlier claim that employees are increasingly cynical regarding management's motivations.

A   The perceived tendency of management to exploit workers discussed in the last sentence would help explain phenomena mentioned earlier—such as increasing interest in entrepreneurship—but it is not presented as an alternative explanation for such phenomena.

B   Nothing in the passage suggests a common misconception that would be corrected by data regarding employee attitudes.

C   The passage does not include any explicit argument that is being challenged by the author.

D   **Correct.** The survey result cited in the final sentence provides specific evidence for the idea that employees often distrust management; in other words, it supports the claim made at the beginning of the final paragraph that employees have grown cynical about management's motivations.

E   There is no question implicit in the preceding sentence; rather, it advances the claim that employers' attitudes are alienating their employees.

The correct answer is D.

Questions 36 to 81 — Difficulty: **Medium**

Questions 36–38 refer to the passage on page 67.

36.   The passage is primarily concerned with

(A)   evaluating the evidence of a major geologic period and determining its duration

(B)   describing an evolutionary phenomenon and speculating about its cause

(C)   explaining the mechanisms through which marine life-forms evolved during a particular period

(D)   analyzing the impact on later life-forms of an important evolutionary development

(E)   contrasting a period of evolutionary change with other such periods

Main Idea

This question asks for an assessment of what the passage as a whole is doing. The passage is mainly concerned with a possible link between certain geological and ecological changes that occurred during the Ordovician period and the Ordovician radiation (when existing marine invertebrate life-forms gave rise to new variations that would eventually lead to new species).

A   The passage is not particularly concerned with determining the length of the period in question.

B   **Correct.** The passage is mainly concerned with a possible link between the evolutionary phenomenon of the Ordovician radiation and certain environmental changes that may have resulted in an enriched pattern of habitats and nutrients that could have fostered that radiation.

C   The passage indicates that the particular mechanisms through which marine life-forms evolved are not well understood.

D   Although the passage indicates that the changes it discusses ultimately did lead to new life-forms, it does not analyze that relationship.

E   The passage does not discuss any period of evolutionary change besides the Ordovician radiation.

The correct answer is B.

37.   Which of the following can be inferred from the passage regarding the geologic changes that occurred during the Ordovician period?

(A)   They were more drastic than those associated with other radiations.

(B)   They may have created conditions favorable to the evolution of many new life-forms.

(C)   They may have caused the extinction of many of the marine species living in shallow waters.

(D)   They may have been a factor in the development of new species adapted to living both on land and in water.

(E)   They hastened the formation of the extensive dry regions found in the western United States.

Inference

The question asks what can be inferred from the passage's claims regarding the geologic changes that took place during the Ordovician period. The passage indicates that during this period the sea level dropped and mountain ranges were formed and that these changes, rather than leading to large-scale extinctions, may have created more favorable habitats providing greater nutrients, which would likely have been favorable to newly evolved life-forms.

A   The passage does not mention other radiations and does not compare the Ordovician geologic changes to geologic changes associated with other radiations.

B   Correct. The passage does suggest that certain geologic changes that occurred during the Ordovician period may have created conditions favorable to the new life-forms associated with the Ordovician radiation.

C   The passage does not indicate whether any marine species became extinct; in fact, it explicitly denies that the geologic changes led to any large-scale extinctions.

D   The passage does not indicate that any new species were adapted to living both on land and in water. It merely discusses marine life-forms.

E   Although these geologic changes did likely create newly dry areas in the western United States, it does not indicate that these areas are *extensive*.

The correct answer is B.

38.   Which of the following best describes the function of the last sentence of the passage?

(A)   It points out that the events described in the passage may be atypical.

(B)   It alludes to the fact that there is disagreement in the scientific community over the importance of the Ordovician radiation.

(C)   It concludes that the evidence presented in the passage is insufficient to support the proposed hypothesis because it comes from a limited geographic area.

(D)   It warns the reader against seeing a connection between the biological and geologic changes described in the passage.

(E)   It alerts the reader that current knowledge cannot completely explain the relationship suggested by the evidence presented in the passage.

Evaluation

The last sentence of the passage functions primarily to indicate that, though certain evidence from the geologic record suggests a possible cause of the Ordovician radiation, the current level of knowledge regarding the relationship between environmental factors and that radiation is not sufficient for a full understanding of that relationship.

A   Although there may be certain geologic or evolutionary aspects of the Ordovician period that are atypical, the final sentence of the passage does not address them.

B   Neither the final sentence nor the rest of the passage addresses any disagreements within the scientific community.

C   Although the final sentence of the passage does indicate that current understanding of the relationship between the environmental factors discussed and the Ordovician radiation is incomplete, it does not indicate that it is because the evidence comes from a limited geographic area that the evidence is insufficient.

D   The last sentence does not advise against seeing a connection between the biological and geologic changes discussed; it merely advises that such a connection is not yet fully understood.

E   **Correct.** The last sentence indicates to the reader that current knowledge is insufficient for fully explaining the relationships among the evidence provided in the passage regarding geologic, ecological, and evolutionary changes.

The correct answer is E.

Questions 39–47 refer to the passage on page 69.

39. The author of the passage draws conclusions about the fur trade in North America from all of the following sources EXCEPT

(A) Cartier's accounts of trading with Native Americans

(B) a seventeenth-century account of European settlements

(C) a sixteenth-century account written by a sailing vessel captain

(D) archaeological observations of sixteenth-century Native American sites

(E) a sixteenth-century account of Native Americans in what is now New England

Supporting Idea

This question asks about the sources mentioned by the author of the passage. Answering the question correctly requires determining which answer choice is NOT referred to in the passage as a source of evidence regarding the North American fur trade.

A   **Correct.** The passage mentions Cartier's voyage but does not refer to Cartier's accounts of his trading.

B   In the first paragraph, Nicolas Denys's 1672 account of European settlements provides evidence of fur trading by sixteenth-century European fishing crews.

C   In the second paragraph, a Portuguese captain's records provide evidence that the fur trade was going on for some time prior to his 1501 account.

D   In the first paragraph, archaeologists' observations of sixteenth-century Native American sites provide evidence of fur trading at that time.

E   In the second paragraph, a 1524 account provides evidence that Native Americans living in what is now New England had become selective about which European goods they would accept in trade for furs.

The correct answer is A.

40. The passage suggests that which of the following is partially responsible for the difficulty in establishing the precise date when the fur trade in North America began?

(A) A lack of written accounts before that of Nicolas Denys in 1672

(B) A lack of written documentation before 1501

(C) Ambiguities in the evidence from Native American sources

(D) Uncertainty about Native American trade networks

(E) Uncertainty about the origin of artifacts supposedly traded by European fishing crews for furs

Inference

The question asks about information implied by the passage. The first paragraph points out the difficulty of establishing exactly when the fur trade between Native Americans and Europeans began. The second paragraph explains that the first written record of the fur trade (at least the earliest known to scholars who study the history of the trade) dates to 1501, but that trading was already well established by that time. Thus, it can be inferred that lack of written records prior to 1501 contributes to the difficulty in establishing an exact date for the beginning of the fur trade.

A   Two written records of the fur trade prior to the account by Nicolas Denys are mentioned in the passage. The passage does not suggest that a lack of written records from before 1672 is a source of the difficulty in establishing the date.

B   **Correct.** The passage indicates that the fur trade was well established by the time of the documentation dating from 1501 but strongly suggests that there is no known earlier documentation regarding that trade, so a lack of records before that time contributes to the difficulty in establishing an exact date.

C   The only Native American sources mentioned in the passage are archaeological sites, and there is no indication of ambiguities at those sites.

D   Native American trade networks are not mentioned in the passage.

E   The passage mentions that fishing crews exchanged parts of their ships for furs and does not suggest any uncertainty about the origin of those artifacts.

The correct answer is B.

41.   Which of the following, if true, most strengthens the author's assertion in the first sentence of the second paragraph?

(A)   When Europeans retraced Cartier's voyage in the first years of the seventeenth century, they frequently traded with Native Americans.

(B)   Furs from beavers, which were plentiful in North America but nearly extinct in Europe, became extremely fashionable in Europe in the final decades of the sixteenth century.

(C)   Firing arms were rarely found on sixteenth-century Native American sites or on European lists of trading goods since such arms required frequent maintenance and repair.

(D)   Europeans and Native Americans had established trade protocols, such as body language assuring one another of their peaceful intentions, that antedate the earliest records of trade.

(E)   During the first quarter of the sixteenth century, an Italian explorer recorded seeing many Native Americans with what appeared to be copper beads, though they may have been made of indigenous copper.

Evaluation

The question depends on evaluating an assertion made in the passage and determining which additional evidence would most strengthen it. The first sentence of the second paragraph claims that the fur trade was well established by the time Europeans sailing the Atlantic coast of America first documented it. The passage then indicates that the first written documentation of the trade dates to 1501. Thus, evidence showing that trade had been going on for some time before 1501 would strengthen (support) the assertion.

A   This evidence shows trade occurring in the first years of the seventeenth century, not prior to the first records from 1501.

B   This evidence shows trade occurring in the final decades of the sixteenth century, not prior to the first records from 1501.

C   This evidence does not indicate that trade took place prior to the first records from 1501.

D   **Correct.** Evidence that trade protocols had developed before the trade was first recorded in 1501 would strengthen support for the assertion that trade was taking place prior to the earliest documentation.

E   Because the copper beads may have been made by Native Americans rather than acquired through trade with other societies, this observation would not provide evidence that trade with Europeans took place prior to 1501.

The correct answer is D.

42. Which of the following best describes the primary function of lines 11–16?

    (A) It offers a reconsideration of a claim made in the preceding sentence.

    (B) It reveals how archaeologists arrived at an interpretation of the evidence mentioned in the preceding sentence.

    (C) It shows how scholars misinterpreted the significance of certain evidence mentioned in the preceding sentence.

    (D) It identifies one of the first significant accounts of seventeenth-century European settlements in North America.

    (E) It explains why Denys's account of seventeenth-century European settlements is thought to be significant.

Evaluation

This question depends on understanding how the last sentence of the first paragraph functions in relation to the larger passage. The first paragraph explains that the earliest Europeans to trade with Native Americans were fishing crews near Newfoundland. The second-to-last sentence of the paragraph describes archaeological artifacts from Native American sites. The last sentence then explains that Nicolas Denys's 1672 account helped archaeologists realize that the artifacts were evidence of trade with fishing crews. Thus, the last sentence of the passage shows how archaeologists learned to interpret the evidence mentioned in the previous sentence.

A   The only claim made in the previous sentence is that archaeologists found a particular type of evidence. The final sentence of the paragraph does not suggest that this claim should be reconsidered.

B   Correct. After reading Denys's account, archaeologists were able to interpret the archaeological evidence mentioned in the previous sentence.

C   The passage suggests that archaeologists correctly interpreted the evidence, not misinterpreted it.

D   Denys's account is mentioned primarily to explain how archaeologists learned to interpret the archaeological evidence, not primarily to identify an important early account of settlements.

E   The passage does not discuss why Denys's account is significant, only that archaeologists used it to help understand the evidence mentioned in the previous sentence.

The correct answer is B.

43. It can be inferred from the passage that the author would agree with which of the following statements about the fur trade between Native Americans and Europeans in the early modern era?

    (A) This trade may have begun as early as the 1480s.

    (B) This trade probably did not continue much beyond the 1530s.

    (C) This trade was most likely at its peak in the mid-1520s.

    (D) This trade probably did not begin prior to 1500.

    (E) There is no written evidence of this trade prior to the seventeenth century.

Inference

The question requires determining which statement can most reasonably be inferred from the information in the passage. The passage argues that it is difficult to determine when the fur trade between Native Americans and Europeans began, since the earliest people to participate in that trade apparently left no written records. The second paragraph notes that at the time of the earliest known record in 1501, trade was already *well underway*. In the final two sentences of the passage, the author mentions an event that occurred in 1534 and then says that by that time the trade may have been going on for *perhaps half a century*.

A **Correct.** The next-to-last sentence of the passage cites evidence of fur trade between Native Americans and Europeans in 1524. In the final sentence of the passage, the author mentions an event that happened a decade after that date—thus in 1534—and expresses the opinion that the trade started *perhaps half a century* (fifty years) before that later date. Fifty years before 1534 would be 1484. This implies that the author accepts that the trade may have begun by the 1480s.

B The passage gives no indication that the author believes trade ended shortly after the 1530s.

C The passage does not discuss when the fur trade was at its peak.

D To the contrary, the passage argues that trade began well before 1501.

E The passage mentions written evidence of the trade from 1501 and 1524.

The correct answer is A.

44. Which of the following can be inferred from the passage about the Native Americans mentioned in line 24?

(A) They had little use for decorative objects such as earrings.

(B) They became increasingly dependent on fishing between 1501 and 1524.

(C) By 1524, only certain groups of Europeans were willing to trade with them.

(D) The selectivity of their trading choices made it difficult for them to engage in widespread trade with Europeans.

(E) The selectivity of their trading choices indicates that they had been trading with Europeans for a significant period of time prior to 1524.

Inference

The question asks about information that can be inferred from the passage. The Native Americans mentioned in the 1524 chronicles accepted only certain kinds of European goods in trade. The passage indicates that these Native Americans *had become selective* about which goods they would accept, which implies that by 1524 they had been trading long enough to determine which European goods were most valuable to them.

A The passage does not imply that these Native Americans had no use for decorative objects, only that they did not desire to obtain such items through trade with Europeans.

B The passage does not suggest that the Native Americans' dependency on fishing changed over time.

C There is no indication that any groups of Europeans were unwilling to trade with these Native Americans.

D The passage notes that the Native Americans were selective in their trade choices but does not suggest that such selectivity made widespread trade difficult.

E **Correct.** The passage notes that by 1524, the Native Americans had become selective about which European goods they would accept, and the passage takes this to indicate that the trade with Europeans significantly predated 1524.

The correct answer is E.

45. The passage supports which of the following statements about sixteenth-century European fishing crews working the waters off Newfoundland?

(A) They wrote no accounts of their fishing voyages.

(B) They primarily sailed under the flag of Portugal.

(C) They exchanged ship parts with Native Americans for furs.

(D) They commonly traded jewelry with Native Americans for furs.

(E) They carried surplus metal implements to trade with Native Americans for furs.

Inference

The question asks which statement is supported by information provided in the passage. The first paragraph states that European fishing crews around Newfoundland were the first Europeans to trade goods for furs with Native Americans in the modern period. The last sentence of the paragraph states that archaeological evidence indicates the crews had dismantled their ships to trade ship parts for furs.

A   The second sentence states that the crews left no written accounts of their trade with Native Americans, but it does not suggest that they left no written accounts of their voyages.

B   The passage mentions one Portuguese vessel but does not suggest that the European crews who fished off Newfoundland were mostly on Portuguese vessels.

C   **Correct.** The last sentence of the first paragraph supports the conclusion that the crews traded ship parts for furs.

D   The passage mentions one instance of a Native American acquiring earrings from Europeans but does not suggest that trades for such goods were common.

E   The passage indicates that fishing crews traded metal implements with Native Americans but does not suggest that they brought surplus implements for that purpose—and in fact mentions that sometimes traded metal articles had been parts of their own ships.

The correct answer is C.

46. Which of the following can be inferred from the passage about evidence pertaining to the fur trade between Native Americans and Europeans in the early modern era?

(A) A lack of written evidence has made it difficult to establish which Europeans first participated in this trade.

(B) In general, the physical evidence pertaining to this trade has been more useful than the written evidence has been.

(C) There is more written evidence pertaining to this trade from the early part of the sixteenth century than from later in that century.

(D) The earliest written evidence pertaining to this trade dates from a time when the trade was already well established.

(E) Some important pieces of evidence pertaining to this trade, such as Denys's 1672 account, were long overlooked by archaeologists.

Inference

This question asks about information that can be inferred from the passage. Any suggestion that Native Americans may have produced written evidence of the early-modern trade with Europeans is absent from the passage. The second paragraph states that by the time Europeans first documented the fur trade, it was already well underway. This statement, in the context of the passage, implies that the earliest written records of the trade date to a time after it was well established.

A   The first paragraph indicates that the first Europeans to participate in the trade were quite certainly fishing crews near Newfoundland.

B   The passage gives no indication that physical evidence of the trade has been more useful than written evidence.

C   Although the passage does not cite written evidence from the late sixteenth century, the passage gives no reason to believe that less written evidence exists from that time.

D   **Correct.** According to the passage, the fur trade was well underway when written evidence of the trade was first documented by Europeans. The passage contains no suggestion that there might have been earlier documentation of that trade by anybody other than Europeans.

E   The passage does not imply that archaeologists overlooked evidence for long periods of time.

The correct answer is D.

47. The passage suggests which of the following about the sixteenth-century Native Americans who traded with Europeans on the coast of what is now called New England?

(A) By 1524, they had become accustomed to exchanging goods with Europeans.

(B) They were unfamiliar with metals before encountering Europeans.

(C) They had no practical uses for European goods other than metals and metal implements.

(D) By 1524, they had become disdainful of European traders because such traders had treated them unfairly in the past.

(E) By 1524, they demanded only the most prized European goods because they had come to realize how valuable furs were on European markets.

Inference

The question asks about what is implied in the passage. The Native Americans trading with Europeans on the coast of what is now called New England are discussed in the 1524 chronicles mentioned in the second paragraph. The passage indicates that these Native Americans *had become selective* about which European goods they would accept in trade, which suggests they had become accustomed to trading with Europeans.

A Correct. By the time the chronicle was written, the Native Americans were familiar enough with trade to be able to specify which European goods they would accept.

B Although the Native Americans chose to trade furs for European metal goods, the passage does not imply they were unfamiliar with any metals prior to encountering Europeans.

C The passage does not suggest why Native Americans preferred certain goods over others.

D The passage does not attribute disdain for European traders to Native Americans.

E There is no indication in the passage that Native Americans were aware of furs' value in European markets.

The correct answer is A.

Questions 48–50 refer to the passage on page 72.

48. The primary purpose of the passage is to

(A) summarize findings in an area of research

(B) discuss different perspectives on a scientific question

(C) outline the major questions in a scientific discipline

(D) illustrate the usefulness of investigating a research topic

(E) reconcile differences between two definitions of a term

Main Idea

The passage discusses two problems confronting researchers studying the genetic bases of animal behavior: the complexity of the control of most behaviors by multiple genes, and divergence between research fields in what counts as a behavioral gene. The passage focuses mainly on the latter issue, discussing how ethologists define "behavioral gene" in a narrower manner than neuroscientists, who define the term broadly. To elucidate the ethologists' approach, two genes are discussed, one a behavioral gene, the other not.

A The passage primarily aims to explain how researchers in two different research areas define "behavioral gene." It does not try to summarize the research findings of either area.

B Correct. The primary purpose of the passage is to identify differing perspectives on the scientific question of how genes control animal behavior.

C The scientific disciplines of genetics, neuroscience, and ethology—all subdisciplines of biology—contain many different "major questions," and the passage does not try to outline the great variety of such questions in any one of those subdisciplines.

D   The topic of the utility of doing research is not part of the passage discussion.

E   An important purpose of the passage is to illustrate divergence among scientific fields in how a key term is defined, but the point is to show how the definitions differ rather than to "reconcile" the difference.

The correct answer is B.

49. The passage suggests that neuroscientists would most likely consider *Shaker* to be which of the following?

(A)   An example of a behavioral gene

(B)   One of multiple genes that control a single behavior

(C)   A gene that, when mutated, causes an alteration in a specific normal behavior without making the organism ill

(D)   A gene of interest to ethologists but of no interest to neuroscientists

(E)   A poor source of information about the nervous system

Application

The passage asserts that ethologists do not regard *Shaker* as a behavioral gene because it merely makes fruit flies exhibit unhealthy behavior (shaking under anesthesia). But neuroscientists, according to the passage, are mainly interested in how genes, via the nervous system, contribute to behavior. The passage suggests that neuroscientists, unlike ethologists, have no reservation about using the term *behavioral gene* to apply to any gene that contributes to behavior. The implication is that neuroscientists would probably regard *Shaker* as a behavioral gene.

A   **Correct.** The passage suggests that neuroscientists would probably regard *Shaker* as a behavioral gene.

B   The passage indicates that research shows *Shaker* is a sufficient cause, in fruit flies, of shaking under anesthesia. Although some organism might display a behavior controlled by *Shaker* in concert with other genes, the passage is silent on any such possibility.

C   The passage lacks information as to whether there is any alteration—one that neuroscientists would likely consider healthy—in a normal behavior if the alteration is caused by a mutation in *Shaker*.

D   The passage indicates that neuroscientists' interest in genetics is part of their effort to understand the nervous system. This seems to imply that neuroscientists might be interested in *Shaker*.

E   The passage is silent on how neuroscientists would evaluate the potential for *Shaker* to contribute to understanding of the nervous system.

The correct answer is A.

50. It can be inferred from the passage that which of the following, if true, would be most likely to influence ethologists' opinions about whether a particular gene in a species is a behavioral gene?

(A)   The gene is found only in that species.

(B)   The gene is extremely difficult to identify.

(C)   The only effect of mutations in the gene is to make the organism ill.

(D)   Neuroscientists consider the gene to be a behavioral gene.

(E)   Geneticists consider the gene to be a behavioral gene.

Application

The passage identifies two criteria that ethologists use in deciding whether a gene should count as a behavioral gene: a mutation in the gene alters a specific normal behavior and the mutation does not merely make the organism ill.

A   The passage is silent on whether either of two genes identified by ethologists in fruit flies are to be found only in fruit flies. The two criteria mentioned used by ethologists carry no implication as to whether any gene unique to a given species would count as a behavioral gene.

B   The difficulty of identifying a gene can obviously be due to many factors, such as limitations in existing scientific techniques, and the passage does not imply that such difficulty increases the likelihood that a gene would count as a behavioral gene for ethologists.

C   **Correct.** The passage implies that if this were found to be true, ethologists would regard it as sufficient reason for not counting the gene as a behavioral gene.

D   A central theme of the passage is that whether ethologists would count a gene as a behavioral gene is largely unaffected by whether neuroscientists do so, given the divergent perspectives of the scientists' respective disciplines.

E   The main contrast in the passage with respect to definitions of the term *behavioral gene* is between ethologists and neuroscientists, and no specific definitional criteria for this term are explicitly attributed to geneticists. However, there is a slight suggestion that since geneticists find that most behaviors are governed by multiple genes, geneticists might regard any gene involved in the governance of a behavior as a behavioral gene. This approach, however, would be unlikely to influence the opinions of ethologists concerning definition.

The correct answer is C.

Questions 51–57 refer to the passage on page 73.

51. The author indicates that tamarin territories are

(A)   surprisingly large

(B)   poorly situated

(C)   unusually abundant in food resources

(D)   incapable of supporting large troops of tamarins

(E)   larger in Peru than in other parts of South America

Supporting Idea

This question depends on understanding what the passage says about tamarin territories. In the second paragraph, the passage claims that the most surprising thing about tamarins is the size of their territories, and it indicates how large these territories are by comparing them to the territories of certain other animals.

A   **Correct.** The passage indicates that the size of tamarins' territories—large in comparison to the territories of several other species—is surprising.

B   The passage gives no indication as to whether tamarin territories are poorly situated.

C   Although the passage does discuss the tamarin diet, it does not indicate how abundant in food sources tamarin territories are.

D   The passage does indicate that relatively few tamarins live per square kilometer, but it does not claim that this is so because the territories are incapable of supporting a larger number of tamarins. In fact, there is some suggestion that the territories would seem to be capable of supporting more, which is one reason the size of the territories is so surprising.

E   The passage does not compare the size of tamarin territories in Peru to tamarin territories elsewhere in South America.

The correct answer is A.

52. The author mentions the spatial requirements of the gray squirrel in order to

(A)   explain why they are so common

(B)   demonstrate the consequences of their nonterritoriality

(C)   emphasize the unusual territorial requirements of the tamarin

(D)   provide an example of a major difference between squirrels and monkeys

(E)   provide an example of an animal with requirements similar to those of the tamarin

Evaluation

The passage mentions the spatial requirements of the gray squirrel as part of its discussion of the surprising size of tamarin territories. Gray squirrel territories are mentioned for the specific purpose of highlighting how much more space tamarins require compared to another animal of roughly equal size.

A   The passage does refer to "the common gray squirrel," but it does not explain why they are so common.

B   The passage does not say anything about the consequences of the gray squirrel's nonterritoriality.

C   **Correct.** The spatial requirements of gray squirrels are mentioned to highlight, by contrast, how expansive the spatial requirements of tamarins are.

D   Although the passage mentions the spatial requirements of the gray squirrel to highlight how different the spatial requirements of one particular type of monkey, the tamarin, are from those of other animals, the passage does not mention the squirrels' spatial requirements to provide an example of a difference between squirrels and monkeys in general.

E   The passage actually does the opposite of this—it mentions the gray squirrel's spatial requirements to provide an example of an animal with requirements vastly different from those of the tamarin.

The correct answer is C.

53.   The author regards the differences between the diets of the tamarins and several larger species as

(A)   generally explicable in terms of territory size

(B)   apparently too small to explain the rarity of tamarins

(C)   wholly predictable on the basis of differences in body size

(D)   a result of the rigid territoriality of tamarins

(E)   a significant factor in determining behavioral differences

Supporting Idea

This question depends on recognizing that the passage rejects the idea that any differences between the diets of tamarins and those of certain larger animals are large enough to explain tamarins' relative rarity. The passage points out that these animals feed on the same fruits, nectar, and small prey, and claims that though the proportions of the fruits consumed varies somewhat, this variation is not sufficient to explain the tamarin's rarity.

A   The author does not seek to explain why these differences in diet—which the passage indicates are minimal—exist. Given that the author indicates that differences in territory size are large and differences in diet are small, it is unlikely, in any case, that the author would regard the former as explaining the latter.

B   **Correct.** The passage indicates that the differences in diet among these animals are too small to explain the rarity of tamarins.

C   The author does not give any indication that the differences in the diets of these animals are predictable based on differences in body size.

D   The author does indicate that tamarins are rather unusual among primates in their rigid territoriality, but there is no indication that this rigid territoriality explains the small differences in diet among tamarins and certain larger animals.

E   The author mentions differences in diet merely to rule out that these differences are large enough to explain tamarins' rarity; these differences are not mentioned as a factor in determining behavioral differences.

The correct answer is B.

54. Which of the following would most probably be regarded by the author as anomalous?

(A) A large primate species that eats mostly plants

(B) A species of small mammals that is fiercely territorial

(C) Two species of small primates that share the same territories

(D) A species of small birds that is more abundant than many species of larger birds

(E) A species of small rodents that requires more living space per individual than most species of larger rodents

Application

This question requires you to understand an underlying principle of the passage and to apply that principle to an instance that is not specifically discussed in the passage. The passage is concerned with how anomalous tamarins are: they are exceptions to the general rule that in general the number of animals in a species is proportional to the average body size of individuals within the species. The author also points out that tamarins are unusual in that the amount of space they require is out of proportion to their body size, suggesting the principle that an animal's spatial requirement is generally proportional to the animal's body size. And, though the passage is generally concerned with comparing tamarins to other primates, the author also compares tamarins' spatial requirements to those of gray squirrels, a type of rodent.

A   The author does not give any indication whether it would be anomalous for a species of large primates to eat mostly plants. The author does not present a general principle about the diets of primates, and says nothing specific about species of large primates.

B   Although the author indicates that the "rigid" territoriality of tamarins is "rather exceptional among primates," the author lists several other primate species that are also territorial. The author does not indicate whether such territoriality is rare among small mammals in general.

C   The author indicates that most primates do not have "such concerted territoriality" as tamarins do, suggesting that the author may not think that two other species of small primates sharing territories would be anomalous.

D   Given that the author indicates that generally the number of individuals within a species is inversely proportional to the average body size of the members of the species, the author would probably expect that a species of small birds would be more abundant than most species of larger birds and would not regard this as anomalous.

E   **Correct.** The author would generally expect that smaller animals would require less living space than larger animals.

The correct answer is E.

55. The author most probably regards the tamarins studied in Manu National Park as

(A) an endangered species

(B) typical tamarins

(C) unusually docile

(D) the most unusual primates anywhere

(E) too small a sample to be significant

Inference

This question requires you to make an inference from what the author says about the tamarins studied in Manu National Park to a claim about how the author most likely regards these tamarins. The author considers certain information that has been gathered about the two tamarin species studied in the park, and on the basis of that, makes claims about tamarins in general (note that the author elsewhere in the passage simply refers to "tamarins" without qualification, i.e., without referring specifically to "the tamarins studied in Manu National Park"). This suggests that the author would regard the tamarins studied in the park as being typical of tamarins generally, at least in the ways discussed.

A   It is possible that the two tamarin species studied in the park are endangered, but apart from noting the surprisingly small number of individuals belonging to the species, there is no information that would suggest that they are endangered, and the mere fact that the number of members is relatively small compared to the number of members in other species is not sufficient to indicate that they are endangered, as that number could nonetheless be stable or even growing.

B   **Correct.** The author does not specifically mention anything that would indicate that these tamarins are atypical of tamarins in general, and appears to make inferences about tamarins in general on the basis of the two species studied in the park. The author would not be justified in making such inferences if the author believed that the tamarins observed in the park were not in fact typical.

C   The author does not give any indication that these species are unusually docile, and in fact suggests the opposite by indicating that tamarins vigorously expel any intruders from their territories.

D   The author does note some ways in which these tamarin species are unusual among primates, but does not indicate that they are "the most unusual primates anywhere." The author, in fact, indicates that in one of the ways that these species are unusual—their relative scarcity despite their small body size—another primate species, the pygmy marmoset, is even more unusual.

E   Because the author appears to make some inferences from information about the tamarins studied in the park to claims about tamarins in general, the author does not seem to regard the tamarins studied in the park as too small a sample to be significant.

The correct answer is B.

56.   Which of the following is NOT mentioned in the passage as a species whose groups display territoriality?

   (A)   Gibbons

   (B)   Siamangs

   (C)   Titi monkeys

   (D)   Squirrel monkeys

   (E)   Night monkeys

Inference

This question requires you, by process of elimination, to identify the species that is NOT explicitly mentioned as being a species displaying territoriality. Each of the species given in the answer choices is explicitly mentioned in the passage, and all but one of these species are explicitly described as displaying territoriality. In lines 38–41, the author states, "concerted territoriality [like that of tamarins] is rather exceptional among primates, though the gibbons and siamangs of Asia show it, as do a few other New World species such as the titi and night monkeys." So, clearly, gibbons, siamangs, titi monkeys, and night monkeys are each said to display territoriality. Squirrel monkeys, the remaining answer choice, are mentioned three different times in the passage (lines 16, 25, 30), but never as displaying territoriality.

A   Gibbons are identified as displaying "concerted territoriality" (line 39).

B   Siamangs are identified as displaying "concerted territoriality" (line 39).

C   Titi monkeys are identified as displaying "concerted territoriality" (line 41).

D   **Correct.** Although squirrel monkeys are mentioned three times in the passage (lines 16, 25, and 30), in none of the instances are they mentioned as displaying territoriality.

E   Night monkeys are identified as displaying "concerted territoriality" (line 41).

The correct answer is D.

57. The primary concern of the passage is to

(A) recommend a policy
(B) evaluate a theory
(C) describe an unusual condition
(D) explain the development of a hypothesis
(E) support one of several competing hypotheses

Main Idea

Answering this question requires identifying an abstract description of the primary purpose of the passage. The passage focuses in different ways on an unusual condition, namely, the anomalous relationship between tamarins' relatively small average body size and the number of individuals in the species.

A   The passage is not concerned with recommending any policy.

B   The passage does not focus on any theory; it considers a phenomenon, but proposes no theory to explain that phenomenon.

C   **Correct.** The passage's primary concern is to describe an unusual phenomenon, namely, how tamarins "break the rule" that, in general, the number of individuals in a species is inversely proportional to the average body size of members of the species.

D   The passage is primarily concerned with a particular, unusual phenomenon, but it offers no hypothesis regarding it, nor does it discuss the development of any such hypothesis.

E   Although the passage gives passing consideration to some hypotheses, its primary concern is to note certain characteristics of tamarins. The passage does not primarily concern itself with any hypotheses.

The correct answer is C.

Questions 58–64 refer to the passage on page 75.

58. It can be inferred from the passage that opponents of labor concessions would most likely describe many plant-relocation decisions made by United States companies as

(A) capricious
(B) self-serving
(C) naive
(D) impulsive
(E) illogical

Evaluation

This question requires you to pick a word that the passage suggests opponents of labor concessions would apply to many plant-relocation decisions made by U.S. companies. The passage indicates that those who oppose labor concessions often do so on the grounds that companies will move their production overseas if it matches their perceived self-interest—regardless of any concessions labor has made in order to preserve jobs. According to the passage, opponents of labor concessions therefore tend to view such plant-relocation decisions as self-serving.

A   The passage does not attribute to opponents of labor concessions the view that corporate decisions are variable in a way that makes them unpredictable.

B   **Correct.** According to the passage, the opponents of labor concessions believe that companies make investment decisions that fit their strategic plans and profit objectives.

C   The passage suggests that the opponents may view plant managers' relocation decisions as based on realistic assessments of corporate interests.

D   The passage does not attribute to the opponents the view that companies make plant-relocation decisions on impulse; rather, it suggests that these opponents tend to see relocation decisions as based on analysis of how relocation would advance predetermined strategies and objectives.

E   According to the passage, the opponents see an inflexible logic governing such relocation decisions, which are based on an assessment of how best to serve companies' interests, as judged by reference to predetermined investment strategies and profit objectives.

The correct answer is B.

59.   It can be inferred from the passage that, until recently, which of the following has been true of United States industry in the twentieth century?

(A)   Unions have consistently participated in major corporate policy decisions.

(B)   Maintaining adequate quality control in manufacturing processes has been a principal problem.

(C)   Union workers have been paid relatively high wages.

(D)   Two-tier wage systems have been the norm.

(E)   Goods produced have been priced beyond the means of most workers.

Inference

This question requires you to draw a conclusion about United States industry in the twentieth century from the information in the passage. The passage indicates that even opponents of labor concessions believe that union workers have traditionally been paid relatively high wages and that high wages underlay much of the success of industry in the United States in the twentieth century.

A   The passage suggests otherwise. It tells us that advocates of labor concessions believe it may eventually be possible for labor to participate in management decisions in a way that was not traditionally the case.

B   The passage mentions "quality circles" as a benefit that, according to some proponents of labor concessions, may eventually be gained in the context of having more say on the shop floor. But that does not imply that quality control in manufacturing has been a major problem.

C   **Correct.** The passage attributes a belief that this was so to opponents of labor concessions.

D   The passage tells us that opponents of labor concessions believe that proposals for two-tier wage systems could become a reality—which indicates that such systems have not been the norm.

E   According to the passage, opponents of labor concessions admit that wages have been relatively high for union workers and that labor and management have long been committed to the idea that workers should be able to afford to purchase the products they make.

The correct answer is C.

60.   The passage provides information to answer which of the following questions?

(A)   What has caused unions to consider wage restraints and reduced benefits?

(B)   Why do analysts study United States labor-management relations?

(C)   How do job-security guarantees operate?

(D)   Are investment and pricing strategies effective in combating imports?

(E)   Do quality circles improve product performance and value?

Evaluation

This question requires you to identify a question that the passage provides an answer to. In paragraph 1, the passage indicates some factors ("twin shocks") that have contributed to a change in the approach of labor unions to negotiations with management.

A   **Correct.** The passage claims that competition from non-union companies and imports of low-priced high-quality products from abroad have induced labor unions to be more flexible in meeting the demands of management.

B   The passage does not address this question either directly or indirectly.

C   According to the passage, proponents of labor concessions claim that job-security guarantees can be negotiated if concessions are made, but the passage provides no further detail that would shed light on how such guarantees operate.

D   The passage is silent on the effectiveness of investment and pricing strategies in combating imports.

E   The passage mentions quality circles, but provides no information on their impact. Presumably, quality circles aim to improve quality, and such improvements would be pointless absent any payoff in "performance and value."

The correct answer is A.

61.   The passage is primarily concerned with the

(A)   reasons for adversarialism between labor and management

(B)   importance of cooperative labor-management relations

(C)   consequences of labor concessions to management

(D)   effects of foreign competition on the United States economy

(E)   effects of nonunion competition on union bargaining strategies

Main Idea

This question asks us to identify the overall theme of the passage, i.e., the topic that motivates the discussion of various subtopics.

A   The traditionally adversarial relationship between labor and management is mentioned in passing, but the reasons for that relationship are not probed.

B   The passage details benefits that some labor unionists perceive in cooperative labor-management relations, but does not assess the importance of such relations.

C   **Correct.** The passage explores this theme by looking at the new approach of some labor unions by discussing the pros and cons of labor concessions as perceived by proponents and opponents of such concessions.

D   The passage alludes to these effects, but no sustained exploration of this topic is present in the passage.

E   The passage alludes to these effects, but no sustained exploration of this topic is present in the passage.

The correct answer is C.

62.   The sentence "If proposals for pay cuts . . . unskilled laborers" (lines 45–52) serves primarily to

(A)   disprove a theory

(B)   clarify an ambiguity

(C)   reconcile opposing views

(D)   present a hypothesis

(E)   contradict accepted data

Evaluation

This question asks you to determine the intended purpose of one of the passage's sentences. This sentence, found in the final paragraph, describes what opponents of labor concessions predict are possible consequences if labor unions agree to pay cuts, two-tier wage systems, or lower wages for newly hired workers. These hypothesized consequences can be summarized as a significant degradation in the overall material welfare of large sections of the population because of grossly unequal distribution of wealth and income such as exist in some less-developed societies.

A   The sentence describes what is perceived as something that could occur if labor unions were to make concessions resulting in reductions in wages. It is not framed as evidence to refute a theory, since it is merely a prediction of what could occur.

B   The sentence does not function in resolving an ambiguity; no ambiguity that the sentence could be meant to resolve is described or suggested.

C   The sentence does nothing to reconcile opposing views; it articulates a vision of a possible future that it attributes to those who oppose wage-reduction concessions by labor unions.

D   Correct. The sentence presents a hypothesis about the possible long-term consequences of labor-union concessions that would result in significantly lower wages.

E   Accepted data can be contradicted only by alternative datasets, but the sentence in question does not provide alternative data, only a prediction of what the future might bring for workers' material welfare if drastic wage reductions were to be conceded by labor unions.

The correct answer is D.

63.   It can be inferred from the passage that opponents of labor concessions believe that if concession bargaining continues, then

(A)   plants will close instead of relocating

(B)   young workers will need continued job retraining

(C)   professional workers will outnumber marginal workers

(D)   wealthy investors will invest in Third World countries instead of the United States

(E)   the social structure of the United States will be negatively affected

Inference

This question concerns the beliefs of opponents of labor concessions, as those beliefs are represented in the passage. The passage attributes to those opponents the view that if the idea of reducing wages gains credence, the U.S. social structure will begin to decline and will eventually be on a par with the social structures of less-developed nations. Moreover, the passage represents the opponents as believing that if labor unions negotiate on the premise that high labor costs are causing a company's problems, eventually wages will be reduced drastically—potentially to Third World levels. In paragraph 1, the passage reports that analysts say that labor unions are currently

forced to favorably consider management demands for "wage restraint" and concessions on benefits.

A   The passage indicates that the opponents believe companies relocate their plants whenever companies perceive this as in accord with their investment strategies and profit objectives.

B   A need for continued retraining of young workers is not a belief attributed by the passage to opponents of labor concessions.

C   The passage, in referring to "a huge mass of marginal workers," attributes a contrary view to opponents of labor concessions.

D   The passage does not attribute this view to opponents of labor concessions.

E   Correct. We learn from the passage that labor unions are engaged in concession bargaining, on topics that include wage restraint. The opponents of labor concessions believe, according to the passage, that eventually the result will be wage reductions, and the ultimate result will be degradation of the U.S. social structure, resulting in a social structure more like that of a less-developed nation.

The correct answer is E.

64.   According to the author, "Sophisticated proponents" (line 13) of concessions do which of the following?

(A)   Support the traditional adversarialism characteristic of labor-management relations.

(B)   Emphasize the benefits unions can gain by granting concessions.

(C)   Focus on thorough analyses of current economic conditions.

(D)   Present management's reasons for demanding concessions.

(E)   Explain domestic economic developments in terms of worldwide trends.

Supporting Idea

This question requires you to identify what the passage says "sophisticated proponents" of concessions do. According to the passage, these sophisticated proponents represent their concessions in a "prolabor light." They suggest that concessions by labor can bargain for profit sharing, retraining rights, and job-security guarantees—and can even bargain for "more say on the shop floor" and a voice in company strategy and decision making.

A   According to the passage, analysts say that labor-management relations are increasingly cooperative rather than adversarial.

B   **Correct.** As explained above, the proponents of labor concessions represent concessions in a prolabor light by detailing the types of labor gains that can come from such concessions.

C   The proponents probably conduct such analyses, but no information about this is given in the passage.

D   Sophisticated proponents may sometimes do this, but the passage emphasizes their focus on the opportunities for labor gains.

E   Sophisticated proponents may sometimes do this, but the passage emphasizes their focus on the opportunities for labor gains.

The correct answer is B.

Questions 65–69 refer to the passage on page 77.

65.   According to the passage, much of the research on Alessandra Strozzi done by the historian mentioned in the second paragraph supports which of the following conclusions?

(A)   Alessandra used her position as her sons' sole guardian to further interests different from those of her sons.

(B)   Alessandra unwillingly sacrificed her own interests in favor of those of her sons.

(C)   Alessandra's actions indicate that her motivations and intentions were those of an independent individual.

(D)   Alessandra's social context encouraged her to take independent action.

(E)   Alessandra regarded her sons' goals and interests as her own.

Supporting Idea

According to the passage, a historian of women in Renaissance Europe attributes to a Florentine widow Alessandra Strozzi "individual intention and authorship of actions" and argues that she had significant individual goals and interests other than those of her sons. But the passage states that much of the historian's research indicates otherwise.

A   According to the passage, the historian's research provides much evidence that Alessandra Strozzi acted primarily to further her sons' interests.

B   The passage does not cite any of the historian's research to suggest that Strozzi was an unwilling champion of her sons' interest.

C   A theme of the passage is that the historian's research provides weak, if any, support for this claim.

D   The historian's research is not invoked in the passage to support this. The passage suggests that such a claim is more compatible with an anthropologist's idea that identity is socially and culturally determined and not necessarily "independent," as various historians assume.

E   **Correct.** The passage states: "much of the historian's own research reveals that Alessandra acted primarily as a champion of her sons' interests, taking their goals as her own."

The correct answer is E.

66.   In the first paragraph, the author of the passage mentions a contention that would be made by an anthropologist most likely in order to

(A)   present a theory that will be undermined in the discussion of a historian's study later in the passage

(B)   offer a perspective on the concept of personhood that can usefully be applied to the study of women in Renaissance Europe

(C)   undermine the view that the individuality of European women of the Renaissance was largely suppressed

(D)   argue that anthropologists have applied the Western concept of individualism in their research

(E)   lay the groundwork for the conclusion that Alessandra's is a unique case among European women of the Renaissance whose lives have been studied by historians

Evaluation

The passage asserts that an anthropologist would contend that "a person can be conceived in ways other than as an 'individual.'" Immediately preceding this assertion, the passage asserts that certain historians think of a person as "an innately bounded unit, autonomous and standing apart from both nature and society." The passage invokes anthropology to support the view that perhaps the findings of those historians regarding individualism among women in Renaissance Europe are biased.

A   Anthropology is invoked to provide a corrective to the findings of the historians mentioned—not to provide a critique of any anthropological theory.

B   Correct. The passage makes the case that the anthropological view may be more useful than the historian's in the study of women in Renaissance Europe.

C   The passage cites no claim by historians that individuality of women in Renaissance Europe was largely suppressed, and the passage presents no argument to critique or refute such a claim.

D   The passage makes no such claim about anthropologists, but does make a similar claim about certain historians.

E   The passage does not state or imply that Strozzi was atypical of women in Renaissance Europe that historians have studied, nor is the anthropological conception of personhood invoked to underpin any such view.

The correct answer is B.

67.   The passage suggests that the historians referred to in line 1 make which of the following assumptions about Renaissance Europe?

(A)   That anthropologists overestimate the importance of the individual in Renaissance European society

(B)   That in Renaissance Europe, women were typically allowed to express their individuality

(C)   That European women of the Renaissance had the possibility of acting independently of the social context in which they lived

(D)   That studying an individual such as Alessandra is the best way to draw general conclusions about the lives of women in Renaissance Europe

(E)   That people in Renaissance Europe had greater personal autonomy than people do currently

Evaluation

The passage suggests that the historians, in their studies of women in Renaissance Europe, held a preconceived notion of personhood—a notion that implied at least the possibility of individual autonomous action unaffected by social context. By implication, the passage ascribes a similar preconception to the historian whose study of Strozzi is discussed.

A   No view concerning anthropologists or their work is attributed, even by implication, to the historians.

B   Even if the historians held a view regarding the scope of what women in Renaissance Europe were typically allowed to do, the passage does not attribute such a view to them.

C   Correct. The passage implies that the historians assumed it was at least sometimes possible for women in Renaissance Europe to act autonomously, unaffected by social context.

D   The passage does not indicate that the historians assumed study of a single individual was the best approach to study of women's lives in Renaissance Europe.

E   The passage neither explicitly nor implicitly claims that the historians assumed women had more personal autonomy in Renaissance Europe than women have currently.

The correct answer is C.

68. It can be inferred that the author of the passage believes which of the following about the study of Alessandra Strozzi done by the historian mentioned in the second paragraph?

(A) Alessandra was atypical of her time and was therefore an inappropriate choice for the subject of the historian's research.

(B) In order to bolster her thesis, the historian adopted the anthropological perspective on personhood.

(C) The historian argues that the boundaries of the conceptual self were not always firm and closed in Renaissance Europe.

(D) In her study, the historian reverts to a traditional approach that is out of step with the work of other historians of Renaissance Europe.

(E) The interpretation of Alessandra's actions that the historian puts forward is not supported by much of the historian's research.

Inference

The passage tells us that the historian who studied Strozzi "attributes individual intention and authorship of actions" to her. But the passage author claims that much of the historian's own research supports the view that, contrary to the historian's interpretation, "Alessandra did not distinguish her personhood from that of her sons"—and therefore that her actions did not primarily express personal autonomy.

A Nothing in the passage implies that this is true or that the passage author believes it was so.

B The passage is in direct contradiction with this claim about the historian, and it strongly suggests that the author of the passage would reject this claim.

C The passage author makes this point concerning "the boundaries of the conceptual self" as part of the critique of the historian's approach.

D The passage author characterizes the historian's approach neither as traditional nor as nontraditional; nor does the passage author contrast the historian's approach with that of any other historian.

E **Correct.** The passage author suggest that much of the historian's research provides support for an interpretation that is incompatible with the historian's own interpretation.

The correct answer is E.

69. The passage suggests that the historian mentioned in the second paragraph would be most likely to agree with which of the following assertions regarding Alessandra Strozzi?

(A) Alessandra was able to act more independently than most women of her time because she was a widow.

(B) Alessandra was aware that her personal motivation was embedded in a social context.

(C) Alessandra had goals and interests similar to those of many other widows in her society.

(D) Alessandra is an example of a Renaissance woman who expressed her individuality through independent action.

(E) Alessandra was exceptional because she was able to effect changes in the social constraints placed upon women in her society.

Application

According to the passage, the historian whose study of Strozzi is discussed "attributes individual intention and authorship of actions" to her. The passage does not discuss whether, or how, the historian may have regarded Strozzi's widowhood as relevant to her exercise of autonomy; nor does the passage discuss the extent to which, if at all, the historian regarded Strozzi's actions, goals, or interests as typical of women in Renaissance Europe.

A The passage provides no evidence as to whether the historian would agree with this.

B The passage does not attribute to the historian, even implicitly, a view that Strozzi's personal motivation was primarily "embedded in a social context"; so the historian would likely believe that Strozzi herself did not see her personal motivation as so embedded.

C   The passage provides no evidence as to whether the historian would regard Strozzi's goals and interests as resembling those of other widows in her society.

D   Correct. The first sentence of the second paragraph indicates that the historian treats Strozzi as an example of a Renaissance woman who expressed her individuality through independent action.

E   The passage provides no evidence that the historian viewed Strozzi as exceptional in effecting any kind of social change.

The correct answer is D.

Questions 70–72 refer to the passage on page 79.

70. According to the passage, which of the following was true of relations between the federal government and Native American tribes?

(A) Some Native American tribes approved of the congressional action of 1871 because it simplified their dealings with the federal government.

(B) Some Native American tribes were more eager to negotiate treaties with the United States after the *Lone Wolf* decision.

(C) Prior to the *Lone Wolf* decision, the Supreme Court was reluctant to hear cases involving agreements negotiated between Congress and Native American tribes.

(D) Prior to 1871, the federal government sometimes negotiated treaties with Native American tribes.

(E) Following 1871, the House exercised more power than did the Senate in the government's dealings with Native American tribes.

Supporting Idea

The question depends on recognizing information implicit in the passage. The passage states that a change occurred when Congress abolished the making of treaties with Native American tribes in 1871. Since that decision represented a change, it would follow that such treaties were negotiated at least sometimes prior to that date.

A   The passage does not suggest that some tribes approved of the decision to abolish making treaties.

B   The passage does not suggest that some tribes were more eager to negotiate treaties after *Lone Wolf,* but it does say such treaties were banned well before then.

C   The passage suggests nothing about the Supreme Court's willingness to hear cases related to Native American tribes before the *Lone Wolf* case.

D   Correct. The passage states that the 1871 federal ban on negotiating treaties with Native American tribes represented a change, which suggests that such treaties had been negotiated, at least sometimes, prior to 1871.

E   The passage states that the House and Senate disputed control over Native American affairs and that this dispute led to the 1871 ban on treaties, but it does not suggest that the House exercised more power than did the Senate after that date.

The correct answer is D.

71. According to the passage, in the case of *Lone Wolf v. Hitchcock,* the Supreme Court decided that

(A) disputes among Native American tribes over the ownership of tribal lands were beyond the jurisdiction of the Court

(B) Congress had the power to allow outsiders to settle on lands occupied by a Native American tribe without obtaining permission from that tribe

(C) Congress had exceeded its authority in attempting to exercise sole power over Native American affairs

(D) the United States was not legally bound by the provisions of treaties previously concluded with Native American tribes

(E) formal agreements between the federal government and Native American tribes should be treated as ordinary legislation rather than as treaties

Supporting Idea

The question requires recognizing specific information presented in the passage. The passage states that in *Lone Wolf,* the Supreme Court rejected an effort by Native American tribes to refuse settlement of their territory by outsiders without their consent. According to the passage, this decision represented an assertion of Congress's power over Native American affairs, in deciding that Congress could allow settlement of Native American lands without the permission of the tribes.

A   The passage does not concern disputes among Native American tribes but rather an effort by those tribes to retain control over their territory and the Supreme Court's rejection of that control.

B   **Correct.** The passage states that the Supreme Court rejected an effort by the tribes to exclude settlers who did not have the tribes' permission and that this represented an assertion of Congress's power over Native American affairs. In other words, the Court decided that Congress could allow such settlement without the tribes' consent.

C   The passage states that the Supreme Court expanded Congress's authority over Native American affairs, not that it decided Congress had exceeded such authority.

D   The passage describes a decision by Congress to abolish making new treaties, but it does not say that the Supreme Court decided that earlier treaties were not binding.

E   According to the passage, *Lone Wolf* concerned questions of tribal sovereignty, not issues of whether agreements between the government and the tribes should be treated as legislation or as treaties.

The correct answer is B.

72. The author of the passage is primarily concerned with

(A)   identifying similarities in two different theories

(B)   evaluating a work of scholarship

(C)   analyzing the significance of a historical event

(D)   debunking a revisionist interpretation

(E)   exploring the relationship between law and social reality

Evaluation

The question requires recognizing the main purpose of the passage. The passage describes a

historical event—the Supreme Court's decision in *Lone Wolf*—and goes on to discuss the ramifications of that decision: ending formal negotiation with Native American tribes and rejecting the need for tribal consent, instead asserting Congress's control over the tribes' affairs.

A   The passage mentions two different views of the relevant history: the contention that the federal government's usurpation of tribal control occurred in 1871 and the author's belief that it occurred in 1903 with *Lone Wolf.* These ideas are presented in opposition, however, and the passage does not point out similarities between them.

B   The passage is mainly concerned with evaluating a historical event, not a work of scholarship.

C   **Correct.** The passage is primarily concerned with analyzing the impact of the *Lone Wolf* decision on the federal government's relationship with Native American tribes.

D   The passage disputes the contention that 1871 marked the end of formal negotiation between Native American tribes and the federal government, but that contention is nowhere characterized as a revisionist interpretation.

E   While the legal decisions discussed in the passage likely affected social reality, those impacts are not explored in the passage.

The correct answer is C.

Questions 73–75 refer to the passage on page 81.

73. According to the passage, which of the following is true of the traditional routes to global expansion?

(A)   They have been supplanted in most service industries by alternative routes.

(B)   They are less attractive to travel agencies since deregulation of the airlines.

(C)   They may represent the most cost-effective means for a travel agency to globalize.

(D)   They may be unsuitable for service agencies that are attempting to globalize.

(E)   They are most likely to succeed in markets that are not actively growing.

Supporting Idea

The question requires recognizing a specific view advanced by the passage. The passage states that service industries face challenges when attempting to globalize that are not addressed by the traditional expansion strategies of acquisition and internal expansion. Also, some service industries perceive a need to rely on local presence and expertise. Therefore, such traditional routes may be unsuitable, and other routes such as partnerships may be preferable.

A   The passage suggests that some service industries are seeking alternative routes, not that traditional routes have been supplanted in most service industries.

B   The passage suggests that the deregulation of airlines had a major impact on the travel industry, not that the deregulation made traditional routes to global expansion less attractive.

C   The passage nowhere suggests that traditional routes are more cost-effective; on the contrary, it notes that high costs are a disadvantage of one traditional route, acquisition.

D   **Correct.** The passage suggests that traditional routes to global expansion may be unsuitable for some service agencies, because providing good service requires local expertise.

E   The passage states that the traditional route of internal expansion may be impossible in markets that are not actively growing, not that traditional routes fare better in markets that are not growing.

The correct answer is D.

74.   The passage suggests that one of the effects of the deregulation of the airlines was

(A)   a decline in the services available to noncommercial travelers

(B)   a decrease in the size of the corporate travel market

(C)   a sharp increase in the number of cooperative alliances among travel agencies

(D)   increased competition in a number of different service industries

(E)   the merging of some companies within the travel industry

Supporting Idea

The item requires recognizing specific information included in the passage. The passage states that the deregulation of airlines in 1978 led to changes including increased corporate demand for travel services and widespread restructuring and *consolidation* in the travel industry. In other words, some companies in the travel industry merged in the aftermath of airline deregulation.

A   The passage makes no mention of any effects on noncommercial travelers.

B   The passage states, on the contrary, that the corporate travel market grew dramatically.

C   The passage states that one result was increased restructuring and consolidation among travel agencies, not that they formed cooperating alliances.

D   The passage does not mention increased competition in a variety of service industries as a result of airline deregulation.

E   **Correct.** The passage states that there was extensive consolidation in the travel industry as a result of the deregulation of airlines; in other words, some travel companies merged.

The correct answer is E.

75.   The author discusses a particular travel agency in the passage most likely in order to

(A)   provide evidence of the pressures on the travel industry to globalize

(B)   demonstrate the limitations of the traditional routes to global expansion

(C)   illustrate an unusual approach to globalizing a service organization

(D)   highlight the difficulties confronting travel agencies that attempt to globalize

(E)   underscore the differences between the service industry and other industries

Evaluation

The item requires assessing the author's purpose in discussing a specific travel agency. The only agency discussed on an individual basis rejected traditional routes to global expansion in favor of forming cooperative partnerships with foreign travel companies. This example illustrates an alternative strategy to global expansion for service companies that find the traditional routes impracticable.

A   The passage discusses pressures on the travel industry to globalize, but it does not mention such pressures in relation to the travel agency discussed as an example.

B   The travel agency used as an example may have adopted their alternative strategy in response to the limitations of traditional routes to globalization, but the agency does not demonstrate such limitations.

C   **Correct.** After a discussion of the drawbacks to traditional globalization strategies for service industries, the author uses the travel agency to illustrate an alternative approach that might be more appropriate.

D   The passage discusses the difficulties facing travel agencies that attempt to globalize, but not in relation to the travel agency brought up as an example.

E   The passage suggests that there are differences between service and other industries, but it does not do so in relation to the travel agency used as an example.

The correct answer is C.

Questions 76–78 refer to the passage on page 82.

76.   The passage suggests that the economists mentioned in line 1 would have expected which of the following to occur during the 1960s in the United States?

(A)   Savings and investment rates to be equal in spite of high real interest rates

(B)   Real interest rates to remain low when the national savings surplus was large

(C)   Investment rates to remain constant while the national savings rate changed

(D)   The national economy to suffer a decline as a result of high national savings rates

(E)   Businesses to be encouraged to save due to high real interest rates

Application

The thinking of many economists about business savings, business investment, and real interest rates is explained in the passage. However, the passage tells us, an event occurred in the 1960s that these economists would have not expected. We are asked what the economists would have expected based on their thinking about interest-rate dynamics.

A   The passage does not explain what the economists would have expected regarding the rates (as opposed to the amounts) of national savings and business investment. The passage does not indicate that if real interest rates were high, the economists' theory would have predicted the rates of national savings and industrial investment to be equal.

B   **Correct.** If total national savings exceeded total business investment, there would be a savings surplus. This occurred during the 1960s. Consistent with their theory, the economists would have expected real interest rates to be low. On the contrary, real interest rates were high.

C   According to the economists' theory as explained in the passage, if total national savings changed while total business investment remained unchanged, real interest rates would have changed. But the passage does not address what the economists would have predicted regarding changes in the rates (as opposed to the totals) of national saving and business investment.

D   The passage provides no information about any implications of the economists' theory regarding the impact on the national economy of high national savings rates.

E   The passage provides no information about what the economists' theory would have predicted regarding the likely response of businesses to high real interest rates.

The correct answer is B.

77. The author of the passage would be most likely to agree with which of the following statements regarding the economists mentioned in line 1?

    (A) Their beliefs are contradicted by certain economic phenomena that occurred in the United States during the 1960s and the 1980s.

    (B) Their theory fails to predict under what circumstances the prices of foreign and domestic goods are likely to increase.

    (C) They incorrectly identify the factors other than savings and investment rates that affect real interest rates.

    (D) Their belief is valid only for the United States economy and not necessarily for other national economies.

    (E) They overestimate the impact of the real interest rate on the national savings and investment rates.

Evaluation

The passage indicates that economic phenomena that occurred in the United States during the 1960s and the 1980s were contrary to the predictions of many economists' theory regarding savings, investment, and real interest rates.

A **Correct.** In the 1960s, real interest rates were higher even with a large national savings surplus; in the period 1980-82, real interest rates went from 2 percent to 7 percent even with national savings and business investment roughly equal. The author of the passage believes that both occurrences were contrary to what the economists' theory predicted.

B Although the passage describes the actual consequences of a drastic rise in real interest rates after 1979, the author also indicates that the economists' theory would have failed to predict correctly how a drastic rise in real interest rates would affect the prices of goods produced in the United States or elsewhere. The passage is silent on whether the economists' theory addressed factors claimed to be predictive of changes in the prices of goods.

C The passage does not indicate that the economists identified any factors other than savings and investment rates that would affect real interest rates. Therefore, it does not indicate that they misidentified any such factors.

D The passage indicates no such restriction on the scope of application of the economists' theory, which is represented in the passage as highly general.

E The author states that *real interest rates may themselves influence swings in the savings and investment rates*. The context of the statement suggests that the author believes that economists may have underestimated how real interest rates impact savings and investment.

The correct answer is A.

78. The passage is primarily concerned with

    (A) contrasting trends in two historical periods

    (B) presenting evidence that calls into question certain beliefs

    (C) explaining the reasons for a common phenomenon

    (D) criticizing evidence offered in support of a well-respected belief

    (E) comparing conflicting interpretations of a theory

Main Idea

The passage discusses a theory held by *many economists* regarding the relationships among business investment, national savings, and real interest rates. The passage presents evidence from economic events in the United States to show that the theory is flawed.

A The passage does not contrast trends in two historical periods. It discusses two historical periods, though not with the goal of contrasting them.

B **Correct.** The passage presents evidence from economic events in the 1960s and the 1980s and concludes that this evidence indicates that *real interest rates respond to influences other than the savings/investment nexus*. The evidence of these events is contrary to predictions of the economists' theory. The main conclusion of the argumentation in the passage is that the theory is flawed.

C The passage cites economic events in the 1960s and 1980s that were not characterized as "common phenomena," and the passage does not explore specific factors that contributed to these phenomena.

D The passage is not primarily focused on debunking the evidence that the economists based their theory on—a theory which may have been "well-respected" at some time but is not characterized as such in the passage.

E The passage does not compare any conflicting interpretations of a theory.

The correct answer is B.

Questions 79–81 refer to the passage on page 83.

79. The primary purpose of the passage is to

(A) offer sociohistorical explanations for the cultural differences between men and women in the United States

(B) examine how the economic roles of women in the United States changed during the nineteenth century

(C) consider differing views held by social scientists concerning women's class status in the United States

(D) propose a feminist interpretation of class structure in the United States

(E) outline specific distinctions between working-class women and women of the upper and middle classes

Main Idea

Various social science models of class in the United States, based on economic status, gender, or occupation, are presented in the passage as differing in their implications regarding women's class status. We are asked what the primary purpose of the passage is.

A The passage is not focused on cultural differences between women and men.

B The passage cites a view that *the gap between women of different economic classes widened in the late nineteenth century*. However, the passage does not primarily address changes in women's economic roles during the nineteenth century.

C **Correct.** The passage surveys a variety of social science analyses of women's class status in the United States.

D Although the passage examines accounts from *some feminist social scientists* concerning women's class status, the primary purpose of the passage is not to propose a feminist interpretation of United States class structure.

E The passage examines views of various feminist analysts regarding class distinctions among women. However, this is not the main purpose of the passage.

The correct answer is C.

80. It can be inferred from the passage that the most recent feminist social science research on women and class seeks to do which of the following?

(A) Introduce a divergent new theory about the relationship between legal status and gender

(B) Illustrate an implicit middle-class bias in earlier feminist models of class and gender

(C) Provide evidence for the position that gender matters more than wealth in determining class status

(D) Remedy perceived inadequacies of both traditional social science models and earlier feminist analyses of class and gender

(E) Challenge the economic definitions of class used by traditional social scientists

Inference

What does the passage imply about the primary goal of most recent feminist social research on women and class? One would expect such more recent research to seek to adjust earlier accounts, both in traditional social science models and feminist models.

A   Historian Mary Ryan points out that identical legal status of working-class and middle-class free married women outweighed any other distinctions. But the passage does not present this as the primary theme of the most recent feminist social science research.

B   The passage does not attribute to the most recent feminist social research, explicitly or by implication, any attempt to illustrate a middle-class bias in earlier feminist models.

C   The passage cites a recent feminist analyst as noting that *the gap between women of different economic classes widened in the late nineteenth century*. This goes against the notion that recent feminist analysts sought to argue that gender outweighed economic position in determining women's class status.

D   Correct. The passage represents the most recent feminist social science analysts as seeking to amend the views of traditional social science models and earlier feminist models regarding women's class status. We read: *Recently, though, other feminist analysts have questioned this model*—namely, the feminist model that regarded women's class as predominantly determined by gender alone. Ann Oakley contests this, arguing that, in the late nineteenth century, differences of economic standing among women contributed to determining women's relative class statuses.

E   This does not reflect what the passage implies about the primary goal of recent feminist social science analysts. One of the most recent feminist analysts, Ann Oakley, suggests that from the late nineteenth century, distinct economic statuses were reflected in distinct social class statuses for women.

The correct answer is D.

81. Which of the following statements best characterizes the relationship between traditional social science models of class and Ryan's model, as described in the passage?

(A)   Ryan's model differs from the traditional model by making gender, rather than economic status, the determinant of women's class status.

(B)   The traditional social science model of class differs from Ryan's in its assumption that women are financially dependent on men.

(C)   Ryan's model of class and the traditional social science model both assume that women work, either within the home or for pay.

(D)   The traditional social science model of class differs from Ryan's in that each model focuses on a different period of American history.

(E)   Both Ryan's model of class and the traditional model consider multiple factors, including wealth, marital status, and enfranchisement, in determining women's status.

Application

How does Ryan's model differ from the traditional social science models? According to the passage, the traditional models were based on women's economic status as derived from their association with men. Ryan advocated a model that regarded women's class as based on gender alone.

A   **Correct.** The passage indicates that Ryan's model involved cleaving women's class status from their association with men and regarding women as one distinct class.

B   The passage does not describe Ryan's model as assuming that women are never "financially dependent on men." According to the passage, Ryan's view is that women's class status is determined by gender and not based on financial dependence on men.

C   The passage does not ascribe to the traditional social science models of class the assumption that all women work either in the home or outside of it for pay. For example, the model as described in the passage would have been consistent with some women who were not themselves employed having all the work in their home done by other people.

D   The passage does not support this view. Ryan's opinions in the passage are represented as applying to the early nineteenth century and later, whereas the *traditional social science model of class* is not clearly located in time.

E   The passage indicates that neither the traditional model nor Ryan's model consider multiple factors in determining women's class status. Ryan is cited as illustrating the view that gender, not economic standing, was the crucial determinant of women's class status in American society. According to the passage, the traditional social science models held that the class status of women was derived exclusively from their economic situation, which was determined, in turn, by their association with men (fathers or husbands).

The correct answer is A.

Questions 82 to 110 — Difficulty: **Hard**

Questions 82–88 refer to the passage on page 85.

82.   According to the passage, conventional spiral galaxies differ from low-surface-brightness galaxies in which of the following ways?

    (A)   They have fewer stars than do low-surface-brightness galaxies.

    (B)   They evolve more quickly than low-surface-brightness galaxies.

    (C)   They are more diffuse than low-surface-brightness galaxies.

    (D)   They contain less helium than do low-surface-brightness galaxies.

    (E)   They are larger than low-surface-brightness galaxies.

Supporting Idea

This question requires recognizing information that is provided in the passage. The first paragraph describes and compares two types of galaxies: conventional galaxies and dim, or low- surface-brightness, galaxies. It states that dim galaxies have the same approximate number of stars as a common type of conventional galaxy but tend to be larger and more diffuse because their mass is spread over wider areas (lines 4-10). The passage also indicates that dim galaxies take longer than conventional galaxies to convert their primordial gases into stars, meaning that dim galaxies evolve much more slowly than conventional galaxies (lines 10-14), which entails

that conventional galaxies evolve more quickly than dim galaxies.

A   The passage states that dim galaxies have approximately the same numbers of stars as a common type of conventional galaxy.

B   **Correct.** The passage indicates that dim galaxies evolve much more slowly than conventional galaxies, which entails that conventional galaxies evolve more quickly.

C   The passage states that dim galaxies are more spread out, and therefore more diffuse, than conventional galaxies.

D   The passage does not mention the relative amounts of helium in the two types of galaxies under discussion.

E   The passage states that dim galaxies tend to be much larger than conventional galaxies.

The correct answer is B.

83.   It can be inferred from the passage that which of the following is an accurate physical description of typical low-surface-brightness galaxies?

    (A)   They are large spiral galaxies containing fewer stars than conventional galaxies.

    (B)   They are compact but very dim spiral galaxies.

    (C)   They are diffuse spiral galaxies that occupy a large volume of space.

    (D)   They are small, young spiral galaxies that contain a high proportion of primordial gas.

    (E)   They are large, dense spirals with low luminosity.

Inference

This question requires drawing an inference from information given in the passage. The first paragraph compares dim galaxies and conventional galaxies. Dim galaxies are described as having the same general shape (lines 4–5) as a common type of conventional galaxy, the spiral galaxy, suggesting that dim galaxies are, themselves, spiral shaped. The passage also indicates that, although both types of galaxies tend to have approximately the same number of stars, dim galaxies tend to be much larger and spread out over larger areas of space (lines 4–10) than conventional galaxies.

A   The passage states that the two types of galaxies have approximately the same number of stars.

B   The passage indicates that dim galaxies are relatively large and spread out.

C   **Correct.** The passage indicates that dim galaxies have the same general shape as spiral galaxies and that their mass is spread out over large areas of space.

D   The passage indicates that dim galaxies are relatively large and spread out.

E   The passage states that dim galaxies have few stars per unit of volume, suggesting that they are not dense but diffuse.

The correct answer is C.

84. It can be inferred from the passage that the "longstanding puzzle" refers to which of the following?

(A) The difference between the rate at which conventional galaxies evolve and the rate at which low-surface-brightness galaxies evolve

(B) The discrepancy between estimates of total baryonic mass derived from measuring helium and estimates based on measuring galactic luminosity

(C) The inconsistency between the observed amount of helium in the universe and the number of stars in typical low-surface-brightness galaxies

(D) Uncertainties regarding what proportion of baryonic mass is contained in intergalactic space and what proportion in conventional galaxies

(E) Difficulties involved in detecting very distant galaxies and in investigating their luminosity

Inference

This question requires drawing an inference from information given in the passage. The second paragraph describes *the long-standing puzzle of the missing baryonic mass in the universe*. The passage states that baryons are the source of galactic luminosity, and so scientists can estimate the amount of baryonic mass in the universe by measuring the luminosity of galaxies (lines 17–21). The puzzle is that spectroscopic measures of helium in the universe suggest that the baryonic mass in the universe is much higher than measures of luminosity would indicate (21–25).

A   The differences between the rates of evolution of the two types of galaxies is not treated as being controversial in the passage.

B   **Correct.** The passage indicates that measurements using spectroscopy and measurements using luminosity result in puzzling differences in estimates of the universe's baryonic mass.

C   The passage does not suggest how helium might relate to the numbers of stars in dim galaxies.

D   The passage indicates that astronomers have speculated that the missing baryonic mass might be discovered in intergalactic space or hard-to-detect galaxies but does not suggest that these speculations are constituents of the long-standing puzzle.

E   The passage does not mention how the distance to galaxies affects scientists' ability to detect these galaxies.

The correct answer is B.

85. The author implies that low-surface-brightness galaxies could constitute an answer to the puzzle discussed in the second paragraph primarily because

(A) they contain baryonic mass that was not taken into account by researchers using galactic luminosity to estimate the number of baryons in the universe

(B) they, like conventional galaxies that contain many baryons, have evolved from massive, primordial gas clouds

(C) they may contain relatively more helium, and hence more baryons, than do galaxies whose helium content has been studied using spectroscopy

(D) they have recently been discovered to contain more baryonic mass than scientists had thought when low-surface-brightness galaxies were first observed

(E) They contain stars that are significantly more luminous than would have been predicted on the basis of initial studies of luminosity in low-surface-brightness galaxies

Inference

This question requires drawing an inference from information given in the passage. The puzzle is that estimates of the baryonic mass of the universe based on luminosity are lower than those based on spectroscopy (lines 21–25). The passage states that astronomers did not notice dim galaxies until recently (lines 2–3) and that these galaxies may help account for the missing baryonic mass in the universe (lines 15–17). The passage also suggests that astronomers measure the luminosity of specific galaxies (lines 19–21). Thus it can be inferred that, prior to their being noticed by astronomers, the luminosity of these dim galaxies was not measured, and their baryonic mass was not taken into account in the estimates of luminosity that led to the long-standing puzzle.

A **Correct.** The passage states that the missing baryonic mass in the universe may be discovered in the dim galaxies that have only recently been noticed by astronomers.

B The passage does not suggest that dim and conventional galaxies both originating from primordial gas clouds help solve the longstanding puzzle of the missing baryonic mass in the universe.

C The passage does not suggest that dim galaxies might contain more helium than do conventional galaxies or that measures of baryonic mass using spectroscopy do not take some dim galaxies into account.

D The passage does not suggest that dim galaxies contain more baryonic mass than scientists originally believed upon discovering these galaxies.

E The passage suggests that scientists measured the luminosity of galaxies, not of individual stars.

The correct answer is A.

86. The author mentions the fact that baryons are the source of stars' luminosity primarily in order to explain

(A) how astronomers determine that some galaxies contain fewer stars per unit volume than do others

(B) how astronomers are able to calculate the total luminosity of a galaxy

(C) why astronomers can use galactic luminosity to estimate baryonic mass

(D) why astronomers' estimates of baryonic mass based on galactic luminosity are more reliable than those based on spectroscopic studies of helium

(E) how astronomers know bright galaxies contain more baryons than do dim galaxies

Evaluation

This question requires understanding how one aspect of the passage relates to the reasoning in a larger portion of the passage. The second paragraph explains that scientists have been puzzled over missing baryonic mass in the universe as measured by luminosity (lines 21–25). Given that baryons are the source of luminosity in the galaxy (lines 17–19), astronomers can estimate the baryonic mass of a galaxy by measuring its luminosity.

A The passage discussion of baryons does not address the number of stars in individual galaxies.

B The passage discusses how the luminosity of galaxies can be used to estimate baryonic mass but does not address how total luminosity is measured.

C **Correct.** The passage indicates that because baryons are the source of galactic luminosity, measuring luminosity can be used to estimate baryonic mass of galaxies.

D The passage suggests that estimates based on luminosity may have been less accurate, not more accurate, than those based on spectroscopy.

E The passage does not indicate that bright galaxies contain more baryons than do dim galaxies.

The correct answer is C.

87. The author of the passage would be most likely to disagree with which of the following statements?

    (A) Low-surface-brightness galaxies are more difficult to detect than are conventional galaxies.

    (B) Low-surface-brightness galaxies are often spiral in shape.

    (C) Astronomers have advanced plausible ideas about where missing baryonic mass might be found.

    (D) Astronomers have devised a useful way of estimating the total baryonic mass in the universe.

    (E) Astronomers have discovered a substantial amount of baryonic mass in intergalactic space.

Inference

This question involves identifying which answer choice potentially conflicts with the information the author has provided in the passage. The second paragraph indicates that astronomers' estimates of the baryonic mass of the universe is lower when measured using luminosity than it is when measured using spectroscopy (lines 21–25). The final sentence states that astronomers have speculated that the missing baryonic mass might be discovered in intergalactic space or in hard-to-detect galaxies (lines 25–29). Although the passage does indicate that the discovery of dim, low-surface-brightness galaxies might help account for the missing baryonic mass (lines 15–17), the passage provides no support for the possibility that baryonic mass has been discovered in intergalactic space.

A   The passage indicates that low-surface-brightness galaxies went unnoticed until recently, unlike conventional galaxies.

B   The passage indicates that low-surface-brightness galaxies have the same general shape as spiral galaxies.

C   The passage describes two possible explanations astronomers have given for the missing baryonic mass, one of which was made more plausible by the discovery of low-surface-brightness galaxies.

D   The passage indicates that astronomers have used spectroscopy to estimate baryonic mass and gives no reason to suspect that this method is not useful.

E   **Correct.** The passage does not indicate that astronomers have found any baryonic mass in intergalactic space.

The correct answer is E.

88. The primary purpose of the passage is to

    (A) describe a phenomenon and consider its scientific significance

    (B) contrast two phenomena and discuss a puzzling difference between them

    (C) identify a newly discovered phenomenon and explain its origins

    (D) compare two classes of objects and discuss the physical properties of each

    (E) discuss a discovery and point out its inconsistency with existing theory

Main Idea

This question requires understanding, in broad terms, the purpose of the passage as a whole. The first paragraph describes a phenomenon: the discovery of dim galaxies and some of their general attributes. The second paragraph describes how this discovery may help astronomers to solve a long-standing puzzle about the baryonic mass of the universe.

A   **Correct.** The passage describes the phenomenon of dim galaxies and describes their significance in solving the longstanding puzzle of the missing baryonic mass in the universe.

B   Although the passage discusses the puzzling difference between the two estimates of baryonic mass, this answer choice does not account for the broader topic of dim galaxies.

C   While the passage identifies the newly discovered phenomenon of dim galaxies, it does not offer a significant explanation for these galaxies' origins.

D   Although the passage compares dim and conventional galaxies in the first paragraph, this answer choice does not account for the important detail that dim galaxies may help solve a long-standing puzzle.

E   The discovery of dim galaxies discussed in the passage is not said to be inconsistent with any existing scientific theory.

The correct answer is A.

Questions 89–91 refer to the passage on page 87.

89.   The passage suggests that, in the early 1990s, Michaels would have been most likely to agree with which of the following statements about the disparity mentioned in lines 3–4?

(A)   This disparity is relatively less extreme in the Northern Hemisphere because of sulfate cooling.

(B)   This disparity is only a short-term phenomenon brought about by sulfate cooling.

(C)   This disparity is most significant in those parts of the world dominated by oceans.

(D)   The extent of this disparity is being masked by the temporary effect of sulfate cooling.

(E)   The disparity confirms that current models of global warming are correct.

Inference

The disparity highlighted in this question is between global warming models and actual climate data—that is, that the models predicted warming that has not occurred. In the early 1990s, according to the passage, Michaels tried to explain this disparity by saying that industrial sulfate emissions had a cooling effect that slowed global warming briefly.

A   The passage does not indicate that Michaels came to distinguish between the Northern and Southern Hemispheres until he began to doubt his early 1990s explanation for the mentioned disparity.

B   **Correct.** Michaels claimed in the early 1990s that the disparity was temporary, and that it occurred due to the cooling effect of sulfate emissions.

C   Santer's contention, not Michaels's, is based on the effect of oceans on global warming.

D   In the early 1990s, Michaels used the idea of sulfate cooling to explain the observed disparity, not to suggest that the disparity itself was larger than observed.

E   In seeking to explain the disparity, Michaels seems to have assumed, in the early 1990s at least, that the models of global warming were correct. But he did not take the disparity as evidence of their correctness.

The correct answer is B.

90.   According to the passage, Santer asserts which of the following about global warming?

(A)   It will become a more serious problem in the Southern Hemisphere than in the Northern Hemisphere in spite of the cooling influence of oceans in the south.

(B)   It is unlikely to be a serious problem in the future because of the pervasive effect of sulfate cooling.

(C)   It will proceed at the same general rate in the Northern and Southern Hemispheres once the temporary influence of sulfate cooling comes to an end.

(D)   Until the late 1980s, it was moderated in the Northern Hemisphere by the effect of sulfate cooling.

(E)   Largely because of the cooling influence of oceans, it has had no discernible impact on the Southern Hemisphere.

Supporting Idea

The second paragraph of the passage discusses Santer's take on global warming. He is concerned with the effect of oceans and of sulfate cooling on this process, and he argues that the rate of warming in the Southern and Northern Hemispheres has been differently affected by each of these. In general, oceans slow warming in the south, while sulfate cooling temporarily slowed warming in the north until the late 1980s.

A   According to the passage, Santer has argued that since 1987 the Northern Hemisphere has warmed more significantly than the Southern Hemisphere.

B   Santer maintains that sulfate cooling complicates our attempts to understand global warming. He notes, however, that sulfate cooling peaked in the Northern Hemisphere in the mid-1900s, and that that hemisphere's warming has increased considerably. So sulfate cooling's effect is not pervasive and has not mitigated the medium- and long-term problem of global warming.

C   Santer argues that, in the absence of sulfate cooling, global warming would occur more slowly in the Southern Hemisphere due to the greater ocean coverage there.

D   Correct. Santer says that sulfate cooling slowed warming in the Northern Hemisphere, but that in 1987, the influence of sulfate cooling was no longer significant.

E   Santer maintains that global warming happens more slowly in the Southern Hemisphere due to the greater ocean coverage there, not that it has no discernible impact there.

The correct answer is D.

91. The passage suggests that Santer and Michaels would be most likely to DISAGREE over which of the following issues?

(A)   Whether climatological data invalidates global warming models

(B)   Whether warming in the Northern Hemisphere has intensified since 1987

(C)   Whether disparities between global warming models and climatological data can be detected

(D)   Whether landmasses warm more rapidly than oceans

(E)   Whether oceans have a significant effect on global climate patterns

Inference

According to the end of the first paragraph, Michaels began to doubt that sulfate cooling had an effect on global warming, and, further, based on the fact that he could not find an answer for why climatological data did not line up with global warming models, he questioned the accuracy of those models. The second paragraph explains that Santer, in contrast, offered a more nuanced explanation for the effect of sulfate cooling, and that based on this explanation, he disputed the claim that climatological data were inconsistent with the models' predictions.

A   Correct. Based on the passage, Santer and Michaels would clearly disagree about whether climatological data invalidate global warming models: Michaels came to question the models on the basis of those data, while Santer found the model predictions were in fact ultimately consistent with the observed data.

B   Both Santer and Michaels accept the idea that warming in the north has accelerated since 1987.

C   Santer and Michaels both offered reasons for why the seeming disparity between models and data occurred—thus they agreed that such disparities were in fact detected.

D   According to the second paragraph, Santer holds that landmasses warm more rapidly than oceans. But the passage offers no indication that Michaels disagrees with this.

E   Santer's argument is based in large part on the effect of oceans on global climate patterns, but nothing in the passage's discussion of Michaels's work indicates that Michaels would disagree that oceans have such an effect.

The correct answer is A.

Questions 92–99 refer to the passage on page 89.

92. According to the passage, Walker and Szalay disagree on which of the following points?

(A) The structure and composition of australopithecine teeth

(B) The kinds of conclusions that can be drawn from the micro-wear patterns on australopithecine teeth

(C) The idea that fruit was a part of the australopithecine diet

(D) The extent to which seed cracking and bone crunching produce similar micro-wear patterns on teeth

(E) The function of the heavy enamel on australopithecine teeth

Supporting Idea

This question refers to the first paragraph, which states that Walker does not agree with Szalay's idea that *the heavy enamel of australopithecine teeth is an adaptation to bone crunching*.

A   According to the passage, Walker and Szalay disagree about the function of heavy enamel on the teeth, not the structure and composition of the teeth.

B   The passage does not indicate that Szalay has anything to say about the micro-wear patterns on the teeth.

C   Walker does, according to the passage, believe that australopithecines ate fruit, but it gives no evidence about whether Szalay believes that they ate at least some fruit.

D   According to the passage, Walker believes that seed cracking and bone crunching produce distinctive micro-wear patterns on teeth, but he does not necessarily believe that they are similar. The passage does not indicate Szalay's position on the difference between micro-wear patterns.

E   **Correct.** The function of the heavy enamel on the teeth is the only idea about which the passage clearly indicates that Walker and Szalay disagree.

The correct answer is E.

93. The passage suggests that Walker's research indicated which of the following about australopithecine teeth?

(A) They had micro-wear characteristics indicating that fruit constituted only a small part of their diet.

(B) They lacked micro-wear characteristics associated with seed eating and bone crunching.

(C) They had micro-wear characteristics that differed in certain ways from the micro-wear patterns of chimpanzees and orangutans.

(D) They had micro-wear characteristics suggesting that the diet of australopithecines varied from one region to another.

(E) They lacked the micro-wear characteristics distinctive of modern frugivores.

Inference

According to the passage, Walker's research focuses on micro-wear patterns on the teeth of australopithecines. He draws several conclusions on the basis of these patterns: first, that australopithecines did not eat hard seeds; next, that they did not crunch bones; and finally, that they ate fruit.

A   The passage indicates that Walker's observation of micro-wear patterns led him to conclude that australopithecines ate mostly fruit, not that *fruit constituted only a small part of their diet*.

B   **Correct.** The first paragraph explains that Walker concluded from micro-wear patterns that australopithecines did not eat hard seeds and did not crunch bones; thus, his research must have indicated that they lacked micro-wear characteristics associated with such activities.

C   According to the passage, the opposite is true: based on the observation that their micro-wear patterns were indistinguishable from those of chimpanzees and orangutans, Walker concluded that australopithecines ate fruit.

D   The second paragraph of the passage complicates Walker's view by suggesting that australopithecines' diet might have varied from one region to another, but the passage says nothing about Walker's research from which to infer that it indicated such variation.

E   Chimpanzees and orangutans are assumed to be frugivores, according to the passage, and Walker's research indicated that australopithecine teeth had micro-wear characteristics identical to theirs.

The correct answer is B.

94.   The passage suggests that which of the following would be true of studies of tooth micro-wear patterns conducted on modern baboons?

(A)   They would inaccurately suggest that some baboons eat more soft-bodied than hard-bodied insects.

(B)   They would suggest that insects constitute the largest part of some baboons' diets.

(C)   They would reveal that there are no significant differences in tooth micro-wear patterns among baboon populations.

(D)   They would inadequately reflect the extent to which some baboons consume certain types of insects.

(E)   They would indicate that baboons in certain regions eat only soft-bodied insects, whereas baboons in other regions eat hard-bodied insects.

Inference

The second paragraph states that modern baboons eat *only soft-bodied insects* and so would not exhibit tooth abrasion to indicate that they were insectivores. Thus, it would be difficult to determine exactly which soft-bodied insects they ate.

A   The passage states that baboons eat only soft-bodied insects—so it is in fact accurate to suggest that all baboons eat more soft-bodied than hard-bodied insects.

B   The passage says that baboons eat only soft-bodied insects. It also suggests that soft-bodied insects do not leave significant enough abrasions on baboons' teeth to provide evidence of this aspect of their diet. Therefore, the tooth-wear patterns would give little or no information regarding what proportion of the baboons' overall diet consists of insects.

C   The passage does not provide grounds for inferring anything about the differences, or lack thereof, among baboon populations in terms of tooth micro-wear patterns.

D   **Correct.** Because soft-bodied insects cause little tooth abrasion, micro-wear patterns would most likely not reflect the extent to which baboons consume soft-bodied insects.

E   The passage states that baboons eat *only soft-bodied insects*. Nothing in the passage suggests that baboons in certain regions eat hard-bodied insects.

The correct answer is D.

95.   The passage suggests which of the following about the micro-wear patterns found on the teeth of omnivorous primates?

(A)   The patterns provide information about what kinds of foods are not eaten by the particular species of primate, but not about the foods actually eaten.

(B)   The patterns of various primate species living in the same environment resemble one another.

(C)   The patterns may not provide information about the extent to which a particular species' diet includes seeds.

(D)   The patterns provide more information about these primates' diet than do the tooth micro-wear patterns of primates who are frugivores.

(E)   The patterns may differ among groups within a species depending on the environment within which a particular group lives.

Inference

This question focuses mainly on the end of the second paragraph, which states that *the diets of current omnivorous primates vary considerably depending on the environments* in which they live. It goes on to conclude that australopithecines, if they were omnivores, would similarly consume varied diets, depending on environment, and exhibit varied tooth micro-wear patterns as well. Thus, it is reasonable to conclude that any omnivorous primates living in different environments and consuming different diets would exhibit varied micro-wear patterns.

A   The passage indicates that the absence of certain types of micro-wear patterns can provide evidence about what foods a species does not eat. It also says that among omnivorous primates, one might expect to find considerable population variation in their tooth micro-wear patterns. Wherever micro-wear patterns are present, they provide evidence about what kinds of foods are eaten.

B   The passage suggests that various primate species living in the same environment might consume a variety of different diets, so there is no reason to conclude that their micro-wear patterns would resemble one another.

C   The passage indicates that seed-eating produces distinctive micro-wear patterns, so the patterns, or lack thereof, on the teeth of any species would most likely provide information about the extent to which the species' diet includes seeds.

D   The end of the first paragraph suggests that frugivores' micro-wear patterns are distinctive; the passage provides no reason to believe that omnivores' diets provide more information.

E   **Correct.** According to the passage, omnivorous primates of a particular species may consume different diets depending on where they live. Thus, their micro-wear patterns may differ on this basis.

The correct answer is E.

96.   It can be inferred from the passage that if studies of tooth micro-wear patterns were conducted on modern baboons, which of the following would most likely be true of the results obtained?

(A)   There would be enough abrasion to allow a determination of whether baboons are frugivorous or insectivorous.

(B)   The results would suggest that insects constitute the largest part of the baboons' diet.

(C)   The results would reveal that there are no significant differences in tooth micro-wear patterns from one regional baboon population to another.

(D)   The results would provide an accurate indication of the absence of some kinds of insects from the baboons' diet.

(E)   The results would be unlikely to provide any indication of what inferences about the australopithecine diet can or cannot be drawn from micro-wear studies.

Inference

The second paragraph states that modern baboons eat soft-bodied insects but not hard-bodied ones—and it is hard-bodied insects, the passage suggests, that would cause particular micro-wear patterns on teeth. So the patterns on modern baboons' teeth most likely do not exhibit the patterns indicating hard-bodied insect consumption.

A   The passage states that baboons' consumption of soft-bodied insects would not show up in the patterns on their teeth—so the abrasion would most likely not provide enough information for a determination of whether baboons are frugivorous or insectivorous.

B   Since soft-bodied insects do not abrade the teeth significantly, it would be difficult to determine, based on micro-wear patterns, the part such insects play in the baboons' diet. Furthermore, the passage does not suggest that micro-wear patterns can indicate the quantity of food an animal might have eaten.

C   There could be differences in tooth micro-wear patterns from one regional baboon population to another if they consumed anything in addition to soft-bodied insects.

D   Correct. Studying tooth micro-wear patterns on baboons' teeth would most likely show that their teeth do not exhibit patterns typical of creatures that consume hard-bodied insects.

E   The passage suggests that based on results from micro-wear patterns on modern baboons' teeth, one cannot infer from micro-wear studies whether australopithecines ate soft-bodied insects.

The correct answer is D.

97.   It can be inferred from the passage that Walker's conclusion about the australopithecine diet would be called into question under which of the following circumstances?

(A)   The tooth enamel of australopithecines is found to be much heavier than that of modern frugivorous primates.

(B)   The micro-wear patterns of australopithecine teeth from regions other than east Africa are analyzed.

(C)   Orangutans are found to have a much broader diet than is currently recognized.

(D)   The environment of east Africa at the time australopithecines lived there is found to have been far more varied than is currently thought.

(E)   The area in which the australopithecine specimens were found is discovered to have been very rich in soft-bodied insects during the period when australopithecines lived there.

Inference

The passage explains that Walker bases his conclusion about the frugivorous nature of the australopithecine diet on the fact that the micro-wear patterns on australopithecine teeth are indistinguishable from those of chimpanzees and orangutans, both of which are presumed to have frugivorous diets.

A   The passage indicates that Walker took into account the fact that australopithecines had relatively heavy tooth enamel and that

he rejected the view that this heaviness was evidence against the hypothesis that they were frugivorous. For all we can tell from the information in the passage, the australopithecines' tooth enamel was already known to be much heavier than that of modern frugivorous primates.

B   It could be the case that analyzing the micro-wear patterns of australopithecine teeth from other regions would yield the same data as those from east Africa.

C   Correct. According to the passage, Walker bases the conclusion that australopithecines were frugivorous on the similarity between their micro-wear patterns and those of modern chimpanzees and orangutans. If orangutans were found to have a diet that included a greater range of non-fruit foods than is currently recognized, then the correspondence between their micro-wear patterns and australopithecines' micro-wear patterns would be consistent with the hypothesis that australopithecines' diet was broader as well.

D   Even if the environment of east Africa were more varied, that would not mean the australopithecines necessarily ate a more varied diet. Many species that live in very varied environments specialize narrowly on particular foods in those environments.

E   Just because many soft-bodied insects might have been available to australopithecines does not mean that australopithecines ate them.

The correct answer is C.

98.   The passage is primarily concerned with

(A)   comparing two research methods for determining a species' dietary habits

(B)   describing and evaluating conjectures about a species' diet

(C)   contrasting several explanations for a species' dietary habits

(D)   discussing a new approach and advocating its use in particular situations

(E)   arguing that a particular research methodology does not contribute useful data

Main Idea

Answering this question depends on identifying the main point of the passage and requires an understanding of the passage as a whole. The passage discusses Walker's dismissal of certain other researchers' hypotheses regarding the diet of the primate species australopithecine. Walker does so on the basis of tooth micro-wear patterns, which lead him to the hypothesis that australopithecines were fruit eaters. However, the passage goes on to point out limitations of the utility of micro-wear studies, and discusses certain considerations which suggest that the australopithecines may have had a more diverse diet.

A The passage primarily focuses on using an analysis of micro-wear patterns to determine australopithecines' dietary habits, so it is not the case that the passage is primarily concerned with comparing two research methods.

B **Correct.** The passage considers Walker's evidence against certain hypotheses regarding the australopithecine diet, as well as his evidence for his own hypothesis, and presents considerations that suggest an alternative hypothesis. Thus, the passage is primarily concerned with describing and evaluating conjectures about the diet of a species—the australopithecines.

C The passage is not so much concerned with contrasting explanations for a species' dietary habits as with describing and evaluating evidence for such explanations.

D The passage gives no indication that the analysis of micro-wear patterns is a new approach.

E The passage does not argue that micro-wear analysis fails to contribute useful data. It merely points out that such analysis has certain limitations.

The correct answer is B.

99. The author of the passage mentions the diets of baboons and other living primates most likely in order to

(A) provide evidence that refutes Walker's conclusions about the foods making up the diets of australopithecines

(B) suggest that studies of tooth micro-wear patterns are primarily useful for determining the diets of living primates

(C) suggest that australopithecines were probably omnivores rather than frugivores

(D) illustrate some of the limitations of using tooth micro-wear patterns to draw definitive conclusions about a group's diet

(E) suggest that tooth micro-wear patterns are caused by persistent, as opposed to occasional, consumption of particular foods

Evaluation

The passage discusses the diets of baboons and other living primates mainly in the second paragraph, which is concerned with explaining the limited utility of micro-wear studies.

A The author raises some doubts about Walker's conclusions but does not go as far as to try to refute them outright. The author argues only that, as the final sentence of the passage states, they may need to be expanded.

B The author discusses the diets of baboons and other living primates in relation to micro-wear research on extinct primates. Nothing in the discussion suggests that micro-wear studies would be more useful for determining the diets of living primates than for providing evidence regarding the diets of earlier primates or of other types of animals. Furthermore, the mention of baboon diets suggests that micro-wear studies may not be very useful for determining the diets of some living primates.

C   The author leaves open the question of whether australopithecines were omnivores or frugivores. The passage suggests that some australopithecines might have been omnivores, if australopithecines' diets varied according to the environments they inhabited. Walker's conclusion regarding east African australopithecines' being frugivores might still hold, however.

D   Correct. The author refers to baboons' diets and those of current omnivorous primates in order to suggest that there might be limitations to Walker's use of tooth micro-wear patterns to determine australopithecines' diet.

E   The passage does not make a distinction between persistent and occasional consumption of particular foods.

The correct answer is D.

Questions 100–103 refer to the passage on page 92.

100. According to the passage, the use of Shortt clocks led to the discovery that

(A)   optical sensing equipment can be used effectively in timekeeping systems

(B)   atomic clocks can be used in place of pendulum clocks in observatories

(C)   tides occur in solid ground as well as in oceans

(D)   the earth's rotation varies from one time of year to another

(E)   pendulums can be synchronized with one another electronically

Supporting Idea

The item requires recognizing information stated in the passage. The second paragraph describes the use of Shortt clocks in astronomical observatories and attributes one discovery to the use of Shortt clocks: "the first indications of seasonal variations in the Earth's rotation." In other words, Shortt clocks enabled the discovery that the Earth's rotation varies at different times of year.

A   The passage mentions the use of optical sensing equipment in a Shortt clock, but it does not characterize the effectiveness of that use as a discovery.

B   The passage refers to the use of atomic clocks in observatories, but it does not suggest that Shortt clocks led to the discovery that atomic clocks could be used instead of pendulum clocks.

C   The passage discusses the fact that tides occur in solid ground, but it does not suggest that the discovery of this phenomenon was enabled by Shortt clocks.

D   Correct. The passage states that the use of Shortt clocks revealed the first evidence of seasonal variations in the rotation of the Earth; in other words, Shortt clocks led to the discovery that the Earth's rotation varies at different times of year.

E   The passage mentions the pendulums in a Shortt clock synchronizing by means of an electrical signal, but it does not suggest that Shortt clocks led to the discovery of such synchronization.

The correct answer is D.

101. The passage most strongly suggests that which of the following is true of the chamber in which a Shortt clock's primary pendulum was housed?

(A)   It contained elaborate mechanisms that were attached to, and moved by, the pendulum.

(B)   It was firmly sealed during normal operation of the clock.

(C)   It was at least partly transparent so as to allow for certain types of visual data output.

(D)   It housed both the primary pendulum and another pendulum.

(E)   It contained a transmitter that was activated at irregular intervals to send a signal to the secondary pendulum.

Inference

The question requires recognizing information strongly implied, but not directly stated, in the passage. The first paragraph states that the primary pendulum in a Shortt clock swung freely in a vacuum chamber. To maintain a vacuum, that chamber necessarily would have been tightly sealed when the clock was operating normally.

A   The passage states that the primary pendulum swung freely, which does not suggest that it was attached to and moving an elaborate mechanism.

B   **Correct.** The passage states that the primary pendulum swung freely in a vacuum chamber. Maintaining a vacuum would necessitate a tight seal, so it follows that the chamber was firmly sealed when the clock was operating normally.

C   The passage implies nothing about the transparency of the chamber housing the primary pendulum.

D   The passage states that the secondary pendulum was housed in a separate cabinet, so a second pendulum in the same cabinet with the primary pendulum is not suggested.

E   The passage describes a signal sent from the secondary pendulum to the primary pendulum, not the other way around.

The correct answer is B.

102. The passage most strongly suggests that its author would agree with which of the following statements about clocks?

(A)   Before 1921, no one had designed a clock that used electricity to aid in its timekeeping functions.

(B)   Atomic clocks depend on the operation of mechanisms that were invented by William Shortt and first used in the Shortt clock.

(C)   No type of clock that keeps time more stably and accurately than a Shortt clock relies fundamentally on the operation of a pendulum.

(D)   Subtle changes in the earth's rotation slightly reduce the accuracy of all clocks used in observatories after 1921.

(E)   At least some mechanical clocks that do not have pendulums are almost identical to Shortt clocks in their mode of operation.

Inference

The question requires recognizing information implied, but not directly stated, in the passage. The author characterizes Shortt's clock as the "ultimate pendulum clock, indeed the ultimate mechanical clock of any kind," which strongly suggests the view that any type of clock superior to a Shortt clock—that is, any clock which kept time more reliably and accurately—must not be mechanical or rely on the operation of a pendulum.

A   The passage states that Shortt clocks were first used in 1921, but it does not imply that earlier clocks did not use electricity.

B   The passage does not suggest that the mechanisms in an atomic clock have any relation to those in a Shortt clock.

C   **Correct.** The author describes Shortt clocks as the ultimate, or best, in the class of pendulum clocks; therefore, the author likely would agree that any clock that kept time more accurately than a Shortt clock would not rely on a pendulum.

D   The passage suggests nothing about the subtle changes in the Earth's rotation affecting all clocks; rather, it states that Shortt clocks first allowed such subtle seasonal changes to be detected.

E   The passage does not discuss mechanical clocks without pendulums, nor would such clocks be almost identical to a pendulum clock, such as a Shortt clock, in their mode of operation.

The correct answer is C.

103. The passage most strongly suggests that the study described in the third paragraph would not have been possible in the absence of

(A)   accurate information regarding the times at which high and low ocean tides occurred at various locations during 1984

(B)   comparative data regarding the use of Shortt clocks in observatories between 1921 and 1932

(C)   a non-Shortt clock that was known to keep time extremely precisely and reliably

(D)   an innovative electric-power source that was not available in the 1920s and 1930s

(E)   optical data-transmission devices to communicate between the U.S. Naval Observatory and other research facilities

Inference

The item requires recognizing information strongly implied, but not directly stated, in the passage. The study discussed in the third paragraph compared a Shortt clock's functioning against that of atomic clocks. Atomic clocks are known to be extraordinarily precise, allowing for the precise comparisons made by the study; it follows that the study would have been impossible without an atomic clock or another non-Shortt clock that was equally precise and reliable.

A   The study discovered slight deviations in the functioning of the Shortt clock caused by tidal distortion in the earth itself, but it did not rely on information regarding ocean tides.

B   The study compared a Shortt clock against atomic clocks; it did not compare the use of Shortt clocks in observatories during a specific period.

C   **Correct.** The study compared a Shortt clock against atomic clocks to determine exactly how accurate a Shortt clock is. Atomic clocks are known to be extremely precise and reliable. It follows that such precise comparisons would have been impossible without either an atomic clock or another non-Shortt clock that was as precise and reliable as an atomic clock.

D   Nothing suggests that the study in question required an innovative power source.

E   The passage states that the study used optical sensing equipment but makes no mention of optical data transmission devices used to communicate between various research facilities.

The correct answer is C.

Questions 104–107 refer to the passage on page 94.

104.   According to the passage, comparable worth principles are different in which of the following ways from other mandates intended to reduce or eliminate pay inequities?

(A)   Comparable worth principles address changes in the pay schedules of male as well as female workers.

(B)   Comparable worth principles can be applied to employees in both the public and the private sector.

(C)   Comparable worth principles emphasize the training and skill of workers.

(D)   Comparable worth principles require changes in the employer's resource allocation.

(E)   Comparable worth principles can be used to quantify the value of elements of dissimilar jobs.

Supporting Idea

The question requires recognizing specific claims presented in the passage. The passage notes that two mandates—the Equal Pay Act of 1963 and Title VII of the Civil Rights Act of 1964—do not compare the value of similar tasks in dissimilar jobs, and then contrasts that limitation with comparable worth principles, which attempt to quantify the value of specific elements of diverse jobs in order to assert that similar work elements, even when found in dissimilar jobs, should be regarded as comparable in value and therefore receive comparable remuneration.

A   The passage mentions comparable worth principles in relation to pay schedules, but it does not specify pay schedules as a point of difference with other mandates.

B   The passage states that both public- and private-sector employers have adopted comparable worth principles, but it does not contrast that adoption with the application of other mandates.

C   The passage suggests that comparable worth principles emphasize the similar training and skills of workers performing dissimilar jobs, but it does not suggest that comparable worth principles differ from other mandates in emphasizing skills and training.

D   While comparable worth principles are likely to require changes in resource allocation, nothing in the passage suggests that other mandates would not also require such changes.

E   **Correct.** The passage notes that other mandates do not attempt to compare the value of tasks performed in dissimilar jobs, then states that comparable worth principles are different because they quantify the value of such job elements as training, responsibility, and work environment, even across different categories of work.

The correct answer is E.

105. According to the passage, which of the following is true of comparable worth as a policy?

(A)   Comparable worth policy decisions in pay-inequity cases have often failed to satisfy the complainants.

(B)   Comparable worth policies have been applied to both public-sector and private-sector employee pay schedules.

(C)   Comparable worth as a policy has come to be widely criticized in the past decade.

(D)   Many employers have considered comparable worth as a policy, but very few have actually adopted it.

(E)   Early implementations of comparable worth policies resulted in only transitory gains in pay equity.

Supporting Idea

The question requires recognizing specific information presented in the passage. In the first paragraph, the passage states that over the last decade, comparable worth policies have been adopted or considered by both private-sector companies and governments on the federal, state, and local levels. In other words, such policies have been applied to both public-sector and private-sector employee pay schedules by the companies and governmental entities discussed.

A   The passage states that other mandates meant to address inequity have failed to satisfy litigants and contrasts this

dissatisfaction with the greater perceived fairness of comparable worth policies.

B   **Correct.** The passage states in the first paragraph that comparable worth policies have been adopted by both private companies and governmental entities, which would mean that such policies were applied to both private-sector and public-sector employee pay.

C   The passage does not mention widespread criticisms of comparable worth policies.

D   The passage states that large numbers of employers have adopted or begun to consider comparable worth policies; nowhere does it suggest that very few employers have adopted such policies after considering them.

E   The passage mentions concerns that the pay gains brought about by comparable worth policies will be transitory, but it goes on to suggest that such concerns are misplaced.

The correct answer is B.

106. It can be inferred from the passage that application of "other mandates" (line 22) would be unlikely to result in an outcome satisfactory to the female employees in which of the following situations?

I.   Males employed as long-distance truck drivers for a furniture company make $3.50 more per hour than do females with comparable job experience employed in the same capacity.

II.   Women working in the office of a cement company contend that their jobs are as demanding and valuable as those of the men working outside in the cement factory, but the women are paid much less per hour.

III.   A law firm employs both male and female paralegals with the same educational and career backgrounds, but the starting salary for male paralegals is $5,000 more than for female paralegals.

(A)   I only

(B)   II only

(C)   III only

(D)   I and II only

(E)   I and III only

Inference

The question requires applying the information supplied by the passage to hypothetical scenarios. The passage states that the "other mandates" referred to in line 22 of the text—such as the Equal Pay Act of 1963 and Title VII of the Civil Rights Act of 1964—do not address the issue of similarly valuable work in dissimilar jobs. Therefore, it can be inferred that they *do* address the issue of pay disparities in similar or identical jobs, like the scenarios described in I and III. It would follow that the female employees described in scenarios I and III would be more likely to be satisfied with the results of applying those mandates, and only the female employees described in scenario II—who seek to correct pay inequities across dissimilar but equally demanding jobs—would likely be dissatisfied.

A   The male and female employees in scenario I are performing identical work with comparable experience but receiving unequal pay—a situation that the passage implies "other mandates" can address adequately.

B   Correct. The male and female employees in scenario II are performing different but equally demanding jobs—exactly the situation that the passage suggests the "other mandates" referred to in line 22 of the text do not address. Therefore, the female employees in this scenario are likely to find the application of such other mandates unsatisfying.

C   The male and female employees in scenario III are performing identical work with identical credentials but receiving unequal pay—a situation that the passage implies "other mandates" can address satisfactorily.

D   As discussed above, the female employees in scenario II are likely to be dissatisfied by the application of "other mandates," but those in scenario I are more likely to be satisfied.

E   As discussed above, the female employees in scenarios I and III are most likely to find that the "other mandates" are sufficient to address their situations.

The correct answer is B.

107. Which of the following best describes an application of the principles of comparable worth as they are described in the passage?

(A)   The current pay, rates of increase, and rates of promotion for female mechanics are compared with those of male mechanics.

(B)   The training, skills, and job experience of computer programmers in one division of a corporation are compared to those of programmers making more money in another division.

(C)   The number of women holding top executive positions in a corporation is compared to the number of women available for promotion to those positions, and both tallies are matched to the tallies for men in the same corporation.

(D)   The skills, training, and job responsibilities of the clerks in the township tax assessor's office are compared to those of the much better paid township engineers.

(E)   The working conditions of female workers in a hazardous-materials environment are reviewed and their pay schedules compared to those of all workers in similar environments across the nation.

Main Idea

The question requires grasping the central principle behind comparable worth policies and then assessing if application of that principle is illustrated by hypothetical scenarios. The passage describes comparable worth as the idea that jobs requiring similar levels of skill, training, and responsibility, or involving similar tasks, should receive similar remuneration, even when those jobs differ from each other in other respects. Therefore, the scenario that illustrates the application of comparable worth will involve the comparison of such elements as skills, training, and responsibilities in two jobs that are otherwise broadly different.

A   Comparable worth principles apply in situations where people are doing work of similar value in dissimilar jobs; in this scenario, the male and female mechanics are doing the same job.

B   Comparable worth principles do not apply in situations where people are doing the same work—programming—in different divisions of a company.

C   Assessing the availability of male and female employees for promotion is not an application of comparable worth principles.

D   Correct. Comparable worth principles are demonstrated in scenarios such as this one, where skills, training, and responsibilities are compared across jobs that are otherwise different; in this case, a comparison between the work performed by tax clerks and by engineers.

E   Comparable worth principles apply to comparisons of the value of work performed in different jobs, not to comparisons of working conditions.

The correct answer is D.

Questions 108–110 refer to the passage on page 96.

108. In lines 14–18, the author implies which of the following about Marseilles trade during the period 1700–1715?

(A)   Reluctance on the part of merchants to import goods taxable at high rates of the *cottimo* probably explains the drop in *cottimo* revenues.

(B)   Even if imports subject to the *cottimo* decreased in volume, the city's total business activity in the Mediterranean was increasing.

(C)   Shifts in trading patterns occurred primarily because ports whose goods were taxed at high rates of the *cottimo* were no longer accessible.

(D)   The total volume of imports increased dramatically, even though imports subject to the *cottimo* generated less revenue.

(E)   The total volume of imports subject to the *cottimo* need not have decreased in order for *cottimo* revenues to decline.

Inference

The question asks what the author implies about Marseilles' trade during 1700–1715, specifically using the information in lines 14–18. Lines 14–18 describe a shift toward trade with

cities, which were subject to lower *cottimo* rates, which in turn would imply that the overall revenue derived from *cottimo* might fall even without a corresponding drop in total imports.

A   Lines 14–18 don't mention *reluctance* or a change in the merchants' psychology regarding tax rates. It states instead that the shift was "due to a shift in trading patterns caused by the war."

B   The passage mentions an increase in grain imports (which are tax-exempt) and trade with low-rate ports. While this suggests that total activity *could* have been increasing, the text in lines 14–18 doesn't establish this. It only implies that a larger share of the *cottimo*-subject trade was now coming from low-rate ports.

C   The text in lines 14–18 attributes the shift to changes "caused by the war," but it does not specify the primary mechanism. The passage never states or implies that high-rate ports became "inaccessible."

D   Lines 14–18 only addresses imports *subject to the cottimo* and how the rate changed for that trade. It doesn't imply a "dramatic" increase in volume.

E   Correct. Lines 14–18 explain that the shift in trading patterns meant merchants favored ports where the *cottimo* rate was lower. If merchants shift a large portion of their trade volume away from high-rate ports and toward low-rate ports, the tax revenue will decrease—which could account for some or all of the documented 30 percent decline—even if the total volume of imports subject to the tax remained constant or even slightly increased.

The correct answer is E.

109. The passage suggests that, in comparison with the period before 1700, which of the following was true of imports to Marseilles in the period 1700–1715?

(A)   Imports declined in volume throughout the period.

(B)   Imports increased in volume throughout the period.

(C)   The percentage of imports that was subject to the *cottimo* increased.

(D)   A larger percentage of imports were food imports.

(E)   A larger percentage of imports came from Mediterranean areas.

Inference

The passage is concerned with identifying reasons why the fact that Marseilles collected a much lower total amount of import taxes, or *cottimo*, during the 1700–1715 period would not necessarily imply that imports overall were significantly lower. The *cottimo* collected during the period under discussion was 30 percent lower than during the preceding years, a fact that would seem to suggest stagnant or decreasing imports, or at least does not imply significant increases. However, the passage also states that Marseilles' "role as a grain importer" grew during the same period, and that most foods—implicitly including grain—were exempt from the tax. Taken together, increased grain imports and stagnant or questionable overall imports would tend to suggest that a larger percentage of total imports during that period were food imports.

A   The central argument of the passage is that overall imports did not necessarily decline during the 1700–1715 period; that imports *did* decline is in no way implied.

B   The passage is concerned with identifying reasons that imports might not have *declined* during that period, but it does not suggest that imports actually *increased*.

C   The argument that lower *cottimo* would not necessarily imply lower imports depends on the suggestion that a lower, not higher, percentage of total imports were subject to the tax.

D   **Correct.** The passage states that Marseilles imported increasing amounts of grain at a period when overall imports seem unlikely to have increased; if food imports increased at a greater rate than did total imports, that would imply that a larger percentage of total imports consisted of food than in the earlier period.

E   The passage implies that the percentage of imports from Mediterranean areas decreased rather than increased at this period, by stating that such imports were the only ones subject to the *cottimo* and by referring to increased trade with other regions.

The correct answer is D.

110.   The author mentions all of the following as factors that could possibly account for the 30 percent decline in revenues in Marseilles during the period 1700–1715 EXCEPT:

(A)   a decline in the city's commercial activity

(B)   increased trade with cities subject to lower rates of the tax

(C)   larger role for the city as an importer of food

(D)   increased focus on trade with non-Mediterranean ports

(E)   a decrease in exports to Middle Eastern ports in the Mediterranean

Supporting Idea

The question requires identifying information clearly excluded from the passage. The passage discusses a number of factors that could have contributed to the fall in total *cottimo*, or import taxes, collected in Marseilles during the 1700–1715 period. These explicitly identified factors include reduced economic activity, increased trade with Middle Eastern cities whose imports were subject to lower rates of taxation, increased untaxed imports of food, and growing trade with ports beyond the Mediterranean. The factors discussed do not include lower exports; since the *cottimo* was a tax on imports, exports would not affect it.

A   While the passage argues against the assumption that lower *cottimo* necessarily resulted from lower economic activity, it does explicitly mention lower economic activity as a possible contributing factor.

B   The passage explicitly includes increased trade with Middle Eastern cities, whose imports were subject to lower rates of *cottimo*, as a factor that could help explain lower *cottimo* during the period under discussion.

C   Marseilles' increased role as a food importer is explicitly cited as a factor that could have reduced *cottimo*.

D   Growing trade with ports beyond the Mediterranean is mentioned as a reason why *cottimo* might have fallen, since imports from non-Mediterranean areas were not subject to the tax.

E   **Correct.** The passage makes no mention of exports to any region as a factor that could account for lower *cottimo*; since *cottimo* was an import tax, exports would be unlikely to affect it in any way.

The correct answer is E.

4.7 Practice Questions: Critical Reasoning

Each of the Critical Reasoning questions is based on a short argument, a set of statements, or a plan of action. For each question, select the best answer of the choices given.

Questions 111 to 148 — Difficulty: Easy

111. Stockholders have been critical of the Flyna Company, a major furniture retailer, because most of Flyna's furniture is manufactured in Country X from local wood, and illegal logging is widespread there. However, Flyna has set up a certification scheme for lumber mills. It has hired a staff of auditors and forestry professionals who review documentation of the wood supply of Country X's lumber mills to ensure its legal origin, make surprise visits to mills to verify documents, and certify mills as approved sources of legally obtained lumber. Flyna uses only lumber from certified mills. Thus, Flyna's claim that its Country X wood supply is obtained legally is justified.

Which of the following, if true, would most undermine the justification provided for Flyna's claim?

(A) Only about one-third of Flyna's inspectors were hired from outside the company.

(B) Country X's government recently reduced its subsidies for lumber production

(C) Flyna has had to pay higher than expected salaries to attract qualified inspectors.

(D) The proportion of Country X's lumber mills inspected each year by Flyna's staff is about 10 percent, randomly selected.

(E) Illegal logging costs Country X's government a significant amount in lost revenue each year.

112. Companies O and P each have the same number of employees who work the same number of hours per week. According to records maintained by each company, the employees of Company O had fewer job-related accidents last year than did the employees of Company P. Therefore, employees of Company O are less likely to have job-related accidents than are employees of Company P.

Which of the following, if true, would most weaken the conclusion?

(A) The employees of Company P lost more time at work due to job-related accidents than did the employees of Company O.

(B) Company P considered more types of accidents to be job-related than did Company O.

(C) The employees of Company P were sick more often than were the employees of Company O.

(D) Several employees of Company O each had more than one job-related accident.

(E) The majority of job-related accidents at Company O involved a single machine.

113. The *XCT* automobile is considered less valuable than the *ZNK* automobile, because insurance companies pay less, on average, to replace a stolen *XCT* than a stolen *ZNK*. Surprisingly, the average amount insurance companies will pay to repair a car involved in a collision is typically higher for the *XCT* than for the *ZNK*. One insurance expert explained that repairs to *XCT* automobiles are especially labor-intensive, and labor is a significant factor in collision repair costs.

Which of the following, if true, most strongly supports the insurance expert's explanation?

(A) *ZNK* automobiles are involved in accidents more frequently than *XCT* automobiles.

(B) The cost of routine maintenance for the *ZNK* is about the same as for the *XCT*.

(C) There are more automobile mechanics who specialize in *XCT* repairs than in *ZNK* repairs.

(D) The ease of repair of *ZNK* automobiles is one factor that adds to their value.

(E) *XCT* automobiles are more likely to be stolen than *ZNK* automobiles.

114. The sustained massive use of pesticides in farming has two effects that are especially pernicious. First, it often kills off the pests' natural enemies in the area. Second, it often unintentionally gives rise to insecticide-resistant pests, since those insects that survive a particular insecticide will be the ones most resistant to it, and they are the ones left to breed.

From the passage above, it can be properly inferred that the effectiveness of the sustained massive use of pesticides can be extended by doing which of the following, assuming that each is a realistic possibility?

(A) Using only chemically stable insecticides

(B) Periodically switching the type of insecticide used

(C) Gradually increasing the quantities of pesticides used

(D) Leaving a few fields fallow every year

(E) Breeding higher-yielding varieties of crop plants

115. Editorial: The mayor plans to deactivate the city's fire alarm boxes, because most calls received from them are false alarms. The mayor claims that the alarm boxes are no longer necessary, since most people now have access to cell phones. But the city's commercial district, where there is the greatest risk of fire, has few residents and few cell towers, so some alarm boxes are still necessary.

Which of the following, if true, most seriously weakens the editorial's argument?

(A) Maintaining the fire alarm boxes costs the city more than 5 million dollars annually.

(B) Commercial buildings have automatic fire alarm systems that are linked directly to the fire department.

(C) The fire department gets less information from an alarm box than it does from a telephone call.

(D) The city's fire department is located much closer to the residential areas than to the commercial district.

(E) On average, almost 25 percent of the cell towers in the city are out of order.

116. Which of the following, if true, most logically completes the argument?

Some dairy farmers in the province of Takandia want to give their cows a synthetic hormone that increases milk production. Many Takandians, however, do not want to buy milk from cows given the synthetic hormone. For this reason Takandia's legislature is considering a measure requiring milk from cows given the hormone to be labeled as such. Even if the measure is defeated, dairy farmers who use the hormone will probably lose customers, since __________.

(A) it has not been proven that any trace of the synthetic hormone exists in the milk of cows given the hormone

(B) some farmers in Takandia who plan to use the synthetic hormone will probably not do so if the measure were passed

(C) milk from cows that have not been given the synthetic hormone can be labeled as such without any legislative action

(D) the legislature's consideration of the bill has been widely publicized

(E) milk that comes from cows given the synthetic hormone looks and tastes the same as milk from cows that have not received the hormone

117. Sparrow Airlines is planning to reduce its costs by cleaning its planes' engines once a month, rather than the industry standard of every six months. With cleaner engines, Sparrow can postpone engine overhauls, which take planes out of service for up to 18 months. Furthermore, cleaning an engine reduces its fuel consumption by roughly 1.2 percent.

The airline's plan assumes that

(A) fuel prices are likely to rise in the near future and therefore cutting fuel consumption is an important goal

(B) the cost of monthly cleaning of an airplane's engines is not significantly greater in the long run than is the cost of an engine overhaul

(C) engine cleaning does not remove an airplane from service

(D) Sparrow Airlines has had greater problems with engine overhauls and fuel consumption than other airlines have

(E) cleaning engines once a month will give Sparrow Airlines a competitive advantage over other airlines

118. Patrick usually provides child care for six children. Parents leave their children at Patrick's house in the morning and pick them up after work. At the end of each workweek, the parents pay Patrick at an hourly rate for the child care provided that week. The weekly income Patrick receives is usually adequate but not always uniform, particularly in the winter, when children are likely to get sick and be unpredictably absent.

Which of the following plans, if put into effect, has the best prospect of making Patrick's weekly income both uniform and adequate?

(A) Pool resources with a neighbor who provides child care under similar arrangements, so that the two of them cooperate in caring for twice as many children as Patrick currently does.

(B) Replace payment by actual hours of child care provided with a fixed weekly fee based upon the number of hours of child care that Patrick would typically be expected to provide.

(C) Hire a full-time helper and invest in facilities for providing child care to sick children.

(D) Increase the hourly rate to a level that would provide adequate income even in a week when half of the children Patrick usually cares for are absent.

(E) Increase the number of hours made available for child care each day, so that parents can leave their children in Patrick's care for a longer period each day at the current hourly rate.

119. Film director: It is true that certain characters and plot twists in my newly released film *The Perfect Heist* are strikingly similar to characters and plot twists in *Thieves*, a movie that came out last year. Based on these similarities, the film studio that produced *Thieves* is now accusing me of taking ideas from that film. The accusation is clearly without merit. All production work on *The Perfect Heist* was actually completed months before *Thieves* was released.

Which of the following, if true, provides the strongest support for the director's rejection of the accusation?

(A) Before *Thieves* began production, its script had been circulating for several years among various film studios, including the studio that produced *The Perfect Heist*.

(B) The characters and plot twists that are most similar in the two films have close parallels in many earlier films of the same genre.

(C) The film studio that produced *Thieves* seldom produces films in this genre.

(D) The director of *Thieves* worked with the director of *The Perfect Heist* on several earlier projects.

(E) The time it took to produce *The Perfect Heist* was considerably shorter than the time it took to produce *Thieves*.

120. Ythex has developed a small diesel engine that produces 30 percent less particulate pollution than the engine made by its main rival, Onez, now widely used in Marania; Ythex's engine is well-suited for use in the thriving warehousing businesses in Marania, though it costs more than the Onez engine. The Maranian government plans to ban within the next two years the use of diesel engines with more than 80 percent of current diesel engine particulate emissions in Marania, and Onez will probably not be able to retool its engine to reduce emissions to reach this target. So if the ban is passed, the Ythex engine ought to sell well in Marania after that time.

Which of the following is an assumption on which the argument above depends?

(A) Marania's warehousing and transshipment business buys more diesel engines of any size than other types of engines.

(B) Ythex is likely to be able to reduce the cost of its small diesel engine within the next two years.

(C) The Maranian government is generally favorable to anti-pollution regulations.

(D) The government's ban on high levels of pollution caused by diesel engines, if passed, will not be difficult to enforce.

(E) The other manufacturers of small diesel engines in Marania, if there are any, have not produced an engine as popular and clean running as Ythex's new engine.

121. Which of the following most logically completes the argument?

     The last members of a now-extinct species of a European wild deer called the giant ceer lived in Ireland about 16,000 years ago. Prehistoric cave paintings in France depict this animal as having a large hump on its back. Fossils of this animal, however do not show any hump. Nevertheless, there is no reason to conclude that the cave paintings are therefore inaccurate in this regard, since ___________.

     (A) some prehistoric cave paintings in France also depict other animals as having a hump

     (B) fossils of the giant deer are much more common in Ireland than in France

     (C) animal humps are composed of fatty tissue, which does not fossilize

     (D) the cave paintings of the giant deer were painted well before 16,000 years ago

     (E) only one currently existing species of deer has any anatomical feature that even remotely resembles a hump

122. Psychologists conducted an experiment in which half of the volunteers were asked to describe an unethical action they had performed, while the other half were asked to describe an ethical action they had performed. Some of the volunteers, chosen at random from each of the two groups, were encouraged to wash their hands afterward. Among those who described unethical actions, those who washed their hands were significantly less likely to volunteer for another, similar experiment than those who did not wash their hands. The researchers concluded that some of the subjects failed to volunteer again in part because of their having described an unethical action.

     Which of the following would, if true, most help to support the researchers' conclusion?

     (A) Among the volunteers who described ethical actions, those who washed their hands were significantly less likely to volunteer for another, similar experiment than those who did not wash their hands.

     (B) The average likelihood of volunteering for another, similar experiment was higher among those who described ethical actions than among those who described unethical actions.

     (C) Most of the volunteers who were encouraged to wash their hands did so.

     (D) The volunteers in the study were not more disposed to washing their hands under normal circumstances than the general population was.

     (E) Equal numbers of volunteers from both groups were encouraged to wash their hands.

123. High levels of fertilizer and pesticides, needed when farmers try to produce high yields of the same crop year after year, pollute water supplies. Experts therefore urge farmers to diversify their crops and to rotate their plantings yearly.

To receive governmental price-support benefits for a crop, farmers must have produced that same crop for the past several years.

The statements above, if true, best support which of the following conclusions?

(A) The rules for governmental support of farm prices work against efforts to reduce water pollution.

(B) The only solution to the problem of water pollution from fertilizers and pesticides is to take farmland out of production.

(C) Farmers can continue to make a profit by rotating diverse crops, thus reducing costs for chemicals, but not by planting the same crop each year.

(D) New farming techniques will be developed to make it possible for farmers to reduce the application of fertilizers and pesticides.

(E) Governmental price supports for farm products are set at levels that are not high enough to allow farmers to get out of debt.

124. Many leadership theories have provided evidence that leaders affect group success rather than the success of particular individuals. So it is irrelevant to analyze the effects of supervisor traits on the attitudes of individuals whom they supervise. Instead, assessment of leadership effectiveness should occur only at the group level.

Which of the following would it be most useful to establish in order to evaluate the argument?

(A) Whether supervisors' documentation of individual supervisees' attitudes toward them is usually accurate

(B) Whether it is possible to assess individual supervisees' attitudes toward their supervisors without thereby changing those attitudes

(C) Whether any of the leadership theories in question hold that leaders should assess other leaders' attitudes

(D) Whether some types of groups do not need supervision in order to be successful in their endeavors

(E) Whether individuals' attitudes toward supervisors affect group success

125. A major health insurance company in Lagolia pays for special procedures prescribed by physicians only if the procedure is first approved as "medically necessary" by a company-appointed review panel. The rule is intended to save the company the money it might otherwise spend on medically unnecessary procedures. The company has recently announced that in order to reduce its costs, it will abandon this rule.

Which of the following, if true, provides the strongest justification for the company's decision?

(A)   Patients often register dissatisfaction with physicians who prescribe nothing for their ailments.

(B)   Physicians often prescribe special procedures that are helpful but not altogether necessary for the health of the patient.

(C)   The review process is expensive and practically always results in approval of the prescribed procedure.

(D)   The company's review process does not interfere with the prerogative of physicians, in cases where more than one effective procedure is available, to select the one they personally prefer.

(E)   The number of members of the company-appointed review panel who review a given procedure depends on the cost of the procedure.

126. Automobile ownership was rare in Sabresia as recently as 30 years ago, but with continuing growth of personal income there, automobile ownership has become steadily more common. Consequently, there are now far more automobiles on Sabresia's roads than there were 30 years ago, and the annual number of automobile accidents has increased significantly. Yet the annual number of deaths and injuries resulting from automobile accidents has not increased significantly.

Which of the following, if true, most helps to explain why deaths and injuries resulting from automobile accidents have not increased significantly?

(A)   Virtually all of the improvements in Sabresia's roads that were required to accommodate increased traffic were completed more than ten years ago.

(B)   With more and more people owning cars, the average number of passengers in a car on the road has dropped dramatically.

(C)   The increases in traffic volume have been most dramatic on Sabresia's highways, where speeds are well above those of other roads.

(D)   Because of a vigorous market in used cars, the average age of cars on the road has actually increased throughout the years of steady growth in automobile ownership.

(E)   Automobile ownership is still much less common in Sabresia than it is in other countries.

127. A child learning to play the piano will not succeed unless the child has an instrument at home on which to practice. However, good-quality pianos, whether new or secondhand, are costly. Buying one is justified only if the child has the necessary talent and perseverance, which is precisely what one cannot know in advance. Consequently, parents should buy an inexpensive secondhand instrument at first and upgrade if and when the child's ability and inclination are proven.

Which of the following, if true, casts the most serious doubt on the course of action recommended for parents?

(A) Learners, particularly those with genuine musical talent, are apt to lose interest in the instrument if they have to play on a piano that fails to produce a pleasing sound.

(B) Reputable piano teachers do not accept children as pupils unless they know that the children can practice on a piano at home.

(C) Ideally, the piano on which a child practices at home should be located in a room away from family activities going on at the same time.

(D) Very young beginners often make remarkable progress at playing the piano at first, but then appear to stand still for a considerable period of time.

(E) In some parents, spending increasing amounts of money on having their children learn to play the piano produces increasing anxiety to hear immediate results.

128. Which of the following most logically completes the market forecaster's argument?

Market forecaster: The price of pecans is high when pecans are comparatively scarce but drops sharply when pecans are abundant. Thus, in high-yield years, growers often store part of their crop in refrigerated warehouses until after the next year's harvest, hoping for higher prices then. Because of bad weather, this year's pecan crop will be very small. Nevertheless, pecan prices this year will not be significantly higher than last year, since __________.

(A) the last time the pecan crop was as small as it was this year, the practice of holding back part of one year's crop had not yet become widely established

(B) last year's pecan harvest was the largest in the last 40 years

(C) pecan prices have remained relatively stable in recent years

(D) pecan yields for some farmers were as high this year as they had been last year

(E) the quality of this year's pecan crop is as high as the quality of any pecan crop in the previous five years

129. Many office buildings designed to prevent outside air from entering have been shown to have elevated levels of various toxic substances circulating through the air inside, a phenomenon known as sick building syndrome. Yet the air in other office buildings does not have elevated levels of these substances, even though those buildings are the same age as the "sick" buildings and have similar designs and ventilation systems.

Which of the following, if true, most helps to explain why not all office buildings designed to prevent outside air from entering have air that contains elevated levels of toxic substances?

(A) Certain adhesives and drying agents used in particular types of furniture, carpets, and paint contribute the bulk of the toxic substances that circulate in the air of office buildings.

(B) Most office buildings with sick building syndrome were built between 1950 and 1990.

(C) Among buildings designed to prevent outside air from entering, houses are no less likely than office buildings to have air that contains elevated levels of toxic substances.

(D) The toxic substances that are found in the air of "sick" office buildings are substances that are found in at least small quantities in nearly every building.

(E) Office buildings with windows that can readily be opened are unlikely to suffer from sick building syndrome.

130. Newsletter: **A condominium generally offers more value for its cost than an individual house because of economies of scale.** The homeowners in a condominium association can collectively buy products and services that they could not afford on their own. And since a professional management company handles maintenance of common areas, **condominium owners spend less time and money on maintenance than individual homeowners do.**

The two portions in **boldface** play which of the following roles in the newsletter's argument?

(A) The first is the argument's main conclusion; the second is another conclusion supporting the first.

(B) The first is a premise, for which no evidence is provided; the second is the argument's only conclusion.

(C) The first is a conclusion supporting the second; the second is the argument's main conclusion.

(D) The first is the argument's only conclusion; the second is a premise, for which no evidence is provided.

(E) Both are premises, for which no evidence is provided, and both support the argument's only conclusion.

131. Platinum is a relatively rare metal vital to a wide variety of industries. Xagor Corporation, a major producer of platinum, has its production plant in a country that will soon begin imposing an export tax on platinum sold and shipped to customers abroad. As a consequence, the price of platinum on the world market is bound to rise.

Which of the following, if true, tends to confirm the conclusion above?

(A) An inexpensive substitute for platinum has been developed and will be available to industry for the first time this month.

(B) The largest of the industries that depend on platinum reported a drop in sales last month.

(C) The producers of platinum in other countries taken together cannot supply enough platinum to meet worldwide demand.

(D) Xagor produced more platinum last month than in any previous month.

(E) New deposits of platinum have been found in the country in which Xagor has its production plant.

132. From 1973 to 1986, growth in the United States economy was over 33 percent, while the percent growth in United States energy consumption was zero. The number of barrels of oil being saved per day by energy-efficiency improvements made since 1973 is now 13 million.

If the information above is correct, which of the following conclusions can properly be drawn on the basis of it?

(A) It is more difficult to find new sources of oil than to institute new energy-conservation measures.

(B) Oil imports cannot be reduced unless energy consumption does not grow at all.

(C) A reduction in the consumption of gasoline was the reason overall energy consumption remained steady.

(D) It is possible for an economy to grow without consuming additional energy.

(E) The development of nontraditional energy sources will make it possible for the United States economy to grow even faster.

133. Although many customers do not make a sufficient effort to conserve water, water companies must also be held responsible for wasteful consumption. Their own policies, in fact, encourage excessive water use, and attempts at conservation will succeed only if the water companies change their practices.

Which of the following, if true, would most strongly support the view above?

(A) Most water companies reduce the cost per unit of water as the amount of water used by a customer increases.

(B) Most water companies keep detailed records of the quantity of water used by different customers.

(C) Most water companies severely curtail the use of water during periods of drought.

(D) Federal authorities limit the range of policies that can be enforced by the water companies.

(E) The price per unit of water charged by the water companies has risen steadily in the last 10 years.

134. Despite legislation designed to stem the accumulation of plastic waste, the plastics industry continued to grow rapidly last year, as can be seen from the fact that sales of the resin that is the raw material for manufacturing plastics grew by 10 percent to $28 billion.

In assessing the support provided by the evidence cited above for the statement that the plastics industry continued to grow, in addition to the information above it would be most useful to know

(A) whether the resin has other uses besides the manufacture of plastics

(B) the dollar amount of resin sales the year before last

(C) the plastics industry's attitude toward the legislation concerning plastic waste

(D) whether sales of all goods and services in the economy as a whole were increasing last year

(E) what proportion of the plastics industry's output eventually contributes to the accumulation of plastic waste

135. Studies of the political orientations of 1,055 college students revealed that the plurality of students in an eastern, big-city, private university was liberal, whereas in a state-supported, southern college, the plurality was conservative. Orientations were independent of the student's region of origin, and the trends were much more pronounced in seniors than in beginning students.

Which of the following hypotheses is best supported by the observations stated above?

(A) The political orientations of college students are more similar to the political orientations of their parents when the students start college than when the students are seniors.

(B) The political orientations of college seniors depend significantly on experiences they have had while in college.

(C) A college senior originally from the South is more likely to be politically conservative than is a college senior originally from the East.

(D) Whether their college is state-supported or private is the determining factor in college students' political orientations.

(E) College students tend to become more conservative politically as they become older and are confronted with pressures for financial success.

136. Diabetics often suffer dangerously low blood sugar levels, which they can correct safely if they notice the symptoms quickly. It has been suggested that **diabetics should be advised to drink moderate amounts of coffee**, since doing so improves their ability to recognize symptoms of low blood sugar quickly. That would be bad advice, however, since drinking even small amounts of coffee can increase the body's need for sugar in unpredictable ways.

In the argument being made, the part that is in **boldface** plays which of the following roles?

(A) Presenting the conclusion toward which the argument as a whole is directed

(B) Providing support for the conclusion of the argument

(C) Offering a reason to take a course of action recommended in the argument

(D) Stating the position to be refuted by the argument

(E) Providing an instance of a general principle articulated in the argument

137. Trancorp currently transports all its goods to Burland Island by truck. The only bridge over the channel separating Burland from the mainland is congested, and trucks typically spend hours in traffic. Trains can reach the channel more quickly than trucks, and freight cars can be transported to Burland by barges that typically cross the channel in an hour. Therefore, to reduce shipping time, Trancorp plans to switch to trains and barges to transport goods to Burland.

Which of the following, if true, casts the most serious doubt on whether Trancorp's plan will succeed?

(A) It does not cost significantly more to transport goods to Burland by truck than it does to transport goods by train and barge.

(B) The number of cars traveling over the bridge into Burland is likely to increase slightly over the next two years.

(C) Because there has been so much traffic on the roads leading to the bridge between Burland and the mainland, these roads are in extremely poor condition.

(D) Barges that arrive at Burland typically wait several hours for their turn to be unloaded.

(E) Most trucks transporting goods into Burland return to the mainland empty.

138. When ducklings are exposed to music, they gain about 6 percent more weight for a given amount of feed than ducklings that are not exposed to music.

    Which of the following, if true, most helps to explain the extra weight gains referred to above?

    (A) Music played for ducklings must be kept at a low level because ducklings exposed to loud music gain less weight than ducklings exposed to no music.

    (B) Ducklings exposed to classical music gained more weight than ducklings exposed to popular music.

    (C) Ducklings are less active when they hear music, so that less of the food they eat is expended in movement and more contributes directly to the ducklings' growth.

    (D) When ducklings gain 6 percent more weight on a given amount of grain, the farmers' profits increase because they can spend less money on grain to feed the ducklings.

    (E) When female ducklings were exposed to music, the percentage of fertile eggs that they laid as adults increased by over 27 percent in comparison to ducklings not exposed to music.

139. X: In order to reduce the amount of plastic in landfills, legislatures should impose a ban on the use of plastics for packaging goods.

    Y: Impossible! Plastic packaging is necessary for public safety. Consumers will lose all of the safety features that plastic offers, chiefly tamper-resistant closures and shatterproof bottles.

    Which of the following best describes the weak point in Y's response to X's proposal?

    (A) Y ignores the possibility that packaging goods in materials other than plastic might provide the same safety features that packaging in plastic offers.

    (B) The economic disadvantages of using plastics as a means of packaging goods are not taken into consideration.

    (C) Y attempts to shift the blame for the large amount of plastic in landfills from the users of plastic packaging to the legislators.

    (D) Y does not consider the concern of some manufacturers that safety features spoil package appearances.

    (E) Y wrongly assumes that X defends the interests of the manufacturers rather than the interests of the consumers.

140. United Lumber will use trees from its forests for two products. The tree trunks will be used for lumber and the branches converted into wood chips to make fiberboard. The cost of this conversion would be the same whether done at the logging site, where the trees are debranched, or at United's factory. However, wood chips occupy less than half the volume of the branches from which they are made.

The information given, if accurate, most strongly supports which of the following?

(A) Converting the branches into wood chips at the logging site would require transporting a fully assembled wood-chipping machine to and from the site.

(B) It would be more economical to debranch the trees at the factory where the fiberboard is manufactured.

(C) The debranching of trees and the conversion of the branches into chips are the only stages in the processing of branches that would be in United's economic advantage to perform at the logging site.

(D) Transportation costs from the logging site to the factory that are determined by volume of cargo would be lower if the conversion into chips is done at the logging site rather than at the factory.

(E) In the wood-processing industry, branches are used only for the production of wood chips for fiberboard.

141. Which of the following most logically completes the passage?

For the past several years, a certain technology has been widely used to transmit data among networked computers. Recently, two data transmission companies, Aptron and Gammatech, have each developed separate systems that allow network data transmission at rates ten times faster than the current technology allows. Although the systems are similarly priced and are equally easy to use, Aptron's product is likely to dominate the market, because __________.

(A) Gammatech has been in the business of designing data transmission systems for several years more than Aptron has

(B) the number of small businesses that need computer networking systems is likely to double over the next few years

(C) it is much more likely that Gammatech's system will be expandable to meet future needs

(D) unlike many data transmission companies, Aptron and Gammatech develop computers in addition to data transmission systems

(E) it is easier for users of the current data transmission technology to switch to Aptron's product than to Gammatech's

142. In Brindon County, virtually all of the fasteners—such as nuts, bolts, and screws—used by workshops and manufacturing firms have for several years been supplied by the Brindon Bolt Barn, a specialist wholesaler. In recent months, many of Brindon County's workshops and manufacturing firms have closed down, and no new ones have opened. Therefore, the Brindon Bolt Barn will undoubtedly show a sharp decline in sales volume and revenue for this year as compared to last year.

The argument depends on assuming which of the following?

(A)   Last year, the Brindon Bolt Barn's sales volume and revenue were significantly higher than they had been the previous year.

(B)   The workshops and manufacturing firms that have remained open have a smaller volume of work to do this year than they did last year.

(C)   Soon the Brindon Bolt Barn will no longer be the only significant supplier of fasteners to Brindon County's workshops.

(D)   The Brindon Bolt Barn's operating expenses have not increased this year.

(E)   The Brindon Bolt Barn is not a company that gets the great majority of its business from customers outside Brindon County.

143. Eurasian water milfoil, a weed not native to Frida Lake, has reproduced prolifically since being accidentally introduced there. In order to eliminate the weed, biologists proposed treating infested parts of the lake with a certain herbicide that is nontoxic for humans and aquatic animals. However, the herbicide might damage populations of certain rare plant species that the lake contains. For this reason, local officials rejected the proposal.

Which of the following, if true, points out the most serious weakness in the officials' grounds for rejecting the biologists' proposal?

(A)   The continuing spread of Eurasian water milfoil in Frida Lake threatens to choke out the lake's rare plant species.

(B)   Because of ecological conditions prevailing in its native habitat, Eurasian water milfoil is not as dominant there as it is in Frida Lake.

(C)   The proliferation of Eurasian water milfoil in Frida Lake has led to reductions in the populations of some species of aquatic animals.

(D)   Although Eurasian water milfoil could be mechanically removed from Frida Lake, eliminating the weed would take far longer this way than it would using herbicides.

(E)   Unless Eurasian water milfoil is completely eliminated from Frida Lake, it will quickly spread again once herbicide treatments or other control measures cease.

144. When airplanes are taken out of service for maintenance, they are often repainted. Having an airplane out of service is extremely costly to an airline, and during repainting, no other maintenance can be done. In an attempt to reduce expenses associated with maintenance, airline officials are considering using a new plastic film, which is applied in sheets, instead of paint. However, the film is more expensive than paint, lasts no longer, and takes as long to apply.

Which of the following, if true, argues most strongly that use of the film will help the airline officials in their attempt to reduce expenses?

(A) While the film is being applied, other workers can do maintenance work on the plane.

(B) Unlike paint, the film gives a milky tone to certain colors.

(C) The film can be applied only by technicians who have received special training.

(D) The metal exteriors of airplanes have to be protected from high temperatures and caustic chemicals such as exhaust gases.

(E) Special ripples in the film reduce a plane's air resistance and thus reduce fuel costs.

145. Almost all the fish sold in Eastville is sold in small seafood stores. Fish at such stores in Eastville's downtown Old Market is much cheaper than similar fish sold at large uptown stores. Old Market vendors buy fish of similar quality from the same wholesalers and at the same prices as uptown vendors do, and their other business expenses are also about the same. Yet the Old Market stores are just as profitable as are the uptown stores.

The statements given, if true, most strongly support which of the following?

(A) Small seafood stores are less profitable than large seafood stores.

(B) Some varieties of fish that are not available at Old Market stores can be found occasionally at large uptown seafood stores.

(C) The amount of fish sold at stores in the Old Market is, on average, much higher than that sold at large uptown stores.

(D) Most of the people who live in uptown Eastville buy fish from their neighborhood stores.

(E) There are many more seafood stores in uptown Eastville than there are in the downtown Old Market.

146. When a certain software update is installed on computer systems, the security programs that normally operate within the system typically respond by disabling key monitoring functions, with the result that the systems become vulnerable to serious security breaches. When systems are installed with both the update and a protective patch, security breaches occur far less frequently. The protective patch is known to counteract many effects of the update and does not itself interfere with normal security programs.

Which of the following hypotheses is best supported by the information given?

(A) Installing the protective patch without the update on systems that are not already vulnerable puts the systems at greater risk of security breaches than installing both the update and the patch does.

(B) The disabling of monitoring functions is the most common cause of security breaches in computer systems.

(C) The protective patch interferes with the tendency of the update to disable key monitoring functions.

(D) For computer systems, increased vulnerability to security breaches is the most harmful effect of installing the update.

(E) If the protective patch is installed along with the update, the version of the update required to achieve its intended performance improvement can generally be reduced.

147. A proposed change to federal income tax laws would eliminate deductions from taxable income for donations a taxpayer has made to charitable and educational institutions. So in particular, if this change were adopted, wealthy individuals would no longer be permitted such deductions. Therefore, many charitable and educational institutions would be forced to reduce services.

Which of the following is an assumption on which the argument depends?

(A) Without the incentives offered by federal income tax laws, at least some wealthy individuals would not donate as much money to charitable and educational institutions as they otherwise would have.

(B) Most charitable and educational institutions are satisfied with the level of services that the contributions they currently receive allow them to provide.

(C) The primary reason for not adopting the proposed change in the federal income tax laws cited above is to protect wealthy individuals from having to pay higher taxes.

(D) Charitable and educational institutions do not currently receive a substantial proportion of their funds from tax monies collected by the government.

(E) Income tax laws should be changed to make donations to charitable and educational institutions the only permissible deductions from taxable income.

148. While airplanes are being repainted, only the painters, wearing special protective gear, can go near them. A newly developed nontoxic plastic film offers an alternative to paint; it can be applied to planes in sheets and requires no special precautions. However, the film takes as long to apply as paint does, and it is neither cheaper nor more durable than paint. Clearly, therefore, airlines have little incentive for switching to the film.

Which of the following, if true, most seriously weakens the argument?

(A) While the plastic film is being applied to a plane, mechanics can perform other maintenance work on the plane.

(B) The plastic film withstands extremes of temperature and corrosive chemicals such as exhaust fumes about as well as aircraft paint does.

(C) The plastic film can be applied properly only by technicians who have received special training.

(D) Standard techniques for detecting metal fatigue through a coat of paint cannot be used on planes covered with the plastic film.

(E) No uses other than that of covering a plane's exterior have as yet been identified for the newly developed plastic film.

Questions 149 to 196 — Difficulty: **Medium**

149. Donations of imported food will be distributed to children in famine-stricken countries in the form of free school meals. The process is efficient because the children are easy to reach at the schools and cooking facilities are often available on site.

Which of the following, if true, casts the most serious doubt on the efficiency of the proposed process?

(A) The emphasis on food will detract from the major function of the schools, which is to educate the children.

(B) A massive influx of donated food will tend to lower the price of food in the areas near the schools.

(C) Supplies of fuel needed for cooking at the schools arrive there only intermittently and in inadequate quantities.

(D) The reduction in farm surpluses in donor countries benefits the donor countries to a greater extent than the recipient countries are benefited by the donations.

(E) The donation of food tends to strengthen the standing of the political party that happens to be in power when the donation is made.

150. *John:* You told me once that no United States citizen who supports union labor should buy an imported car. Yet you are buying an Alma. Since Alma is one of the biggest makers of imports, I infer that you no longer support unions.

Harry: I still support labor unions. Even though Alma is a foreign car company, the car I am buying, the Alma Deluxe, is designed, engineered, and manufactured in the United States.

Harry's method of defending his purchase of an Alma is to

(A) disown the principle he formerly held

(B) show that John's argument involves a false unstated assumption

(C) contradict John's conclusion without challenging John's reasoning in drawing that conclusion

(D) point out that one of the statements John makes in support of his argument is false

(E) claim that his is a special case in which the rule need not apply

151. Public-sector (government-owned) companies are often unprofitable and a drain on the taxpayer. Such enterprises should be sold to the private sector, where competition will force them either to be efficient and profitable or else to close.

Which of the following, if true, identifies a flaw in the policy proposed above?

(A) The revenue gained from the sale of public-sector companies is likely to be negligible compared to the cost of maintaining them.

(B) By buying a public-sector company and then closing the company and selling its assets, a buyer can often make a profit.

(C) The services provided by many public-sector companies must be made available to citizens, even when a price that covers costs cannot be charged.

(D) Some unprofitable private-sector companies have become profitable after being taken over by the government to prevent their closing.

(E) The costs of environmental protection, contributions to social programs, and job-safety measures are the same in the public and private sectors.

152. After receiving numerous complaints from residents about loud, highly amplified music played at local clubs, Middletown is considering a law that would prohibit clubs located in residential areas from employing musical groups that consist of more than three people.

The likelihood that the law would be effective in reducing noise would be most seriously diminished if which of the following were true?

(A) Groups that consist of more than three musicians are usually more expensive for clubs to hire than are groups that consist of fewer than three musicians.

(B) In towns that have passed similar laws, many clubs in residential areas have relocated to nonresidential areas.

(C) Most of the complaints about the music have come from people who do not regularly attend the clubs.

(D) Much of the music popular at the local clubs can be played only by groups of at least four musicians.

(E) Amplified music played by fewer than three musicians generally is as loud as amplified music played by more than three musicians.

153. The town council of North Tarrytown favored changing the name of the town to Sleepy Hollow. Council members argued that making the town's association with Washington Irving and his famous "legend" more obvious would increase tourism and result immediately in financial benefits for the town's inhabitants.

The council members' argument requires the assumption that

(A) most of the inhabitants would favor a change in the name of the town

(B) many inhabitants would be ready to supply tourists with information about Washington Irving and his "legend"

(C) the town can accomplish, at a very low cost per capita, the improvements in tourist facilities that an increase in tourism would require

(D) other towns in the region have changed their names to reflect historical associations and have, as a result, experienced a rise in tourism

(E) the immediate per capita cost to inhabitants of changing the name of the town would be less than the immediate per capita revenue they would receive from the change

154. Premature babies who receive regular massages are more active than premature babies who do not. Even when all the babies drink the same amount of milk, the massaged babies gain more weight than do the unmassaged babies. This is puzzling because a more active person generally requires a greater food intake to maintain or gain weight.

Which of the following, if true, best reconciles the apparent discrepancy described above?

(A) Increased activity leads to increased levels of hunger, especially when food intake is not also increased.

(B) Massage increases premature babies' curiosity about their environment, and curiosity leads to increased activity.

(C) Increased activity causes the intestines of premature babies to mature more quickly, enabling the babies to digest and absorb more of the nutrients in the milk they drink.

(D) Massage does not increase the growth rate of babies over one year old, if the babies had not been previously massaged.

(E) Premature babies require a daily intake of nutrients that is significantly higher than that required by babies who were not born prematurely.

155. In Australia, in years with below-average rainfall, less water goes into rivers and more water is extracted from rivers for drinking and irrigation. Consequently, in such years, water levels drop considerably and the rivers flow more slowly. Because algae grow better the more slowly the water in which they are growing moves, such years are generally beneficial to populations of algae. But, by contrast, populations of algae drop in periods of extreme drought.

Which of the following, if true, does most to explain the contrast?

(A) Algae grow better in ponds and lakes than in rivers.

(B) The more slowly water moves, the more conducive its temperature is to the growth of algae.

(C) Algae cannot survive in the absence of water.

(D) Algae must be filtered out of water before it can be used for drinking.

(E) The larger the population of algae in a body of water, the less sunlight reaches below the surface of the water.

156. Which of the following, if true, most logically completes the politician's argument?

United States politician: Although the amount of United States goods shipped to Mexico doubled in the year after tariffs on trade between the two countries were reduced, it does not follow that the reduction in tariffs caused the sales of United States goods to companies and consumers in Mexico to double that year, because

_____.

(A) many of the United States companies that produced goods that year had competitors based in Mexico that had long produced the same kind of goods

(B) most of the increase in goods shipped by United States companies to Mexico was in parts shipped to the companies' newly relocated subsidiaries for assembly and subsequent shipment back to the United States

(C) marketing goods to a previously unavailable group of consumers is most successful when advertising specifically targets those consumers, but developing such advertising often takes longer than a year

(D) the amount of Mexican goods shipped to the United States remained the same as it had been before the tariff reductions

(E) there was no significant change in the employment rate in either of the countries that year

157. Budget constraints have made police officials consider reassigning a considerable number of officers from traffic enforcement to work on higher-priority, serious crimes. Reducing traffic enforcement for this reason would be counterproductive, however, in light of the tendency of criminals to use cars when engaged in the commission of serious crimes. An officer stopping a car for a traffic violation can make a search that turns up evidence of serious crime.

Which of the following, if true, most strengthens the argument given?

(A) An officer who stops a car containing evidence of the commission of a serious crime risks a violent confrontation, even if the vehicle was stopped only for a traffic violation.

(B) When the public becomes aware that traffic enforcement has lessened, it typically becomes lax in obeying traffic rules.

(C) Those willing to break the law to commit serious crimes are often in committing such crimes unwilling to observe what they regard as the lesser constraints of traffic law.

(D) The offenders committing serious crimes who would be caught because of traffic violations are not the same group of individuals as those who would be caught if the arresting officers were reassigned from traffic enforcement.

(E) The great majority of persons who are stopped by officers for traffic violations are not guilty of any serious crimes.

158. Conventional wisdom suggests vaccinating elderly people first in flu season, because they are at greatest risk of dying if they contract the virus. This year's flu virus poses particular risk to elderly people and almost none at all to younger people, particularly children. Nevertheless, health professionals are recommending vaccinating children first against the virus rather than elderly people.

Which of the following, if true, provides the strongest reason for the health professionals' recommendation?

(A) Children are vulnerable to dangerous infections when their immune systems are severely weakened by other diseases.

(B) Children are particularly unconcerned with hygiene and therefore are the group most responsible for spreading the flu virus to others.

(C) The vaccinations received last year will confer no immunity to this year's flu virus.

(D) Children who catch one strain of the flu virus and then recover are likely to develop immunity to at least some strains with which they have not yet come in contact.

(E) Children are no more likely than adults to have immunity to a particular flu virus if they have never lived through a previous epidemic of the same virus.

159. Pro-Tect Insurance Company has recently been paying out more on car-theft claims than it expected. Cars with special antitheft devices or alarm systems are much less likely to be stolen than are other cars. Consequently Pro-Tect, as part of an effort to reduce its annual payouts, will offer a discount to holders of car-theft policies if their cars have antitheft devices or alarm systems.

Which of the following, if true, provides the strongest indication that the plan is likely to achieve its goal?

(A) The decrease in the risk of car theft conferred by having a car alarm is greatest when only a few cars have such alarms.

(B) The number of policyholders who have filed a claim in the past year is higher for Pro-Tect than for other insurance companies.

(C) In one or two years, the discount that Pro-Tect is offering will amount to more than the cost of buying certain highly effective antitheft devices.

(D) Currently, Pro-Tect cannot legally raise the premiums it charges for a given amount of insurance against car theft.

(E) The amount Pro-Tect has been paying out on car-theft claims has been greater for some models of car than for others.

160. While the total enrollment of public elementary and secondary schools in Sondland is one percent higher this academic year than last academic year, the number of teachers there increased by three percent. Thus, the Sondland Education Commission's prediction of a teacher shortage as early as next academic year is unfounded.

Which of the following, if true, most seriously weakens the claim that the prediction of a teacher shortage as early as next academic year is unfounded?

(A) Funding for public elementary schools in Sondland is expected to increase over the next ten years.

(B) Average salaries for Sondland's teachers increased at the rate of inflation from last academic year to this academic year.

(C) A new law has mandated that there be ten percent more teachers per pupil in Sondland's public schools next academic year than there were this academic year.

(D) In the past, increases in enrollments in public elementary and secondary schools in Sondland have generally been smaller than increases in the number of teachers.

(E) Because of reductions in funding, the number of students enrolling in teacher-training programs in Sondland is expected to decline beginning in the next academic year.

161. A newly discovered painting seems to be the work of one of two 17th-century artists, either the northern German Johannes Drechen or the Frenchman Louis Birelle, who sometimes painted in the same style as Drechen. Analysis of the carved picture frame, which has been identified as the painting's original 17th-century frame, showed that it is made of wood found widely in northern Germany at the time, but rare in the part of France where Birelle lived. This shows that the painting is most likely the work of Drechen.

Which of the following is an assumption that the argument requires?

(A) The frame was made from wood local to the region where the picture was painted.

(B) Drechen is unlikely to have ever visited the home region of Birelle in France.

(C) Sometimes a painting so closely resembles others of its era that no expert is able to confidently decide who painted it.

(D) The painter of the picture chose the frame for the picture.

(E) The carving style of the picture frame is not typical of any specific region of Europe.

162. Meat from chickens contaminated with salmonella bacteria can cause serious food poisoning. Capsaicin, the chemical that gives chili peppers their hot flavor, has antibacterial properties. Chickens do not have taste receptors for capsaicin and will readily eat feed laced with capsaicin. When chickens were fed such feed and then exposed to salmonella bacteria, relatively few of them became contaminated with salmonella.

In deciding whether the feed would be useful in raising salmonella-free chicken for retail sale, it would be most helpful to determine which of the following?

(A) Whether feeding capsaicin to chickens affects the taste of their meat

(B) Whether eating capsaicin reduces the risk of salmonella poisoning for humans

(C) Whether chicken is more prone to salmonella contamination than other kinds of meat

(D) Whether appropriate cooking of chicken contaminated with salmonella can always prevent food poisoning

(E) Whether capsaicin can be obtained only from chili peppers

163. Which of the following most logically completes the passage?

Leaf beetles damage willow trees by stripping away their leaves, but a combination of parasites and predators generally keeps populations of these beetles in check. Researchers have found that severe air pollution results in reduced predator populations. The parasites, by contrast, are not adversely affected by pollution; nevertheless, the researchers' discovery probably does explain why leaf beetles cause particularly severe damage to willows in areas with severe air pollution, since __________.

(A) neither the predators nor the parasites of leaf beetles themselves attack willow trees

(B) the parasites that attack leaf beetles actually tend to be more prevalent in areas with severe air pollution than they are elsewhere

(C) the damage caused by leaf beetles is usually not enough to kill a willow tree outright

(D) where air pollution is not especially severe, predators have much more impact on leaf-beetle populations than parasites do

(E) willows often grow in areas where air pollution is especially severe

164. On May 1st, in order to reduce the number of overdue books, a children's library instituted a policy of forgiving fines and giving bookmarks to children returning all of their overdue books. On July 1st, there were twice as many overdue books as there had been on May 1st, although a record number of books had been returned during the interim.

Which of the following, if true, most helps to explain the apparent inconsistency in the results of the library's policy?

(A) The librarians did not keep accurate records of how many children took advantage of the grace period, and some of the children returning overdue books did not return all of their overdue books.

(B) Although the grace period enticed some children to return all of their overdue books, it did not convince all of the children with overdue books to return all of their books.

(C) The bookmarks became popular among the children, so in order to collect the bookmarks, many children borrowed many more books than they usually did and kept them past their due date.

(D) The children were allowed to borrow a maximum of five books for a two-week period, and hence each child could keep a maximum of fifteen books beyond their due date within a two-month period.

(E) Although the library forgave overdue fines during the grace period, the amount previously charged the children was minimal; hence, the forgiveness of the fines did not provide enough incentive for them to return their overdue books.

165. A certain species of desert lizard digs tunnels in which to lay its eggs. The eggs must incubate inside the tunnel for several weeks before hatching, and they fail to hatch if they are disturbed at any time during this incubation period. Yet these lizards guard their tunnels for only a few days after laying their eggs.

Which of the following, if true, most helps explain why there is no need for lizards to guard their tunnels for more than a few days?

(A) The eggs are at risk of being disturbed only during the brief egg-laying season when many lizards are digging in a relatively small area.

(B) The length of the incubation period varies somewhat from one tunnel to another.

(C) Each female lizard lays from 15 to 20 eggs, only about 10 of which hatch even if the eggs are not disturbed at any time during the incubation period.

(D) The temperature and humidity within the tunnels will not be suitable for the incubating eggs unless the tunnels are plugged with sand immediately after the eggs are laid.

(E) The only way to disturb the eggs of this lizard species is by opening up one of the tunnels in which they are laid.

166. Most banks that issue credit cards charge interest rates on credit card debt that are ten percentage points higher than the rates those banks charge for ordinary consumer loans. These banks' representatives claim the difference is fully justified, since it simply covers the difference between the costs to these banks associated with credit card debt and those associated with consumer loans.

Which of the following, if true, most seriously calls into question the reasoning offered by the banks' representatives?

(A) Some lenders that are not banks offer consumer loans at interest rates that are even higher than most banks charge on credit card debt.

(B) Most car rental companies require that their customers provide signed credit card charge slips or security deposits.

(C) Two to three percent of the selling price of every item bought with a given credit card goes to the bank that issued that credit card.

(D) Most people need not use credit cards to buy everyday necessities, but could buy those necessities with cash or pay by check.

(E) People who pay their credit card bills in full each month usually pay no interest on the amounts they charge.

167. Often patients with ankle fractures that are stable, and thus do not require surgery, are given follow-up x-rays because their orthopedists are concerned about possibly having misjudged the stability of the fracture. When a number of follow-up x-rays were reviewed, however, all the fractures that had initially been judged stable were found to have healed correctly. Therefore, it is a waste of money to order follow-up x-rays of ankle fractures initially judged stable.

Which of the following, if true, most strengthens the argument?

(A) Doctors who are general practitioners rather than orthopedists are less likely than orthopedists to judge the stability of an ankle fracture correctly.

(B) Many ankle injuries for which an initial x-ray is ordered are revealed by the x-ray not to involve any fracture of the ankle.

(C) X-rays of patients of many different orthopedists working in several hospitals were reviewed.

(D) The healing of ankle fractures that have been surgically repaired is always checked by means of a follow-up x-ray.

(E) Orthopedists routinely order follow-up x-rays for fractures of bones other than ankle bones.

168. In setting environmental standards for industry and others to meet, it is inadvisable to require the best results that state-of-the-art technology can achieve. Current technology is able to detect and eliminate even extremely minute amounts of contaminants, but at a cost that is exorbitant relative to the improvement achieved. So it would be reasonable instead to set standards by taking into account all of the current and future risks involved.

The argument given concerning the reasonable way to set standards presupposes that

(A) industry currently meets the standards that have been set by environmental authorities

(B) there are effective ways to take into account all of the relevant risks posed by allowing different levels of contaminants

(C) the only contaminants worth measuring are generated by industry

(D) it is not costly to prevent large amounts of contaminants from entering the environment

(E) minute amounts of some contaminants can be poisonous

169. The chemical adenosine is released by brain cells when those cells are active. Adenosine then binds to more and more sites on cells in certain areas of the brain, as the total amount released gradually increases during wakefulness. During sleep, the number of sites to which adenosine is bound decreases. Some researchers have hypothesized that it is the cumulative binding of adenosine to a large number of sites that causes the onset of sleep.

Which of the following, if true, provides the most support for the researchers' hypothesis?

(A) Even after long periods of sleep when adenosine is at its lowest concentration in the brain, the number of brain cells bound with adenosine remains very large.

(B) Caffeine, which has the effect of making people remain wakeful, is known to interfere with the binding of adenosine to sites on brain cells.

(C) Besides binding to sites in the brain, adenosine is known to be involved in biochemical reactions throughout the body.

(D) Some areas of the brain that are relatively inactive nonetheless release some adenosine.

(E) Stress resulting from a dangerous situation can preserve wakefulness even when brain levels of bound adenosine are high.

170. A two-year study beginning in 1977 found that, among 85-year-old people, those whose immune systems were weakest were twice as likely to die within two years as others in the study. The cause of their deaths, however, was more often heart disease, against which the immune system does not protect, than cancer or infections, which are attacked by the immune system.

Which of the following, if true, would offer the best prospects for explaining deaths in which weakness of the immune system, though present, played no causal role?

(A) There were twice as many infections among those in the study with the weakest immune systems as among those with the strongest immune systems.

(B) The majority of those in the study with the strongest immune systems died from infection or cancer by 1987.

(C) Some of the drugs that had been used to treat the symptoms of heart disease had a side effect of weakening the immune system.

(D) Most of those in the study who survived beyond the two-year period had recovered from a serious infection sometime prior to 1978.

(E) Those in the study who survived into the 1980s had, in 1976, strengthened their immune systems through drug therapy.

171. Most scholars agree that King Alfred (A.D. 849–899) personally translated a number of Latin texts into Old English. One historian contends that Alfred also personally penned his own law code, arguing that the numerous differences between the language of the law code and Alfred's translations of Latin texts are outweighed by the even more numerous similarities. Linguistic similarities, however, are what one expects in texts from the same language, the same time, and the same region. Apart from Alfred's surviving translations and law code, there are only two other extant works from the same dialect and milieu, so it is risky to assume here that linguistic similarities point to common authorship.

The passage above proceeds by

(A) providing examples that underscore another argument's conclusion

(B) questioning the plausibility of an assumption on which another argument depends

(C) showing that a principle if generally applied would have anomalous consequences

(D) showing that the premises of another argument are mutually inconsistent

(E) using argument by analogy to undermine a principle implicit in another argument

172. Aroca City currently funds its public schools through taxes on property. **In place of this system, the city plans to introduce a sales tax of 3 percent on all retail sales in the city.** Critics protest that 3 percent of current retail sales falls short of the amount raised for schools by property taxes. The critics are correct on this point. **Nevertheless, implementing the plan will probably not reduce the money going to Aroca's schools.** Several large retailers have selected Aroca City as the site for huge new stores, and these are certain to draw large numbers of shoppers from neighboring municipalities, where sales are taxed at rates of 6 percent and more. In consequence, retail sales in Aroca City are bound to increase substantially.

In the argument given, the two portions in **boldface** play which of the following roles?

(A) The first presents a plan that the argument concludes is unlikely to achieve its goal; the second expresses that conclusion.

(B) The first presents a plan that the argument concludes is unlikely to achieve its goal; the second presents evidence in support of that conclusion.

(C) The first presents a plan that the argument contends is the best available; the second is a conclusion drawn by the argument to justify that contention.

(D) The first presents a plan one of whose consequences is at issue in the argument; the second is the argument's conclusion about that consequence.

(E) The first presents a plan that the argument seeks to defend against a certain criticism; the second is that criticism.

173. Which of the following most logically completes the argument?

     A photograph of the night sky was taken with the camera shutter open for an extended period. The normal motion of stars across the sky caused the images of the stars in the photograph to appear as streaks. However, one bright spot was not streaked. Even if the spot were caused, as astronomers believe, by a celestial object, that object could still have been moving across the sky during the time the shutter was open, since ______.

     (A)　the spot was not the brightest object in the photograph

     (B)　the photograph contains many streaks that astronomers can identify as caused by noncelestial objects

     (C)　stars in the night sky do not appear to shift position relative to each other

     (D)　the spot could have been caused by an object that emitted a flash that lasted for only a fraction of the time that the camera shutter was open

     (E)　if the camera shutter had not been open for an extended period, it would have recorded substantially fewer celestial objects

174. Economist: Paying extra for fair-trade coffee—coffee labeled with the Fairtrade logo—is intended to help poor farmers, because they receive a higher price for the fair-trade coffee they grow. But this practice may hurt more farmers in developing nations than it helps. By raising average prices for coffee, it encourages more coffee to be produced than consumers want to buy. This lowers prices for non-fair-trade coffee and thus lowers profits for non-fair-trade coffee farmers.

     To evaluate the strength of the economist's argument, it would be most helpful to know which of the following?

     (A)　Whether there is a way of alleviating the impact of the increased average prices for coffee on non-fair-trade coffee farmers' profits

     (B)　What proportion of coffee farmers in developing nations produce fair-trade coffee

     (C)　Whether many coffee farmers in developing nations also derive income from other kinds of farming

     (D)　Whether consumers should pay extra for fair-trade coffee if doing so lowers profits for non-fair-trade coffee farmers

     (E)　How fair-trade coffee farmers in developing nations could be helped without lowering profits for non-fair-trade coffee farmers

175. Since smoking-related illnesses are a serious health problem in Country X, and since addiction to nicotine prevents many people from quitting smoking, the government of Country X plans to reduce the maximum allowable quantity of nicotine per cigarette by half over the next five years. However, reducing the quantity of nicotine per cigarette will probably cause people addicted to nicotine to smoke more cigarettes. Therefore, implementing this plan is unlikely to reduce the incidence of smoking-related illnesses.

Which of the following, if true, most strongly supports the argument about the consequences of implementing the Country X government's plan?

(A) Over half of the nonsmoking adults in Country X have smoked cigarettes in the past.

(B) If the Country X government's plan is implemented, the brands of cigarettes sold in Country X will differ less from each other than they do now in terms of their nicotine content.

(C) Inexpensive, smoke-free sources of nicotine, such as nicotine gum and nicotine skin patches, have recently become available in Country X.

(D) Many smokers in Country X already spend a large proportion of their disposable income on cigarettes.

(E) The main cause of smoking-related illnesses is not nicotine but the tar in cigarette smoke.

176. In 1983, Argonia's currency, the argon, underwent a reduction in value relative to the world's strongest currencies. This reduction resulted in a significant increase in Argonia's exports over 1982 levels. In 1987, a similar reduction in the value of the argon led to another increase in Argonia's exports. Faced with the need to increase exports yet again, Argonia's finance minister has proposed another reduction in the value of the argon.

Which of the following, if true, most strongly supports the prediction that the finance minister's plan will NOT result in a significant increase in Argonia's exports next year?

(A) The value of the argon rose sharply last year against the world's strongest currencies.

(B) In 1988, the argon lost a small amount of its value, and Argonian exports rose slightly in 1989.

(C) The value of Argonia's exports was lower last year than it was the year before.

(D) All of Argonia's export products are made by factories that were operating at full capacity last year, and new factories would take years to build.

(E) Reductions in the value of the argon have almost always led to significant reductions in the amount of goods and services that Argonians purchase from abroad.

177. Transnational cooperation among corporations is experiencing a modest resurgence among United States firms, even though projects undertaken by two or more corporations under a collaborative agreement are less profitable than projects undertaken by a single corporation. The advantage of transnational cooperation is that such joint international projects may allow United States firms to win foreign contracts that they would not otherwise be able to win.

Which of the following is information provided by the passage?

(A) Transnational cooperation involves projects too big for a single corporation to handle.

(B) Transnational cooperation results in a pooling of resources leading to high-quality performance.

(C) Transnational cooperation has in the past been both more common and less common than it is now among United States firms.

(D) Joint projects between United States and foreign corporations are not profitable enough to be worth undertaking.

(E) Joint projects between United States and foreign corporations benefit only those who commission the projects.

178. Temporary-services firms supply trained workers to other companies on a temporary basis. Temporary-services firms lose business when the economy shows signs of beginning to weaken. They gain business when the economy begins to recover but often lose business again when the economy stabilizes. These firms have begun to gain business in the present weak economy. The economy therefore must be beginning to recover.

Which of the following is an assumption on which the argument depends?

(A) Temporary-services firms are more likely to regain old clients than to acquire new ones when the economy begins to recover.

(B) Temporary-services firms do not gain business when an already weak economy worsens.

(C) New companies do not often hire temporary help until they have been in business for some time.

(D) Companies that use workers from temporary-services firms seldom hire those workers to fill permanent positions.

(E) Temporary-services firms can most easily find qualified new workers when the economy is at its weakest.

179. Wolves generally avoid human settlements. For this reason, domestic sheep, though essentially easy prey for wolves, are not usually attacked by them. In Hylantia prior to 1910, farmers nevertheless lost considerable numbers of sheep to wolves each year. Attributing this to the large number of wolves, in 1910, the government began offering rewards to hunters for killing wolves. From 1910 to 1915, large numbers of wolves were killed. Yet wolf attacks on sheep increased significantly.

Which of the following, if true, most helps to explain the increase in wolf attacks on sheep?

(A) Populations of deer and other wild animals that wolves typically prey on increased significantly in numbers from 1910 to 1915.

(B) Prior to 1910, there were no legal restrictions in Hylantia on the hunting of wolves.

(C) After 1910, hunters shot and wounded a substantial number of wolves, thereby greatly diminishing these wolves' ability to prey on wild animals.

(D) Domestic sheep are significantly less able than most wild animals to defend themselves against wolf attacks.

(E) The systematic hunting of wolves encouraged by the program drove many wolves in Hylantia to migrate to remote mountain areas uninhabited by humans.

180. Paint on a new airliner is usually applied in two stages: first, a coat of primer, and then a top coat. A new process requires no primer, but instead uses two layers of the same newly developed coating, with each layer of the new coating having the same thickness and weight as a traditional top coat. Using the new process instead of the old process increases the price of a new aircraft considerably.

Which of the following, if true, most strongly indicates that it is in an airline's long-term economic interest to purchase new airliners painted using the new process rather than the old process?

(A) Although most new airliners are still painted using the old process, aircraft manufacturers now offer a purchaser of any new airliner the option of having it painted using the new process instead.

(B) A layer of primer on an airliner weighs more than a layer of the new coating would by an amount large enough to make a difference to that airliner's load-bearing capacity.

(C) A single layer of the new coating provides the aluminum skin of the airliner with less protection against corrosion than does a layer of primer of the usual thickness.

(D) Unlike the old process, the new process was originally invented for use on spacecraft, which are subject to extremes of temperature to which airliners are never exposed.

(E) Because the new coating has a viscosity similar to that of a traditional top coat, aircraft manufacturers can apply it using the same equipment as is used for a traditional top coat.

181. Because of steep increases in the average price per box of cereal over the last 10 years, overall sales of cereal have recently begun to drop. In an attempt to improve sales, one major cereal manufacturer reduced the wholesale prices of its cereals by 20 percent. Since most other cereal manufacturers have announced that they will follow suit, it is likely that the level of overall sales of cereal will rise significantly.

Which of the following would it be most useful to establish in evaluating the argument?

(A) Whether the high marketing expenses of the highly competitive cereal market led to the increase in cereal prices

(B) Whether cereal manufacturers use marketing techniques that encourage brand loyalty among consumers

(C) Whether the variety of cereals available on the market has significantly increased over the last 10 years

(D) Whether the prices that supermarkets charge for these cereals will reflect the lower prices the supermarkets will be paying the manufacturers

(E) Whether the sales of certain types of cereal have declined disproportionately over the last 10 years

182. Crowding on Mooreville's subway frequently leads to delays, because it is difficult for passengers to exit from the trains. Over the next ten years, the Mooreville Transit Authority projects that subway ridership will increase by 20 percent. The authority plans to increase the number of daily train trips by only 5 percent over the same period. Officials predict that this increase is sufficient to ensure that the incidence of delays due to crowding does not increase.

Which of the following, if true, provides the strongest grounds for the officials' prediction?

(A) The population of Mooreville is not expected to increase significantly in the next ten years.

(B) The Transit Authority also plans a 5 percent increase in the number of bus trips on routes that connect to subways.

(C) The Transit Authority projects that the number of Mooreville residents who commute to work by automobile will increase in the next ten years.

(D) Most of the projected increase in ridership is expected to occur in off-peak hours when trains now are sparsely used.

(E) The 5 percent increase in the number of train trips can be achieved without an equal increase in Transit Authority operational costs.

183. Though sucking zinc lozenges has been promoted as a treatment for the common cold, research has revealed no consistent effect. Recently, however, a zinc gel applied nasally has been shown to greatly reduce the duration of colds. Since the gel contains zinc in the same form and concentration as the lozenges, the greater effectiveness of the gel must be due to the fact that cold viruses tend to concentrate in the nose, not the mouth.

Which of the following, if true, most seriously weakens the argument?

(A) Experimental subjects who used the zinc gel not only had colds of shorter duration but also had less severe symptoms than did those who used a gel that did not contain zinc.

(B) The mechanism by which zinc affects the viruses that cause the common cold has not been conclusively established.

(C) To make them palatable, zinc lozenges generally contain other ingredients, such as citric acid, that can interfere with the chemical activity of zinc.

(D) No zinc-based cold remedy can have any effect unless it is taken or applied within 48 hours of the initial onset of cold symptoms.

(E) Drug-company researchers experimenting with a nasal spray based on zinc have found that it has much the same effect on colds as the gel does.

184. In each of the past five years, Barraland's prison population has increased. Yet, according to official government statistics, for none of those years has there been either an increase in the number of criminal cases brought to trial or an increase in the rate at which convictions have been obtained. Clearly, therefore, the percentage of people convicted of crimes who are being given prison sentences is on the increase.

Which of the following, if true, most seriously weakens the argument?

(A) In Barraland, the range of punishments that can be imposed instead of a prison sentence is wide.

(B) Over the last ten years, overcrowding in the prisons of Barraland has essentially been eliminated as a result of an ambitious program of prison construction.

(C) Ten years ago, Barraland reformed its criminal justice system, imposing longer minimum sentences for those crimes for which a prison sentence had long been mandatory.

(D) Barraland has been supervising convicts on parole more closely in recent years, with the result that parole violations have become significantly less frequent.

(E) The number of people in Barraland who feel that crime is on the increase is significantly greater now than it was five years ago.

185. TrueSave is a mail-order company that ships electronic products from its warehouses to customers worldwide. The company's shipping manager is proposing that customer orders be packed with newer, more expensive packing materials that virtually eliminate damage during shipping. The manager argues that overall costs would essentially remain unaffected, since the extra cost of the new packing materials roughly equals the current cost of replacing products returned by customers because they arrived in damaged condition.

Which of the following would it be most important to ascertain in determining whether implementing the shipping manager's proposal would have the argued-for effect on costs?

(A) Whether the products shipped by TrueSave are more vulnerable to incurring damage during shipping than are typical electronic products

(B) Whether electronic products are damaged more frequently in transit than are most other products shipped by mail-order companies

(C) Whether a sizable proportion of returned items are returned because of damage already present when those items were packed for shipping

(D) Whether there are cases in which customers blame themselves for product damage that, though present on arrival of the product, is not discovered until later

(E) Whether TrueSave continually monitors the performance of the shipping companies it uses to ship products to its customers

186. Business Consultant: **Some corporations shun the use of executive titles** because they fear that the use of titles indicating position in the corporation tends to inhibit communication up and down the corporate hierarchy. Since an executive who uses a title is treated with more respect by outsiders, however, use of a title can facilitate an executive's dealings with external businesses. Clearly, **corporations should adopt the compromise of encouraging their executives to use their corporate titles externally but not internally,** since even if it is widely known that the corporation's executives use titles outside their organization, this knowledge does not by itself inhibit communication within the corporation.

In the consultant's reasoning, the two portions in **boldface** play which of the following roles?

(A) The first describes a strategy that has been adopted to avoid a certain problem; the second expresses the consultant's assessment of the significance of that problem.

(B) The first describes a strategy that has been adopted to avoid a certain problem; the second is a judgment that the consultant uses to argue that the strategy is ineffective.

(C) The first describes a strategy that has a drawback that the consultant points out; the second presents a strategy that, according to the consultant, would achieve the same end while avoiding that drawback.

(D) The first describes a practice for which the consultant seeks to provide a justification; the second is a consideration offered as part of that justification.

(E) The first describes a policy that the consultant concludes is misguided; the second is introduced to explain why that policy was adopted.

187. For new restaurant managers, a number of organizations offer food-safety certification courses. Although people can manage a restaurant without having taken such a course, the courses are effective in promoting safe food-handling practices. Their effectiveness is demonstrated by the fact that about a third of restaurant managers have taken such a course; only eight percent of restaurants cited for serious health-code violations are managed by someone who has done so.

Which of the following, if true, most strengthens the force of the support offered for the effectiveness of the courses?

(A) It is more difficult to maintain food safety in large restaurants than in small ones.

(B) New restaurant managers who are most likely to take a food-safety course are those who already have several years of experience working in restaurants.

(C) The various food-safety courses that are available differ considerably in both the material they cover and the amount of hands-on training they require.

(D) Most serious health-code violations involve improper food storage rather than poor cooking techniques.

(E) In terms of hours worked per week and number of meals served annually, managers who have taken a food-safety course are no different from those who have not.

188. Ms. Rayner found that her ten-year-old son, Mitchell, often failed to complete his homework even though she responded by giving him brief time-outs. She decided to try calmly explaining to him why completing homework was important instead of using time-outs. After three months of this approach, Mitchell still sometimes failed to complete his homework. Ms. Rayner concluded that explaining the importance of homework to Mitchell was no more effective than using time-outs in reducing his failure to complete homework.

Which of the following, if true by the end of the three months, would most call into question Ms. Rayner's conclusion?

(A) Mitchell was more likely to fail to complete his homework in public settings, such as after-school programs, than he had been before.

(B) Ms. Rayner decided to investigate the effectiveness of systematically rewarding Mitchell whenever he completed his homework, as an alternative to using time-outs or explanations.

(C) Ms. Rayner herself had rarely been given time-outs when she failed to complete assignments as a child.

(D) Mitchell was failing to complete his homework less often than he had been when his mother had used time-outs.

(E) Mitchell reacted negatively after explanations just as often as he had after time-outs.

189. A lack of a particular nutrient in the soil during the earliest stage of plant growth has been identified as the cause of a certain crop defect. In order to help reduce the occurrence of this defect, the government has proposed that this nutrient—normally found in such materials as organic compost and untreated topsoil—be added to commercially sold fertilizer used for a wide range of crops.

Which of the following, if true, most strongly supports the claim that the government's proposal, if implemented, will achieve its goal?

(A) The nutrient is an important component of soil health for many types of plants.

(B) Many farmers begin planting before soil testing can identify nutrient deficiencies in the earliest stages of growth.

(C) Both organic compost and untreated topsoil contain a wide variety of beneficial substances.

(D) Small quantities of the nutrient are already present in some fertilizers that are widely used.

(E) The nutrient plays an important role in the development of plant root systems.

190. Historian: Frobisher, a sixteenth-century English explorer, had soil samples from an island in Canada assessed for gold content. **The assessments found high gold content**, and Elizabeth I consequently funded two mining expeditions, which were both unsuccessful. **Modern analysis of the island's soil indicates much lower gold content** than Frobisher's reports indicated, and some scholars have therefore hypothesized that the methods used to assess the gold content of Frobisher's samples were inaccurate. This conclusion would be reasonable only if one could be sure that neither Frobisher nor anyone else had added gold to the samples before they were assessed.

In the historian's argument, the two **boldfaced** portions play which of the following roles?

(A) The first provides evidence in favor of the historian's position; the second presents evidence that has been used to support an opposing position.

(B) The first provides evidence in favor of a hypothesis that the historian critiques; the second provides evidence against that hypothesis.

(C) The first provides evidence that has been used to support one of two alternative courses of action; the second is a reason given for abandoning that course of action.

(D) The first and the second are both pieces of evidence that the argument characterizes as discredited by the circumstances in which they were obtained.

(E) The first and the second are two pieces of evidence that point to a discrepancy, the explanation of which is the issue that the argument addresses.

191. A particular accounting error frequently occurs in large corporations when financial reports are prepared using a certain spreadsheet template. Although small businesses often use the same type of spreadsheet template, this accounting error is only rarely detected in small businesses. This fact, however, does not indicate that most small businesses are less susceptible to the error, since __________.

   (A) large corporations and small businesses are not the only organizations that use the type of spreadsheet template associated with the error

   (B) the accounting error has been identified in organizations that did not use the spreadsheet template typically associated with the error

   (C) familiarity with spreadsheet software can reduce the likelihood of certain accounting errors

   (D) both large corporations and small businesses typically require more than a year of financial reporting before the error becomes evident, and small businesses, unlike large corporations, often change their accounting systems within the first year

   (E) the spreadsheet template associated with the error generally constitutes a larger proportion of the reporting tools used by small businesses than by large corporations

192. In the past, most children who went sledding in the winter in Verland used wooden sleds with runners and steering bars. Ten years ago, smooth plastic sleds became popular; they go faster than wooden sleds but are harder to steer. The concern that plastic sleds are more dangerous is clearly borne out by the fact that the number of children injured while sledding was much higher last winter than it was ten years ago.

Which of the following, if true in Verland, most seriously undermines the force of the evidence cited?

   (A) A few children still use traditional wooden sleds.

   (B) Most sledding injuries occur when a sled collides with a tree, a rock, or another sled.

   (C) Very few children wear any kind of protective gear, such as helmets, while sledding.

   (D) Because plastic sleds are less expensive than wooden sleds, many more children own a sled now than did ten years ago.

   (E) Because the traditional wooden sleds can carry more than one rider, an accident involving a wooden sled can result in several children being injured.

193. A particular software malfunction has been observed frequently in large enterprise systems but only rarely in personal computers. Both enterprise systems and personal computers often use the type of third-party application identified as the source of the malfunction. Systems affected by the malfunction typically take more than a year of continuous use before the problem becomes apparent; however, personal computers, unlike enterprise systems, are generally replaced or upgraded within their first year of use.

Which of the following is most strongly supported by the information provided?

(A) The malfunction cannot be transmitted to mobile devices by personal computers.

(B) There is no way to determine whether a personal computer is affected by the malfunction before the problem becomes apparent.

(C) A failure to observe the malfunction in personal computer populations is not good evidence that personal computers are resistant to the malfunction.

(D) A system affected by the malfunction but not yet exhibiting problems cannot cause the malfunction in another system using the same application.

(E) The third-party application is probably not the only source of the malfunction.

194. Last year a record number of new manufacturing jobs were created. Will this year bring another record? Well, any new manufacturing job is created either within an existing company or by the start-up of a new company. **Within existing firms, new jobs have been created this year at well below last year's record pace.** At the same time, there is considerable evidence that the number of new companies starting up will be no higher this year than it was last year, and there is no reason to think that **the new companies starting up this year will create more jobs per company than did last year's start-ups.** So clearly, the number of new jobs created this year will fall short of last year's record.

In the argument given, the two portions in **boldface** play which of the following roles?

(A) The first is a claim that the argument challenges; the second presents an explicit assumption that has served as the basis for that claim.

(B) The first is a claim that the argument challenges; the second is a claim that has been advanced in order to challenge the main conclusion of the argument.

(C) The first provides evidence to support the main conclusion of the argument; the second is a judgment advanced in support of that main conclusion.

(D) The first provides evidence to support the main conclusion of the argument; the second presents a possible objection that the argument discounts.

(E) The first is a claim that has been advanced in support of a position that the argument opposes; the second is a possible objection to that claim.

195. Astronomer: **Observations of the Shoemaker–Levi comet on its collision course with Jupiter showed that the comet broke into fragments before entering Jupiter's atmosphere in 1994, but they did not show how big those fragments were.** In hopes of gaining some indication of the fragments' size, astronomers studied spectrographic analyses of Jupiter's outer atmosphere. After the fragments' entry, these analyses revealed unprecedented traces of sulfur. **The fragments themselves almost certainly contained no sulfur**, but many astronomers believe that the cloud layer below Jupiter's outer atmosphere does contain sulfur. Since sulfur would have seeped into the outer atmosphere if comet fragments had penetrated this cloud layer, it is likely that some of the fragments were at least large enough to have passed through Jupiter's outer atmosphere without being burned up.

In the astronomer's argument, the two portions in **boldface** play which of the following roles?

(A) The first is a claim that the astronomer seeks to show is true; the second acknowledges a consideration that weighs against the truth of that claim.

(B) The first is a claim that the astronomer seeks to show is false; the second acknowledges a consideration that weighs in favor of the truth of that claim.

(C) The first reports observations that the astronomer argues have certain implications; the second is one of those implications.

(D) The first introduces the issue that the argument addresses; the second is a judgment advanced in support of the conclusion of the argument.

(E) The first provides evidence in support of the conclusion of the argument; the second acknowledges a consideration that weighs against that conclusion.

196. Historian: In the Drindian Empire, censuses were conducted annually to determine the population of each village. **Village census records for the last half of the 1600s are remarkably complete.** This very completeness makes one point stand out: In five different years, villages overwhelmingly reported significant population declines. Tellingly, each of those five years immediately followed an increase in a certain Drindian tax. **This tax, which was assessed on villages, was computed by the central government using the annual census figures.** Obviously, whenever the tax went up, villages had an especially powerful economic incentive to minimize the number of people they recorded, and concealing the size of a village's population from government census takers would have been easy. Therefore, the reported declines probably did not happen.

In the historian's argument, the two portions in **boldface** play which of the following roles?

(A) The first provides evidence to support the main conclusion of the historian's argument; the second presents that conclusion.

(B) The first is a claim which the historian seeks to evaluate; the second presents evidence in order to call that claim into question.

(C) The first is a consideration that is advanced to counter evidence that weighs against the historian's conclusion; the second provides evidence to support that conclusion.

(D) The first provides a context for certain evidence that supports the position that the historian seeks to establish; the second provides evidence to support the main conclusion of the argument.

(E) The first provides a context for certain evidence that supports the position that the historian seeks to establish; the second is the main conclusion of the argument.

Questions 197 to 253 — Difficulty: **Hard**

197. Twenty-five years ago, 2,000 married people were asked to rank four categories—spouses, friends, jobs, and housework—according to the amount of time each category demanded. A recent follow-up survey indicates that a majority of those same people rank housework higher on the list now than they did twenty-five years ago. Yet most of the respondents also claim that housework has become less demanding of their time over the last twenty-five years.

Which of the following, if true, helps to explain the apparent discrepancy?

(A)   Some of the people surveyed were married to other people in the survey.

(B)   Many of the most time-consuming aspects of people's lives do not appear as categories on either survey.

(C)   Most of those who responded to the follow-up survey have retired in the last twenty-five years.

(D)   At the time of the follow-up survey, some of the people surveyed did no housework.

(E)   Many of the respondents to the follow-up survey claim that they now spend much more time with their friends than they did twenty-five years ago.

198. In Cecropia, inspections of fishing boats that estimate the number of fish they are carrying are typically conducted upon their return to port. The high numbers so obtained have led the government to conclude that the coastal waters are being overfished. To allow commercial fishing stocks to recover, the government is considering introducing annual quotas on the number of fish that each fishing boat can catch. Compliance with the quotas would be determined by the established system of inspections.

Which of the following, if true, raises the most serious doubts about whether the government's proposed plan would succeed?

(A)   Some commercial fishing boats in Cecropia are large enough to catch their entire annual quota in only a few months of fishing.

(B)   The quotas would have to be reduced if more boats began fishing in Cecropia's coastal waters.

(C)   Because fish prices will rise if the quotas go into effect, it is unlikely that the quotas will significantly change the number of boats fishing Cecropia's coastal waters.

(D)   The procedure that inspectors use to estimate the number of fish a boat is carrying often results in a slight overcount.

(E)   Quotas encourage fishers to bring only the most commercially valuable fish into port and to discard less valuable fish, most of them dead or dying.

199. Consultant: **A significant number of complex repair jobs carried out by Ace Repairs have to be redone under the company's warranty, but when those repairs are redone they are invariably successful.** Since we have definitely established that **there is no systematic difference between the mechanics who are assigned to do the initial repairs and those who are assigned to redo unsatisfactory jobs**, it is clear that inadequacies in the initial repairs cannot be attributed to the mechanics' lack of competence. Rather, it is likely that complex repairs require a level of focused attention that the company's mechanics apply consistently only to repair jobs that have been inadequately done on the first try.

In the consultant's reasoning, the two portions in **boldface** play which of the following roles?

(A) The first is a claim that the consultant rejects as false; the second is evidence that forms the basis for that rejection.

(B) The first is part of an explanation that the consultant offers for a certain finding; the second is that finding.

(C) The first presents a pattern whose explanation is at issue in the reasoning; the second provides evidence to rule out one possible explanation of that pattern.

(D) The first presents a pattern whose explanation is at issue in the reasoning; the second is evidence that has been used to challenge the explanation presented by the consultant.

(E) The first is the position the consultant seeks to establish; the second is offered as evidence for that position.

200. A library currently has only coin-operated photocopy machines, which cost 10 cents per copy. Library administrators are planning to refit most of those machines with card readers. The library will sell prepaid copy cards that allow users to make 50 copies at 9 cents per copy. Administrators believe that, despite the convenience of copy cards and their lower per-copy cost, the number of copies made in the library will be essentially unchanged after the refit.

On the assumption that administrators' assessment is correct, which of the following predictions about the effect of the refit is most strongly supported by the information given?

(A) Library patrons will only purchase a copy card on days when they need to make 50 or more copies.

(B) No library patrons will increase their usage of the library's photocopy machines once the refit has been made.

(C) If most of the copy cards sold in the library are used to their full capacity, the number of people using the library's photocopy machines over a given period will fall.

(D) Revenues from photocopying will decrease unless most library patrons choose to use the remaining coin-operated machines in preference to the card-reader equipped ones.

(E) Revenues from photocopying will increase if copy cards that are purchased are, on average, used to significantly less than 90 percent of their capacity.

201. Harvester-ant colonies live for fifteen to twenty years, though individual worker ants live only a year. The way a colony behaves changes steadily in a predictable pattern as the colony grows older and larger. For the first few years, the foragers behave quite aggressively, searching out and vigorously defending new food sources, but once a colony has reached a certain size, its foragers become considerably less aggressive.

If the statements above are true, which of the following can most properly be concluded on the basis of them?

(A) As a result of pressure from neighbors, some colonies do not grow larger as they become older.

(B) Unpredictable changes in a colony's environment can cause changes in the tasks that the colony must perform if it is to continue to survive.

(C) The reason a mature colony goes out of existence is that younger, more aggressive colonies successfully outcompete it for food.

(D) The pattern of changing behavior that a colony displays does not arise from a change in the behavior of any individual worker ant or group of worker ants.

(E) A new colony comes into existence when a group of young, aggressive workers leaves a mature colony and sets up on its own.

202. To improve customer relations, several big retailers have recently launched "smile initiatives," requiring their employees to smile whenever they have contact with customers. These retailers generally have low employee morale, which is why they have to enforce smiling. However, studies show that customers can tell fake smiles from genuine smiles and that fake smiles prompt negative feelings in customers. So the smile initiatives are unlikely to achieve their goal.

The argument relies on which of the following as an assumption?

(A) The smile initiatives have achieved nearly complete success in getting employees to smile while they are around customers.

(B) Customers' feelings about fake smiles are no better than their feelings about the other facial expressions employees with low morale are likely to have.

(C) The feelings that employees generate in retail customers are a principal determinant of the amount of money customers will spend at a retailer.

(D) At the retailers who have launched the smile initiatives, none of the employees gave genuine smiles to customers before the initiatives were launched.

(E) Customers rarely, if ever, have a negative reaction to a genuine smile from a retail employee.

203. Many economists hold that keeping taxes low helps to spur economic growth, and that low taxes thus lead to greater national prosperity. But Country X, which has unusually high taxes, has greater per-capita income than the neighboring Country Y, which has much lower taxes. Some politicians have concluded from this that high taxes do not hinder national prosperity.

The politicians' reasoning is most vulnerable to criticism on which of the following grounds?

(A) It overlooks the possibility that even if Country X reduced its taxes, it would not experience greater national prosperity in the long term.

(B) It confuses a claim that a factor does not hinder a given development with the claim that the same factor promotes that development.

(C) It fails to adequately address the possibility that Country X and Country Y differ in relevant respects other than taxation.

(D) It fails to take into account that the per-capita income of a country does not determine its rate of economic growth.

(E) It assumes that the economists' thesis must be correct despite a clear counterexample to that thesis.

204. Mayor: The financial livelihood of our downtown businesses is in jeopardy. There are few available parking spaces close to the downtown shopping area, so if we are to spur economic growth in our city, we must build a large parking ramp no more than two blocks from downtown.

Which of the following, if true, most seriously weakens the mayor's reasoning?

(A) The city budget is not currently large enough to finance the construction of a new parking ramp.

(B) There are other more significant reasons for the financial woes of downtown businesses in addition to a lack of nearby parking spaces.

(C) Building a parking ramp as much as four blocks from downtown would be sufficient to greatly increase the number of shoppers to downtown businesses.

(D) Explosive growth is most often associated with large suburban shopping malls, not small businesses.

(E) Some additional parking spaces could be added to the downtown area without the construction of a parking ramp.

205. Compact fluorescent light (CFL) bulbs are growing in market share as a replacement for the standard incandescent light bulb. However, an even newer technology is emerging: the light-emitting diode (LED) bulb. Like CFL bulbs, LED bulbs are energy efficient, and they can last around fifty thousand hours, about five times as long as most CFL bulbs. Yet, a single LED bulb costs much more than five CFL bulbs.

The information in the passage above most supports which of the following conclusions?

(A) LED bulbs are most likely to be used in locations where light bulbs would be difficult or costly to replace.

(B) CFL bulbs will need to come down further in price in order to compete with LED bulbs.

(C) LED bulbs are most likely to be used in locations where there is frequent accidental breakage of bulbs.

(D) CFL bulb designs are likely to advance to the point where they can last as long as LED bulbs.

(E) LED bulbs are likely to drop in price, to the point of being competitive with CFL bulbs.

206. Colorless diamonds can command high prices as gemstones. A type of less valuable diamonds can be treated to remove all color. Only sophisticated tests can distinguish such treated diamonds from naturally colorless ones. However, only 2 percent of diamonds mined are of the colored type that can be successfully treated, and many of those are of insufficient quality to make the treatment worthwhile. Surely, therefore, the vast majority of colorless diamonds sold by jewelers are naturally colorless.

A serious flaw in the reasoning of the argument is that

(A) comparisons between the price diamonds command as gemstones and their value for other uses are omitted

(B) information about the rarity of treated diamonds is not combined with information about the rarity of naturally colorless, gemstone diamonds

(C) the possibility that colored diamonds might be used as gemstones, even without having been treated, is ignored

(D) the currently available method for making colorless diamonds from colored ones is treated as though it were the only possible method for doing so

(E) the difficulty that a customer of a jeweler would have in distinguishing a naturally colorless diamond from a treated one is not taken into account

207. The Sumpton town council recently voted to pay a prominent artist to create an abstract sculpture for the town square. Critics of this decision protested that town residents tend to dislike most abstract art, and any art in the town square should reflect their tastes. But a town council spokesperson dismissed this criticism, pointing out that other public abstract sculptures that the same sculptor has installed in other cities have been extremely popular with those cities' local residents.

The statements above most strongly suggest that the main point of disagreement between the critics and the spokesperson is whether

(A) it would have been reasonable to consult town residents on the decision

(B) most Sumpton residents will find the new sculpture to their taste

(C) abstract sculptures by the same sculptor have truly been popular in other cities

(D) a more traditional sculpture in the town square would be popular among local residents

(E) public art that the residents of Sumpton would find desirable would probably be found desirable by the residents of other cities

208. Boreal owls range over a much larger area than do other owls of similar size. The reason for this behavior is probably that the small mammals on which owls feed are especially scarce in the forests where boreal owls live, and the relative scarcity of prey requires the owls to range more extensively to find sufficient food.

Which of the following, if true, most helps to confirm the explanation above?

(A) Some boreal owls range over an area eight times larger than the area over which any other owl of similar size ranges.

(B) Boreal owls range over larger areas in regions where food of the sort eaten by small mammals is sparse than they do in regions where such food is abundant.

(C) After their young hatch, boreal owls must hunt more often than before in order to feed both themselves and their newly hatched young.

(D) Sometimes individual boreal owls hunt near a single location for many weeks at a time and do not range farther than a few hundred yards.

(E) The boreal owl requires less food, relative to its weight, than is required by members of other owl species.

209. Microbiologist: A lethal strain of salmonella recently showed up in a European country, causing an outbreak of illness that killed two people and infected twenty-seven others. Investigators blame the severity of the outbreak on the overuse of antibiotics, since the salmonella bacteria tested were shown to be drug-resistant. But this is unlikely because patients in the country where the outbreak occurred cannot obtain antibiotics to treat illness without a prescription, and the country's doctors prescribe antibiotics less readily than do doctors in any other European country.

Which of the following, if true, would most weaken the microbiologist's reasoning?

(A) Physicians in the country where the outbreak occurred have become hesitant to prescribe antibiotics since they are frequently in short supply.

(B) People in the country where the outbreak occurred often consume foods produced from animals that eat antibiotics-laden livestock feed.

(C) Use of antibiotics in two countries that neighbor the country where the outbreak occurred has risen over the past decade.

(D) Drug-resistant strains of salmonella have not been found in countries in which antibiotics are not generally available.

(E) Salmonella has been shown to spread easily along the distribution chains of certain vegetables, such as raw tomatoes.

210. Historian: Newton developed mathematical concepts and techniques that are fundamental to modern calculus. Leibniz developed closely analogous concepts and techniques. It has traditionally been thought that these discoveries were independent. Researchers have, however, recently discovered notes of Leibniz's that discuss one of Newton's books on mathematics. Several scholars have argued that since **the book includes a presentation of Newton's calculus concepts and techniques**, and since the notes were written before Leibniz's own development of calculus concepts and techniques, it is virtually certain **that the traditional view is false.** A more cautious conclusion than this is called for, however. Leibniz's notes are limited to early sections of Newton's book, sections that precede the ones in which Newton's calculus concepts and techniques are presented.

In the historian's reasoning, the two portions in **boldface** play which of the following roles?

(A) The first is a claim that the historian rejects; the second is a position that that claim has been used to support.

(B) The first is evidence that has been used to support a conclusion about which the historian expresses reservations; the second is that conclusion.

(C) The first provides evidence in support of a position that the historian defends; the second is that position.

(D) The first and the second each provide evidence in support of a position that the historian defends.

(E) The first has been used in support of a position that the historian rejects; the second is a conclusion that the historian draws from that position.

211. Images from ground-based telescopes are invariably distorted by the Earth's atmosphere. Orbiting space telescopes, however, operating above Earth's atmosphere, should provide superbly detailed images. Therefore, ground-based telescopes will soon become obsolete for advanced astronomical research purposes.

Which of the following statements, if true, would cast the most doubt on the conclusion drawn above?

(A) An orbiting space telescope due to be launched this year is far behind schedule and over budget, whereas the largest ground-based telescope was both within budget and on schedule.

(B) Ground-based telescopes located on mountain summits are not subject to the kinds of atmospheric distortion which, at low altitudes, make stars appear to twinkle.

(C) By careful choice of observatory location, it is possible for large-aperture telescopes to avoid most of the kind of wind turbulence that can distort image quality.

(D) When large-aperture telescopes are located at high altitudes near the equator, they permit the best Earth-based observations of the center of the Milky Way Galaxy, a prime target of astronomical research.

(E) Detailed spectral analyses, upon which astronomers rely for determining the chemical composition and evolutionary history of stars, require telescopes with more light-gathering capacity than space telescopes can provide.

212. Generally scientists enter their field with the goal of doing important new research and accept as their colleagues those with similar motivation. Therefore, when any scientist wins renown as an expounder of science to general audiences, most other scientists conclude that this popularizer should no longer be regarded as a true colleague.

The explanation offered above for the low esteem in which scientific popularizers are held by research scientists assumes that

(A) serious scientific research is not a solitary activity, but relies on active cooperation among a group of colleagues

(B) research scientists tend not to regard as colleagues those scientists whose renown they envy

(C) a scientist can become a famous popularizer without having completed any important research

(D) research scientists believe that those who are well known as popularizers of science are not motivated to do important new research

(E) no important new research can be accessible to or accurately assessed by those who are not themselves scientists

213. Urban planner: When a city loses population due to migration, property taxes in that city tend to rise. This is because there are then fewer residents paying to maintain an infrastructure that was designed to support more people. Rising property taxes, in turn, drive more residents away, compounding the problem. Since the city of Stonebridge is starting to lose population, the city government should therefore refrain from raising property taxes.

Which of the following, if true, would most weaken the urban planner's argument?

(A) If Stonebridge does not raise taxes on its residents to maintain its infrastructure, the city will become much less attractive to live in as that infrastructure decays.

(B) Stonebridge at present benefits from grants provided by the national government to help maintain certain parts of its infrastructure.

(C) If there is a small increase in property taxes in Stonebridge and a slightly larger proportion of total revenue than at present is allocated to infrastructure maintenance, the funding will be adequate for that purpose.

(D) Demographers project that the population of a region that includes Stonebridge will start to increase substantially within the next several years.

(E) The property taxes in Stonebridge are significantly lower than those in many larger cities.

214. Which of the following most logically completes the argument?

Utrania was formerly a major petroleum exporter, but in recent decades economic stagnation and restrictive regulations inhibited investment in new oil fields. In consequence, Utranian oil exports dropped steadily as old fields became depleted. Utraria's currently improving economic situation, together with less-restrictive regulations, will undoubtedly result in the rapid development of new fields. However, it would be premature to conclude that the rapid development of new fields will result in higher oil exports, because
__________.

- (A) the price of oil is expected to remain relatively stable over the next several years
- (B) the improvement in the economic situation in Utrania is expected to result in a dramatic increase in the proportion of Utranians who own automobiles
- (C) most of the investment in new oil fields in Utrania is expected to come from foreign sources
- (D) new technology is available to recover oil from old oil fields formerly regarded as depleted
- (E) many of the new oil fields in Utrania are likely to be as productive as those that were developed during the period when Utrania was a major oil exporter

215. The use of growth-promoting antibiotics in hog farming can weaken their effectiveness in treating humans because such use can spread resistance to those antibiotics among microorganisms. But now the Smee Company, one of the largest pork marketers, may stop buying pork raised on feed containing these antibiotics. Smee has 60 percent of the pork market, and farmers who sell to Smee would certainly stop using antibiotics in order to avoid jeopardizing their sales. So if Smee makes this change, it will probably significantly slow the decline in antibiotics' effectiveness for humans.

Which of the following, if true, would most strengthen the argument above?

- (A) Other major pork marketers will probably stop buying pork raised on feed containing growth-promoting antibiotics if Smee no longer buys such pork.
- (B) The decline in hog growth due to discontinuation of antibiotics can be offset by improved hygiene.
- (C) Authorities are promoting the use of antibiotics to which microorganisms have not yet developed resistance.
- (D) A phaseout of use of antibiotics for hogs in one country reduced usage by over 50 percent over five years.
- (E) If Smee stops buying pork raised with antibiotics, the firm's costs will probably increase.

216. In order to reduce dependence on imported oil, the government of Jalica has imposed minimum fuel-efficiency requirements on all new cars, beginning this year. The more fuel-efficient a car, the less pollution it produces per mile driven. As Jalicans replace their old cars with cars that meet the new requirements, annual pollution from car traffic is likely to decrease in Jalica.

Which of the following, if true, most seriously weakens the argument?

(A) In Jalica, domestically produced oil is more expensive than imported oil.

(B) The Jalican government did not intend the new fuel-efficiency requirement to be a pollution-reduction measure.

(C) Some pollution-control devices mandated in Jalica make cars less fuel-efficient than they would be without those devices.

(D) The new regulation requires no change in the chemical formulation of fuel for cars in Jalica.

(E) Jalicans who get cars that are more fuel-efficient tend to do more driving than before.

217. Plantings of cotton bioengineered to produce its own insecticide against bollworms, a major cause of crop failure, sustained little bollworm damage until this year. This year the plantings are being seriously damaged by bollworms. Bollworms, however, are not necessarily developing resistance to the cotton's insecticide. Bollworms breed on corn, and last year more corn than usual was planted throughout cotton-growing regions. So it is likely that the cotton is simply being overwhelmed by corn-bred bollworms.

In evaluating the argument, which of the following would it be most useful to establish?

(A) Whether corn could be bioengineered to produce the insecticide

(B) Whether plantings of cotton that does not produce the insecticide are suffering unusually extensive damage from bollworms this year

(C) Whether other crops that have been bioengineered to produce their own insecticide successfully resist the pests against which the insecticide was to protect them

(D) Whether plantings of bioengineered cotton are frequently damaged by insect pests other than bollworms

(E) Whether there are insecticides that can be used against bollworms that have developed resistance to the insecticide produced by the bioengineered cotton

218. Typically during thunderstorms most lightning strikes carry a negative electric charge; only a few carry a positive charge. Thunderstorms with unusually high proportions of positive-charge strikes tend to occur in smoky areas near forest fires. The fact that smoke carries positively charged smoke particles into the air above a fire suggests the hypothesis that the extra positive strikes occur because of the presence of such particles in the storm clouds.

Which of the following, if discovered to be true, most seriously undermines the hypothesis?

(A) Other kinds of rare lightning also occur with unusually high frequency in the vicinity of forest fires.

(B) The positive-charge strikes that occur near forest fires tend to be no more powerful than positive strikes normally are.

(C) A positive-charge strike is as likely to start a forest fire as a negative-charge strike is.

(D) Thunderstorms that occur in drifting clouds of smoke have extra positive-charge strikes weeks after the charge of the smoke particles has dissipated.

(E) The total number of lightning strikes during a thunderstorm is usually within the normal range in the vicinity of a forest fire.

219. Since 1990 the percentage of bacterial sinus infections in Aqadestan that are resistant to the antibiotic perxicillin has increased substantially. Bacteria can quickly develop resistance to an antibiotic when it is prescribed indiscriminately or when patients fail to take it as prescribed. Since perxicillin has not been indiscriminately prescribed, health officials hypothesize that the increase in perxicillin-resistant sinus infections is largely due to patients' failure to take this medication as prescribed.

Which of the following, if true of Aqadestan, provides most support for the health officials' hypothesis?

(A) Resistance to several other commonly prescribed antibiotics has not increased since 1990 in Aqadestan.

(B) A large number of Aqadestanis never seek medical help when they have a sinus infection.

(C) When it first became available, perxicillin was much more effective in treating bacterial sinus infections than any other antibiotic used for such infections at the time.

(D) Many patients who take perxicillin experience severe side effects within the first few days of their prescribed regimen.

(E) Aqadestani health clinics provide antibiotics to their patients at cost.

220. Psychologist: In a study, researchers gave 100 volunteers a psychological questionnaire designed to measure their self-esteem. The researchers then asked each volunteer to rate the strength of his or her own social skills. The volunteers with the highest levels of self-esteem consistently rated themselves as having much better social skills than did the volunteers with moderate levels. This suggests that attaining an exceptionally high level of self-esteem greatly improves one's social skills.

The psychologist's argument is most vulnerable to criticism on which of the following grounds?

(A)   It fails to adequately address the possibility that many of the volunteers may not have understood what the psychological questionnaire was designed to measure.

(B)   It takes for granted that the volunteers with the highest levels of self-esteem had better social skills than did the other volunteers, even before the former volunteers had attained their high levels of self-esteem.

(C)   It overlooks the possibility that people with very high levels of self-esteem may tend to have a less accurate perception of the strength of their own social skills than do people with moderate levels of self-esteem.

(D)   It relies on evidence from a group of volunteers that is too small to provide any support for any inferences regarding people in general.

(E)   It overlooks the possibility that factors other than level of self-esteem may be of much greater importance in determining the strength of one's social skills.

221. Political advertisement: Mayor Delmont's critics complain about the jobs that were lost in the city under Delmont's leadership. Yet the fact is that not only were more jobs created than were eliminated, but each year since Delmont took office the average pay for the new jobs created has been higher than that year's average pay for jobs citywide. So it stands to reason that throughout Delmont's tenure the average paycheck in this city has been getting steadily bigger.

Which of the following, if true, most seriously weakens the argument in the advertisement?

(A)   The unemployment rate in the city is higher today than it was when Mayor Delmont took office.

(B)   The average pay for jobs in the city was at a ten-year low when Mayor Delmont took office.

(C)   Each year during Mayor Delmont's tenure, the average pay for jobs that were eliminated has been higher than the average pay for jobs citywide.

(D)   Most of the jobs eliminated during Mayor Delmont's tenure were in declining industries.

(E)   The average pay for jobs in the city is currently lower than it is for jobs in the suburbs surrounding the city.

222. To prevent a newly built dam on the Chiff River from blocking the route of fish migrating to breeding grounds upstream, the dam includes a fish pass, a mechanism designed to allow fish through the dam. Before the construction of the dam and fish pass, several thousand fish a day swam upriver during spawning season. But in the first season after the project's completion, only 300 per day made the journey. Clearly, the fish pass is defective.

Which of the following, if true, most seriously weakens the argument?

(A) Fish that have migrated to the upstream breeding grounds do not return down the Chiff River again.

(B) On other rivers in the region, the construction of dams with fish passes has led to only small decreases in the number of fish migrating upstream.

(C) The construction of the dam stirred up potentially toxic river sediments that were carried downstream.

(D) Populations of migratory fish in the Chiff River have been declining slightly over the last 20 years.

(E) During spawning season, the dam releases sufficient water for migratory fish below the dam to swim upstream.

223. People with a college degree are more likely than others to search for a new job while they are employed. There are proportionately more people with college degrees among managers and other professionals than among service and clerical workers. Surprisingly, however, 2009 figures indicate that people employed as managers and other professionals were no more likely than people employed as service and clerical workers to have searched for a new job.

Which of the following, if true, most helps to resolve the apparent paradox?

(A) People generally do not take a new job that is offered to them while they are employed unless the new job pays better.

(B) Some service and clerical jobs pay more than some managerial and professional jobs.

(C) People who felt they were overqualified for their current positions were more likely than others to search for a new job.

(D) The percentage of employed people who were engaged in job searches declined from 2005 to 2009.

(E) In 2009 employees with no college degree who retired were more likely to be replaced by people with a college degree if they retired from a managerial or professional job than from a service or clerical job.

224. To reduce traffic congestion, City X's transportation bureau plans to encourage people who work downtown to sign a form pledging to carpool or use public transportation for the next year. Everyone who signs the form will get a coupon for a free meal at any downtown restaurant.

For the transportation bureau's plan to succeed in reducing traffic congestion, which of the following must be true?

(A) Everyone who signs the pledge form will fully abide by the pledge for the next year.

(B) At least some people who work downtown prefer the restaurants downtown to those elsewhere.

(C) Most downtown traffic congestion in City X results from people who work downtown.

(D) The most effective way to reduce traffic congestion downtown would be to persuade more people who work there to carpool or use public transportation.

(E) At least some people who receive the coupon for a free meal will sometimes carpool or use public transportation during the next year.

225. When new laws imposing strict penalties for misleading corporate disclosures were passed, they were hailed as initiating an era of corporate openness. As an additional benefit, given the increased amount and accuracy of information disclosed under the new laws, it was assumed that analysts' predictions of corporate performance would become more accurate. Since the passage of the laws, however, the number of inaccurate analysts' predictions has not in fact decreased.

Which of the following would, if true, best explain the discrepancy outlined above?

(A) The new laws' definition of "misleading information" can be interpreted in more than one way.

(B) The new laws require corporations in all industries to release information at specific times of the year.

(C) Even before the new laws were passed, the information most corporations released was true.

(D) Analysts base their predictions on information they gather from many sources, not just corporate disclosures.

(E) The more pieces of information corporations release, the more difficult it becomes for anyone to organize them in a manageable way.

226. Economist: Even with energy conservation efforts, current technologies cannot support both a reduction in carbon dioxide emissions and an expanding global economy. Attempts to restrain emissions without new technology will stifle economic growth. Therefore, increases in governmental spending on research into energy technology will be necessary if we wish to reduce carbon dioxide emissions without stifling economic growth.

Which of the following is an assumption the economist's argument requires?

(A) If research into energy technology does not lead to a reduction in carbon dioxide emissions, then economic growth will be stifled.

(B) Increased governmental spending on research into energy technology will be more likely to reduce carbon dioxide emissions without stifling growth than will nongovernmental spending.

(C) An expanding global economy may require at least some governmental spending on research into energy technology.

(D) Attempts to restrain carbon dioxide emissions without new technology could ultimately cost more than the failure to reduce those emissions would cost.

(E) Restraining carbon dioxide emissions without stifling economic growth would require both new energy technology and energy conservation efforts.

227. Researchers have developed a technology that uses sound as a means of converting heat into electrical energy. Converters based on this technology can be manufactured small enough to be integrated into consumer electronics, where they will absorb significant quantities of heat. A group of engineers is now designing converters to be sold to laptop computer manufacturers, who are expected to use the electrical output of the converters to conserve battery power in their computers.

Which of the following would, if true, provide the strongest evidence that the engineers' plan will be commercially successful for their group?

(A) The sound that is used by the converters is generated by the converters themselves.

(B) Most laptop computer manufacturers today receive fewer complaints than in previous years regarding shortness of operating time on a single battery charge.

(C) The overheating of microprocessors in laptop computers presents a major technological challenge that manufacturers are prepared to meet at significant expense.

(D) Although battery technology has improved significantly, the average capacity of laptop computer batteries has not.

(E) Electrical power generated by the converters can be used to power the fans installed to cool computers' components.

228. According to a widely held economic hypothesis, imposing strict environmental regulations reduces economic growth. This hypothesis is undermined by the fact that the states with the strictest environmental regulations also have the highest economic growth. This fact does not show that environmental regulations promote growth, however, since ___________.

Which of the following, if true, provides evidence that most logically completes the argument above?

(A) those states with the strictest environmental regulations invest the most in education and job training

(B) even those states that have only moderately strict environmental regulations have higher growth than those with the least-strict regulations

(C) many states that are experiencing reduced economic growth are considering weakening their environmental regulations

(D) after introducing stricter environmental regulations, many states experienced increased economic growth

(E) even those states with very weak environmental regulations have experienced at least some growth

229. The prairie vole, a small North American grassland rodent, breeds year-round, and a group of voles living together consists primarily of an extended family, often including two or more litters. Voles commonly live in large groups from late autumn through winter; from spring through early autumn, however, most voles live in far smaller groups. The seasonal variation in group size can probably be explained by a seasonal variation in mortality among young voles.

Which of the following, if true, provides the strongest support for the explanation offered?

(A) It is in the spring and early summer that prairie vole communities generally contain the highest proportion of young voles.

(B) Prairie vole populations vary dramatically in size from year to year.

(C) The prairie vole subsists primarily on broad-leaved plants that are abundant only in spring.

(D) Winters in the prairie voles' habitat are often harsh, with temperatures that drop well below freezing.

(E) Snakes, a major predator of young prairie voles, are active only from spring through early autumn.

230. From 1980 to 1989, total consumption of fish in the country of Jurania increased by 4.5 percent, and total consumption of poultry products there increased by 9.0 percent. During the same period, the population of Jurania increased by 6 percent, in part due to immigration to Jurania from other countries in the region.

If the statements above are true, which of the following must also be true on the basis of them?

(A) During the 1980s in Jurania, profits of wholesale distributors of poultry products increased at a greater rate than did profits of wholesale distributors of fish.

(B) For people who immigrated to Jurania during the 1980s, fish was less likely to be a major part of their diet than was poultry.

(C) In 1989, Juranians consumed twice as much poultry as fish.

(D) For a significant proportion of Jurania's population, both fish and poultry products were a regular part of their diet during the 1980s.

(E) Per capita consumption of fish in Jurania was lower in 1989 than in 1980.

231. Junior biomedical researchers have long assumed that their hirings and promotions depend significantly on the amount of their published work. People responsible for making hiring and promotion decisions in the biomedical research field, however, are influenced much more by the overall impact that a candidate's scientific publications have on his or her field than by the number of those publications.

The information above, if accurate, argues most strongly AGAINST which of the following claims?

(A) Even biomedical researchers who are just beginning their careers are expected to already have published articles of major significance to the field.

(B) Contributions to the field of biomedical research are generally considered to be significant only if the work is published.

(C) The potential scientific importance of not-yet-published work is sometimes taken into account in decisions regarding the hiring or promotion of biomedical researchers.

(D) People responsible for hiring or promoting biomedical researchers can reasonably be expected to make a fair assessment of the overall impact of a candidate's publications on his or her field.

(E) Biomedical researchers can substantially increase their chances of promotion by fragmenting their research findings so that they are published in several journals instead of one.

232. Rabbits were introduced to Tambor Island in the nineteenth century. Overgrazing by the enormous rabbit population now menaces the island's agriculture. The government proposes to reduce the population by using a virus that has caused devastating epidemics in rabbit populations elsewhere. There is, however, a small chance that the virus will infect the bilby, an endangered native herbivore. The government's plan, therefore, may serve the interests of agriculture but will clearly increase the threat to native wildlife.

The argument above assumes which of the following?

(A) There is less chance that the virus will infect domestic animals on Tambor than that it will infect wild animals of species native to the island.

(B) Overgrazing by rabbits does not pose the most significant current threat to the bilby.

(C) There is at least one alternative means of reducing the rabbit population that would not involve any threat to the bilby.

(D) There are no species of animals on the island that prey on the rabbits.

(E) The virus that the government proposes to use has been successfully used elsewhere to control populations of rabbits.

233. Which of the following provides the most logical completion of the argument?

Many of Vebrol Corporation's department heads will retire this year. The number of junior employees with the qualifications Vebrol will require for promotion to department head is equal to only half the expected vacancies. Vebrol is not going to hire department heads from outside the company, have current department heads take over more than one department, or reduce the number of its departments. So some departments will be without department heads next year, since Vebrol will not __________.

(A) promote more than one employee from any department to serve as heads of departments

(B) promote any current department heads to higher-level managerial positions

(C) have any managers who are currently senior to department heads serve as department heads

(D) reduce the responsibilities of each department

(E) reduce the average number of employees per department

234. Ecologist: The Scottish Highlands were once the site of extensive forests, but these forests have mostly disappeared and been replaced by peat bogs. The common view is that the Highlands' deforestation was caused by human activity, especially agriculture. However, **agriculture began in the Highlands less than 2,000 years ago.** Peat bogs, which consist of compressed decayed vegetable matter, build up by only about one foot per 1,000 years and, **throughout the Highlands, remains of trees in peat bogs are almost all at depths greater than four feet.** Since climate changes that occurred between 7,000 and 4,000 years ago favored the development of peat bogs rather than the survival of forests, the deforestation was more likely the result of natural processes than of human activity.

In the ecologist's argument, the two portions in **boldface** play which of the following roles?

(A) The first is evidence that has been used in support of a position that the ecologist rejects; the second is a finding that the ecologist uses to counter that evidence.

(B) The first is evidence that, in light of the evidence provided in the second, serves as grounds for the ecologist's rejection of a certain position.

(C) The first is a position that the ecologist rejects; the second is evidence that has been used in support of that position.

(D) The first is a position that the ecologist rejects; the second provides evidence in support of that rejection.

(E) The first is a position for which the ecologist argues; the second provides evidence to support that position.

235. Beets and carrots are higher in sugar than many other vegetables. They are also high on the glycemic index, a scale that measures the rate at which a food increases blood sugar levels. But while nutritionists usually advise people to avoid high-sugar and high-glycemic-index foods, despite any nutritional benefits they may confer, they are not very concerned about the consumption of beets and carrots.

Which of the following, if true, would best explain the nutritionists' lack of concern?

(A) Foods with added sugar are much higher in sugar, and have a larger effect on blood sugar levels, than do beets and carrots.

(B) Most consumption of beets and carrots occurs in combination with higher-protein foods, which reduce blood sugar fluctuations.

(C) Beets and carrots contain many nutrients, such as folate, beta-carotene, and vitamin C, of which many people fail to consume optimal quantities.

(D) The glycemic index measures the extent to which a food increases blood sugar levels as compared to white bread, a food that is much less healthy than beets and carrots.

(E) Nutritionists have only recently come to understand that a food's effect on blood sugar levels is an important determinant of that food's impact on a person's health.

236. Biologist: Species with broad geographic ranges probably tend to endure longer than species with narrow ranges. The broader a species' range, the more likely that species is to survive the extinction of populations in a few areas. Therefore, it is likely that the proportion of species with broad ranges tends to gradually increase with time.

The biologist's conclusion follows logically from the above if which of the following is assumed?

(A)   There are now more species with broad geographic ranges than with narrow geographic ranges.

(B)   Most species can survive extinctions of populations in a few areas as long as the species' geographic range is not very narrow.

(C)   If a population of a species in a particular area dies out, that species generally does not repopulate that area.

(D)   If a characteristic tends to help species endure longer, then the proportion of species with that characteristic tends to gradually increase with time.

(E)   Any characteristic that makes a species tend to endure longer will make it easier for that species to survive the extinction of populations in a few areas.

237. In a certain rural area, people normally dispose of household garbage by burning it. Burning household garbage releases toxic chemicals known as dioxins. New conservation regulations will require a major reduction in packaging—specifically, paper and cardboard packaging—for products sold in the area. Since such packaging materials contain dioxins, one result of the implementation of the new regulations will surely be a reduction in dioxin pollution in the area.

Which of the following, if true, most seriously weakens the argument?

(A)   Garbage containing large quantities of paper and cardboard can easily burn hot enough for some portion of the dioxins that it contains to be destroyed.

(B)   Packaging materials typically make up only a small proportion of the weight of household garbage, but a relatively large proportion of its volume.

(C)   Per-capita sales of products sold in paper and cardboard packaging are lower in rural areas than in urban areas.

(D)   The new conservation regulations were motivated by a need to cut down on the consumption of paper products in order to bring the harvesting of timber into a healthier balance with its regrowth.

(E)   It is not known whether the dioxins released by the burning of household garbage have been the cause of any serious health problems.

238. For individuals newly hired as data analysts, a number of organizations offer formal data-analysis training programs. Although individuals can work as data analysts without having completed such a program, the programs are purportedly effective in teaching sound data-analysis practices. Evidence for their effectiveness is provided by the following data: Whereas approximately one-third of employed data analysts have completed such a program, only eight percent of analysts whose work resulted in serious reporting errors have done so.

Which of the following, if true, most seriously weakens the conclusion drawn from the data above?

(A) Employers generally offer higher salaries to data analysts who have completed a formal data-analysis training program.

(B) Newly hired data analysts who are most likely to complete a training program are those who already have several years of experience working with data in related roles.

(C) Although formal data-analysis training programs are offered by a number of different organizations, they are generally similar in both content and instructional approach.

(D) Most serious reporting errors result from faulty data supplied to analysts rather than from mistakes made by the analysts themselves.

(E) In terms of workload and average number of reports produced annually, data analysts who have completed a training program do not differ from those who have not.

239. Some farmers have recently begun planting cotton grown from genetically modified seed designed to increase resistance to insect pests. Compared with farmers using ordinary seed, those using the modified seed required only slightly less insecticide per acre to control pests. The modified seed, however, costs more per acre than ordinary seed. On the basis of these facts, some analysts conclude that switching to the modified seed would be unlikely to benefit most cotton farmers economically.

Which of the following, if true, would most seriously weaken the analysts' conclusion?

(A) Many of the farmers who tried the modified seed had previously grown other crops using genetically modified seed.

(B) The insecticides typically used on ordinary cotton are substantially more expensive per unit than those typically used on other crops.

(C) For most cotton farmers, cotton accounts for the largest share of their total farm revenue.

(D) Farmers who tried the modified seed planted approximately the same average acreage of cotton as farmers who used ordinary seed.

(E) Farmers who tried the modified seed had previously spent significantly more per acre on insecticides than most farmers using ordinary seed.

240. Which of the following most logically completes the argument?

Ten years ago, the country of Benovia adopted new workplace safety regulations requiring protective equipment, improved training procedures, and upgraded machinery safeguards for all new manufacturing facilities. In the last few years, the annual number of factory workers hospitalized overnight or longer for injuries sustained on the job has been significantly lower than it was before the regulations went into effect. This evidence does not show that the regulations have made manufacturing work safer, however, since __________.

(A) over the last ten years, production quotas have increased at many of Benovia's largest manufacturing plants

(B) of the patients treated at hospitals in Benovia, the percentage being treated for workplace injuries has not decreased in the last few years

(C) five years ago, hospitals in Benovia adopted stricter criteria for determining when a patient needs to stay overnight

(D) most manufacturing facilities currently operating in Benovia were built or upgraded within the past ten years

(E) the proportion of factory workers who regularly bypass safety procedures has changed very little since the new regulations were adopted

241. People's television-viewing habits could be monitored by having television sets, when on, send out low-level electromagnetic waves that are reflected back to the television sets. The reflected waves could then be analyzed to determine how many people are within the viewing area of the television sets. Critics fear adverse health effects of such a monitoring system, but a proponent responds, "The average dose of radiation is less than one chest x-ray. As they watch, viewers won't feel a thing."

Which of the following, if true, is the most direct criticism of the proponent's response?

(A) The system cannot determine whether persons in the viewing area are paying attention to what is being broadcast.

(B) It is possible to gather reasonably useful data on who is watching programs by having selected families keep diaries of television watching.

(C) Some of those who would watch television sets with the monitoring device on are already ill with conditions that keep them at home.

(D) Even recipients of large, harmful doses of radiation do not sense the radiation as it strikes the body.

(E) Because it would invade privacy, acceptance of the monitoring device would have to be voluntary on the part of viewing families, and that restriction would skew the results.

242. Smithtown University's fundraisers succeeded in getting donations from 80 percent of the potential donors they contacted. This success rate, exceptionally high for university fundraisers, does not indicate that they were doing a good job. On the contrary, since the people most likely to donate are those who have donated in the past, good fundraisers constantly try less-likely prospects in an effort to expand the donor base. The high success rate shows insufficient canvassing effort.

Which of the following, if true, provides the most support for the argument?

(A) Smithtown University's fundraisers were successful in their contacts with potential donors who had never given before about as frequently as were fundraisers for other universities in their contacts with such people.

(B) This year the average size of the donations to Smithtown University from new donors whom the university's fundraisers had contacted was larger than the average size of donations from donors who had given to the university before.

(C) This year most of the donations that came to Smithtown University from people who had previously donated to it were made without the university's fundraisers having made any contact with the donors.

(D) The majority of the donations that fundraisers succeeded in getting for Smithtown University this year were from donors who had never given to the university before.

(E) More than half of the money raised by Smithtown University's fundraisers came from donors who had never previously donated to the university.

243. Scientists typically do their most creative work before the age of forty. It is commonly thought that this happens because **aging by itself brings about a loss of creative capacity.** However, studies show that **a disproportionately large number of the scientists who produce highly creative work beyond the age of forty entered their field at an older age than is usual.** Since by the age of forty the large majority of scientists have been working in their field for at least fifteen years, the studies' finding strongly suggests that the real reason why scientists over forty rarely produce highly creative work is not that they have simply aged but rather that they generally have spent too long in a given field.

In the argument given, the two portions in **boldface** play which of the following roles?

(A) The first is the position that the argument as a whole opposes; the second is an objection that has been raised against a position defended in the argument.

(B) The first is a claim that has been advanced in support of a position that the argument opposes; the second is a finding that has been used in support of that position.

(C) The first is an explanation that the argument challenges; the second is a finding that has been used in support of that explanation.

(D) The first is an explanation that the argument challenges; the second is a finding on which that challenge is based.

(E) The first is an explanation that the argument defends; the second is a finding that has been used to challenge that explanation.

244. Insect infestations in certain cotton-growing regions of the world have caused dramatic increases in the price of cotton on the world market. By contrast, the price of soybeans has long remained stable. Knowing that cotton plants mature quickly, many soybean growers in Ortovia plan to cease growing soybeans and begin raising cotton instead, thereby taking advantage of the high price of cotton to increase their income significantly, at least over the next several years.

Which of the following, if true, most seriously weakens the plan's chances for success?

(A) The cost of raising soybeans has increased significantly over the past several years and is expected to continue to climb.

(B) Tests of a newly developed, inexpensive pesticide have shown it to be both environmentally safe and effective against the insects that have infested cotton crops.

(C) In the past several years, there has been no sharp increase in the demand for cotton and for goods made out of cotton.

(D) Few consumers would be willing to pay significantly higher prices for cotton goods than they are now paying.

(E) The species of insect that has infested cotton plants has never been known to attack soybean plants.

245. A particular logistics routing protocol used in large distribution networks often leads to shipment delays because packages that normally remain within local sorting hubs tend to be redirected into long-distance transit routes, eventually congesting regional distribution centers. When a routing override system, which counteracts certain effects of the protocol, is implemented along with the protocol, shipment delays occur far less frequently. Therefore, the routing override system probably disables the mechanism by which the protocol causes packages to be redirected into long-distance transit routes.

Which of the following is an assumption on which the argument depends?

(A) The routing override system does not directly remove packages once they have entered long-distance transit routes.

(B) Factors other than the redirection of packages into long-distance transit routes can cause shipment delays.

(C) The routing override system does not reduce overall delivery efficiency.

(D) For logistics networks, increased shipment delays are the most harmful effect of using the routing protocol.

(E) Distribution networks in which the routing override system but not the routing protocol is used are no more likely to experience shipment delays than networks in which neither system is used.

246. A manufacturer of specialized computer workstations formerly made nearly all of its sales to corporate customers at prices well below the list price. Because surveys showed that other potential customers were being deterred by its relatively high list prices, the manufacturer, in an effort to increase its sales, reduced those prices to a level closer to what its customers had been paying. This move attracted some new customers, but overall the manufacturer's sales actually fell.

Which of the following, if true, most helps explain why the manufacturer's sales fell instead of rising?

(A)   The manufacturer's new list prices were no lower than those of most of its competitors.

(B)   Demand for specialized computer workstations has been increasing steadily for several years.

(C)   Corporations rarely employ people who lack extensive knowledge about the prices of equipment as buyers of such equipment.

(D)   Customers differ significantly in the proportions of their resources they are willing to devote to specialized equipment such as computer workstations.

(E)   Buyers who purchase equipment such as computer workstations for their employers typically receive bonuses for negotiating large discounts from the list price.

247. In countries where companies offer financial bonuses for employee suggestions that improve efficiency, reports of such suggestions are twice as frequent as they are in countries where no bonuses are offered. **At present, there is no reliable way to determine whether a reported suggestion would genuinely lead to improved efficiency**, so it is true that low-quality or insincere suggestions cannot be readily identified. Nevertheless, these facts do not warrant a conclusion that has been drawn by some commentators: **that in the countries with higher rates of reported suggestions, half of the reported suggestions are of little real value**. What these commentators are overlooking is that in countries where no bonuses are offered, employees often have little incentive to submit suggestions that could in fact improve efficiency.

In the argument given, the two **boldfaced** portions play which of the following roles?

(A)   The first is a judgment advanced in support of the main conclusion of the argument; the second is that main conclusion.

(B)   Each is a judgment advanced in support of the main conclusion of the argument.

(C)   The first is an intermediate conclusion drawn in order to challenge a position opposed by the argument; the second is the position taken by the argument.

(D)   The first is a position that the argument accepts as true; the second states a claim that the argument disputes.

(E)   The first states the position taken by the argument; the second is a consideration presented in order to support that position.

248. Certainly, pesticides can on occasion adversely affect the environment in localities distant from where the pesticide has actually been used. Nevertheless, regulation of pesticide use should take place not at the national level but at the local level. It is in the areas where pesticides are actually applied that they have their most serious effects. **Just how serious these effects are depends on local conditions** such as climate, soil type, and water supply. And **local officials are much more likely than national legislators to be truly knowledgeable about such local conditions.**

In the argument given, the two **boldface** portions play which of the following roles?

(A) The first provides support for the conclusion of the argument; the second states that conclusion.

(B) The first states the conclusion of the argument; the second provides support for that conclusion.

(C) The first identifies grounds for a potential objection to the conclusion of the argument; the second states that conclusion.

(D) The first identifies grounds for a potential objection to the conclusion of the argument; the second provides support for that conclusion.

(E) Each provides support for the conclusion of the argument.

249. Cork stoppers for bottled wine can leak, crumble, or become moldy. As a result, winemakers are forced to discard what are often significant proportions of their inventory of bottled wine. **High-quality plastic stoppers cannot leak, crumble, or mold.** Plastic stoppers will also soon enjoy a price advantage. Prices for cork and plastic stoppers are now about even, but the price of cork is expected to rise sharply in the near future. Nevertheless, **most winemakers who have not already switched to plastic stoppers remain committed to cork stoppers.** It is clear, therefore, that those winemakers' business decisions are shaped primarily by considerations other than a commitment to keeping expenses low.

In the argument given, the two portions in **boldface** play which of the following roles?

(A) The first is evidence that has been used to support a position that the argument challenges; the second is that challenged position.

(B) The first is evidence that has been used to support a position that the argument challenges; the second is evidence on which that challenge is based.

(C) The first and the second each provide evidence in support of the main conclusion of the argument.

(D) The first provides evidence in support of the main conclusion of the argument; the second is an objection that has been raised against that main conclusion.

(E) The first provides evidence in support of the main conclusion of the argument; the second is a conclusion drawn in order to support that main conclusion.

250. Historian: Newton developed mathematical concepts and techniques that are fundamental to modern calculus. Leibniz developed closely analogous concepts and techniques. It has traditionally been thought that these discoveries were independent. Researchers have, however, recently discovered notes of Leibniz's that discuss one of Newton's books on mathematics. Several scholars have argued that since **the book includes a presentation of Newton's calculus concepts and techniques**, and since the notes were written before Leibniz's own development of calculus concepts and techniques, **it is virtually certain that the traditional view is false**. A more cautious conclusion than this is called for, however. Leibniz's notes are limited to early sections of Newton's book, sections that precede the ones in which Newton's calculus concepts and techniques are presented.

In the historian's reasoning, the two **boldfaced** portions play which of the following roles?

(A) The first is a claim that has been advanced as a hypothesis in arguing for the position the historian rejects; the second is that position.

(B) The first is evidence that has been used to support a conclusion that the historian criticizes; the second is that conclusion.

(C) The first provides evidence in support of an intermediate conclusion drawn in order to support the position that the historian defends; the second is that intermediate conclusion.

(D) The first provides evidence in support of the position that the historian defends; the second provides evidence to support that position.

(E) The first is the position taken by the argument; the second is evidence that has been used to support that position.

251. Business Consultant: **Some corporations shun the use of executive titles** because they fear that the use of titles indicating position in the corporation tends to inhibit communication up and down the corporate hierarchy. Since an executive who uses a title is treated with more respect by outsiders, however, use of a title can facilitate an executive's dealings with external businesses. Clearly, **corporations should adopt the compromise of encouraging their executives to use their corporate titles externally but not internally**, since even if it is widely known that the corporation's executives use titles outside the organization, this knowledge does not by itself inhibit communication within the corporation.

In the consultant's reasoning, the two portions in **boldface** play which of the following roles?

(A) The first describes a strategy that has been adopted to avoid a certain problem; the second expresses the consultant's assessment of the significance of that problem.

(B) The first describes a strategy that has been adopted to avoid a certain problem; the second is a judgment that the consultant uses to argue that the strategy is ineffective.

(C) The first describes a strategy that has a drawback that the consultant points out; the second presents a strategy that, according to the consultant, would achieve the same end while avoiding that drawback.

(D) The first describes a practice for which the consultant seeks to provide a justification; the second is a consideration offered as part of that justification.

(E) The first describes a policy that the consultant concludes is misguided; the second is introduced to explain why that policy was adopted.

252. Since it has become known that several of a bank's top executives have been buying shares in their own bank, the bank's depositors, who had been worried by rumors that the bank faced impending financial collapse, have been greatly relieved. They reason that since **top executives evidently have faith in the bank's financial soundness**, those worrisome rumors must be false. **They might well be overoptimistic**, however, since corporate executives have sometimes bought shares in their own company in a calculated attempt to dispel negative rumors about the company's health.

In the argument given, the two **boldfaced** portions play which of the following roles?

(A) The first summarizes the evidence used in the reasoning called into question by the argument; the second states the counterevidence on which the argument relies.

(B) The first summarizes the evidence used in the reasoning called into question by the argument; the second is an intermediate conclusion supported by that evidence.

(C) The first is an intermediate conclusion that forms part of the reasoning called into question by the argument; the second is evidence that undermines the support for this intermediate conclusion.

(D) The first is an intermediate conclusion that forms part of the reasoning called into question by the argument; the second is the main conclusion of the argument.

(E) The first is an intermediate conclusion that forms part of the reasoning called into question by the argument; the second states a further conclusion supported by this intermediate conclusion.

253. **In countries where automobile insurance includes compensation for whiplash injuries sustained in automobile accidents, reports of having suffered such injuries are twice as frequent as they are in countries where whiplash is not covered.** Some commentators have argued, correctly, that since there is presently no objective test for whiplash, **spurious reports of whiplash injuries cannot be readily identified.** These commentators are, however, wrong to draw the further conclusion that in the countries with the higher rates of reported whiplash injuries, half of the reported cases are spurious: clearly, in countries where automobile insurance does not include compensation for whiplash, people often have little incentive to report whiplash injuries that they actually have suffered.

In the argument given, the two **boldfaced** portions play which of the following roles?

(A) The first is a finding whose accuracy is evaluated in the argument; the second is an intermediate conclusion drawn to support the judgment reached by the argument on the accuracy of that finding.

(B) The first is a finding whose accuracy is evaluated in the argument; the second is evidence that has been used to challenge the accuracy of that finding.

(C) The first is a finding whose implications are at issue in the argument; the second is an intermediate conclusion that has been used to support a conclusion that the argument criticizes.

(D) The first is a claim that the argument disputes; the second is a narrower claim that the argument accepts.

(E) The first is a claim that has been used to support a conclusion that the argument accepts; the second is that conclusion.

4.8 Answer Key: Critical Reasoning

111.	D	140.	D	169.	B	198.	E	227.	C
112.	B	141.	E	170.	C	199.	C	228.	A
113.	D	142.	E	171.	B	200.	E	229.	E
114.	B	143.	A	172.	D	201.	D	230.	E
115.	B	144.	A	173.	D	202.	B	231.	E
116.	C	145.	C	174.	B	203.	C	232.	B
117.	B	146.	C	175.	E	204.	C	233.	C
118.	B	147.	A	176.	D	205.	A	234.	B
119.	B	148.	A	177.	C	206.	B	235.	B
120.	E	149.	C	178.	B	207.	B	236.	D
121.	C	150.	B	179.	C	208.	B	237.	A
122.	B	151.	C	180.	B	209.	B	238.	B
123.	A	152.	E	181.	D	210.	B	239.	E
124.	E	153.	E	182.	D	211.	E	240.	C
125.	C	154.	C	183.	C	212.	D	241.	D
126.	B	155.	C	184.	C	213.	A	242.	A
127.	A	156.	B	185.	C	214.	B	243.	D
128.	B	157.	C	186.	C	215.	A	244.	B
129.	A	158.	B	187.	E	216.	E	245.	A
130.	A	159.	C	188.	D	217.	B	246.	E
131.	C	160.	C	189.	B	218.	D	247.	D
132.	D	161.	A	190.	E	219.	D	248.	E
133.	A	162.	A	191.	D	220.	C	249.	C
134.	A	163.	D	192.	D	221.	C	250.	B
135.	B	164.	C	193.	C	222.	C	251.	C
136.	D	165.	A	194.	D	223.	C	252.	D
137.	D	166.	C	195.	D	224.	E	253.	C
138.	C	167.	C	196.	D	225.	E		
139.	A	168.	B	197.	C	226.	B		

4.9 Answer Explanations: Critical Reasoning

The following discussion is intended to familiarize you with the most efficient and effective approaches to Critical Reasoning questions. The particular questions in this chapter are generally representative of the kinds of Critical Reasoning questions you will encounter on the GMAT exam. Remember that it is the problem-solving strategy that is important, not the specific details of a particular question.

Questions 111 to 148 — Difficulty: Easy

111. Stockholders have been critical of the Flyna Company, a major furniture retailer, because most of Flyna's furniture is manufactured in Country X from local wood, and illegal logging is widespread there. However, Flyna has set up a certification scheme for lumber mills. It has hired a staff of auditors and forestry professionals who review documentation of the wood supply of Country X's lumber mills to ensure its legal origin, make surprise visits to mills to verify documents, and certify mills as approved sources of legally obtained lumber. Flyna uses only lumber from certified mills. Thus, Flyna's claim that its Country X wood supply is obtained legally is justified.

Which of the following, if true, would most undermine the justification provided for Flyna's claim?

(A) Only about one-third of Flyna's inspectors were hired from outside the company.

(B) Country X's government recently reduced its subsidies for lumber production.

(C) Flyna has had to pay higher than expected salaries to attract qualified inspectors.

(D) The proportion of Country X's lumber mills inspected each year by Flyna's staff is about 10 percent, randomly selected.

(E) Illegal logging costs Country X's government a significant amount in lost revenue each year.

Argument Evaluation

Situation The Flyna Company sells furniture mostly made in Country X from local wood. Illegal logging is widespread in Country X. Flyna has set up a certification scheme for lumber mills. Specialized staff make surprise visits to Country X mills, inspect documentation to ensure that the wood supply has a legal origin, and certify mills as approved sources for legally obtained lumber. Flyna uses only lumber from certified mills. According to the argument, Flyna's claim that its wood supply is legally obtained is justified.

Reasoning *What additional information would, if true, most undermine the justification for Flyna' claim that its Country X wood is legally obtained?* Clearly, much depends on the thoroughness of the certification scheme. For example, the staff auditing the mills would need to be qualified for the job and meticulous in meeting their responsibilities. The auditing visits would need to be frequent enough, and not predictable by mill management. Flyna would need to be genuinely committed to ensuring legality of wood sources; it would need to monitor its staff to ensure that they were doing their jobs effectively.

A This suggests that Flyna could make good judgments as to the competence and trustworthiness of most of the inspectors hired to certify lumber mills.

B This could provide a perverse incentive to loggers to violate legal restrictions on logging. However, this would not undercut Flyna's justification for its claim that its system ensures that all its lumber is legally sourced.

C   This has no bearing on whether Flyna's certification system will be effective in guaranteeing that Flyna's lumber is legally sourced. We are not told, for example, that Flyna has been unable to find enough qualified inspectors for the certification system to be effective.

D   **Correct.** This means that 90 percent of Country X's certified lumber mills are not inspected in any particular year. Moreover, since the selection of the 10 percent of lumber mills to be inspected in a given year is random, some lumber mills might go for much longer than ten years without inspection; during this period, many of those mills might fall below certification standards and even use lumber illegally obtained.

E   This indicates that a significant amount of illegal logging occurs in Country X; this suggests that it is possible that some illegally sourced wood could find its way to lumber mills that Flyna uses and has certified. But the information given here is not sufficiently specific to indicate that the Flyna certification system would fail to prevent the company's use of illegally sourced wood.

The correct answer is D.

112. Companies O and P each have the same number of employees who work the same number of hours per week. According to records maintained by each company, the employees of Company O had fewer job-related accidents last year than did the employees of Company P. Therefore, employees of Company O are less likely to have job-related accidents than are employees of Company P.

Which of the following, if true, would most weaken the conclusion?

(A)   The employees of Company P lost more time at work due to job-related accidents than did the employees of Company O.

(B)   Company P considered more types of accidents to be job-related than did Company O.

(C)   The employees of Company P were sick more often than were the employees of Company O.

(D)   Several employees of Company O each had more than one job-related accident.

(E)   The majority of job-related accidents at Company O involved a single machine.

Argument Evaluation

Situation   Two companies, O and P, have identical numbers of employees working identical numbers of hours. According to the companies' records, O's workers experienced fewer job-related accidents than did P's workers over the same period. According to the argument, it follows that O's workers are less likely to suffer job-related accidents than are P's workers.

Reasoning   *Which of the statements provided would weaken the argument that workers at O are safer from job-related accidents than are workers at P?* In reviewing the statements, the key phrase here is *According to records maintained at each company.* On the face of it, differing numbers of job-related accidents among identical numbers of workers over an identical timeframe would necessarily imply differing *rates* of such accidents—unless the two companies construe what counts as a job-related accident differently. O's workers may not actually have a lower rate of such accidents, or be safer from such accidents in the future, if their company chooses not to class their accidents as job-related. Therefore, identifying such a discrepancy in how the two companies classify accidents would weaken the conclusion.

A   P's workers losing more time to job-related injuries would be a reasonable expectation if the conclusion is correct; it does not weaken support for that conclusion.

B   **Correct.** If P defines job-related accidents more broadly than does O, that fact would undermine the argument for the conclusion that O's workers genuinely suffer job-related accidents at a lower rate.

C   Relative rates of sickness at the two companies have no bearing on their relative rates of accidents.

D   Absent detailed information about whether P's workers also suffer multiple accidents per worker, this fact does not affect the conclusion that O's workers are safer than P's.

E   The fact that a specific machine was particularly dangerous would not affect the conclusion about rates of accidents at the two companies.

The correct answer is B.

113. The *XCT* automobile is considered less valuable than the *ZNK* automobile, because insurance companies pay less, on average, to replace a stolen *XCT* than a stolen *ZNK*. Surprisingly, the average amount insurance companies will pay to repair a car involved in a collision is typically higher for the *XCT* than for the *ZNK*. One insurance expert explained that repairs to *XCT* automobiles are especially labor-intensive, and labor is a significant factor in collision repair costs.

Which of the following, if true, most strongly supports the insurance expert's explanation?

(A) *ZNK* automobiles are involved in accidents more frequently than *XCT* automobiles.

(B) The cost of routine maintenance for the *ZNK* is about the same as for the *XCT*.

(C) There are more automobile mechanics who specialize in *XCT* repairs than in *ZNK* repairs.

(D) The ease of repair of *ZNK* automobiles is one factor that adds to their value.

(E) *XCT* automobiles are more likely to be stolen than *ZNK* automobiles.

Argument Evaluation

Situation   Two automobile models *XCT* and *ZNK* are compared with respect to (1) what insurance companies pay on average to replace a stolen vehicle and (2) what insurance companies pay on average to repair a crashed vehicle. On (1), insurance companies pay less for XCTs than for ZNKs. On (2), insurance companies pay more for repairing XCTs than ZNKs. An insurance expert explains that repairs to XCTs are especially labor-intensive; this tends to raise the cost of repairs.

Reasoning   *Which piece of new information most strongly supports the expert's explanation for the fact that the replacement value is greater for the car that has lower repair costs?* We should look for information that supplements the explanation in a way that shows the coherence of the two facts given regarding insurance payments for the two cars.

A   The frequency of accidents is not directly relevant to the higher cost of collision repair for those *XCTs* that are involved in collisions.

B   This information is not directly relevant to the higher cost of collision repair for *XCTs*. It neither undermines nor supports the claim that *XCT* labor costs are higher per crashed vehicle and does not help support that claim as an explanation for the discrepancy in question.

C   This neither supports nor undermines the expert's explanation. If we had information concerning the supply of *XCT* mechanics and *ZNK* mechanics relative to the demand for each, we would have some evidence that could throw light on differences in labor costs.

D   **Correct.** *ZNK*s are more valuable because buyers know that total repair costs will be lower. This is reflected in the market value of *ZNK*s compared to that of *XCT*s. Replacing a stolen *XCT* costs insurance companies less than replacing a stolen *ZNK* because the lower market value of *XCT*s is related in the high cost of collision repair.

E   This is unlikely to lower the market value of *XCT*s. The market value of *XCT*s is the factor that determines how much it costs to replace a stolen *XCT*.

The correct answer is D.

114. The sustained massive use of pesticides in farming has two effects that are especially pernicious. First, it often kills off the pests' natural enemies in the area. Second, it often unintentionally gives rise to insecticide-resistant pests, since those insects that survive a particular insecticide will be the ones most resistant to it, and they are the ones left to breed.

From the passage above, it can be properly inferred that the effectiveness of the sustained massive use of pesticides can be extended by doing which of the following, assuming that each is a realistic possibility?

(A)   Using only chemically stable insecticides

(B)   Periodically switching the type of insecticide used

(C)   Gradually increasing the quantities of pesticides used

(D)   Leaving a few fields fallow every year

(E)   Breeding higher-yielding varieties of crop plants

Evaluation of a Plan

Situation   Continued high-level pesticide use often kills off the targeted pests' natural enemies. In addition, the pests that survive the application of the pesticide may become resistant to it, and these pesticide-resistant pests will continue breeding.

Reasoning   What can be done to prolong the effectiveness of pesticide use? *It can be inferred that the ongoing use of a particular pesticide will not continue to be effective against the future generations of pests with an inherent resistance to that pesticide.* What would be effective against these future generations? If farmers periodically change the particular pesticide they use, then pests resistant to one kind of pesticide might be killed by another. This would continue, with pests being killed off in cycles as the pesticides are changed. It is also possible that this rotation might allow some of the pests' natural enemies to survive, at least until the next cycle.

A   Not enough information about chemically stable insecticides is given to make a sound inference.

B   **Correct.** This statement properly identifies an action that could extend the effectiveness of pesticide use.

C   Gradually increasing the amount of the pesticides being used will not help the situation since the pests are already resistant to it.

D   Continued use of pesticides is assumed as part of the argument. Since pesticides would be unnecessary for fallow fields, this suggestion is irrelevant.

E   Breeding higher-yielding varieties of crops does nothing to extend the effectiveness of the use of pesticides.

The correct answer is B.

115. Editorial: The mayor plans to deactivate the city's fire alarm boxes, because most calls received from them are false alarms. The mayor claims that the alarm boxes are no longer necessary, since most people now have access to cell phones. But the city's commercial district, where there is the greatest risk of fire, has few residents and few cell towers, so some alarm boxes are still necessary.

Which of the following, if true, most seriously weakens the editorial's argument?

(A)   Maintaining the fire alarm boxes costs the city more than 5 million dollars annually.

(B)   Commercial buildings have automatic fire alarm systems that are linked directly to the fire department.

(C)   The fire department gets less information from an alarm box than it does from a telephone call.

(D)   The city's fire department is located much closer to the residential areas than to the commercial district.

(E)   On average, almost 25 percent of the cell towers in the city are out of order.

Argument Evaluation

Situation   Due to many false alarms from fire alarm boxes, the mayor intends to turn off the boxes and rely on cell phones for reporting fires. A shortage of cell towers in the commercial district suggests some alarm boxes are still necessary.

Reasoning   *What would weaken the argument that alarm boxes are necessary?* The argument relies on the dearth of cell towers in the commercial district to conclude that alarm boxes are needed in order to report fires. If, however, there was some alternative way to alert the fire department to fires in the commercial district, that fact would undermine the suggestion that the commercial district needs alarm boxes.

A   The cost of the alarm boxes has no bearing on whether or not they are necessary.

B   **Correct.** The argument relies on a shortage of cell towers in the commercial district to conclude that alarm boxes are necessary for reporting fires; if, however, commercial buildings have an alternative way to alert the fire department, such as the alarm systems described here, then that would undermine the argument that the commercial district needs alarm boxes.

C   The lack of detailed information conveyed by alarm boxes does not undermine the contention that such boxes are still necessary in some areas.

D   The location of the fire department is not relevant to the question of whether the city needs alarm boxes.

E   A high percentage of nonfunctional cell towers would tend to strengthen an argument for alarm boxes, not weaken it.

The correct answer is B.

116. Which of the following, if true, most logically completes the argument?

Some dairy farmers in the province of Takandia want to give their cows a synthetic hormone that increases milk production. Many Takandians, however, do not want to buy milk from cows given the synthetic hormone. For this reason Takandia's legislature is considering a measure requiring milk from cows given the hormone to be labeled as such. Even if the measure is defeated, dairy farmers who use the hormone will probably lose customers, since __________.

(A) it has not been proven that any trace of the synthetic hormone exists in the milk of cows given the hormone

(B) some farmers in Takandia who plan to use the synthetic hormone will probably not do so if the measure were passed

(C) milk from cows that have not been given the synthetic hormone can be labeled as such without any legislative action

(D) the legislature's consideration of the bill has been widely publicized

(E) milk that comes from cows given the synthetic hormone looks and tastes the same as milk from cows that have not received the hormone

Argument Construction

Situation   In Takandia, some of the dairy farmers are interested in increasing the amount of milk their cows produce by giving the animals a synthetic hormone. A significant percentage of consumers prefer not to buy milk from cows dosed with the hormone; lawmakers are considering a requirement that such milk carry an identifying label. Even without the labels, however, farmers using the hormone on their cows are likely to have fewer customers buy their milk.

Reasoning   *What would cause a declining share of customers?* The argument states that even if the milk from hormone-dosed cows continues to be unlabeled, fewer customers will probably buy it. That outcome would be likely if customers had another way to identify the milk they prefer—for example, labels on milk from *untreated* cows—so that they could choose the milk from untreated cows instead of milk that does not provide any information about whether the cows were treated. In other words, labeling the untreated milk provides that milk a competitive advantage over treated milk, and that advantage will probably reduce market share for treated milk.

A   Lack of proof that the hormone is in the milk would not be expected to *decrease* market share of such milk; indeed, farmers could use that fact to try to persuade customers to buy it.

B   The fact that required labels might dissuade farmers from using the hormone would have no effect on their potential sales in the *absence* of required labels.

C   **Correct.** If farmers who *don't* use the hormone can label their milk and thereby allow customers to identify the milk they prefer, those labels would provide milk from untreated cows with a competitive advantage. That advantage would be likely to reduce the share of customers who would buy milk from treated cows, even if that milk was not specifically labeled.

D   Publicity regarding potential label requirements would not be likely to cause declining sales in the absence of such requirements.

E   The fact that milk from treated cows looks and tastes the same would not be expected to reduce its share of customers.

The correct answer is C.

117. Sparrow Airlines is planning to reduce its costs by cleaning its planes' engines once a month, rather than the industry standard of every six months. With cleaner engines, Sparrow can postpone engine overhauls, which take planes out of service for up to 18 months. Furthermore, cleaning an engine reduces its fuel consumption by roughly 1.2 percent.

The airline's plan assumes that

(A) fuel prices are likely to rise in the near future and therefore cutting fuel consumption is an important goal

(B) the cost of monthly cleaning of an airplane's engines is not significantly greater in the long run than is the cost of an engine overhaul

(C) engine cleaning does not remove an airplane from service

(D) Sparrow Airlines has had greater problems with engine overhauls and fuel consumption than other airlines have

(E) cleaning engines once a month will give Sparrow Airlines a competitive advantage over other airlines

Evaluation of a Plan

Situation   Sparrow Airlines plans to clean the engines of its planes monthly rather than every six months. The goal is to reduce its costs.

Reasoning   *Which statement provides an assumption underlying the plan?* The plan will enable Sparrow to postpone engine overhauls, which put a plane out of service for up to 18 months. The monthly cleaning will reduce its fuel consumption by 1.2 percent. But suppose the long-run cost of monthly cleanings were greater than the cost of an engine overhaul, then the rationale for the airline's plan would fail.

A   Nothing in the information provided indicates that this is assumed in the plan.

B   **Correct.** The plan makes sense only if this is assumed. If the long-run total cost of monthly cleaning significantly exceeded the total cost of engine overhaul—which would include, in the long run, more frequent downtime of 18 months if the plan were not adopted—then it seems likely that the projected benefit of postponement of engine overhauls would not be compensated for by the 1.2 percent fuel-cost savings.

C   The plan does not have to assume this. Perhaps monthly engine cleaning requires only one day of down time.

D   This is perhaps a good reason for Sparrow to put in place the proposed cost-saving plan, but it is not an assumption that the plan requires for it to make sense.

E   The plan does not have to assume this, even if Sparrow's cost saving were to result in a competitive advantage. Sparrow's plan could equally be aimed at simply removing a competitive disadvantage. The issue of competition is not addressed in the given information.

The correct answer is B.

118. Patrick usually provides child care for six children. Parents leave their children at Patrick's house in the morning and pick them up after work. At the end of each workweek, the parents pay Patrick at an hourly rate for the child care provided that week. The weekly income Patrick receives is usually adequate but not always uniform, particularly in the winter, when children are likely to get sick and be unpredictably absent.

Which of the following plans, if put into effect, has the best prospect of making Patrick's weekly income both uniform and adequate?

(A)   Pool resources with a neighbor who provides child care under similar arrangements, so that the two of them cooperate in caring for twice as many children as Patrick currently does.

(B)   Replace payment by actual hours of child care provided with a fixed weekly fee based upon the number of hours of child care that Patrick would typically be expected to provide.

(C)   Hire a full-time helper and invest in facilities for providing child care to sick children.

(D)   Increase the hourly rate to a level that would provide adequate income even in a week when half of the children Patrick usually cares for are absent.

(E)   Increase the number of hours made available for child care each day, so that parents can leave their children in Patrick's care for a longer period each day at the current hourly rate.

Evaluation of a Plan

Situation   At the end of the workweek, Patrick is paid a certain amount for each hour of child care he has provided. Patrick usually receives adequate weekly income under this arrangement, but in the winter Patrick's income fluctuates, because children are unpredictably absent due to illness.

Reasoning   *Which plan would be most likely to meet the two goals of uniform weekly income and adequate weekly income?* Patrick must find a way to ensure that his weekly income is both adequate—that is, not reduced significantly from current levels—and uniform—that is, not subject to seasonal or other fluctuations. A successful plan would thus most likely be one that does not increase Patrick's costs. Further, the plan need not increase Patrick's weekly income; it must merely ensure that that income is more reliable. It should therefore also provide some way to mitigate the unexpected loss of income from children's absences.

A   This plan might raise Patrick's income slightly, because he and the neighbor might pay out less in costs if they pool their resources. But this plan would have no effect on the problem that unpredictable absences pose for Patrick's weekly income.

B   **Correct.** This statement properly identifies a plan that would most likely keep Patrick's income adequate (he would probably receive approximately the same amount of money per child as he does now) and uniform (he would receive the money regardless of whether a child was present or absent).

C   While this plan might somewhat mitigate the unpredictability in Patrick's income that results from sick children's absences—because parents would be less likely to keep sick children at home—it would increase Patrick's costs. Paying a helper and investing in different facilities would reduce Patrick's income and might thus result in that income being inadequate.

D   Under this plan, if we assume that parents did not balk at the increase in Patrick's hourly rate and find alternative child care, Patrick's income would most likely be adequate. But this plan would not help make Patrick's weekly income uniform. His income would continue to fluctuate when children are absent. Remember, there are two goals with regard to Patrick's income: adequacy and uniformity.

E   This plan might increase Patrick's income, in that he might be paid for more hours of child care each week. The goals here, however, are to make Patrick's weekly income both adequate and uniform, and this plan does not address the issue of uniformity.

The correct answer is B.

119. Film director: It is true that certain characters and plot twists in my newly released film *The Perfect Heist* are strikingly similar to characters and plot twists in *Thieves*, a movie that came out last year. Based on these similarities, the film studio that produced *Thieves* is now accusing me of taking ideas from that film. The accusation is clearly without merit. All production work on *The Perfect Heist* was actually completed months before *Thieves* was released.

Which of the following, if true, provides the strongest support for the director's rejection of the accusation?

(A)   Before *Thieves* began production, its script had been circulating for several years among various film studios, including the studio that produced *The Perfect Heist*.

(B)   The characters and plot twists that are most similar in the two films have close parallels in many earlier films of the same genre.

(C)   The film studio that produced *Thieves* seldom produces films in this genre.

(D)   The director of *Thieves* worked with the director of *The Perfect Heist* on several earlier projects.

(E)   The time it took to produce *The Perfect Heist* was considerably shorter than the time it took to produce *Thieves*.

Argument Evaluation

Situation   A film director is accused of stealing ideas from a recent movie, *Thieves*, and using those ideas in their own newer movie, *The Perfect Heist*. The director admits that there are similarities but denies the charge of plagiarism on the grounds that work on *The Perfect Heist* was complete before *Thieves* came out.

Reasoning   *What factor would support the contention that* The Perfect Heist *did not copy* Thieves? *If it can be shown that* The Perfect Heist *had likely sources for its ideas other than* Thieves*, that would tend to support the director's contention that* The Perfect Heist *did not steal ideas from the earlier film.*

A   If the director could have read or heard about the *Thieves* script at any point in the last several years, that would tend to support the accusation of copying and to undermine the director's dismissal of that accusation.

B   **Correct.** If the disputed ideas are tropes common to many earlier films, then that would tend to suggest that both *Thieves* and *The Perfect Heist* drew their ideas from those earlier films and support the assertion that *The Perfect Heist* did not copy *Thieves*.

C   The fact that the studio behind *Thieves* rarely works in the heist genre has no bearing on whether or not *The Perfect Heist* copied *Thieves*.

D   The fact that the two directors have worked together in the past neither supports nor undermines the accusation that one copied the other.

E   The relative production time of the two movies is not relevant to the question of whether one copied the other.

The correct answer is B.

120. Ythex has developed a small diesel engine that produces 30 percent less particulate pollution than the engine made by its main rival, Onez, now widely used in Marania; Ythex's engine is well-suited for use in the thriving warehousing businesses in Marania, although it costs more than the Onez engine. The Maranian government plans to ban within the next two years the use of diesel engines with more than 80 percent of current diesel engine particulate emissions in Marania, and Onez will probably not be able to retool its engine to reduce emissions to reach this target. So if the ban is passed, the Ythex engine ought to sell well in Marania after that time.

Which of the following is an assumption on which the argument above depends?

(A) Marania's warehousing and transshipment business buys more diesel engines of any size than other types of engines.

(B) Ythex is likely to be able to reduce the cost of its small diesel engine within the next two years.

(C) The Maranian government is generally favorable to anti-pollution regulations.

(D) The government's ban on high levels of pollution caused by diesel engines, if passed, will not be difficult to enforce.

(E) The other manufacturers of small diesel engines in Marania, if there are any, have not produced an engine as popular and clean-running as Ythex's new engine.

Argument Evaluation

Situation   Two companies, Ythex and Onez, produce diesel engines in Marania. Ythex has developed a small engine that produces less particulate pollution than the engine made by Onez, its main rival. The Maranian government will put a new maximum particulate-emission level in force within two years, but Onez will not be able to meet this target.

Reasoning   *What would have to be assumed for the argument to support the prediction that Ythex's engine will sell well in two years when the new maximum particulate level is introduced?* To answer this, one might ask, for example: Will the maximum level be efficiently enforced? Will Ythex have any rivals other than Onez that will compete in the low-pollution diesel market?

A   This tells us that there is a significant market for diesel engines, but this not an assumption that the reasoning depends on. The reasoning focuses only on the market for diesel engines and does not address the relative sizes of the market for diesel engines and that for non-diesel engines.

B   If this is true, it provides additional support for the conclusion that Ythex's engine will sell well in two years. However, it is not an assumption on which the reasoning relies.

C   This information is peripheral to the reasoning and not an assumption on which the reasoning relies. Adding it to the information given would not make the reasoning more logically compelling.

D   The ban might be quite difficult to enforce, but a more important issue is whether the ban will be effectively enforced (so the reasoning does have to assume that the ban would be at least somewhat effective). No assumption about the relative difficulty of enforcing the ban needs to be made for the reasoning to be logically compelling.

E   **Correct.** Are there one or more diesel engines from other companies that will be able to compete effectively with Ythex's engine when the ban is introduced? For the reasoning to be logically compelling, it needs to be assumed that the answer is no.

The correct answer is E.

121. Which of the following most logically completes the argument?

The last members of a now-extinct species of a European wild deer called the giant deer lived in Ireland about 16,000 years ago. Prehistoric cave paintings in France depict this animal as having a large hump on its back. Fossils of this animal, however, do not show any hump. Nevertheless, there is no reason to conclude that the cave paintings are therefore inaccurate in this regard, since __________.

(A)   some prehistoric cave paintings in France also depict other animals as having a hump

(B)   fossils of the giant deer are much more common in Ireland than in France

(C)   animal humps are composed of fatty tissue, which does not fossilize

(D)   the cave paintings of the giant deer were painted well before 16,000 years ago

(E)   only one currently existing species of deer has any anatomical feature that even remotely resembles a hump

Argument Construction

Situation   Representations found in prehistoric cave paintings in France of the now-extinct giant deer species—the last members of which lived in Ireland about 16,000 years ago—depict the deer as having a hump on its back. Fossils of the deer, however, do not feature a hump.

Reasoning   *What point would most logically complete the argument? That is, what would show that the cave paintings are not inaccurate even though fossils of the giant deer show no hump?* How could it be the case that the paintings show a hump while the fossils do not? One way in which this could be so is if the humps are not part of the fossils—that is, if there is some reason why a hump would not be preserved with the rest of an animal's remains.

A   We do not know whether these other cave paintings accurately depict the animals as having humps, so this provides no reason to think that the depictions of giant deer are accurate.

B   Where giant deer fossils are found has no bearing on whether cave paintings of giant deer that show a hump on the animal's back are inaccurate. It could be that this suggests that the painters responsible for the representations would not be very familiar with the species; if this were so, it would give some reason to conclude that the representations were inaccurate.

C   **Correct.** This statement properly identifies a point that logically completes the argument. A hump would not be found as part of a giant deer's fossilized remains if the humps were fatty tissue that would not be fossilized.

D   That the cave paintings were painted well before 16,000 years ago shows that they were executed before the giant deer became extinct, but this does not help to explain the discrepancy between the paintings' depiction of a hump on the deer's back and the fossil record's lack of such a hump. It could be that even though the cave painters coexisted with the giant deer, they were not sufficiently familiar with them to depict them accurately.

E   That currently existing species of deer lack humps, or even that one species does have a feature resembling a hump, has little bearing on whether cave paintings in France accurately depict the giant deer as having a hump.

The correct answer is C.

122. Psychologists conducted an experiment in which half of the volunteers were asked to describe an unethical action they had performed, while the other half were asked to describe an ethical action they had performed. Some of the volunteers, chosen at random from each of the two groups, were encouraged to wash their hands afterward. Among those who described unethical actions, those who washed their hands were significantly less likely to volunteer for another, similar experiment than those who did not wash their hands. The researchers concluded that some of the subjects failed to volunteer again in part because of their having described an unethical action.

Which of the following would, if true, most help to support the researchers' conclusion?

(A)   Among the volunteers who described ethical actions, those who washed their hands were significantly less likely to volunteer for another, similar experiment than those who did not wash their hands.

(B)   The average likelihood of volunteering for another, similar experiment was higher among those who described ethical actions than among those who described unethical actions.

(C)   Most of the volunteers who were encouraged to wash their hands did so.

(D)   The volunteers in the study were not more disposed to washing their hands under normal circumstances than the general population was.

(E)   Equal numbers of volunteers from both groups were encouraged to wash their hands.

Argument Evaluation

Situation   In an experiment, volunteers in one group were asked to describe an unethical action they had performed; volunteers in another group were asked to describe an ethical action they had performed. Some of the volunteers, randomly selected from each group, were encouraged to wash their hands afterwards. Among those who had described unethical actions, those who washed their hands were significantly less likely to volunteer for another, similar experiment than were those who did not wash their hands. The researchers concluded that some of the volunteers declined to volunteer again because of their having described an unethical action.

Reasoning   *Which new information most strongly supports the researchers' conclusion?* The researchers offered an answer to the following question in their conclusion: What caused some subjects not to volunteer again for another, similar experiment? The researchers concluded that one causal factor was having described an unethical action. This conclusion is based only on data about those who had described their unethical actions; the data showed that the hand washers among them were less likely to volunteer again than were those who did not wash their hands. This data, by itself, seems to provide at best weak support for the researchers' conclusion. The hypothesis could be strengthened by data comparing those who had described their ethical actions with those who had described their unethical ones.

A   This information slightly weakens the researchers' conclusion in that it suggests that the decision not to volunteer for future experiments could have been due entirely to the hand washing rather than partly to the participants' having described unethical actions.

B   **Correct.** This information does not refer to hand washing but provides a comparison between those who described an ethical action and those who described an unethical one, with respect to the likelihood of their volunteering for another, similar experiment. The fact that those who described ethical actions were more likely than the others to volunteer for subsequent experiments provides some evidence that describing an unethical action could have been a factor, along with the hand washing, that caused the observed difference in the volunteering rate. This additional evidence is only prima facie, though; it would be weakened if we also knew that among those who described ethical actions, the hand washers were just as unlikely to volunteer again as were those who washed their hands after describing unethical actions.

C   This information about hand washing is largely irrelevant to the researchers' conclusion, which is focused on the hypothesis that having described an unethical action made some participants less likely to volunteer again. It provides only very slight, conjectural support in that it is inconsistent with a hypothesis that so few actually washed their hands that they constituted a statistically insignificant sample.

D   The researchers' conclusion is not about the general population, so the information in this answer choice could only be relevant if such a generalization were the goal.

E   Like answer choice C, this information about hand washing is largely irrelevant to the researchers' conclusion, which is focused on the hypothesis that having described an unethical action made some participants less likely to volunteer again. It provides only very slight, conjectural support in that it is inconsistent with a hypothesis that one or more of the groups being compared was too small to be statistically significant.

The correct answer is B.

123. High levels of fertilizer and pesticides, needed when farmers try to produce high yields of the same crop year after year, pollute water supplies. Experts therefore urge farmers to diversify their crops and to rotate their plantings yearly.

To receive governmental price-support benefits for a crop, farmers must have produced that same crop for the past several years.

The statements above, if true, best support which of the following conclusions?

(A) The rules for governmental support of farm prices work against efforts to reduce water pollution.

(B) The only solution to the problem of water pollution from fertilizers and pesticides is to take farmland out of production.

(C) Farmers can continue to make a profit by rotating diverse crops, thus reducing costs for chemicals, but not by planting the same crop each year.

(D) New farming techniques will be developed to make it possible for farmers to reduce the application of fertilizers and pesticides.

(E) Governmental price supports for farm products are set at levels that are not high enough to allow farmers to get out of debt.

Argument Construction

Situation   Farmers are urged to rotate crops annually because the chemicals they must use when continuing to produce the same crops pollute water supplies. On the other hand, farmers may receive federal price-support benefits only if they have been producing the same crop for the past several years.

Reasoning   *What conclusion can be drawn from this information?* Farmers wish to receive the price-support benefits offered by the government, so they grow the same crop for several years. In order to continue getting good yields, they use the high levels of chemicals necessary when the same crop is grown from year to year. The result is water pollution. The government's rules for price-support benefits work against the efforts to reduce water pollution.

A   **Correct.** This statement properly identifies the conclusion supported by the evidence.

B   The experts cited in the passage believe that the rotation of crops is the solution, not the removal of farmland from production.

C   The conclusion that farmers cannot make a profit by producing the same crop year after year is not justified by the information given in the premises. The information given suggests that this conclusion would actually be false, since these farmers would benefit by price-support measures for such a crop.

D   No information in the passage supports a conclusion about farming techniques other than crop diversification and rotation, which are clearly existing farming techniques and not new or yet to be developed.

E   This conclusion is unwarranted because there is no information in the two statements about the levels of the price supports and of the farmers' debts.

The correct answer is A.

124. Many leadership theories have provided evidence that leaders affect group success rather than the success of particular individuals. So it is irrelevant to analyze the effects of supervisor traits on the attitudes of individuals whom they supervise. Instead, assessment of leadership effectiveness should occur only at the group level.

Which of the following would it be most useful to establish in order to evaluate the argument?

(A)   Whether supervisors' documentation of individual supervisees' attitudes toward them is usually accurate

(B)   Whether it is possible to assess individual supervisees' attitudes toward their supervisors without thereby changing those attitudes

(C)   Whether any of the leadership theories in question hold that leaders should assess other leaders' attitudes

(D)   Whether some types of groups do not need supervision in order to be successful in their endeavors

(E)   Whether individuals' attitudes toward supervisors affect group success

Argument Evaluation

Situation   Many leadership theories have provided evidence that leaders affect the success of groups but not of individuals.

Reasoning   *What would be most helpful to know in order to evaluate how well the stated fact supports the conclusion that leadership effectiveness should be assessed only at the group level without considering supervisors' influence on the attitudes of the individuals they supervise?* Even if leaders do not affect the success of the individuals they lead, they might still affect those individuals' attitudes. And those attitudes in turn might affect group success. If so, the argument would be weak. So any evidence about the existence or strength of these possible effects in the relationship between supervisors and their supervisees would be helpful in evaluating the argument.

A   How accurately supervisors document their supervisees' attitudes is not clearly relevant to how much the supervisors affect those attitudes, nor to how much the attitudes affect group success.

B   Even if assessing supervisees' attitudes would in itself change those attitudes, the person doing the assessment might be able to predict this change and take it into account. Thus, considering individual supervisees' attitudes might still be worthwhile.

C   The argument is not about interactions among leaders, but rather about interactions between supervisors and supervisees.

D   The argument is not about groups without supervisors, or whether certain groups might be effective without a supervisor, but rather about how to assess the effectiveness of supervisors in groups that do have them.

E   **Correct**. As explained above, if individual supervisees' attitudes affect group success, the argument would be weak. And probably individual supervisees' attitudes toward their supervisors are influenced by those supervisors. So knowing whether individual attitudes toward supervisors affect group success would be helpful in evaluating the argument

The correct answer is E.

125. A major health insurance company in Lagolia pays for special procedures prescribed by physicians only if the procedure is first approved as "medically necessary" by a company-appointed review panel. The rule is intended to save the company the money it might otherwise spend on medically unnecessary procedures. The company has recently announced that in order to reduce its costs, it will abandon this rule.

Which of the following, if true, provides the strongest justification for the company's decision?

(A) Patients often register dissatisfaction with physicians who prescribe nothing for their ailments.

(B) Physicians often prescribe special procedures that are helpful but not altogether necessary for the health of the patient.

(C) The review process is expensive and practically always results in approval of the prescribed procedure.

(D) The company's review process does not interfere with the prerogative of physicians, in cases where more than one effective procedure is available, to select the one they personally prefer.

(E) The number of members of the company-appointed review panel who review a given procedure depends on the cost of the procedure.

Evaluation of a Plan

Situation   In order to cut costs, a major health insurance company is abandoning a rule stating that it will pay for special procedures only if the procedure is approved as medically necessary by a review panel.

Reasoning   *What piece of information would most help to justify the company's decision?* For the company to save money, it would need to be in some way cutting its costs by abandoning the rule. Under what circumstances might the rule cost, rather than save, the company money? The panel itself might be expensive to convene, for example. Further, the cost savings achieved by the panel might be minimal if the panel did not deny significant numbers of procedures.

A   This suggests that patients might be pressuring their physicians to prescribe certain unnecessary procedures for their ailments, which in turn suggests that the panel is reviewing these procedures and denying them. But if so, then the panel is probably saving the insurance company money, so abandoning the panel's review would not reduce the company's costs.

B   This suggests that certain procedures that are being prescribed by physicians are not medically necessary, which in turn suggests that the panel reviewing these procedures may be denying them. If this is the case, then the panel is probably saving the insurance company a significant amount of money, so abandoning the panel's review may well increase rather than decrease the company's costs.

C   **Correct.** This statement properly identifies information that would help to justify the company's decision.

D   Even if the panel does not interfere with physicians' choices when more than one medically effective procedure is available, the panel may still be denying pay for many procedures that are not medically necessary. In such cases the panel may be saving the insurance company money, and abandoning the review process would not reduce the company's costs.

E   This suggests that the more expensive the procedure under review, the more expensive the panel itself is. Even so, if the panel denies payment for very expensive procedures, it may nonetheless save the company significantly more than the company has to pay to convene the panel, so abandoning the review process would not reduce the company's costs.

The correct answer is C.

126. Automobile ownership was rare in Sabresia as recently as 30 years ago, but with continuing growth of personal income there, automobile ownership has become steadily more common. Consequently, there are now far more automobiles on Sabresia's roads than there were 30 years ago, and the annual number of automobile accidents has increased significantly. Yet the annual number of deaths and injuries resulting from automobile accidents has not increased significantly.

Which of the following, if true, most helps to explain why deaths and injuries resulting from automobile accidents have not increased significantly?

(A) Virtually all of the improvements in Sabresia's roads that were required to accommodate increased traffic were completed more than ten years ago.

(B) With more and more people owning cars, the average number of passengers in a car on the road has dropped dramatically.

(C) The increases in traffic volume have been most dramatic on Sabresia's highways, where speeds are well above those of other roads.

(D) Because of a vigorous market in used cars, the average age of cars on the road has actually increased throughout the years of steady growth in automobile ownership.

(E) Automobile ownership is still much less common in Sabresia than it is in other countries.

Argument Construction

Situation   Many more cars are on Sabresia's roads than 30 years ago; and there are also many more car accidents. Yet the annual number of deaths and injuries resulting from car accidents has not increased much, which is quite puzzling.

Reasoning   *What factor could help explain the puzzling fact that the increase in car accidents was not reflected in a similar increase in deaths and injuries from car accidents?* One (but perhaps unlikely) possibility is that a significantly greater proportion of the recent annual number of car accidents consisted of merely minor accidents, unlike 30 years ago. Another possibility is that cars are currently much better engineered for driver and passenger safety than 30 years ago. Yet a third possibility is that the total number of people traveling by car—passengers and drivers—has not increased significantly despite the large increase in the number of cars. This would mean that the average occupancy of a car has greatly decreased; so, even though the number of car accidents has significantly increased, the average number of people per car involved in an accident would have decreased significantly. On average, this would mean significantly fewer deaths and injuries per accident.

A   This throws little light on the central puzzle: why the current number of car accidents is significantly higher than 30 years ago, while the number of deaths and injuries in car accidents is not. The fact that there has been a significant increase in car accidents suggests that the roads were not made as safe as they could have been, and this just deepens the puzzle about the lack of a significant increase in deaths and injuries.

B   **Correct**. This implies that the average number of passengers per car accident is significantly less, and this helps explain why the total number of deaths and injuries has not increased significantly.

C   This information does not help explain the mismatch between increased accident numbers and relatively stable death-and-injury numbers. High-speed car accidents would likely have caused more fatalities, on average, than other car accidents; so, given that the increase in traffic volume has been greatest on Sabresia's high-speed roads, one would expect a significant increase in the number of accidents, and consequently in the number of deaths and injuries. But this expectation has not been fulfilled.

D   This does not help explain the surprisingly stable death-and-injury numbers in contrast with the significantly increased number of car accidents. The increase in average age of cars on the road might contribute to the increased number of accidents if older cars are more likely to be dangerously defective than newer ones.

E   The central puzzle already described involves no comparisons between Sabresia and other countries, so this information is irrelevant to explaining the puzzling discrepancy.

The correct answer is B.

127. A child learning to play the piano will not succeed unless the child has an instrument at home on which to practice. However, good-quality pianos, whether new or secondhand, are costly. Buying one is justified only if the child has the necessary talent and perseverance, which is precisely what one cannot know in advance. Consequently, parents should buy an inexpensive secondhand instrument at first and upgrade if and when the child's ability and inclination are proven.

Which of the following, if true, casts the most serious doubt on the course of action recommended for parents?

(A) Learners, particularly those with genuine musical talent, are apt to lose interest in the instrument if they have to play on a piano that fails to produce a pleasing sound.

(B) Reputable piano teachers do not accept children as pupils unless they know that the children can practice on a piano at home.

(C) Ideally, the piano on which a child practices at home should be located in a room away from family activities going on at the same time.

(D) Very young beginners often make remarkable progress at playing the piano at first, but then appear to stand still for a considerable period of time.

(E) In some parents, spending increasing amounts of money on having their children learn to play the piano produces increasing anxiety to hear immediate results.

Evaluation of a Plan

Situation   Children learning the piano need to have a piano on which to practice at home. Purchasing a high-quality piano is costly, and justified only if the child has talent and will persevere, which is hard to predict at an early stage. Parents should make do with a secondhand piano until the child's ability and inclination are proven.

Reasoning   *Which of the statements given would cast the most serious doubt on the recommendation given to parents?* Suppose that a child, because possessed of very high musical talent, is especially sensitive to imprecisions in tuning or imperfections of tone in a secondhand, less expensive piano (presumably Mozart would have been so!). This could, over time, make the child less interested in using the piano—especially if the child had the opportunity to hear music on far superior pianos. The result could be total loss of interest in learning to play the piano.

A   **Correct.** This, if true, would be a good reason to provide the child with the chance to practice regularly on a superior piano.

B   The issue is whether it would be best to provide the child with a superior piano at home, not whether it would be important to provide some piano at home.

C   This is irrelevant to the point at issue, which concerns how high a quality of piano should parents provide at home if they desire optimal development of the child's potential for piano musicianship.

D   Fluctuations in the pace of learning the piano are possible, but not relevant to the central question raised about the quality of the piano to be provided.

E   Investing so much in a piano, to the extent that doing so causes financial and psychological stress, might not be beneficial overall. However, if buying a new piano and buying a used piano are equally feasible financially for a given family, the question concerns which option would most achieve the objective of optimally developing the child's potential for piano musicianship.

The correct answer is A.

128. Which of the following most logically completes the market forecaster's argument?

Market forecaster: The price of pecans is high when pecans are comparatively scarce but drops sharply when pecans are abundant. Thus, in high-yield years, growers often store part of their crop in refrigerated warehouses until after the next year's harvest, hoping for higher prices then. Because of bad weather, this year's pecan crop will be very small. Nevertheless, pecan prices this year will not be significantly higher than last year, since __________.

(A) the last time the pecan crop was as small as it was this year, the practice of holding back part of one year's crop had not yet become widely established

(B) last year's pecan harvest was the largest in the last 40 years

(C) pecan prices have remained relatively stable in recent years

(D) pecan yields for some farmers were as high this year as they had been last year

(E) the quality of this year's pecan crop is as high as the quality of any pecan crop in the previous five years

Argument Construction

Situation   The price of pecans fluctuates based on the fluctuations in market supplies. When pecan farmers have a large harvest, they tend to save some of the crop in refrigerated storage until the following year, hoping to get higher prices then. This year's crop will be very small. But prices are not predicted to be significantly higher than last year.

Reasoning   *What can most reasonably complete the argument by filling in the blank?* In other words, what would be the best reason for the prediction about this year's prices? This year's prices will be determined by the total market supply of pecans; this will include not only freshly harvested pecans but also pecans that were kept in storage from last year's harvest. Information about the relative size of last year's harvest could be partial evidence for a prediction about this year's prices.

A   What this tells us, in effect, is that previous experience with very poor harvests provide a poor guide about this year's total market supply, since the practice of refrigerated storage of pecans had not existed then.

B   **Correct.** This tells us that there was probably an unprecedented quantity of pecans in refrigerated storage from last year, so it is likely that the market supply of pecans this year will be relatively normal despite the poor harvest. This means that this year's prices will not be much higher than last year's; last year, the total pecan harvest was enormous and market supply probably relatively large.

C   This creates a general expectation of prices not being inordinately high this year, but since the harvest this year was "very small," such a general expectation could remain unfulfilled, absent countervailing factors.

D   This information is too vague to be useful. What percentage of farmers obtained satisfactory yields? Were these yields on farms that were by far the largest or the smallest?

E   The reasoning is silent on the issue of pecan quality, even though perceived quality could perhaps affect prices obtained. The additional information does not tell us that this year's quality is better than that found in recent harvests.

The correct answer is B.

129. Many office buildings designed to prevent outside air from entering have been shown to have elevated levels of various toxic substances circulating through the air inside, a phenomenon known as sick building syndrome. Yet the air in other office buildings does not have elevated levels of these substances, even though those buildings are the same age as the "sick" buildings and have similar designs and ventilation systems.

Which of the following, if true, most helps to explain why not all office buildings designed to prevent outside air from entering have air that contains elevated levels of toxic substances?

(A) Certain adhesives and drying agents used in particular types of furniture, carpets, and paint contribute the bulk of the toxic substances that circulate in the air of office buildings.

(B) Most office buildings with sick building syndrome were built between 1950 and 1990.

(C) Among buildings designed to prevent outside air from entering, houses are no less likely than office buildings to have air that contains elevated levels of toxic substances.

(D) The toxic substances that are found in the air of "sick" office buildings are substances that are found in at least small quantities in nearly every building.

(E) Office buildings with windows that can readily be opened are unlikely to suffer from sick building syndrome.

Argument Evaluation

Situation Many office buildings designed to prevent outside air from entering have elevated levels of toxic substances in their interior air, but other such buildings similar in age, design, and ventilation do not.

Reasoning *What would help to explain the difference in air quality among buildings similar in age, design, and ventilation?* If office buildings are designed to prevent outside air from entering, toxic substances emitted into the interior air might not be ventilated out quickly, and thus might become more concentrated inside the building. But if such toxic substances are not emitted into a building's interior air in the first place, they will not become concentrated there, even if the building is poorly ventilated. So any factor that suggests why toxic substances are emitted into the interior air of some buildings but not others of similar age and design would help to explain the difference in the buildings' air quality.

A **Correct.** Some buildings may have these types of furniture, carpets, and paint, while other buildings similar in age, design, and ventilation do not.

B Since all these buildings were built during the same period, this does not help to explain the difference in air quality among buildings similar in age.

C The passage concerns air quality in office buildings only, not in houses.

D This does not help to explain why these toxic substances are more concentrated in some office buildings than in others.

E The passage concerns the differences in air quality only among office buildings that were designed to prevent outside air from entering.

The correct answer is A.

130. Newsletter: **A condominium generally offers more value for its cost than an individual house because of economies of scale.** The homeowners in a condominium association can collectively buy products and services that they could not afford on their own. And since a professional management company handles maintenance of common areas, **condominium owners spend less time and money on maintenance than individual homeowners do.**

The two portions in **boldface** play which of the following roles in the newsletter's argument?

(A)   The first is the argument's main conclusion; the second is another conclusion supporting the first.

(B)   The first is a premise, for which no evidence is provided; the second is the argument's only conclusion.

(C)   The first is a conclusion supporting the second; the second is the argument's main conclusion.

(D)   The first is the argument's only conclusion; the second is a premise, for which no evidence is provided.

(E)   Both are premises, for which no evidence is provided, and both support the argument's only conclusion.

Argument Construction

Situation   Homeowners in a condominium association can buy products and services collectively. A management company handles maintenance of condominium common areas.

Reasoning   *What roles are played in the argument by the statement that a condominium generally offers more value for its cost than a house because of economies of scale and by the statement that condominium owners spend less time and money on maintenance than owners of individual homes do?* In the passage, the first sentence (the first **boldfaced** statement) is a generalization. The second sentence provides an example of the economies of scale mentioned in the first sentence, so it helps support the first sentence as a conclusion. In the third sentence, the word *since* indicates that the first clause is a premise supporting the second clause (the second **boldfaced** statement) as a conclusion. That conclusion itself provides another example of the economies of scale mentioned in the first sentence, so it also helps support that first sentence as a conclusion.

A   **Correct.** As explained above, the first **boldfaced** statement is supported by the rest of the statements in the argument, so it is the main conclusion. The second **boldfaced** statement supports the first, but is itself a conclusion supported by the *since* clause preceding it.

B   The second and third sentences in the argument provide examples of economies of scale. These examples are evidence supporting the first **boldfaced** statement as a conclusion.

C   Since the second **boldfaced** statement provides evidence of the economies of scale described by the first, it supports the first as a conclusion.

D   The *since* clause immediately preceding the second **boldfaced** statement provides evidence that supports it, so the second **boldfaced** statement is a conclusion.

E   Both the second and the third sentences of the argument support the first **boldfaced** statement as a conclusion. And the *since* clause immediately preceding the second **boldfaced** statement supports it as a conclusion.

The correct answer is A.

131. Platinum is a relatively rare metal vital to a wide variety of industries. Xagor Corporation, a major producer of platinum, has its production plant in a country that will soon begin imposing an export tax on platinum sold and shipped to customers abroad. As a consequence, the price of platinum on the world market is bound to rise.

Which of the following, if true, tends to confirm the conclusion above?

(A) An inexpensive substitute for platinum has been developed and will be available to industry for the first time this month.

(B) The largest of the industries that depend on platinum reported a drop in sales last month.

(C) The producers of platinum in other countries taken together cannot supply enough platinum to meet worldwide demand.

(D) Xagor produced more platinum last month than in any previous month.

(E) New deposits of platinum have been found in the country in which Xagor has its production plant.

Argument Evaluation

Situation   Xagor Corporation produces platinum, a rare metal vital to many industries. Xagor's plant is in a country that will soon impose an export tax on platinum. The world market price of platinum is predicted to rise.

Reasoning   *Which of the pieces of information given, if true, would most tend to confirm the prediction given?* The conclusion of the argument is a causal prediction: the world market price of platinum will increase because of the export tax on platinum. The argument tells us that a wide range of industries need platinum, so the introduction of taxes on exported platinum would likely make that platinum more expensive for the importing industries. This, in turn, would likely raise the world market price of platinum. But what if those industries could get all their platinum from countries that did not tax platinum exports? Then the world market price might not rise if exports from those countries could adequately fulfill market demand.

A   This information tends to undermine the reasoning and does not confirm the conclusion. If a less expensive platinum-substitute were to be developed, the world market price of platinum would tend to decline.

B   This information somewhat weakens support for the conclusion. It suggests that overall demand for platinum might decline, at least temporarily, which would tend to lower the world market price of platinum.

C   **Correct.** This information strengthens the support for the conclusion. It indicates that some platinum subject to the export tax will almost certainly be exported and will cost importers more than before. This would tend to cause the world market price of platinum to rise, especially since platinum producers in other countries could remain competitive and still raise their prices.

D   This information could indicate a possible upswing in platinum production, which could increase the total world supply of platinum. If the supply increased relative to world demand, the world market price of platinum could decrease, not increase as the argument's conclusion predicts.

E   This information suggests a possible increase in the world market supply of platinum, which would tend to reduce the world market price, provided world demand for platinum did not also increase at least proportionately.

The correct answer is C.

132. From 1973 to 1986, growth in the United States economy was over 33 percent, while the percent growth in United States energy consumption was zero. The number of barrels of oil being saved per day by energy-efficiency improvements made since 1973 is now 13 million.

If the information above is correct, which of the following conclusions can properly be drawn on the basis of it?

(A) It is more difficult to find new sources of oil than to institute new energy-conservation measures.

(B) Oil imports cannot be reduced unless energy consumption does not grow at all.

(C) A reduction in the consumption of gasoline was the reason overall energy consumption remained steady.

(D) It is possible for an economy to grow without consuming additional energy.

(E) The development of nontraditional energy sources will make it possible for the United States economy to grow even faster.

Argument Construction

Situation   From 1973 to 1986, the United States economy grew over 33 percent while energy consumption did not grow. Energy improvements have made dramatic savings in annual oil consumption since 1973.

Reasoning   *If the given information in the passage is true, which answer choice must be true based on that information?* To find that statement, look for the one that has the closest relevance to the information given. All of the answer choices refer to topics at least loosely associated with the topics discussed in the given information. But four of them introduce extraneous information, while just one relies solely on the given information, simply making explicit something implicit in that information.

A   Nothing in the given information even implicitly depends on contrasting the relative difficulty of finding new oil with the difficulty of instituting new energy-conservation measures.

B   Nothing in the given information refers, even implicitly, to oil imports, so this statement does not follow logically from the given information.

C   This is new information that, if true, would help explain why there was zero percent growth in energy consumption in the period under discussion. But this new information could easily be false even if the given information is true. For instance, gasoline consumption could have held steady but the consumption of petroleum diesel or heating oil could have been reduced significantly.

D   **Correct.** This statement must be true if the given information is accurate. If something of a given kind has occurred, then it must be possible for that kind of thing to occur. The given information cites an example of an economy that had 33 percent economic growth along with zero percent growth in energy consumption.

E   The given information may be entirely accurate even if this claim is false. Even if this claim is true, the given information does not address, even implicitly, the development of nontraditional sources.

The correct answer is D.

133. Although many customers do not make a sufficient effort to conserve water, water companies must also be held responsible for wasteful consumption. Their own policies, in fact, encourage excessive water use, and attempts at conservation will succeed only if the water companies change their practices.

Which of the following, if true, would most strongly support the view above?

(A)   Most water companies reduce the cost per unit of water as the amount of water used by a customer increases.

(B)   Most water companies keep detailed records of the quantity of water used by different customers.

(C)   Most water companies severely curtail the use of water during periods of drought.

(D)   Federal authorities limit the range of policies that can be enforced by the water companies.

(E)   The price per unit of water charged by the water companies has risen steadily in the last 10 years.

Argument Evaluation

Situation   Water companies have policies that encourage excessive water use. Water conservation cannot succeed unless water companies change their practices.

Reasoning   *Which answer choice would indicate that water companies' policies and practices lead to wasteful water use?* If the companies have policies or practices that reduce customers' incentive to consume less water, then wasteful water consumption would be more likely to occur. Water companies would be contributing to wasteful water use and should be held accountable for that waste if water conservation is to succeed.

A   **Correct.** Water companies' charging customers less per additional unit of water consumed is likely to reduce customers' incentive to avoid wasteful water use. So water companies bear some responsibility for wasteful water use.

B   This shows that water companies have adequate data to indicate trends in customers' water consumption. But this does not, by itself, indicate that water companies incentivize wasteful consumption.

C   This indicates that water companies likely curtail wasteful water use during droughts, which somewhat weakens the argument.

D   This information is too nonspecific to allow us to judge whether the federal authorities' regulatory regime directly or indirectly contributes to wasteful water use.

E   If anything, this information tends to weaken the argument. Over a 10-year period, because most economies experience inflation, increases in the price per unit of water would naturally occur, absent special countervailing factors. But if the increases were large, they would, if anything, tend to reduce wasteful water use.

The correct answer is A.

134. Despite legislation designed to stem the accumulation of plastic waste, the plastics industry continued to grow rapidly last year, as can be seen from the fact that sales of the resin that is the raw material for manufacturing plastics grew by 10 percent to $28 billion.

In assessing the support provided by the evidence cited above for the statement that the plastics industry continued to grow, in addition to the information above it would be most useful to know

(A) whether the resin has other uses besides the manufacture of plastics

(B) the dollar amount of resin sales the year before last

(C) the plastics industry's attitude toward the legislation concerning plastic waste

(D) whether sales of all goods and services in the economy as a whole were increasing last year

(E) what proportion of the plastics industry's output eventually contributes to the accumulation of plastic waste

Argument Evaluation

Situation   There is legislation meant to slow the accumulation of plastic waste. Last year, however, the plastics industry continued to grow rapidly. Sales of the resin that is the raw material for plastics grew in monetary terms by 10 percent.

Reasoning   *What additional information should we seek in order to evaluate the evidence offered for the conclusion that the plastics industry continued to grow rapidly last year?* The evidence offered is that sales of resin from which plastics can be made increased 10 percent over the preceding year. For example, we could inquire whether the resin is used exclusively for plastics manufacture. If this were found NOT to be so, then the evidence presented would be of little use in showing that the plastics industry grew rapidly last year.

A   **Correct.** Knowing whether this is so is crucial for judging the evidential value of last year's growth in sales of resin.

B   This information is implicit in the given information and is therefore not additional information.

C   The central issue is whether the information about last year's resin sales is good evidence of the plastics industry growth. The question as to whether that industry favors curtailment of plastics pollution has little if any relevance to that issue.

D   If the answer to this *whether*-question is yes, there was presumably some inflation in the currency, so the increase in nominal monetary value of resin sales may or may not reflect very strong evidence of growth in the plastics industry. If the answer to the question is no, the increase in resin sales could be evidence of growth but is not necessarily so. In either case, we would need further information, so either answer to the question would not be useful for assessing the evidence.

E   Knowing the answer to this could be important, but it is irrelevant in determining the evidential value of the information about growth in resin sales last year.

The correct answer is A.

135. Studies of the political orientations of 1,055 college students revealed that the plurality of students in an eastern, big-city, private university was liberal, whereas in a state-supported, southern college, the plurality was conservative. Orientations were independent of the student's region of origin, and the trends were much more pronounced in seniors than in beginning students.

Which of the following hypotheses is best supported by the observations stated above?

(A) The political orientations of college students are more similar to the political orientations of their parents when the students start college than when the students are seniors.

(B) The political orientations of college seniors depend significantly on experiences they have had while in college.

(C) A college senior originally from the South is more likely to be politically conservative than is a college senior originally from the East.

(D) Whether their college is state-supported or private is the determining factor in college students' political orientations.

(E) College students tend to become more conservative politically as they become older and are confronted with pressures for financial success.

Argument Evaluation

Situation Studies of a total of 1,055 college students in an eastern big-city private university and in a state-supported southern college found that, in the sample, the political orientation of most students in the private college was liberal and that of most students in the southern college was conservative. Among the liberal students identified in the private college and among the conservative students identified in the state-supported college, significantly more were seniors than beginning students.

Reasoning *What would best explain the trends observed in the college students' political orientations?* Five hypotheses to explain the trends are offered, and we are asked to identify the hypothesis that is most supported by the information already given about the studies. It should be noted that the information given is very limited, whereas the hypotheses offered involve quite broad generalizations, so whatever support is provided by the given information for any of these will at best be quite weak from a statistician's perspective. We should look for the hypothesis that makes the least ambitious claim and draws most closely on the given information.

A The given information, without unjustified introduction of unstated assumptions, provides no insight into the political orientations of the students' parents.

B **Correct.** Among the five hypotheses offered, this makes the least ambitious claim. Although its scope extends to college seniors in general (and in a statistical sense goes far beyond the evidence provided in the given information), it is the best supported of the five because it deviates least from the information we have. It is a good inference that the students' political re-orientation occurred as a result of the "experiences they have had while in college"—even if some of the truly mind-changing experiences were obtained in activities unrelated to their college life (e.g., speaking with fellow workers in a part-time restaurant job).

C We are given no information about the students' places of origin. The passage states: "orientations were independent of the student's region of origin."

D The given information provides no information regarding which among a multiplicity of conceivable influences contributed most strongly to the students' political orientations.

E We are not told in the given information that the students were "confronted with pressures for financial success"—although it is a truism that they were becoming older in their progress toward graduation.

The correct answer is B.

136. Diabetics often suffer dangerously low blood sugar levels, which they can correct safely if they notice the symptoms quickly. It has been suggested that **diabetics should be advised to drink moderate amounts of coffee**, since doing so improves their ability to recognize symptoms of low blood sugar quickly. That would be bad advice, however, since drinking even small amounts of coffee can increase the body's need for sugar in unpredictable ways.

In the argument being made, the part that is in **boldface** plays which of the following roles?

(A) Presenting the conclusion toward which the argument as a whole is directed

(B) Providing support for the conclusion of the argument

(C) Offering a reason to take a course of action recommended in the argument

(D) Stating the position to be refuted by the argument

(E) Providing an instance of a general principle articulated in the argument

Argument Evaluation

Situation   Diabetics need to recognize the signs of dangerously low blood sugar to address low sugar levels promptly. Because moderate coffee consumption heightens diabetics' awareness of symptoms indicating low blood sugar, some people advise that diabetics consume coffee. However, even limited coffee consumption can also destabilize blood sugar levels unpredictably.

Reasoning   *What role does the advice for diabetics to drink coffee play in an argument about safe strategies for avoiding dangerous drops in blood sugar?* Since drinking coffee heightens diabetics' awareness of the symptoms of low blood pressure, the argument might be expected to endorse the advice that diabetics should drink coffee in moderation. The following sentence, however, suggests that coffee consumption could be dangerous for diabetics by destabilizing their blood sugar levels.

A   The recommendation in **boldface** is described as bad advice in the following sentence, so it is not the argument's conclusion.

B   The advice for diabetics to drink coffee does not support the conclusion that drinking coffee could be risky for them.

C   The **boldfaced** text advises a course of action but does not offer a reason to follow any course of action.

D   **Correct.** The recommendation that diabetics should drink moderate amounts of coffee is refuted by the following sentence, which suggests that even small amounts of coffee could cause unpredictable shifts in their sugar requirements.

E   The recommendation for diabetics to drink moderate amounts of coffee is specific advice and not a general principle.

The correct answer is D.

137. Trancorp currently transports all its goods to Burland Island by truck. The only bridge over the channel separating Burland from the mainland is congested, and trucks typically spend hours in traffic. Trains can reach the channel more quickly than trucks, and freight cars can be transported to Burland by barges that typically cross the channel in an hour. Therefore, to reduce shipping time, Trancorp plans to switch to trains and barges to transport goods to Burland.

Which of the following, if true, casts the most serious doubt on whether Trancorp's plan will succeed?

(A) It does not cost significantly more to transport goods to Burland by truck than it does to transport goods by train and barge.

(B) The number of cars traveling over the bridge into Burland is likely to increase slightly over the next two years.

(C) Because there has been so much traffic on the roads leading to the bridge between Burland and the mainland, these roads are in extremely poor condition.

(D) Barges that arrive at Burland typically wait several hours for their turn to be unloaded.

(E) Most trucks transporting goods into Burland return to the mainland empty.

Evaluation of a Plan

Situation Trancorp's shipments to Burland Island are slowed by congestion on the one bridge that connects the island to the mainland. To address this problem, the company plans to transport goods to Burland Island by a combination of trains and barges, which can reach the island more quickly.

Reasoning *Since the goal of Trancorp's plan is to reduce shipping times by switching to trains and barges for transport, what would be most likely to interfere with that goal's achievement?* Trancorp is attempting to reduce shipping times to Burland Island by switching from trucks to trains and barges, so any factors that significantly slow shipping by trains and barges cast doubt on their plan's success.

A Trancorp's goal is to reduce shipping times, not shipping costs, so the costs of different shipping methods do not cast doubt on the plan's success.

B Increasing congestion on the bridge to Burland would make the plan to reduce shipping times by avoiding that bridge more likely to succeed, not less.

C The poor condition of roads to Burland Island would make the plan to reduce shipping times by avoiding those roads more likely to succeed, not less.

D **Correct.** If waiting time for barges to be unloaded adds several hours to the total shipping time by train and barge, that delay may cancel out the time otherwise saved by switching to trains and barges, making Trancorp's plan less likely to succeed.

E The plan concerns having goods transported to Burland Island, not carrying goods back from there, so the emptiness of returning trucks has no bearing on that plan's success.

The correct answer is D.

138. When ducklings are exposed to music, they gain about 6 percent more weight for a given amount of feed than ducklings that are not exposed to music.

Which of the following, if true, most helps to explain the extra weight gains referred to above?

(A)   Music played for ducklings must be kept at a low level because ducklings exposed to loud music gain less weight than ducklings exposed to no music.

(B)   Ducklings exposed to classical music gained more weight than ducklings exposed to popular music.

(C)   Ducklings are less active when they hear music, so that less of the food they eat is expended in movement, and more contributes directly to the ducklings' growth.

(D)   When ducklings gain 6 percent more weight on a given amount of grain, the farmers' profits increase because they can spend less money on grain to feed the ducklings.

(E)   When female ducklings were exposed to music, the percentage of fertile eggs that they laid as adults increased by over 27 percent in comparison to ducklings not exposed to music.

Argument Construction

Situation   Ducklings that are exposed to music gain more weight from a given amount of feed than ducklings that aren't exposed to music.

Reasoning   *What factor is most likely to contribute to the additional weight gains observed in ducklings exposed to music?* Because the amount of food given to ducklings exposed to music is the same as the amount given to ducklings not exposed to music, other factors must account for the music-exposed ducklings' greater weight gains.

A   The effects of variable musical volume on ducklings' weight gains would not help explain those gains.

B   Variable duckling weight gains promoted by different types of music does not provide an explanation for those gains.

C   **Correct.** If ducklings exposed to music are less active and therefore burn fewer calories, then the lesser activity of such ducklings would provide a likely explanation for their higher weight gains.

D   The greater profits of farmers is a consequence of the ducklings' increased weight gains and does not provide any explanation for those weight gains.

E   The gain in egg fertility observed in ducks with early musical exposure does not explain the greater weight gains in music-exposed ducklings.

The correct answer is C.

139. X: In order to reduce the amount of plastic in landfills, legislatures should impose a ban on the use of plastics for packaging goods.

Y: Impossible! Plastic packaging is necessary for public safety. Consumers will lose all of the safety features that plastic offers, chiefly tamper-resistant closures and shatterproof bottles.

Which of the following best describes the weak point in Y's response to X's proposal?

(A) Y ignores the possibility that packaging goods in materials other than plastic might provide the same safety features that packaging in plastic offers.

(B) The economic disadvantages of using plastics as a means of packaging goods are not taken into consideration.

(C) Y attempts to shift the blame for the large amount of plastic in landfills from the users of plastic packaging to the legislators.

(D) Y does not consider the concern of some manufacturers that safety features spoil package appearances.

(E) Y wrongly assumes that X defends the interests of the manufacturers rather than the interests of the consumers.

Argument Evaluation

Situation   X believes that plastic packaging should be banned to reduce plastic waste in landfills, but Y argues that plastic packaging is essential for public safety because of the safety features offered by plastic.

Reasoning   *What is the weak point in Y's response to X's proposal, based on the claim that plastic packaging is necessary for public safety?* Since Y's argument is that plastic packaging offers essential safety features and therefore should not be eliminated, Y's argument would be undermined by information that those safety features could be provided without the use of plastic.

A   **Correct.** Y's argument states that plastic is essential for providing safety features, which would allow the argument to be refuted by any evidence that those features can be created with other materials.

B   Possible economic disadvantages of using plastic do not weaken Y's argument or undermine the claim that plastic is necessary for public safety.

C   Y's argument does not address the roles of either legislators or consumers in creating plastic waste in landfills.

D   Whether or not safety features spoil package appearance is irrelevant to the argument that plastic is necessary to provide such features.

E   Y's argument that plastic is essential for public safety does not imply that X favors the interests of manufacturers over those of consumers.

The correct answer is A.

140. United Lumber will use trees from its forests for two products. The tree trunks will be used for lumber and the branches converted into wood chips to make fiberboard. The cost of this conversion would be the same whether done at the logging site, where the trees are debranched, or at United's factory. However, wood chips occupy less than half the volume of the branches from which they are made.

The information given, if accurate, most strongly supports which of the following?

(A) Converting the branches into wood chips at the logging site would require transporting a fully assembled wood-chipping machine to and from the site.

(B) It would be more economical to debranch the trees at the factory where the fiberboard is manufactured.

(C) The debranching of trees and the conversion of the branches into chips are the only stages in the processing of branches that would be in United's economic advantage to perform at the logging site.

(D) Transportation costs from the logging site to the factory that are determined by volume of cargo would be lower if the conversion into chips is done at the logging site rather than at the factory.

(E) In the wood-processing industry, branches are used only for the production of wood chips for fiberboard.

Argument Construction

Situation   United Lumber creates two products from trees: lumber from trunks and wood-chip-composed fiberboard from branches. Though converting the branches into wood chips costs the same whether done at the logging site or at the factory, the wood chips take up half the space that the branches take up before conversion.

Reasoning   *What is most likely to be true if the cost of converting branches to wood chips is equal at the logging site and the factory, but the total volume of the branches is greatly reduced by converting them into wood chips?* The information states that the cost of conversion is the same at both locations, so the significant variable is the reduced volume of the branches after conversion into chips.

A   While converting branches to chips might well require machinery onsite, nothing suggests that such machinery would require transport fully assembled.

B   No information is provided about the cost of debranching at the logging site compared to the cost of debranching at the factory.

C   The information states that converting branches to chips reduces volume, which might benefit United if performed at the logging site, but nothing implies that other steps in the process would not also be advantageous if performed at the site.

D   Correct. Since converting the branches into chips greatly reduces their total volume, it follows that shipping costs determined by volume would also be reduced if the conversion were done at the logging site.

E   The information states that United converts branches into wood chips for fiberboard, but it does not imply that the wood-processing industry in general uses branches exclusively to make fiberboard.

The correct answer is D.

141. Which of the following most logically completes the passage?

For the past several years, a certain technology has been widely used to transmit data among networked computers. Recently, two data transmission companies, Aptron and Gammatech, have each developed separate systems that allow network data transmission at rates ten times faster than the current technology allows. Although the systems are similarly priced and are equally easy to use, Aptron's product is likely to dominate the market, because __________.

(A) Gammatech has been in the business of designing data transmission systems for several years more than Aptron has

(B) the number of small businesses that need computer networking systems is likely to double over the next few years

(C) it is much more likely that Gammatech's system will be expandable to meet future needs

(D) unlike many data transmission companies, Aptron and Gammatech develop computers in addition to data transmission systems

(E) it is easier for users of the current data transmission technology to switch to Aptron's product than to Gammatech's

Argument Construction

Situation   Two companies, Aptron and Gammatech, have both developed data transmission systems that are much faster than the previously available systems. Moreover, the two new systems are comparable in performance, price, and ease of use.

Reasoning   *Since the systems developed by Gammatech and Aptron are similar in price and ease of use, what other factor supports the prediction that Aptron's system is more likely to dominate the market?* The statement predicts that Aptron's system will dominate the market but implicitly rules out two explanations— price and ease of use—for that prediction. Therefore, there is likely to be another factor that justifies the prediction.

A   Gammatech's greater experience in the field would not make Aptron more likely to dominate the market.

B   Increased demand for networking systems would be likely to benefit both companies, not Aptron in particular.

C   If Gammatech's system is more likely to meet future needs, that would be a factor that might help Gammatech, not Aptron, dominate the market.

D   If both companies make the same products in addition to data transmission systems, that would not be likely in itself to help one company outperform the other in the market.

E   **Correct.** If it is easier to convert to Aptron's system than to Gammatech's, which might include some conversions from an earlier Gammatech system to the newest Aptron system, that would provide a logical reason for the prediction that Aptron will be likely to dominate the market.

The correct answer is E.

142. In Brindon County, virtually all of the fasteners—such as nuts, bolts, and screws—used by workshops and manufacturing firms have for several years been supplied by the Brindon Bolt Barn, a specialist wholesaler. In recent months, many of Brindon County's workshops and manufacturing firms have closed down, and no new ones have opened. Therefore, the Brindon Bolt Barn will undoubtedly show a sharp decline in sales volume and revenue for this year as compared to last year.

The argument depends on assuming which of the following?

(A) Last year, the Brindon Bolt Barn's sales volume and revenue were significantly higher than they had been the previous year.

(B) The workshops and manufacturing firms that have remained open have a smaller volume of work to do this year than they did last year.

(C) Soon the Brindon Bolt Barn will no longer be the only significant supplier of fasteners to Brindon County's workshops.

(D) The Brindon Bolt Barn's operating expenses have not increased this year.

(E) The Brindon Bolt Barn is not a company that gets the great majority of its business from customers outside Brindon County.

Argument Construction

Situation   Brindon County has seen a recent steep decline in the number of its workshops and manufacturing firms. This will result in a significant decline in Brindon Bolt Barn's sales, given that Brindon Bolt Barn supplied these defunct businesses with parts.

Reasoning   *What assumption underlies the argument that Brindon Bolt Barn's decreasing sales in Brindon County will necessarily lead to a steep decline in Brindon Bolt Barn's sales overall?* A sharp decline in overall sales due to reduced demand in Brindon County would be likely only if Brindon Bolt Barn did not have enough sales elsewhere to offset that reduction by a significant amount.

A   Brindon Bolt Barn's higher sales last year would not be expected to lead to sharply lower sales this year.

B   If Brindon Bolt Barn relies heavily on sales in Brindon County, then a large number of workshop closures in the county could well be enough to cause sharply declining sales, even without the additional factor of lower demand from the surviving workshops.

C   The argument suggests that the decline is sales will be caused by decreasing demand, not by increasing competition.

D   Steady operating expenses would not be expected to lead to sharply decreasing sales.

E   **Correct.** The argument assumes that Brindon Bolt Barn relies heavily on sales in Brindon County; if a great majority of its products are sold outside the county, then a sharp decline in local sales would not necessarily lead to a sharp decline in overall sales.

The correct answer is E.

143. Eurasian water milfoil, a weed not native to Frida Lake, has reproduced prolifically since being accidentally introduced there. In order to eliminate the weed, biologists proposed treating infested parts of the lake with a certain herbicide that is nontoxic for humans and aquatic animals. However, the herbicide might damage populations of certain rare plant species that the lake contains. For this reason, local officials rejected the proposal.

Which of the following, if true, points out the most serious weakness in the officials' grounds for rejecting the biologists' proposal?

(A) The continuing spread of Eurasian water milfoil in Frida Lake threatens to choke out the lake's rare plant species.

(B) Because of ecological conditions prevailing in its native habitat, Eurasian water milfoil is not as dominant there as it is in Frida Lake.

(C) The proliferation of Eurasian water milfoil in Frida Lake has led to reductions in the populations of some species of aquatic animals.

(D) Although Eurasian water milfoil could be mechanically removed from Frida Lake, eliminating the weed would take far longer this way than it would using herbicides.

(E) Unless Eurasian water milfoil is completely eliminated from Frida Lake, it will quickly spread again once herbicide treatments or other control measures cease.

Evaluation of a Plan

Situation Invasive Eurasian water milfoil is spreading rapidly in Frida Lake. Biologists want to control the milfoil with an herbicide safe for people and aquatic animals, but because it is potentially harmful to rare native plants, officials declined to use this herbicide.

Reasoning *Since officials rejected the plan to kill the invasive milfoil in Frida Lake with herbicide because of that herbicide's risk to rare plant species in the same lake, what factor would significantly weaken those grounds for rejection?* Rejecting the plan to use herbicide to kill milfoil because of the herbicide's risk to native plants only makes sense if the milfoil itself does not present a greater risk than the herbicide does.

A **Correct.** The risk that milfoil could completely choke out the rare native plant species might well be greater than the risk that the milfoil-killing herbicide could damage those rare species, which would present a serious weakness in the officials' grounds for rejecting the herbicide's use.

B Eurasian water milfoil's behavior in its native habitat has no bearing on the decision not to use herbicide against it in Frida Lake.

C The officials refused the use of milfoil-killing herbicide on the specific grounds that the herbicide could damage native plants, so milfoil's damage to native animal species might support the use of herbicide, but it does not weaken the officials' stated grounds for refusing to use it.

D The possibility of removing milfoil from Frida Lake by means other than the herbicide would tend to support the officials' decision, not weaken it.

E The possibility of milfoil quickly returning to Frida Lake if eradication is incomplete has no bearing on whether or not officials were right to reject the use of herbicide against milfoil.

The correct answer is A.

144. When airplanes are taken out of service for maintenance, they are often repainted. Having an airplane out of service is extremely costly to an airline, and during repainting, no other maintenance can be done. In an attempt to reduce expenses associated with maintenance, airline officials are considering using a new plastic film, which is applied in sheets, instead of paint. However, the film is more expensive than paint, lasts no longer, and takes as long to apply.

Which of the following, if true, argues most strongly that use of the film will help the airline officials in their attempt to reduce expenses?

(A) While the film is being applied, other workers can do maintenance work on the plane.

(B) Unlike paint, the film gives a milky tone to certain colors.

(C) The film can be applied only by technicians who have received special training.

(D) The metal exteriors of airplanes have to be protected from high temperatures and caustic chemicals such as exhaust gases.

(E) Special ripples in the film reduce a plane's air resistance and thus reduce fuel costs.

Argument Evaluation

Situation   During the period when airplanes are grounded for maintenance, they are often repainted. The repainting process prevents other maintenance from being done until it is complete, and having a plane grounded is expensive for the airline. To reduce maintenance costs, airline officials are considering replacing paint with a new plastic film that is more expensive, no more durable, and equally time-consuming to apply.

Reasoning   *What additional factor would make the use of the plastic film in place of paint reduce maintenance costs?* The information provided compares the plastic film to paint in three respects: it has greater cost, equal or lower durability, and equal application time. These factors taken together would tend to increase maintenance costs, not reduce them, unless the plastic film significantly reduced maintenance costs in some additional respect.

A   **Correct.** The information establishes that having a plane grounded for maintenance is very expensive; therefore, if other maintenance work can be done during application of the film, but not during painting, that is a factor that suggests using the film could reduce maintenance costs by significantly reducing the amount of time a plane must stay grounded for maintenance.

B   Whether or not the plastic film gives a milky tone to certain colors is not relevant to the question of whether using the film can reduce maintenance costs.

C   If the plastic film requires specially trained technicians to apply it, that factor would be more likely to increase maintenance costs—assuming such technicians command higher salaries than do painters—than it would be to lower such costs.

D   Because there is no information about whether paint or the plastic film offers more protection to airplanes' metal surfaces, it is impossible to determine whether the fact that planes need such protection is germane to the question of whether the film can lower maintenance costs.

E   The fact that the use of the plastic film can reduce fuel costs would make it a more attractive option for airlines, but reduced fuel costs have no bearing on the specific question of whether the plastic film can reduce *maintenance* costs.

The correct answer is A.

145. Almost all the fish sold in Eastville is sold in small seafood stores. Fish at such stores in Eastville's downtown Old Market is much cheaper than similar fish sold at large uptown stores. Old Market vendors buy fish of similar quality from the same wholesalers and at the same prices as uptown vendors do, and their other business expenses are also about the same. Yet the Old Market stores are just as profitable as the uptown stores.

The statements given, if true, most strongly support which of the following?

(A) Small seafood stores are less profitable than large seafood stores.

(B) Some varieties of fish that are not available at Old Market stores can be found occasionally at large uptown seafood stores.

(C) The amount of fish sold at stores in the Old Market is, on average, much higher than that sold at large uptown stores.

(D) Most of the people who live in uptown Eastville buy fish from their neighborhood stores.

(E) There are many more seafood stores in uptown Eastville than there are in the downtown Old Market.

Argument Evaluation

Situation There are two types of stores that sell fish in Eastville: cheaper stores in the Old Market downtown, and more expensive stores uptown. The two types of stores sell fish of comparable quality and wholesale price and have comparable expenses in other respects. Nonetheless, the Old Market stores are as profitable as those uptown.

Reasoning *What can be inferred from the information given?* The information states that the two types of fish stores are similar in every respect except their retail prices: The downtown stores charge much less. Therefore, the downtown stores must have a much lower profit margin per unit than do the uptown stores. In order to achieve comparable total profits with a lower profit margin, the downtown stores must therefore have a significantly greater sales volume than the uptown stores do.

A The information in no way supports an inference that small stores are less profitable than large ones.

B There is nothing whatsoever to suggest that the uptown stores offer a wider range of fish for sale.

C **Correct.** If the downtown stores operate at a significantly lower profit margin per unit than do the uptown stores, but nonetheless achieve equal profits, it follows that they must sell a much greater quantity of fish.

D Nothing supports an inference regarding the location where uptown Eastville residents buy fish.

E There is nothing to suggest that there are more fish stores uptown than downtown.

The correct answer is C.

146. When a certain software update is installed on computer systems, the security programs that normally operate within the system typically respond by disabling key monitoring functions, with the result that the systems become vulnerable to serious security breaches. When systems are installed with both the update and a protective patch, security breaches occur far less frequently. The protective patch is known to counteract many effects of the update and does not itself interfere with normal security programs.

Which of the following hypotheses is best supported by the information given?

(A) Installing the protective patch without the update on systems that are not already vulnerable puts the systems at greater risk of security breaches than installing both the update and the patch does.

(B) The disabling of monitoring functions is the most common cause of security breaches in computer systems.

(C) The protective patch interferes with the tendency of the update to disable key monitoring functions.

(D) For computer systems, increased vulnerability to security breaches is the most harmful effect of installing the update.

(E) If the protective patch is installed along with the update, the version of the update required to achieve its intended performance improvement can generally be reduced.

Argument Evaluation

Situation   Installing a particular software update on computer systems typically causes the systems' security programs to disable key monitoring functions, which in turn makes the systems vulnerable to serious security breaches. When a protective patch is installed together with the update, security breaches occur much less frequently. The patch is known to counteract many effects of the update and does not itself interfere with normal security programs.

Reasoning   To identify the hypothesis best supported by the information, the correct answer must explain *why adding the protective patch reduces the frequency of security breaches* without introducing unsupported assumptions. Since the patch counteracts the effects of the update and does not directly affect security programs, the most reasonable conclusion is that the patch *blocks the update's tendency to disable monitoring functions*, thereby preventing the chain of events that leads to breaches.

A   This choice is unsupported. The information given says nothing about the effects of installing the patch alone. Without evidence about the patch's independent impact, no comparison between patch-only systems and systems with both components can be made.

B   This option makes an unjustified generalization. The evidence only concerns breaches occurring after a specific update is installed, not the causes of security breaches in general. No information is provided about breach causes across all systems.

C   **Correct.** The evidence directly supports this hypothesis. The update triggers a process that leads to security breaches, and the patch both counteracts the update's effects and reduces breaches. Since the patch is not harmful to security programs, the most logical explanation is that it blocks the update's tendency to disable monitoring functions, preventing the vulnerability from arising.

D   This choice goes beyond the evidence. While increased vulnerability is identified as one harmful effect, the passage does not compare it with other possible harms. Therefore, the claim that it is the *most* harmful effect is not supported.

E   This option introduces a new idea—reducing the update's version or intensity—that is not discussed in the passage.

The correct answer is C.

147. A proposed change to federal income tax laws would eliminate deductions from taxable income for donations a taxpayer has made to charitable and educational institutions. So in particular, if this change were adopted, wealthy individuals would no longer be permitted such deductions. Therefore, many charitable and educational institutions would be forced to reduce services.

Which of the following is an assumption on which the argument depends?

(A) Without the incentives offered by federal income tax laws, at least some wealthy individuals would not donate as much money to charitable and educational institutions as they otherwise would have.

(B) Most charitable and educational institutions are satisfied with the level of services that the contributions they currently receive allow them to provide.

(C) The primary reason for not adopting the proposed change in the federal income tax laws cited above is to protect wealthy individuals from having to pay higher taxes.

(D) Charitable and educational institutions do not currently receive a substantial proportion of their funds from tax monies collected by the government.

(E) Income tax laws should be changed to make donations to charitable and educational institutions the only permissible deductions from taxable income.

Argument Evaluation

Situation   There is a proposal to eliminate tax deductions for donations to charities and educational institutions. In that case, the wealthy would not be able to claim these tax deductions. The argument concludes that, in that case, charities and educational institutions would be compelled to curtail their services.

Reasoning: *What assumption is implied by the conclusion?* The argument makes a logical leap: If wealthy people cannot deduct charitable contributions, then charities will have to reduce operations. This leap implies an assumption that, if wealthy people *cannot* claim charitable deductions, then they will donate less money to charity. Otherwise, the charities and educational institutions would be unaffected by the change in tax law.

A   **Correct.** The argument states that if wealthy people cannot claim tax deductions for charitable donations, then charities will have to curtail operations; that leap rests on the assumption that eliminating the deduction would reduce donations.

B   How charities and educational institutions feel about their *current* level of operations has no bearing on the argument that eliminating charitable deductions would *reduce* those operations.

C   The argument suggests, if anything, that the reason not to adopt the proposal is that it would damage charities, not that it would negatively affect the wealthy; in any case, a need to protect the wealthy from tax liabilities is in no way a necessary assumption of the argument.

D   The argument states that eliminating the charitable deduction would force charities to reduce operations, not *end* operations; the charities could, therefore, receive a "substantial proportion" of their funding from any number of other sources, including from money raised by taxation.

E   While the argument can reasonably be read as implying a preference for continuing to allow charitable deductions, nothing suggests the assumption that they should be the *only* deductions.

The correct answer is A.

148. While airplanes are being repainted, only the painters, wearing special protective gear, can go near them. A newly developed nontoxic plastic film offers an alternative to paint; it can be applied to planes in sheets and requires no special precautions. However, the film takes as long to apply as paint does, and it is neither cheaper nor more durable than paint. Clearly, therefore, airlines have little incentive for switching to the film.

Which of the following, if true, most seriously weakens the argument?

(A)   While the plastic film is being applied to a plane, mechanics can perform other maintenance work on the plane.

(B)   The plastic film withstands extremes of temperature and corrosive chemicals such as exhaust fumes about as well as aircraft paint does.

(C)   The plastic film can be applied properly only by technicians who have received special training.

(D)   Standard techniques for detecting metal fatigue through a coat of paint cannot be used on planes covered with the plastic film.

(E)   No uses other than that of covering a plane's exterior have as yet been identified for the newly developed plastic film.

Argument Evaluation

Situation   Repainting planes makes those planes inaccessible to everyone but painters wearing protective gear. A new nontoxic film can be used instead of paint; it takes a similar amount of time to apply and is also comparable in terms of price and durability. The argument concludes that airlines will not have compelling reasons to use the film instead.

Reasoning   *What additional factor would make the film beneficial to airlines?* The argument concludes that airlines have "little incentive" to use the nontoxic plastic film instead of paint. If, then, there was an additional benefit to using the film, then that would seriously weaken the argument by showing that airlines might well have an incentive to switch.

A   **Correct.** If mechanics can do other maintenance work while the plastic film is being applied—but not while the paint is being applied because of the safety measures the paint necessitates—then the plastic film would indeed provide a considerable benefit to airlines in the form of more efficient maintenance. The benefit in turn would weaken the argument by directly counteracting the claim that airlines lack much incentive to switch.

B   If the film is merely comparable to paint in additional important respects, that does not suggest an incentive to switch to the film and therefore does not weaken the argument.

C   The fact that the film needs to be applied by trained technicians might—or might not—be a factor adding to the cost of using it, and could conceivably make it more expensive to use than paint, *if* those technicians are paid more than painters; on the balance it seems likely to either strengthen the argument or else be a neutral factor.

D   If the plastic film makes it more difficult to detect metal fatigue, then that factor would weigh in favor of continuing to use paint and strengthen the argument rather than weakening it.

E   Whether or not there are uses for the film other than covering planes has no bearing on the benefits of using that film *on* planes.

The correct answer is A.

Questions 149 to 196 — Difficulty: **Medium**

149. Donations of imported food will be distributed to children in famine-stricken countries in the form of free school meals. The process is efficient because the children are easy to reach at the schools and cooking facilities are often available on site.

Which of the following, if true, casts the most serious doubt on the efficiency of the proposed process?

(A) The emphasis on food will detract from the major function of the schools, which is to educate the children.

(B) A massive influx of donated food will tend to lower the price of food in the areas near the schools.

(C) Supplies of fuel needed for cooking at the schools arrive there only intermittently and in inadequate quantities.

(D) The reduction in farm surpluses in donor countries benefits the donor countries to a greater extent than the recipient countries are benefited by the donations.

(E) The donation of food tends to strengthen the standing of the political party that happens to be in power when the donation is made.

Evaluation of a Plan

Situation   On grounds of efficiency, it has been proposed that food donated to famine-stricken countries be distributed free to children through the schools. Many of the country's children attend school. Many schools have cooking facilities. Distributing the food through the schools is thus an efficient way of providing nutrition, at least to the children.

Reasoning   *What would most cast doubt on the efficiency of the proposed distribution method?* The rationale offered for the method is twofold. First, many of the country's children attend school. Secondly, many schools have cooking facilities. Any additional information that weakens the significance of either of these two parts of the rationale would cast doubt on the efficiency of the proposed distribution process.

A   This information does not cast significant doubt on the rationale. Of course, providing nutrition might take some time that could otherwise be devoted to teaching and would in that sense perhaps "detract" from the schools' main mission. However, the focus of the given information is on the efficiency of food distribution through the schools, presumably as compared with other methods of distribution that would provide children with adequate nutrition. The trade-off involving some loss of teaching time may be rendered less significant by the fact that children lacking adequate nutrition cannot learn well.

B   This effect, if it occurred, could damage local markets but could also in the short term make locally grown food more available to those who need it. However, the point at issue is whether the rationale for distributing donated food through the schools to improve children's nutrition sufficiently indicates that this distribution method is efficient for that purpose.

C   **Correct.** This information indicates that one part of the rationale given for the efficiency of the distribution method should carry less weight. If the "cooking facilities" at the schools are often inoperable due to lack of fuel, then some of the food to be distributed (for example, staples such as corn, millet, rice, or sorghum) may not be consumable.

D   This information fails to address the central issue, which is the relative efficiency of the proposed distribution method for donated food, to improve children's nutrition.

E   This addresses a possible effect of any food donation and fails to focus on the central issue identified in the foregoing discussion.

The correct answer is C.

150. *John:* You told me once that no United States citizen who supports union labor should buy an imported car. Yet you are buying an Alma. Since Alma is one of the biggest makers of imports, I infer that you no longer support unions.

Harry: I still support labor unions. Even though Alma is a foreign car company, the car I am buying the Alma Deluxe, is designed, engineered, and manufactured in the United States.

Harry's method of defending his purchase of an Alma is to

(A) disown the principle he formerly held

(B) show that John's argument involves a false unstated assumption

(C) contradict John's conclusion without challenging John's reasoning in drawing that conclusion

(D) point out that one of the statements John makes in support of his argument is false

(E) claim that his is a special case in which the rule need not apply

Evaluation of a Plan

Situation   Harry has bought a car manufactured by Alma, a company among the largest makers of cars imported to the United States. From that fact John infers that Harry no longer holds a principle he formerly professed: that nobody who supports U.S. union labor should buy an imported car. Harry responds by clarifying that the Alma Deluxe he is buying is entirely a U.S. product.

Reasoning   *What method has Harry used to show that his purchasing an Alma is not inconsistent with his principles?* Harry does this by showing that John is incorrectly assuming that the car Harry is purchasing has been imported.

A   Harry does not disown the principle he formerly held; rather, he tries to show that his purchase is consistent with it.

B   **Correct.** John mistakenly assumes—without asserting—that the Alma that Harry is buying must be an imported car, and Harry indicates that this assumption is false.

C   Harry challenges John's conclusion but he also challenges John's reasoning, by indicating that it relies on a false unstated assumption.

D   John does not state the assumption that Harry indicates is false, but Harry recognizes that the assumption in question is unstated.

E   Harry does not claim this; he claims, rather, that the new Alma he is purchasing is not imported and so his purchase does not violate his principle concerning union labor.

The correct answer is B.

151. Public-sector (government-owned) companies are often unprofitable and a drain on the taxpayer. Such enterprises should be sold to the private sector, where competition will force them either to be efficient and profitable or else to close.

Which of the following, if true, identifies a flaw in the policy proposed above?

(A) The revenue gained from the sale of public-sector companies is likely to be negligible compared to the cost of maintaining them.

(B) By buying a public-sector company and then closing the company and selling its assets, a buyer can often make a profit.

(C) The services provided by many public-sector companies must be made available to citizens, even when a price that covers costs cannot be charged.

(D) Some unprofitable private-sector companies have become profitable after being taken over by the government to prevent their closing.

(E) The costs of environmental protection, contributions to social programs, and job-safety measures are the same in the public and private sectors.

Evaluation of a Plan

Situation   A policy position is advocated, i.e., that unprofitable public-sector companies that burden taxpayers should be sold to the private sector. As private-sector companies, they would either become efficient and profitable or go out of business.

Reasoning   *In what way is the policy position flawed?* The rationale given for the policy is that unprofitable public-sector companies burden taxpayers and privatizing them would subject them to competition—which would force them either to become efficient and profitable or to go out of business. But one of the characteristics of some public-sector companies is that they must provide certain services in market segments where provision of the services cannot become profitable. For example, provision of transportation services in sparsely populated rural areas is likely to be unprofitable because utilization of the services is insufficient to cover the cost of those services at a price that the market can bear.

A   This information does not clearly indicate a flaw, since elimination of an exorbitant recurring cost by selling off, even at a very low price, an inefficient public company could be financially rational, even if not rational in other ways.

B   This scenario could result in the non-provision of services that should be provided in the public interest, but it represents an aberration relative to the privatization policy described and does not indicate an essential flaw in that policy.

C   **Correct.** This information indicates an essential flaw in the privatization policy described, since private companies are unlikely to provide services, even those needed by the public, in situations where provision of those services is unprofitable.

D   This information indicates that some government-controlled companies can be profitable even when those companies were not profitable when in the private sector. But this does not indicate a flaw in the reasoning concerning privatization.

E   This information offers no help in identifying a flaw in the argument. The types of costs listed are only some of the costs that companies incur and may not be the most significant cost factors in determining whether a company is profitable or not.

The correct answer is C.

152. After receiving numerous complaints from residents about loud, highly amplified music played at local clubs, Middletown is considering a law that would prohibit clubs located in residential areas from employing musical groups that consist of more than three people.

The likelihood that the law would be effective in reducing noise would be most seriously diminished if which of the following were true?

(A) Groups that consist of more than three musicians are usually more expensive for clubs to hire than are groups that consist of fewer than three musicians.

(B) In towns that have passed similar laws, many clubs in residential areas have relocated to nonresidential areas.

(C) Most of the complaints about the music have come from people who do not regularly attend the clubs.

(D) Much of the music popular at the local clubs can be played only by groups of at least four musicians.

(E) Amplified music played by fewer than three musicians generally is as loud as amplified music played by more than three musicians.

Evaluation of a Plan

Situation   Middletown is considering a law to eliminate a nuisance that residents have complained about: loud, highly amplified music at local clubs. The proposed law would address this by prohibiting the clubs to have groups of more than three musicians playing at the club.

Reasoning   *Which statement, if true, would be the strongest indication that the proposed law would fail to reduce the noise that residents complained of?* The proposed limit on group size depends on the assumption that the music played by a group of three musicians or fewer would not be loud enough to bother Middletown's residents. If this assumption is false, for example if some of the smaller groups felt a need to use powerful amplification, the proposed law would be unlikely to be eliminate the nuisance by reducing the noise sufficiently.

A   We are given no information about whether Middletown, in framing its proposal, gave any consideration to the costs the clubs incur in hiring groups of various sizes. If the clubs' costs but not their revenues were to decrease by hiring smaller groups, they would likely obey the new law. However, this by itself would not indicate success for the noise abatement program.

B   If the Middletown clubs were to relocate to nonresidential areas as a result of the law, this would contribute to the law's effectiveness in alleviating the noise disturbance.

C   The proposal for the law is motivated by Middletown's need to respond to "numerous" resident complaints. If relatively few complaints come from residents who regularly attend the clubs, it may be because most of those residents either like loud music or are insensitive to it. But this has no bearing on whether the proposed law would be effective in addressing the noise level that bothers numerous other residents.

D   This could make the law less acceptable to the clubs or their patrons. If the law proved unacceptable, an unacceptable frequency of violation might result unless the law is well designed for effective enforcement. But perhaps the law will be well designed for effective enforcement. Nothing in the passage suggests otherwise.

E   **Correct.** This indicates that the size of a musical group generally has little impact on the volume of sound that the group produces. The proposed law is therefore likely to be ineffective in reducing the noise residents complained about.

The correct answer is E.

153. The town council of North Tarrytown favored changing the name of the town to Sleepy Hollow. Council members argued that making the town's association with Washington Irving and his famous "legend" more obvious would increase tourism and result immediately in financial benefits for the town's inhabitants.

The council members' argument requires the assumption that

(A) most of the inhabitants would favor a change in the name of the town

(B) many inhabitants would be ready to supply tourists with information about Washington Irving and his "legend"

(C) the town can accomplish, at a very low cost per capita, the improvements in tourist facilities that an increase in tourism would require

(D) other towns in the region have changed their names to reflect historical associations and have, as a result, experienced a rise in tourism

(E) the immediate per capita cost to inhabitants of changing the name of the town would be less than the immediate per capita revenue they would receive from the change

Evaluation of a Plan

Situation Members of the North Tarrytown town council argued for changing the town's name to Sleepy Hollow (the name of a fictitious place in stories by early nineteenth-century author Washington Irving). The goal was to increase tourism.

Reasoning *What unstated assumption is required for the council members' argument to be logically compelling?* Their argument was that people who associate the name Sleepy Hollow with the author Washington Irving would come to visit the town because of that association. The resulting influx of tourists would provide additional spending that would "immediately" result in financial benefits for the town's inhabitants. There would not be such immediate benefits if the additional spending did not outweigh the costs of the name change.

A This information about the popular acceptability of the name-change strategy could provide additional logical support for the proposal, but the information is not strictly required for the council members' reasoning to logically succeed.

B If this occurred, it could benefit tourists and help enhance the town's reputation as a tourist venue, thus helping the name-change plan attain its goals. But an assumption that this would occur is not necessary for the logical success of the council members' reasoning.

C This could make it more likely that the proposed name-change strategy would attain its financial goals. But the council members' reasoning does not have to assume that the relevant costs would be "very low."

D This information, if true, would help dispel any doubts as to whether the proposed name change would attain its goals. But it is not information that is necessary for the council members' reasoning to logically succeed.

E **Correct.** To be logically successful, the council members' reasoning requires that this be assumed. Part of the council members' reasoning is that the proposed name change would "result immediately in financial benefits for the town's inhabitants." This result will not occur unless the immediate costs associated with implementing the change are less than the revenue accruing to the town's inhabitants as a result. In the medium and long term, the name change could provide increased financial benefits to the town's inhabitants, but the council members' reasoning requires that those benefits flow immediately.

The correct answer is E.

154. Premature babies who receive regular massages are more active than premature babies who do not. Even when all the babies drink the same amount of milk, the massaged babies gain more weight than do the unmassaged babies. This is puzzling because a more active person generally requires a greater food intake to maintain or gain weight.

Which of the following, if true, best reconciles the apparent discrepancy described above?

(A) Increased activity leads to increased levels of hunger, especially when food intake is not also increased.

(B) Massage increases premature babies' curiosity about their environment, and curiosity leads to increased activity.

(C) Increased activity causes the intestines of premature babies to mature more quickly, enabling the babies to digest and absorb more of the nutrients in the milk they drink.

(D) Massage does not increase the growth rate of babies over one year old, if the babies had not been previously massaged.

(E) Premature babies require a daily intake of nutrients that is significantly higher than that required by babies who were not born prematurely.

Argument Construction

Situation   Premature babies who receive regular massages are more active and gain more weight than unmassaged premature babies do, even when they drink the same amount of milk.

Reasoning   *What would help to explain how the massaged babies could be more active than the unmassaged babies and yet still gain more weight without consuming more milk?* If the massaged babies are burning more calories than unmassaged babies through their extra activity, but are not consuming more calories in the form of milk, then how are they gaining more weight than the unmassaged babies? Possible explanations could cite factors suggesting how the massaged babies might not actually burn more calories despite their greater activity; how they might consume or absorb more calories even without consuming more milk; or how they might gain more weight without extra calorie intake.

A   Increased hunger without increased food intake would not help to explain why the massaged babies are gaining more weight.

B   This only helps to explain why the massaged babies are more active, not why they are gaining more weight without consuming more milk.

C   **Correct.** This suggests that the increased activity of the massaged babies could increase their calorie and nutrient intake from a given amount of milk, thereby explaining how they could gain extra weight without drinking more milk.

D   This suggests that the apparent discrepancy is only present in premature babies under one year old, but it does not explain why that discrepancy exists.

E   The passage does not compare premature babies to babies that were not born prematurely, but rather only compares premature babies that are massaged to premature babies that are not massaged.

The correct answer is C.

155. In Australia, in years with below-average rainfall, less water goes into rivers and more water is extracted from rivers for drinking and irrigation. Consequently, in such years, water levels drop considerably and the rivers flow more slowly. Because algae grow better the more slowly the water in which they are growing moves, such years are generally beneficial to populations of algae. But, by contrast, populations of algae drop in periods of extreme drought.

Which of the following, if true, does most to explain the contrast?

(A) Algae grow better in ponds and lakes than in rivers.

(B) The more slowly water moves, the more conducive its temperature is to the growth of algae.

(C) Algae cannot survive in the absence of water.

(D) Algae must be filtered out of water before it can be used for drinking.

(E) The larger the population of algae in a body of water, the less sunlight reaches below the surface of the water.

Argument Construction

Situation The quantity of water in Australian rivers greatly diminishes in years of below-average rainfall. When river levels become very low, the rivers flow more slowly. The low flow favors rapid algae growth. However, in periods of extreme drought, algae populations drop.

Reasoning *What information would most help to explain the two contrasting trends in algae growth?* The information given indicates that algae proliferate when rivers flow slowly. When the water levels become extremely low, algae populations decrease. In periods of extreme drought, presumably some rivers retain little or no water.

A This has no obvious relevance to explaining the contrast in the algae growth trends.

B Nothing in the given information is explicit about the effects of water temperature and how that changes in rivers with changes in rainfall rates.

C **Correct.** This information could help explain the decrease in algae populations during periods of extreme drought. It seems quite probable that during such periods, at least parts of some riverbeds would dry out.

D This information does not help explain the contrasting trends in algae growth. Algae filtered out of river water to be used for drinking might not be returned to rivers, and this conceivably could affect algae populations. But it seems likely, based on the given information, that this would occur mainly during low-rainfall non-drought periods, when proliferation of algae has increased, so the impact on algae populations would probably be minimal.

E This information is clearly irrelevant to the contrast that needs to be explained.

The correct answer is C.

156. Which of the following, if true, most logically completes the politician's argument?

United States politician: Although the amount of United States goods shipped to Mexico doubled in the year after tariffs on trade between the two countries were reduced, it does not follow that the reduction in tariffs caused the sales of United States goods to companies and consumers in Mexico to double that year, because __________.

(A) many of the United States companies that produced goods that year had competitors based in Mexico that had long produced the same kind of goods

(B) most of the increase in goods shipped by United States companies to Mexico was in parts shipped to the companies' newly relocated subsidiaries for assembly and subsequent shipment back to the United States

(C) marketing goods to a previously unavailable group of consumers is most successful when advertising specifically targets those consumers, but developing such advertising often takes longer than a year

(D) the amount of Mexican goods shipped to the United States remained the same as it had been before the tariff reductions

(E) there was no significant change in the employment rate in either of the countries that year

Argument Construction

Situation   The politician suggests that tariffs on trade between Mexico and the United States were reduced during a certain year and notes that, in the year after that year, the amount of United States goods shipped to Mexico doubled. It may seem from this that the decrease in tariffs, because they may have reduced the prices of United States goods to Mexican companies and consumers, caused Mexican companies and consumers to double their purchases of United States goods in the year after the reduction in tariffs. This might explain the doubling of shipments of goods to Mexico. However, the politician argues that the decrease in tariffs did *not* cause the purchase of United States goods by Mexican companies and consumers to double.

Reasoning   *What possible facts would indicate that the decrease in tariffs may not have caused Mexican companies and consumers to double their purchases of United States goods?* The task in this question is to complete an argument that purports to show that a certain inference—that sales of United States goods to companies and consumers in Mexico increased as a result of the tariff decrease—does not follow logically from the fact that shipments of United States goods to Mexico doubled after the decrease in tariffs. Although it is not necessary to show that sales of United States goods to companies and consumers in Mexico did not double, any statement that would significantly decrease the strength of this inference may provide a reasonable answer to our question.

A   The argument that the politician is criticizing concerns a change in a certain year that purportedly caused another purported change in the next year. This answer choice, about longstanding relationships between United States and Mexican companies, does not address these changes.

B   **Correct.** If the statement in this answer choice is true, then we cannot, on the basis of an increase in shipments of goods to Mexico, infer that these goods were purchased by Mexican companies and consumers. The statement thus directly supports the politician's argument.

C   The argument that the politician is criticizing has to do with purported changes in purchasing behavior by Mexican companies and consumers, due to an increase in tariffs. This answer choice, being entirely concerned with the effectiveness of marketing and advertising, does not address the argument.

D   Although this answer choice may suggest that the change in tariffs did not cause a significant change in shipments of Mexican goods to the United States, it does not address the matter of shipments of United States goods to Mexico.

E   This answer choice addresses an aspect that would be of interest when examining the effects of the change in tariffs. But it does not address the purported change that is addressed by the politician's argument.

The correct answer is B.

157. Budget constraints have made police officials consider reassigning a considerable number of officers from traffic enforcement to work on higher-priority, serious crimes. Reducing traffic enforcement for this reason would be counterproductive, however, in light of the tendency of criminals to use cars when engaged in the commission of serious crimes. An officer stopping a car for a traffic violation can make a search that turns up evidence of serious crime.

Which of the following, if true, most strengthens the argument given?

(A) An officer who stops a car containing evidence of the commission of a serious crime risks a violent confrontation, even if the vehicle was stopped only for a traffic violation.

(B) When the public becomes aware that traffic enforcement has lessened, it typically becomes lax in obeying traffic rules.

(C) Those willing to break the law to commit serious crimes are often in committing such crimes unwilling to observe what they regard as the lesser constraints of traffic law.

(D) The offenders committing serious crimes who would be caught because of traffic violations are not the same group of individuals as those who would be caught if the arresting officers were reassigned from traffic enforcement.

(E) The great majority of persons who are stopped by officers for traffic violations are not guilty of any serious crimes.

Argument Construction

Situation   Budget constraints have made police officials consider reassigning many officers from traffic enforcement to work on serious crimes. But criminals often drive when committing serious crimes, and police who stop cars for traffic violations can find evidence of those crimes.

Reasoning   *What additional information, when combined with the argument provided, would suggest that it would be counterproductive to reassign officers from traffic enforcement to work on serious crimes?* The argument implicitly reasons that because officers working on traffic enforcement can turn up evidence of serious crimes by searching cars that commit traffic violations, reassigning those officers would hinder police efforts to prevent serious crime, even if the officers were reassigned to work directly on serious crime. The argument could be strengthened by information suggesting that traffic enforcement may increase the probability that evidence relating to serious crimes will be discovered.

A   If anything, this risk of violence might discourage traffic enforcement officers from stopping and searching as many cars, thus reducing their effectiveness at preventing serious crimes.

B   This suggests that reassigning officers from traffic enforcement to work on serious crimes would increase the number of unpunished minor traffic violations, not the number of unpunished serious crimes.

C   **Correct.** This suggests that people committing serious crimes often commit traffic violations as well, increasing the likelihood that traffic enforcement officers will stop and search their cars and find evidence of those crimes.

D   The question at issue is not whether the same offenders would be caught if the officers were reassigned, but rather whether more or fewer offenders would be caught.

E   This weakens the argument by suggesting that most work by traffic enforcement officers is unrelated to preventing serious crimes.

The correct answer is C.

158. Conventional wisdom suggests vaccinating elderly people first in flu season, because they are at greatest risk of dying if they contract the virus. This year's flu virus poses particular risk to elderly people and almost none at all to younger people, particularly children. Nevertheless, health professionals are recommending vaccinating children first against the virus rather than elderly people.

     Which of the following, if true, provides the strongest reason for the health professionals' recommendation?

     (A) Children are vulnerable to dangerous infections when their immune systems are severely weakened by other diseases.

     (B) Children are particularly unconcerned with hygiene and therefore are the group most responsible for spreading the flu virus to others.

     (C) The vaccinations received last year will confer no immunity to this year's flu virus.

     (D) Children who catch one strain of the flu virus and then recover are likely to develop immunity to at least some strains with which they have not yet come in contact.

     (E) Children are no more likely than adults to have immunity to a particular flu virus if they have never lived through a previous epidemic of the same virus.

Argument Construction

Situation   Although this year's flu virus poses particular risk to elderly people and almost no risk to children, health professionals are recommending vaccinating children before elderly people, contrary to what conventional wisdom recommends.

Reasoning   *What would help justify the health professionals' recommendation?* Since children will experience almost no risk from the virus, vaccinating them first for their own sake appears unnecessary. However, individuals at no personal risk from a virus can still transmit it to more-vulnerable individuals. If children are especially likely to transmit the virus, it could be reasonable to vaccinate them first in order to protect others, including elderly people, by preventing the virus from spreading.

A   This might be a reason to vaccinate certain children with severely weakened immune systems, if their weak immune systems would even respond effectively to the vaccine. However, it is not clearly a reason to vaccinate the vast majority of children.

B   **Correct.** This suggests that children are especially likely to transmit the virus even if it does not endanger them. So as explained above, it provides a good reason for the health professionals' recommendation.

C   This might be a good reason to vaccinate everyone, but it is not clearly a reason to vaccinate children before vaccinating elderly people.

D   If anything, this would suggest that there might be a reason not to vaccinate children against this year's strain at all: unvaccinated children who catch this year's strain, which the argument claims is relatively harmless to children, may develop immunity to more dangerous strains that might arise in the future.

E   The argument claims that this year's virus poses almost no risk to children. So even if they are not technically immune to it, it does not affect them significantly enough to justify vaccinating them before vaccinating elderly people.

The correct answer is B.

159. Pro-Tect Insurance Company has recently been paying out more on car-theft claims than it expected. Cars with special antitheft devices or alarm systems are much less likely to be stolen than are other cars. Consequently Pro-Tect, as part of an effort to reduce its annual payouts, will offer a discount to holders of car-theft policies if their cars have antitheft devices or alarm systems.

Which of the following, if true, provides the strongest indication that the plan is likely to achieve its goal?

(A) The decrease in the risk of car theft conferred by having a car alarm is greatest when only a few cars have such alarms.

(B) The number of policyholders who have filed a claim in the past year is higher for Pro-Tect than for other insurance companies.

(C) In one or two years, the discount that Pro-Tect is offering will amount to more than the cost of buying certain highly effective antitheft devices.

(D) Currently, Pro-Tect cannot legally raise the premiums it charges for a given amount of insurance against car theft.

(E) The amount Pro-Tect has been paying out on car-theft claims has been greater for some models of car than for others.

Evaluation of a Plan

Situation   An insurance company is paying more money on car-theft claims than anticipated. To reduce these payments, the company is planning to offer discounts to customers whose cars have antitheft devices or alarm systems, because such cars are less likely to be stolen.

Reasoning   *What piece of information would indicate that the plan is likely to succeed?* Pro-Tect wishes to reduce its annual payouts, and one way for that to happen is for fewer cars insured by Pro-Tect to be stolen. To help accomplish this, Pro-Tect is offering discounts to policyholders whose cars are so equipped, because cars equipped with antitheft devices or alarm systems are less likely to be stolen than are cars without such devices. What would interfere with the success of Pro-Tect's plan? Car owners would probably resist investing in antitheft devices or alarm systems if the cost of such systems is higher than the discount they will receive. So if Pro-Tect sets the discount at a level that makes installing antitheft devices seem like a bargain to car owners, the plan will most likely succeed.

A   Pro-Tect's plan is designed to increase the number of cars equipped with car alarms. If having more cars equipped with car alarms reduces those alarms' effectivity in preventing thefts, then Pro-Tect's plan is unlikely to achieve its goal.

B   Pro-Tect's claims in relation to those of other insurance companies are not relevant to whether Pro-Tect's plan to reduce its own car-theft claims will achieve its goal.

C   **Correct.** This statement suggests that Pro-Tect's plan will provide an effective incentive for car owners to install antitheft devices; this statement therefore properly identifies information that indicates the plan is likely to achieve its goal.

D   Because Pro-Tect's plan does not involve raising the premiums it charges, restrictions on its ability to do so are irrelevant to whether that plan will achieve its goal.

E   Pro-Tect's plan does not distinguish among different models of car, so this statement indicates nothing about whether the proposed plan will succeed.

The correct answer is C.

160. While the total enrollment of public elementary and secondary schools in Sondland is one percent higher this academic year than last academic year, the number of teachers there increased by three percent. Thus, the Sondland Education Commission's prediction of a teacher shortage as early as next academic year is unfounded.

Which of the following, if true, most seriously weakens the claim that the prediction of a teacher shortage as early as next academic year is unfounded?

(A) Funding for public elementary schools in Sondland is expected to increase over the next ten years.

(B) Average salaries for Sondland's teachers increased at the rate of inflation from last academic year to this academic year.

(C) A new law has mandated that there be 10 percent more teachers per pupil in Sondland's public schools next academic year than there were this academic year.

(D) In the past, increases in enrollments in public elementary and secondary schools in Sondland have generally been smaller than increases in the number of teachers.

(E) Because of reductions in funding, the number of students enrolling in teacher-training programs in Sondland is expected to decline beginning in the next academic year.

Argument Evaluation

Situation In Sondland's public schools this academic year, the number of students is one percent higher and the number of teachers three percent higher than they were last academic year. For this reason, the Sondland Education Commission's prediction of a teacher shortage as early as next academic year is questionable.

Reasoning *What evidence would most weaken support for the claim that there will be no teacher shortage next academic year?* A teacher shortage will arise next academic year if the number of teachers needed will exceed the number of teachers employed. This will happen if the number of teachers needed increases without a sufficient increase in the number employed, or if the number employed decreases without a sufficient decrease in the number needed. Evidence that either or both of these changes will occur next academic year is evidence that the predicted shortage will occur, so any such evidence will weaken support for the claim that the prediction is unfounded.

A Increased funding will likely allow more teachers to be hired but will not necessarily increase the need for teachers, so it does not support the prediction of a teacher shortage (and indeed it very slightly undermines the prediction). Also, the funding is expected to increase over ten years, not necessarily next year. Furthermore, we are not told who expects this increase or why. Their expectation may be unjustifiable.

B A salary increase at the rate of inflation is equivalent to no change in the salary's actual value. The absence of a change in real salary in the past academic year does not by itself support any prediction of a change in the number of teachers needed or employed next academic year.

C **Correct.** The schools will need a lot more teachers next academic year to satisfy this mandate. It may be difficult for the schools to hire enough teachers in time. This provides at least some reason to predict that a teacher shortage will result.

D This means the number of students per teacher has been generally declining. It does not suggest that next academic year the number of teachers needed will increase, nor that the number employed will decrease.

E This does support the prediction that a shortage of trained teachers will arise eventually. But the declining number of students in teacher-training programs next academic year probably will not reduce the number of teachers available to teach during that same year.

The correct answer is C.

161. A newly discovered painting seems to be the work of one of two 17th-century artists, either the northern German Johannes Drechen or the Frenchman Louis Birelle, who sometimes painted in the same style as Drechen. Analysis of the carved picture frame, which has been identified as the painting's original 17th-century frame, showed that it is made of wood found widely in northern Germany at the time, but rare in the part of France where Birelle lived. This shows that the painting is most likely the work of Drechen.

Which of the following is an assumption that the argument requires?

(A) The frame was made from wood local to the region where the picture was painted.

(B) Drechen is unlikely to have ever visited the home region of Birelle in France.

(C) Sometimes a painting so closely resembles others of its era that no expert is able to confidently decide who painted it.

(D) The painter of the picture chose the frame for the picture.

(E) The carving style of the picture frame is not typical of any specific region of Europe.

Argument Construction

Situation   A 17th-century painting has been discovered that was either by Johannes Drechen from northern Germany or by French artist Louis Birelle. The painting's original picture frame is made of wood widely found in 17th-century northern Germany but rare in the French region where Birelle lived. So the painting was probably the work of Drechen.

Reasoning   *Which answer choice is an assumption required by the argument?* If the painting is correctly attributed to Drechen, then the wood that the frame was made from probably came from the region where Drechen lived and did his painting. The argument assumes that the specific wood used in the frame came from northern Germany rather than from some other place where that wood might have been found, and where (for all we know) Birelle might have visited.

A   **Correct.** Without an assumption equivalent to this, the argument would fail.

B   This is not a required assumption (unlike, for example, the following: Drechen did not give the picture frame to Birelle as a gift).

C   This is a truism but is not required to make the argument's conclusion well supported.

D   This does not need to be assumed; Drechen could, for example, have simply asked a local frame-maker to make a frame for his picture.

E   Neither the affirmation nor the denial of this statement is needed to underpin the argument.

The correct answer is A.

162. Meat from chickens contaminated with salmonella bacteria can cause serious food poisoning. Capsaicin, the chemical that gives chili peppers their hot flavor, has antibacterial properties. Chickens do not have taste receptors for capsaicin and will readily eat feed laced with capsaicin. When chickens were fed such feed and then exposed to salmonella bacteria, relatively few of them became contaminated with salmonella.

In deciding whether the feed would be useful in raising salmonella-free chicken for retail sale, it would be most helpful to determine which of the following?

(A) Whether feeding capsaicin to chickens affects the taste of their meat
(B) Whether eating capsaicin reduces the risk of salmonella poisoning for humans
(C) Whether chicken is more prone to salmonella contamination than other kinds of meat
(D) Whether appropriate cooking of chicken contaminated with salmonella can always prevent food poisoning
(E) Whether capsaicin can be obtained only from chili peppers

Argument Evaluation

Situation   Chickens will readily eat feed laced with capsaicin, which appears to protect them from contamination with salmonella bacteria that can cause food poisoning.

Reasoning   *What information would help determine whether using the feed would be an effective strategy for raising salmonella-free chicken for retail sale?* In order for the strategy to be effective, it must be economically feasible for farmers to raise chickens using the feed, and there must be enough consumer demand for chickens raised this way. So any information about factors likely to affect either the economic feasibility of raising the chickens or consumer demand for them could be helpful in determining how useful the feed would be.

A   **Correct.** If chicken producers tried to market meat from capsaicin-fed chickens without knowing whether the taste is affected, they would risk alienating consumers. Of course, if they found that the taste is affected, they would then need to do further investigations to determine how consumers would likely respond to the difference. If consumers did not like the taste, this could negatively affect demand for the chickens. In that case, using the feed would not be an effective way to raise chickens for retail sale.

B   There are two ways this might be considered relevant. First, it might be thought that because capsaicin reduces the risk of salmonella poisoning in humans, it will also do so in chickens; but we already have good evidence of that in the argument. Second, it might be thought that, if the capsaicin does not produce chickens that are totally salmonella free, then if any capsaicin remains in the chickens, it will help prevent any humans who consume the chicken from getting salmonella poisoning. But the relevant issue is whether the capsaicin will make the chickens salmonella free, not whether humans will be protected whether the chickens are salmonella free or not.

C   The susceptibility of other types of meat to salmonella contamination would not affect the usefulness of the feed for preventing such contamination in chicken.

D   Presumably many people do not cook contaminated chicken appropriately, so consumers could still benefit from salmonella-free chicken whether or not appropriate cooking methods could prevent food poisoning.

E   Regardless of whether capsaicin can be obtained from other sources, chili peppers may be a perfectly viable source.

The correct answer is A.

163. Which of the following most logically completes the passage?

Leaf beetles damage willow trees by stripping away their leaves, but a combination of parasites and predators generally keeps populations of these beetles in check. Researchers have found that severe air pollution results in reduced predator populations. The parasites, by contrast, are not adversely affected by pollution; nevertheless, the researchers' discovery probably does explain why leaf beetles cause particularly severe damage to willows in areas with severe air pollution, since __________.

(A) neither the predators nor the parasites of leaf beetles themselves attack willow trees

(B) the parasites that attack leaf beetles actually tend to be more prevalent in areas with severe air pollution than they are elsewhere

(C) the damage caused by leaf beetles is usually not enough to kill a willow tree outright

(D) where air pollution is not especially severe, predators have much more impact on leaf-beetle populations than parasites do

(E) willows often grow in areas where air pollution is especially severe

Argument Construction

Situation Leaf beetles damage willow trees, but predators and parasites keep leaf beetle populations in check. Air pollution reduces populations of predators but not of parasites. Leaf beetles damage willows especially severely in areas with severe air pollution.

Reasoning *What would support the conclusion that air pollution's effects on the predator populations (but not on the parasite populations) explains why leaf beetles damage willows the most in areas with severe air pollution?* The word *since* preceding the blank space at the end of the passage indicates that the space should be filled with a premise supporting the conclusion stated immediately before the *since.* To support this conclusion, it would help to have evidence that predators play a predominant role in keeping leaf beetle populations in check, and thus that the reduction of predator populations by air pollution could be sufficient to enable leaf beetle populations to grow and cause especially severe damage.

A The fact that neither the predators nor the parasites directly contribute to harming the trees offers no reason to conclude that a difference in how they are affected by pollution would contribute to the harm that the beetles cause to the trees.

B If the parasites are more prevalent in areas with severe air pollution, then they are more likely to keep leaf beetle populations in check in those areas, despite the reduced predator populations. Thus, the decline in predator populations would more likely be insufficient to explain why the leaf beetles cause more damage in those areas.

C This observation is irrelevant to whether the decline in predator populations explains why leaf beetles damage willow trees more severely in areas with severe air pollution.

D **Correct.** This indicates that predators play a predominant role in keeping leaf beetle populations in check, so, as explained above, it supports the argument's conclusion.

E This is not clearly relevant to whether the decline in predator populations explains why leaf beetles damage willow trees more severely in areas with severe air pollution. The argument's conclusion could just as easily be true regardless of whether willows grow in such polluted areas frequently or infrequently.

The correct answer is D.

164. On May 1st, in order to reduce the number of overdue books, a children's library instituted a policy of forgiving fines and giving bookmarks to children returning all of their overdue books. On July 1st, there were twice as many overdue books as there had been on May 1st, although a record number of books had been returned during the interim.

Which of the following, if true, most helps to explain the apparent inconsistency in the results of the library's policy?

(A) The librarians did not keep accurate records of how many children took advantage of the grace period, and some of the children returning overdue books did not return all of their overdue books.

(B) Although the grace period enticed some children to return all of their overdue books, it did not convince all of the children with overdue books to return all of their books.

(C) The bookmarks became popular among the children, so in order to collect the bookmarks, many children borrowed many more books than they usually did and kept them past their due date.

(D) The children were allowed to borrow a maximum of five books for a two-week period, and hence each child could keep a maximum of fifteen books beyond their due date within a two-month period.

(E) Although the library forgave overdue fines during the grace period, the amount previously charged the children was minimal; hence, the forgiveness of the fines did not provide enough incentive for them to return their overdue books.

Argument Construction

Situation   After a library started forgiving fines and giving bookmarks to children who returned all their overdue books, the number of books returned greatly increased, but so did the number of overdue books.

Reasoning   *Why might the policy have simultaneously increased the number of overdue books and the number of books being returned?* In order to increase both these numbers, the policy must have resulted in more books being checked out, kept past their due dates, and then returned. But why would the policy have promoted that behavior? One possibility is that it rewarded the behavior. The policy involved giving children bookmarks as rewards for returning overdue books, while removing the fines that penalized the children for doing so. If the children liked the bookmarks, they might have tried to get more of them by deliberately checking books out in order to keep them past their due dates before returning them to get the bookmarks.

A   Failing to keep accurate records of the number of children would not clearly increase the number of books being returned. And the policy change did not apply to children who returned only some of their overdue books.

B   This suggests that the policy had limited effects, but does not help to explain why it had apparently inconsistent effects.

C   **Correct.** This explains how the policy gave the children a motive to check out and return more books while also allowing them to keep more of the books past the due dates.

D   This restriction would have limited the number of overdue books and thus would not help to explain why that number increased.

E   This suggests that the policy had little effect but does not help to explain why it had apparently inconsistent effects.

The correct answer is C.

165. A certain species of desert lizard digs tunnels in which to lay its eggs. The eggs must incubate inside the tunnel for several weeks before hatching, and they fail to hatch if they are disturbed at any time during this incubation period. Yet these lizards guard their tunnels for only a few days after laying their eggs.

Which of the following, if true, most helps explain why there is no need for lizards to guard their tunnels for more than a few days?

(A) The eggs are at risk of being disturbed only during the brief egg-laying season when many lizards are digging in a relatively small area.

(B) The length of the incubation period varies somewhat from one tunnel to another.

(C) Each female lizard lays from 15 to 20 eggs, only about 10 of which hatch even if the eggs are not disturbed at any time during the incubation period.

(D) The temperature and humidity within the tunnels will not be suitable for the incubating eggs unless the tunnels are plugged with sand immediately after the eggs are laid.

(E) The only way to disturb the eggs of this lizard species is by opening up one of the tunnels in which they are laid.

Argument Construction

Situation   Lizards of a certain species dig tunnels in which they lay their eggs. Although the eggs fail to hatch if disturbed during their several weeks of incubation, the lizards guard the tunnels for only a few days after laying the eggs.

Reasoning   *What would help to explain why the lizards have to guard their tunnels for only a few days?* For the lizards to survive as a species, their behaviors must ensure that enough of their eggs hatch. Thus, they must successfully prevent enough of their eggs from being disturbed in the tunnels throughout the several weeks of incubation. If guarding the tunnels for only a few days accomplishes this, then some other factor must prevent the eggs from being disturbed during the remaining weeks. Evidence of any such factor would help to explain why the lizards do not have to guard the tunnels longer. For example, to protect the eggs without guarding them, the lizards might conceal the tunnel entrances after the first few days. Or animals likely to disturb the eggs might only be present for those first days, in which case there would be nothing for the lizards to guard against thereafter.

A   **Correct.** This suggests that the only creatures likely to disturb the eggs are other lizards of the same species digging tunnels to lay their own eggs at around the same time. If so, each lizard can safely leave its eggs unguarded after a few days because all the other lizards will have finished digging.

B   Even if the incubation period varies somewhat, the passage says it always lasts several weeks. So this does not explain why the lizards have to guard the tunnels for only a few days.

C   If many eggs fail to hatch even when undisturbed, that is all the more reason for the lizards to protect the remaining eggs from disturbance throughout the incubation period so that at least some will hatch. So it does not explain why the lizards guard their tunnels only for a few days.

D   Whether or not immediately plugging the tunnels with sand is enough to protect the eggs, this behavior does not explain why the lizards subsequently guard the tunnels for a few days and then leave for the rest of the incubation period.

E   Even if it is impossible to disturb the eggs without opening the tunnels, that does not explain why the lizards guard the tunnels for a few days and then leave for the rest of the incubation period.

The correct answer is A.

166. Most banks that issue credit cards charge interest rates on credit card debt that are ten percentage points higher than the rates those banks charge for ordinary consumer loans. These banks' representatives claim the difference is fully justified, since it simply covers the difference between the costs to these banks associated with credit card debt and those associated with consumer loans.

Which of the following, if true, most seriously calls into question the reasoning offered by the banks' representatives?

(A) Some lenders that are not banks offer consumer loans at interest rates that are even higher than most banks charge on credit card debt.

(B) Most car rental companies require that their customers provide signed credit card charge slips or security deposits.

(C) Two to three percent of the selling price of every item bought with a given credit card goes to the bank that issued that credit card.

(D) Most people need not use credit cards to buy everyday necessities, but could buy those necessities with cash or pay by check.

(E) People who pay their credit card bills in full each month usually pay no interest on the amounts they charge.

Argument Evaluation

Situation   Banks that issue credit cards tend to charge interest rates on the associated debt that are ten percentage points higher than the rates associated with "ordinary" consumer loans (consumer loans that are not associated with credit cards). Representatives of these banks have offered a justification of this practice, based on a claim that this difference in interest rates "simply covers the difference" in costs, to the banks, associated with these respective types of loans (loans associated with credit cards and consumer loans that are not associated with credit cards).

Reasoning   *What additional facts would indicate a flaw in the bank representatives' argument?* Given the description of the bank representatives' argument, we may assume that, by their estimation, the costs to banks associated with credit card debt are greater than the costs associated with other consumer loans. The representatives' argument, that the difference in interest rates "simply covers" this difference in costs, may then be seen as an argument that all of the extra money that the banks collect from the higher interest rates is *necessary* if the banks are to cover this difference in costs. If we can find a fact whereby the ten percentage point difference is not necessary to cover the difference in costs, then we may be able to "call into question" the bank representatives' argument.

A   The point of this response to the bank representatives' argument would seem to be that the relatively high interest rates on credit debt may be justified because certain other businesses charge even higher interest rates on consumer loans. Regardless of the merits of this response, it appears intended to *support* the argument of the representatives, whereas our task is to identify a fact that could be used to criticize the argument.

B   This purported fact does not address the argument concerning the interest rates on credit-card debt.

C   **Correct.** If two to three percent of the value of purchases made on credit cards goes to the issuing banks, then this money could be used to cover some of the difference in costs described by the bank representatives. The interest rates on credit cards could therefore be somewhat lower than they actually are, with the difference in costs nevertheless still fully covered. The difference in interest rates of ten percentage points may therefore not be necessary.

D   This point might be used in support of an argument that consumers have a genuine choice as to whether to use credit cards, and that they are therefore responsible for the higher rates of interest that they pay for credit-card debt. Such an argument would seem to *support* the position of bank representatives.

E   As with the point in answer choice D, this point might seem to suggest that consumers bear some of the responsibility for the higher interest rates they pay, thus perhaps mitigating the responsibility of the banks. The point might thus seem to *support* the position of the banks' representatives.

The correct answer is C.

167. Often patients with ankle fractures that are stable, and thus do not require surgery, are given follow-up x-rays because their orthopedists are concerned about possibly having misjudged the stability of the fracture. When a number of follow-up x-rays were reviewed, however, all the fractures that had initially been judged stable were found to have healed correctly. Therefore, it is a waste of money to order follow-up x-rays of ankle fractures initially judged stable.

Which of the following, if true, most strengthens the argument?

(A) Doctors who are general practitioners rather than orthopedists are less likely than orthopedists to judge the stability of an ankle fracture correctly.

(B) Many ankle injuries for which an initial x-ray is ordered are revealed by the x-ray not to involve any fracture of the ankle.

(C) X-rays of patients of many different orthopedists working in several hospitals were reviewed.

(D) The healing of ankle fractures that have been surgically repaired is always checked by means of a follow-up x-ray.

(E) Orthopedists routinely order follow-up x-rays for fractures of bones other than ankle bones.

Argument Evaluation

Situation   Often patients with ankle fractures that their orthopedists have judged not to require surgery are given follow-up x-rays to check whether the fracture healed correctly. An examination of a sample of those x-rays found that the ankle had, in each case, healed properly.

Reasoning   *The question is which of the answer choices, if true, would most strengthen the argument.* The argument is based on data concerning follow-up x-rays, each of which revealed no problem with the orthopedist's initial judgment that the ankle fracture was stable (and would heal without surgery). This invites the question whether the follow-up x-rays are really needed. The argument concludes that they are a waste of money. But was the x-ray data truly representative of orthopedists generally? After all, some orthopedists—perhaps more experienced, better-trained, or employed at a facility with better staff or facilities—may be much better than others at judging ankle fractures. If we add the information that the data for the conclusion comes from many orthopedists working at many different hospitals, we have greater assurance that the x-ray data is representative, and the argument will be made much stronger.

A   Neither the study nor the conclusion that is drawn from it concerns general practitioners, so this point is irrelevant.

B   Naturally many ankle injuries do not involve fractures—x-rays may sometimes be used to determine this—but the argument concerns only cases where there have been ankle fractures.

C   **Correct.** This shows that the sample of x-ray data examined was probably sufficiently representative of cases of ankle fracture judged to be stable by orthopedists.

D   The argument does not concern cases of ankle fracture that have been surgically repaired.

E   The argument concerns only x-rays of ankles. From the information given here, we cannot infer that orthopedists are generally wasteful in routinely ordering follow-up x-rays.

The correct answer is C.

168. In setting environmental standards for industry and others to meet, it is inadvisable to require the best results that state-of-the-art technology can achieve. Current technology is able to detect and eliminate even extremely minute amounts of contaminants, but at a cost that is exorbitant relative to the improvement achieved. So it would be reasonable instead to set standards by taking into account all of the current and future risks involved.

The argument given concerning the reasonable way to set standards presupposes that

(A) industry currently meets the standards that have been set by environmental authorities

(B) there are effective ways to take into account all of the relevant risks posed by allowing different levels of contaminants

(C) the only contaminants worth measuring are generated by industry

(D) it is not costly to prevent large amounts of contaminants from entering the environment

(E) minute amounts of some contaminants can be poisonous

Argument Construction

Situation State-of-the-art technology can detect and eliminate even tiny amounts of environmental contaminants, but at a cost that is exorbitant relative to its benefits.

Reasoning *What must be true in order for the argument's premises to support its conclusion?* The argument is that environmental standards requiring the best results that state-of-the-art technology can provide are unreasonably expensive relative to their benefits, so it would be reasonable instead to set environmental standards that take into account all present and future risks from contaminants. In order for the premise to support the conclusion, the environmental standards based on present and future risks would have to be less expensive relative to their benefits than the *best results* environmental standards are. Furthermore, setting the *current and future risks* environmental standards cannot be reasonable unless it is feasible to assess present and future risks as those standards require.

A The argument does not say which standards, if any, environmental authorities have set. In any case, such standards could be reasonable or unreasonable regardless of whether industry currently meets them.

B **Correct.** If taking future risks into account were infeasible, then applying the *current and future risks* standards would also be infeasible. And setting those standards would be unreasonable if they could not feasibly be applied.

C According to the stimulus, the proposed *current and future risks* standards would apply to industry *and others*. So those standards could be reasonable even if the unspecified *others* also generated contaminants worth measuring, and even if the standards required measuring those contaminants.

D Even if it were costly to prevent large amounts of contaminants from entering the environment, the benefits of doing so to prevent present and future risks might outweigh the costs.

E The *current and future risks* standards could take into account any poisoning risks posed by minute amounts of contaminants.

The correct answer is B.

169. The chemical adenosine is released by brain cells when those cells are active. Adenosine then binds to more and more sites on cells in certain areas of the brain, as the total amount released gradually increases during wakefulness. During sleep, the number of sites to which adenosine is bound decreases. Some researchers have hypothesized that it is the cumulative binding of adenosine to a large number of sites that causes the onset of sleep.

Which of the following, if true, provides the most support for the researchers' hypothesis?

(A) Even after long periods of sleep when adenosine is at its lowest concentration in the brain, the number of brain cells bound with adenosine remains very large.

(B) Caffeine, which has the effect of making people remain wakeful, is known to interfere with the binding of adenosine to sites on brain cells.

(C) Besides binding to sites in the brain, adenosine is known to be involved in biochemical reactions throughout the body.

(D) Some areas of the brain that are relatively inactive nonetheless release some adenosine.

(E) Stress resulting from a dangerous situation can preserve wakefulness even when brain levels of bound adenosine are high.

Argument Evaluation

Situation Adenosine is released from brain cells that are active. The amount of adenosine released increases during wakefulness, and it binds to more and more sites on cells in certain brain locations. The number of sites to which it is bound decreases during sleep. Researchers have hypothesized that the cumulative binding of adenosine to many sites causes the onset of sleep.

Reasoning *Which answer choice most strongly supports the hypothesis?* If the hypothesis is correct, then some factor that impedes the binding of adenosine should be closely associated with wakefulness. Therefore, finding some such factor, and observing that it is accompanied by wakefulness when the factor operates, would tend to confirm the hypothesis.

A Without further, more specific information, this piece of information suffices neither to confirm nor to refute the hypothesis.

B **Correct.** A finding that caffeine, known to induce wakefulness, inhibits adenosine from binding to sites on brain cells helps confirm the hypothesis.

C This piece of information lacks a clear relevance to the hypothesized impact on sleep, and therefore does not help confirm the hypothesis.

D This information lacks a clear relevance to the hypothesized impact on sleep, and therefore does not help confirm the hypothesis.

E What this indicates is that stress may impede the hypothesized sleep-inducing effect of adenosine. It does not refute the hypothesis but does not confirm it either.

The correct answer is B.

170. A two-year study beginning in 1977 found that, among 85-year-old people, those whose immune systems were weakest were twice as likely to die within two years as others in the study. The cause of their deaths, however, was more often heart disease, against which the immune system does not protect, than cancer or infections, which are attacked by the immune system.

Which of the following, if true, would offer the best prospects for explaining deaths in which weakness of the immune system, though present, played no causal role?

(A) There were twice as many infections among those in the study with the weakest immune systems as among those with the strongest immune systems.

(B) The majority of those in the study with the strongest immune systems died from infection or cancer by 1987.

(C) Some of the drugs that had been used to treat the symptoms of heart disease had a side effect of weakening the immune system.

(D) Most of those in the study who survived beyond the two-year period had recovered from a serious infection sometime prior to 1978.

(E) Those in the study who survived into the 1980s had, in 1976, strengthened their immune systems through drug therapy.

Argument Construction

Situation This question presents a puzzling scenario and asks us to find a possible fact that could make the situation less puzzling. The scenario involves a study that was conducted a few decades ago on a certain group of older adults. Those with the weakest immune systems were much more likely to die within two years than were the other individuals in the study. However, among the individuals with the weakest immune systems, death was more often by heart disease, from which the immune system does not protect, than from cancer or infections, for which a strong immune system is protective.

Reasoning *For the participants in the study with the weakest immune systems, what might best explain the deaths that were not due to weakness of the immune system?* We might expect that the people with the weakest immune systems would be more likely to die from diseases that a strong immune system would protect them from than from other diseases. An explanation of the deaths that were not due to weakness of the immune system would explain why this is not the case.

A This point is irrelevant. The hypothesis that the participants in the study with the weakest immune systems had more infections than did the other participants does not explain why those participants died from conditions that were not infections.

B Our question involves identifying a possible explanation for the deaths of the participants in the study with the weakest immune systems. This answer choice, about the deaths of those with strong immune systems, is thus irrelevant.

C **Correct.** This answer choice suggests that those with heart disease—which would not have been due to weakness of the immune system—would have nevertheless had a weaker immune system due to the administration of certain drugs. Those with heart disease may for this reason have been among those with the weakest immune systems. If the individuals with weak immune systems due to treatment for heart disease formed a large-enough portion of the patients with the weakest immune systems, then we would have an explanation for why those with the weakest immune systems were more likely to die from heart disease than from infections or cancer.

D This answer choice is not specific enough for us to use in the explanation we are looking for. For example, the "serious" infections in question may have occurred well before the 1977 study. Furthermore, there may appear to be no significant relationship between having had a serious infection and death from a condition that was not an infection.

E This answer choice is also not specific enough to be a factor that might reasonably offer the explanation we are looking for. For example, given the information in this answer choice, it could have been the case that all of the participants had the drug therapy.

The correct answer is C.

171. Most scholars agree that King Alfred (A.D. 849–899) personally translated a number of Latin texts into Old English. One historian contends that Alfred also personally penned his own law code, arguing that the numerous differences between the language of the law code and Alfred's translations of Latin texts are outweighed by the even more numerous similarities. Linguistic similarities, however, are what one expects in texts from the same language, the same time, and the same region. Apart from Alfred's surviving translations and law code, there are only two other extant works from the same dialect and milieu, so it is risky to assume here that linguistic similarities point to common authorship.

The passage above proceeds by

(A)   providing examples that underscore another argument's conclusion

(B)   questioning the plausibility of an assumption on which another argument depends

(C)   showing that a principle if generally applied would have anomalous consequences

(D)   showing that the premises of another argument are mutually inconsistent

(E)   using argument by analogy to undermine a principle implicit in another argument

Argument Evaluation

Situation   A historian argues that King Alfred must have written his own law code, since there are more similarities than differences between the language in the law code and that in Alfred's translations of Latin texts. Apart from Alfred's translations and law code, there are only two other extant works in the same dialect and from the same milieu.

Reasoning   *How does the reasoning in the passage proceed?* The first sentence presents a claim that is not disputed in the passage. The second sentence presents a historian's argument. Implicitly citing the undisputed claim in the passage's first sentence as evidence, the historian proposes an analogy between the law code and Alfred's translations, arguing on the basis of this analogy that Alfred wrote the law code. The third sentence of the passage casts doubt on this analogy, pointing out that it could plausibly apply to texts that Alfred did not write. The fourth sentence suggests that too few extant texts are available as evidence to rule out the possibility raised in the third sentence. Thus, the third and fourth sentences are intended to undermine the historian's argument.

A   As explained above, the passage is intended to undermine the conclusion of the historian's argument, not to *underscore* (emphasize) it.

B   **Correct.** The passage's third and fourth sentences question the plausibility of the historian's assumption that no one but Alfred would have been likely to write a text whose language has more similarities to than differences from the language in Alfred's translations.

C   Although there might well be anomalous consequences from generalizing the assumption on which the historian's argument relies, the passage does not mention or allude to any such consequences.

D   The passage does not mention, or suggest the existence of, any inconsistencies among the premises of the historian's argument.

E   Although the historian argues by analogy, the passage does not itself argue by analogy; it does not suggest any specific counteranalogy to undermine the historian's argument.

The correct answer is B.

172. Aroca City currently funds its public schools through taxes on property. **In place of this system, the city plans to introduce a sales tax of 3 percent on all retail sales in the city.** Critics protest that 3 percent of current retail sales falls short of the amount raised for schools by property taxes. The critics are correct on this point. **Nevertheless, implementing the plan will probably not reduce the money going to Aroca's schools.** Several large retailers have selected Aroca City as the site for huge new stores, and these are certain to draw large numbers of shoppers from neighboring municipalities, where sales are taxed at rates of 6 percent and more. In consequence, retail sales in Aroca City are bound to increase substantially.

In the argument given, the two portions in **boldface** play which of the following roles?

(A) The first presents a plan that the argument concludes is unlikely to achieve its goal; the second expresses that conclusion.

(B) The first presents a plan that the argument concludes is unlikely to achieve its goal; the second presents evidence in support of that conclusion.

(C) The first presents a plan that the argument contends is the best available; the second is a conclusion drawn by the argument to justify that contention.

(D) The first presents a plan one of whose consequences is at issue in the argument; the second is the argument's conclusion about that consequence.

(E) The first presents a plan that the argument seeks to defend against a certain criticism; the second is that criticism.

Argument Evaluation

Situation   Aroca City plans to switch the source of its public school funding from property taxes to a new local sales tax.

Reasoning   *What argumentative roles do the two portions in **boldface** play in the passage?* The first **boldfaced** portion simply describes the city's plan. The next two sentences in the passage describe an observation some critics have made in objecting to the plan and say that the observation is correct. But then the second **boldfaced** portion rejects the critics' implicit conclusion that the plan will reduce school funding. The final two sentences in the passage present reasons to accept the statement in the second **boldfaced** portion, so they are premises supporting it as a conclusion.

A   The argument concludes that the plan is unlikely to reduce funding for the schools. The passage does not mention the plan's goal, but presumably that goal is not to reduce school funding.

B   The second **boldfaced** portion presents the argument's conclusion, not evidence to support the conclusion. The passage does not mention the plan's goal, but presumably that goal is not to reduce school funding.

C   The passage does not say whether the plan is better than any other possible school funding plans.

D   Correct. The plan's likely effect on the amount of school funding is at issue in the argument, whose conclusion is that the plan probably will not reduce that funding.

E   The second **boldfaced** portion does not criticize the plan, but rather rejects a criticism of the plan by stating that the plan will probably not reduce school funding.

The correct answer is D.

173. Which of the following most logically completes the argument?

A photograph of the night sky was taken with the camera shutter open for an extended period. The normal motion of stars across the sky caused the images of the stars in the photograph to appear as streaks. However, one bright spot was not streaked. Even if the spot were caused, as astronomers believe, by a celestial object, that object could still have been moving across the sky during the time the shutter was open, since _________.

(A)   the spot was not the brightest object in the photograph

(B)   the photograph contains many streaks that astronomers can identify as caused by noncelestial objects

(C)   stars in the night sky do not appear to shift position relative to each other

(D)   the spot could have been caused by an object that emitted a flash that lasted for only a fraction of the time that the camera shutter was open

(E)   if the camera shutter had not been open for an extended period, it would have recorded substantially fewer celestial objects

Argument Construction

Situation   In a photograph of the night sky taken with the camera shutter open for an extended period, the images of stars appeared as streaks because of the stars' normal motion across the sky, but one bright spot was not streaked.

Reasoning   *What would most strongly suggest that a celestial object moving across the sky could have caused the spot?* An object moving across the sky that was bright throughout the time the camera shutter was open should have appeared as a streak in the photograph, just as the stars did. But if the moving object was bright for only a very brief moment, and thus not for an extended time while the camera shutter was open, the object's movement may not have been captured in the photograph, and thus would appear in the photograph as an unstreaked bright spot.

A   The argument is not about how bright the spot was compared to other objects in the photograph.

B   Streaks caused by noncelestial objects such as satellites or airplanes do not explain how only one of many celestial objects moving across the sky could have produced the unstreaked spot.

C   The passage indicates that the stars were shifting position relative to the camera, not relative to one another. In any case, this observation does not help to explain how a celestial object that may not have been a star but that was moving across the sky could have produced the unstreaked spot in the photograph.

D   **Correct.** As explained above, a moving celestial object that only produced a momentary flash of light would produce an unstreaked bright spot in the photograph.

E   This may be true, given that fewer celestial objects might have moved into the camera's range of view if the camera shutter had not been open as long. But it does not provide any evidence that a moving celestial object could have produced the unstreaked spot.

The correct answer is D.

174. Economist: Paying extra for fair-trade coffee—coffee labeled with the Fairtrade logo—is intended to help poor farmers, because they receive a higher price for the fair-trade coffee they grow. But this practice may hurt more farmers in developing nations than it helps. By raising average prices for coffee, it encourages more coffee to be produced than consumers want to buy. This lowers prices for non-fair-trade coffee and thus lowers profits for non-fair-trade coffee farmers.

To evaluate the strength of the economist's argument, it would be most helpful to know which of the following?

(A) Whether there is a way of alleviating the impact of the increased average prices for coffee on non-fair-trade coffee farmers' profits

(B) What proportion of coffee farmers in developing nations produce fair-trade coffee

(C) Whether many coffee farmers in developing nations also derive income from other kinds of farming

(D) Whether consumers should pay extra for fair-trade coffee if doing so lowers profits for non-fair-trade coffee farmers

(E) How fair-trade coffee farmers in developing nations could be helped without lowering profits for non-fair-trade coffee farmers

Argument Evaluation

Situation   Poor farmers receive higher prices for fair-trade coffee. But paying extra for fair-trade coffee lowers prices for non-fair-trade coffee and thus lowers profits for non-fair-trade coffee farmers.

Reasoning   *What would be most helpful to know to evaluate how well the economist's observations support the conclusion that buying fair-trade coffee hurts more farmers in developing nations than it helps?* The economist suggests that buying fair-trade coffee benefits farmers who grow it because they receive higher prices, but that it hurts non-fair-trade coffee farmers by reducing their profits. So to know whether the practice hurts more farmers in developing nations than it helps, it would be helpful to know whether developing nations have more farmers who produce non-fair-trade coffee than produce fair-trade coffee.

A   Even if there were some potential way of alleviating the negative impact from buying fair-trade coffee on non-fair-trade coffee farmers, it still could be that the practice hurts more developing-nation farmers than it helps. Alleviating the negative impact does not entail that there is no negative impact.

B   **Correct.** If fewer than half of these farmers produce fair-trade coffee, then the economist's observations do suggest that buying fair-trade coffee hurts more coffee farmers in developing nations than it helps. But if more than half do, those observations suggest the contrary.

C   Although knowing this could be helpful in determining how intensely many farmers are economically affected by people buying fair-trade coffee, it is not helpful in determining whether more farmers are hurt than are helped.

D   The argument's conclusion is only about the economic impact of buying fair-trade coffee, not about how consumers should or should not respond to that impact.

E   Knowing how the fair-trade coffee farmers could potentially be helped without hurting the other coffee farmers is irrelevant to assessing whether the practice of buying fair-trade coffee hurts more developing-nation farmers than it helps.

The correct answer is B.

175. Since smoking-related illnesses are a serious health problem in Country X, and since addiction to nicotine prevents many people from quitting smoking, the government of Country X plans to reduce the maximum allowable quantity of nicotine per cigarette by half over the next five years. However, reducing the quantity of nicotine per cigarette will probably cause people addicted to nicotine to smoke more cigarettes. Therefore, implementing this plan is unlikely to reduce the incidence of smoking-related illnesses.

Which of the following, if true, most strongly supports the argument about the consequences of implementing the Country X government's plan?

(A) Over half of the nonsmoking adults in Country X have smoked cigarettes in the past.

(B) If the Country X government's plan is implemented, the brands of cigarettes sold in Country X will differ less from each other than they do now in terms of their nicotine content.

(C) Inexpensive, smoke-free sources of nicotine, such as nicotine gum and nicotine skin patches, have recently become available in Country X.

(D) Many smokers in Country X already spend a large proportion of their disposable income on cigarettes.

(E) The main cause of smoking-related illnesses is not nicotine but the tar in cigarette smoke.

Argument Construction

Situation   Country X plans to mandate that the nicotine content of cigarettes be reduced by half to encourage a reduction in smoking. The goal is to reduce the incidence of illnesses caused by cigarette smoking. Is there information given that suggests a likelihood that this goal will not be attained?

Reasoning   We're given the information that people addicted to nicotine would probably smoke more cigarettes after Country X's plan has been implemented. The argument concludes that the incidence of smoking-related illnesses is therefore unlikely to be reduced. The option providing the strongest support for that conclusion is (E): the information that tar, not nicotine, is the main contributor to smoking-related illnesses.

A   This information suggests that cigarette smoking is a well-established practice in Country X. But it does not address the question of whether the government's plan will succeed.

B   This information indicates that cigarette smokers in Country X will have less choice regarding the average quantity of nicotine per cigarette smoked, but it does not suggest that addicted smokers will smoke less, on average, than they do now. Having greater uniformity in the average quantity of nicotine per cigarette, however, does not support the contention that the government's plan to reduce smoking-related illness will fail.

C   This information suggests a way in which cigarette smoking rates could decline, though it does not indicate any likelihood that such a decline would occur.

D   This information suggests how strong the incentive to smoke cigarettes is for many smokers in Country X. But it does not indicate that mandating lower nicotine levels will reduce smoking or smoking-related illnesses.

E   **Correct.** This option adds important information to the argument regarding a key causal factor showing that smoking even nicotine-reduced cigarettes would likely not reduce the incidence of illnesses caused by cigarette smoking in Country X, unless the average rate of cigarette smoking were to decline significantly. A premise of the argument indicates that people addicted to nicotine would probably smoke more cigarettes, on average, to feed their addiction. If this occurred, more tar from cigarette smoking would enter the lungs, which suggests that a reduction in illnesses caused by smoking cigarettes would be unlikely to occur.

The correct answer is E.

176. In 1983, Argonia's currency, the argon, underwent a reduction in value relative to the world's strongest currencies. This reduction resulted in a significant increase in Argonia's exports over 1982 levels. In 1987, a similar reduction in the value of the argon led to another increase in Argonia's exports. Faced with the need to increase exports yet again, Argonia's finance minister has proposed another reduction in the value of the argon.

Which of the following, if true, most strongly supports the prediction that the finance minister's plan will NOT result in a significant increase in Argonia's exports next year?

(A)   The value of the argon rose sharply last year against the world's strongest currencies.

(B)   In 1988, the argon lost a small amount of its value, and Argonian exports rose slightly in 1989.

(C)   The value of Argonia's exports was lower last year than it was the year before.

(D)   All of Argonia's export products are made by factories that were operating at full capacity last year, and new factories would take years to build.

(E)   Reductions in the value of the argon have almost always led to significant reductions in the amount of goods and services that Argonians purchase from abroad.

Argument Construction

Situation   Two drops in the value of Argonia's currency, the argon, during the 1980s both led to increased exports. To stimulate a new surge in exports, the finance minister suggests lowering the value of the argon again.

Reasoning   *What supports the prediction that a weak argon may not increase exports?* Drops in the value of the argon have led to increases in Argonian exports in the past, so the finance minister's plan to increase exports by weakening the currency is reasonable *unless* some additional factor undermines the plan's odds of success. Therefore, identifying such a factor would support the prediction that the finance minister's plan will not increase exports.

A   The fact that the argon's value rose last year does not in itself support the prediction that lowering the argon's value will not increase exports.

B   A small decline in the argon's value leading to a slight increase in Argonian exports would tend to support the idea that the minister's plan to increase exports by weakening the currency will succeed; it does not support the prediction that the plan will fail.

C   Recent decreases in the value of Argonia's exports have no bearing on whether the finance minister's plan to increase exports will succeed or fail.

D   Correct. The prediction that the finance minister's plan to increase exports will fail would be more likely to be correct *if* the factories which make exports are already working at full capacity, and therefore would be unable to make significantly more goods to meet the increased demand stimulated by a weaker currency. Exports could not increase without additional goods to export.

E   The fact that a weaker argon reduces Argonia's imports has no bearing on whether a weaker argon would successfully stimulate exports.

The correct answer is D.

177. Transnational cooperation among corporations is experiencing a modest resurgence among United States firms, even though projects undertaken by two or more corporations under a collaborative agreement are less profitable than projects undertaken by a single corporation. The advantage of transnational cooperation is that such joint international projects may allow United States firms to win foreign contracts that they would not otherwise be able to win.

Which of the following is information provided by the passage?

(A) Transnational cooperation involves projects too big for a single corporation to handle.

(B) Transnational cooperation results in a pooling of resources leading to high-quality performance.

(C) Transnational cooperation has in the past been both more common and less common than it is now among United States firms.

(D) Joint projects between United States and foreign corporations are not profitable enough to be worth undertaking.

(E) Joint projects between United States and foreign corporations benefit only those who commission the projects.

Argument Construction

Situation   The passage states that cooperative transnational projects have recently had a resurgence among US firms; the advantage of such cooperative projects is that companies working together may win international contracts they could not win separately, and the disadvantage is that profits for each firm are lower than profits derived from independent projects.

Reasoning   *Which fact is included in the passage?* The key phrase in the passage is *modest resurgence*. A resurgence, or rebirth, in any area can only occur if that area previously enjoyed more popularity, then fell out of favor. If it had never been popular in the past, its increase would be a novelty and not a resurgence. Moreover, if the current resurgence equaled or surpassed previous levels of transnational cooperation, that increase would be robust, not modest. Therefore, the passage includes the information that transnational cooperation was first more popular than currently, then less so, before making the modest resurgence discussed.

A   The passage states that corporations may be more likely to win contracts for cooperative projects, not that they could not handle those projects on their own.

B   The passage states that transnational cooperation helps firms secure contracts, not that it results in quality work.

C   **Correct**. If transnational cooperation among corporations is experiencing a *modest resurgence*, as stated in the passage, then, by definition, such cooperation must have once been more common, experienced a falling-off, and then increased again to a current level somewhere between the two previous levels. In other words, such cooperation was both more common and less common at different points in the past.

D   The passage states that joint projects are less profitable than individual projects, not that they are not profitable enough to be worthwhile.

E   The passage never states that joint projects benefit only those who commission them.

The correct answer is C.

178. Temporary-services firms supply trained workers to other companies on a temporary basis. Temporary-services firms lose business when the economy shows signs of beginning to weaken. They gain business when the economy begins to recover but often lose business again when the economy stabilizes. These firms have begun to gain business in the present weak economy. The economy therefore must be beginning to recover.

Which of the following is an assumption on which the argument depends?

(A) Temporary-services firms are more likely to regain old clients than to acquire new ones when the economy begins to recover.

(B) Temporary-services firms do not gain business when an already weak economy worsens.

(C) New companies do not often hire temporary help until they have been in business for some time.

(D) Companies that use workers from temporary-services firms seldom hire those workers to fill permanent positions.

(E) Temporary-services firms can most easily find qualified new workers when the economy is at its weakest.

Argument Construction

Situation   Temporary-services firms lose business when the economy appears to be starting to weaken, but they gain business when the economy begins to recover (though as the economy stabilizes, in many instances the firms will lose business again). Because these firms have started gaining new business in the current weak economy, an economic recovery must have begun.

Reasoning   *On what assumption does the argument depend?* The argument states that temporary-services firms will *lose* business as the economy *begins* to weaken and *gain* business as the economy *begins* to recover. Nothing in the argument rules out the possibility that these firms may also gain business during a period of increased weakening. If these firms did gain business during times when a weak economy gets even worse, then the argument's conclusion—that the economy must be strengthening—would not follow. So, the argument must assume that these firms do *not* gain business during such times.

A   Whether the clients are old or new is not relevant to the argument that an overall increase in hiring temporary workers necessarily implies an improving economy.

B   **Correct.** If the argument did not assume this—that temporary-services firms do not at least sometimes gain business when an already weak economy worsens—then the mere fact that such firms *have* gained business recently would not be good reason to infer that the economy is recovering.

C   Even if new companies regularly hire temporary help before they have been in business for some time, it still could be the case that the gaining of business by temporary-services firms indicates economic recovery.

D   Nothing in the argument makes any assumptions about the frequency with which companies that use temporary-services workers hire those workers to fill permanent positions.

E   The *availability* of temporary workers has no bearing on whether or not *demand* for such workers necessarily implies that the weak economy is improving.

The correct answer is B.

179. Wolves generally avoid human settlements. For this reason, domestic sheep, though essentially easy prey for wolves, are not usually attacked by them. In Hylantia prior to 1910, farmers nevertheless lost considerable numbers of sheep to wolves each year. Attributing this to the large number of wolves, in 1910, the government began offering rewards to hunters for killing wolves. From 1910 to 1915, large numbers of wolves were killed. Yet wolf attacks on sheep increased significantly.

Which of the following, if true, most helps to explain the increase in wolf attacks on sheep?

(A) Populations of deer and other wild animals that wolves typically prey on increased significantly in numbers from 1910 to 1915.

(B) Prior to 1910, there were no legal restrictions in Hylantia on the hunting of wolves.

(C) After 1910, hunters shot and wounded a substantial number of wolves, thereby greatly diminishing these wolves' ability to prey on wild animals.

(D) Domestic sheep are significantly less able than most wild animals to defend themselves against wolf attacks.

(E) The systematic hunting of wolves encouraged by the program drove many wolves in Hylantia to migrate to remote mountain areas uninhabited by humans.

Argument Construction

Situation   Significant numbers of wolf attacks on sheep in Hylantia prior to 1910 led the Hylantia government to adopt a wolf-reduction program that year. Although large numbers of wolves were killed over the next five years, wolf attacks on sheep nonetheless increased.

Reasoning   *Since Hylantia's wolf population was presumably reduced by significant killing of wolves from 1910 to 1915, what other factor would help explain increasing wolf attacks on sheep during the same period?* Hylantia's reduction of its wolf population did not lead to the desired result of reducing wolf attacks on sheep, but on the contrary increased such attacks. Therefore, some additional factor should account for the unexpected increase.

A   Increasing availability of other prey animals would be likely to decrease wolf attacks on sheep, not increase such attacks.

B   A lack of hunting restrictions before 1910 would not help explain increasing attacks after 1910.

C   **Correct.** If the population of injured wolves with a limited ability to hunt wild prey greatly increased after 1910, that would help explain why wolves increased their attacks on easier prey such as sheep at that time.

D   The ability of sheep to defend themselves would not change in the period from 1910–1915 and so would not have any effect on the rate of wolf attacks during that time.

E   Driving wolves to remote regions far from human populations would probably decrease, not increase, attacks on domestic animals such as sheep.

The correct answer is C.

180. Paint on a new airliner is usually applied in two stages: first, a coat of primer, and then a top coat. A new process requires no primer, but instead uses two layers of the same newly developed coating, with each layer of the new coating having the same thickness and weight as a traditional top coat. Using the new process instead of the old process increases the price of a new aircraft considerably.

Which of the following, if true, most strongly indicates that it is in an airline's long-term economic interest to purchase new airliners painted using the new process rather than the old process?

(A)   Although most new airliners are still painted using the old process, aircraft manufacturers now offer a purchaser of any new airliner the option of having it painted using the new process instead.

(B)   A layer of primer on an airliner weighs more than a layer of the new coating would by an amount large enough to make a difference to that airliner's load-bearing capacity.

(C)   A single layer of the new coating provides the aluminum skin of the airliner with less protection against corrosion than does a layer of primer of the usual thickness.

(D)   Unlike the old process, the new process was originally invented for use on spacecraft, which are subject to extremes of temperature to which airliners are never exposed.

(E)   Because the new coating has a viscosity similar to that of a traditional top coat, aircraft manufacturers can apply it using the same equipment as is used for a traditional top coat.

Evaluation of a Plan

Situation   A new coating for airliners has been developed. Instead of a coat of primer followed by a top coat, the new coating is applied in two coats, each of which is equal in weight and thickness to an application of top coat. Coating the airliner in this way makes purchasing a new airliner more expensive.

Reasoning   *Since the new painting process adds significant expense, what additional factors could make that expense economically beneficial in the long term?* The added expense of the new painting process would seem to make it a poor economic choice for airlines, unless some other factor would be likely to make using the new paint increase revenue over time, sufficiently to justify the added cost.

A   The ready availability of the new process does not make that process economically beneficial to airlines.

B   **Correct.** If the new process reduces an airliner's weight enough to increase its load-bearing capacity, the extra revenue generated by the greater loads might be enough to outweigh, over time, the additional upfront cost.

C   If the new process provides inferior protection than does the old process, that would not help make the new process economically beneficial.

D   The new process's utility in space has no bearing on its economic advantages for airlines.

E   The ability of aircraft manufacturers to use their old equipment for the new process might help keep the cost of the new process from going even higher, but it does not provide airlines with an incentive to choose the more expensive paint.

The correct answer is B.

181. Because of steep increases in the average price per box of cereal over the last 10 years, overall sales of cereal have recently begun to drop. In an attempt to improve sales, one major cereal manufacturer reduced the wholesale prices of its cereals by 20 percent. Since most other cereal manufacturers have announced that they will follow suit, it is likely that the level of overall sales of cereal will rise significantly.

Which of the following would it be most useful to establish in evaluating the argument?

(A)   Whether the high marketing expenses of the highly competitive cereal market led to the increase in cereal prices

(B)   Whether cereal manufacturers use marketing techniques that encourage brand loyalty among consumers

(C)   Whether the variety of cereals available on the market has significantly increased over the last 10 years

(D)   Whether the prices that supermarkets charge for these cereals will reflect the lower prices the supermarkets will be paying the manufacturers

(E)   Whether the sales of certain types of cereal have declined disproportionately over the last 10 years

Evaluation of a Plan

Situation   Increasing cereal prices over the past decade have led to decreasing sales. In an effort to reverse this trend, one cereal manufacturer is significantly lowering wholesale prices. Because other manufacturers have said they will do the same, lower wholesale prices will lead to higher cereal sales.

Reasoning   *What additional factor would be likely to affect the argument that lower wholesale cereal prices will lead to higher cereal sales?* To determine whether the lower wholesale cereal prices set by manufacturers will indeed lead to higher retail sales of cereal, it would be useful to determine if any other factors would be likely to interfere in the expected causative relation between lower wholesale prices and higher demand. Since the information specifies that the lower prices are wholesale, one variable that could affect the argument is retail pricing.

A   Even if increased marketing expenses was one factor that contributed to higher cereal prices, this would not affect the argument that lowering wholesale prices will lead to higher sales.

B   Brand loyalty might affect the market share of various cereal brands, but it would not be likely to lead to decreases or increases in cereal sales overall.

C   The variety of available cereals is not relevant to the question of whether decreasing wholesale prices will promote cereal sales.

D   **Correct.** If supermarkets failed to lower their retail prices to reflect the decrease in wholesale prices, retail sales and ultimately wholesale sales would probably not increase. On the other hand, a lowering of retail cereal prices would likely boost retail and wholesale sales volume.

E   The greater sales decreases of specific cereals would not affect the argument that lower wholesale prices will lead to higher total sales of cereals.

The correct answer is D.

182. Crowding on Mooreville's subway frequently leads to delays, because it is difficult for passengers to exit from the trains. Over the next ten years, the Mooreville Transit Authority projects that subway ridership will increase by 20 percent. The authority plans to increase the number of daily train trips by only 5 percent over the same period. Officials predict that this increase is sufficient to ensure that the incidence of delays due to crowding does not increase.

Which of the following, if true, provides the strongest grounds for the officials' prediction?

(A) The population of Mooreville is not expected to increase significantly in the next ten years.

(B) The Transit Authority also plans a 5 percent increase in the number of bus trips on routes that connect to subways.

(C) The Transit Authority projects that the number of Mooreville residents who commute to work by automobile will increase in the next ten years.

(D) Most of the projected increase in ridership is expected to occur in off-peak hours when trains now are sparsely used.

(E) The 5 percent increase in the number of train trips can be achieved without an equal increase in Transit Authority operational costs.

Evaluation of a Plan

Situation   Crowding on Mooreville's subway makes it difficult for passengers to exit the trains, which in turn leads to delays. Officials plan to address an anticipated 20 percent increase in ridership over the coming decade with a 5 percent increase in trains, and these officials predict that this increase in trains will be sufficient to prevent more crowding-related delays.

Reasoning   *What factor could support the prediction that a greater increase in ridership than in the number of trains over the next ten years will not lead to increased crowding over the same period?* A 20 percent increase in ridership, with only a 5 percent increase in train trips to accommodate the additional passengers, would be expected to significantly increase crowding, unless an additional reason justified the prediction that it would not increase, and might even reduce, crowding and the resulting delays.

A   Constant population does not support the prediction that a larger percentage increase in ridership than in available trains will not lead to increased crowding.

B   An increase in bus trips that connect to subways would not necessarily affect crowding caused by a 20 percent increase in ridership on those subways.

C   An increase in commuting by car, without a corresponding decrease in subway ridership, would not support the prediction that subway crowding won't increase.

D   Correct. If the projected increase in ridership mainly affects trains that have space available to accommodate the added passengers, then that would provide support for the prediction that a greater percentage increase in riders than in train trips will not lead to greater crowding and delays.

E   Constant operational costs would not support the prediction that crowding will not increase.

The correct answer is D.

183. Though sucking zinc lozenges has been promoted as a treatment for the common cold, research has revealed no consistent effect. Recently, however, a zinc gel applied nasally has been shown to greatly reduce the duration of colds. Since the gel contains zinc in the same form and concentration as the lozenges, the greater effectiveness of the gel must be due to the fact that cold viruses tend to concentrate in the nose, not in the mouth.

Which of the following, if true, most seriously weakens the argument?

(A) Experimental subjects who used the zinc gel not only had colds of shorter duration but also had less severe symptoms than did those who used a gel that did not contain zinc.

(B) The mechanism by which zinc affects the viruses that cause the common cold has not been conclusively established.

(C) To make them palatable, zinc lozenges generally contain other ingredients, such as citric acid, that can interfere with the chemical activity of zinc.

(D) No zinc-based cold remedy can have any effect unless it is taken or applied within 48 hours of the initial onset of cold symptoms.

(E) Drug-company researchers experimenting with a nasal spray based on zinc have found that it has much the same effect on colds as the gel does.

Argument Evaluation

Situation Sucking zinc lozenges has not been shown to fight colds effectively, but application of a nasal zinc gel is demonstrably effective. Both the gel and the lozenges contain the same type and concentration of zinc, so the greater efficacy of the nasal gel must be because cold viruses are present in higher levels in the nose than in the mouth.

Reasoning *What additional factor could weaken the argument that, since zinc-based remedies fight colds, but nasal-gel zinc fights colds more effectively than does oral-lozenge zinc, that difference must be explained by higher concentrations of cold virus in the nose than in the mouth?* The argument that the virus's high concentrations in the nose must account for the greater effectiveness of nasal zinc gel over oral zinc lozenges only holds if no other factor could explain that difference in effectiveness; therefore, identifying another explanation for that difference weakens the argument.

A The greater effectiveness of zinc gel versus a control would not explain the greater effectiveness of zinc gel versus zinc lozenges.

B Uncertainty regarding the mechanism by which zinc fights colds is not relevant to the question of why zinc lozenges are less effective than zinc gel.

C **Correct.** The presence of other ingredients in zinc lozenges that can interfere with zinc's activity could help explain why zinc lozenges are less effective than zinc gel and thereby weaken the argument that the virus's distribution must be the reason for differences in effectiveness.

D The importance of early treatment with zinc has no bearing on the question of why nasal zinc gel works better than oral zinc lozenges.

E The equal effectiveness of nasal spray and nasal gel does not provide any explanation for why nasal gel is more effective than oral lozenges.

The correct answer is C.

184. In each of the past five years, Barraland's prison population has increased. Yet, according to official government statistics, for none of those years has there been either an increase in the number of criminal cases brought to trial or an increase in the rate at which convictions have been obtained. Clearly, therefore, the percentage of people convicted of crimes who are being given prison sentences is on the increase.

Which of the following, if true, most seriously weakens the argument?

(A) In Barraland, the range of punishments that can be imposed instead of a prison sentence is wide.

(B) Over the last ten years, overcrowding in the prisons of Barraland has essentially been eliminated as a result of an ambitious program of prison construction.

(C) Ten years ago, Barraland reformed its criminal justice system, imposing longer minimum sentences for those crimes for which a prison sentence had long been mandatory.

(D) Barraland has been supervising convicts on parole more closely in recent years, with the result that parole violations have become significantly less frequent.

(E) The number of people in Barraland who feel that crime is on the increase is significantly greater now than it was five years ago.

Argument Evaluation

Situation   Barraland has seen annual increases in its prison population over a five-year period. However, over the same period, there has not been a corresponding increase in the number of people convicted of crimes, which indicates that a larger percentage of prison sentences handed down to convicted people must account for the increase.

Reasoning   *What additional factor could weaken the argument that, since the annual number of convicted people in Barraland has not increased over the last five years, a greater percentage of such convicts receiving prison sentences must be responsible for the increasing prison population during the same period?* The argument that a higher rate of prison sentences must be responsible for a higher prison population only holds if there are no other factors contributing to that increase in population, so identifying such an additional factor weakens the argument.

A   Sentencing options other than prison would not account for an increasing prison population over the last five years.

B   The lack of overcrowding in Barraland's prisons is not relevant to the question of why its prison population has increased.

C   **Correct.** Longer prison sentences would provide an alternative explanation for increasing prison population and thereby weaken the argument that an increasing percentage of the people sentenced to prison must be responsible.

D   Lower rates of parole violations would not account for the increasing prison population.

E   A general sense that crime is increasing, absent a corresponding increase in criminal convictions, would not explain an increasing prison population.

The correct answer is C.

185. TrueSave is a mail-order company that ships electronic products from its warehouses to customers worldwide. The company's shipping manager is proposing that customer orders be packed with newer, more expensive packing materials that virtually eliminate damage during shipping. The manager argues that overall costs would essentially remain unaffected, since the extra cost of the new packing materials roughly equals the current cost of replacing products returned by customers because they arrived in damaged condition.

Which of the following would it be most important to ascertain in determining whether implementing the shipping manager's proposal would have the argued-for effect on costs?

(A) Whether the products shipped by TrueSave are more vulnerable to incurring damage during shipping than are typical electronic products

(B) Whether electronic products are damaged more frequently in transit than are most other products shipped by mail-order companies

(C) Whether a sizable proportion of returned items are returned because of damage already present when those items were packed for shipping

(D) Whether there are cases in which customers blame themselves for product damage that, though present on arrival of the product, is not discovered until later

(E) Whether TrueSave continually monitors the performance of the shipping companies it uses to ship products to its customers

Evaluation of a Plan

Situation   TruSave's shipping manager wants to switch to new, more costly packing materials that will prevent their products from being damaged during shipping. The manager argues that the additional cost will be offset by a reduction in returns of broken items.

Reasoning   *If the increased cost of switching to better packing materials is roughly equal to the cost of items returned due to damage, what additional factors might affect the cost-effectiveness of the proposed switch?* Returns due to damage cost TrueSave roughly the same amount as would better packaging. Since the better packaging only protects against damage during shipping, returns due to damage prior to shipping would add support to the manager's argument that switching to better packaging would not affect overall costs.

A   Higher rates of damage to TrueSave's shipments would not affect the overall cost of switching to better packaging.

B   The comparative rates of damage to electronics versus other products would not affect the overall cost of switching to better packaging.

C   **Correct.** If a significant proportion of total damage is found to occur before shipping, and therefore would not be prevented by better packaging during shipping, that finding would support the manager's argument that the switch to better packaging would not affect total costs.

D   Cases of consumers wrongly blaming themselves for damage would not affect the question of whether or not switching to better packaging would affect total costs, since those consumers presumably do not return their items.

E   TrueSave's attentiveness to the performance of its shipping companies would not affect the overall cost of switching to better packaging.

The correct answer is C.

186. Business Consultant: **Some corporations shun the use of executive titles** because they fear that the use of titles indicating position in the corporation tends to inhibit communication up and down the corporate hierarchy. Since an executive who uses a title is treated with more respect by outsiders, however, use of a title can facilitate an executive's dealings with external businesses. Clearly, **corporations should adopt the compromise of encouraging their executives to use their corporate titles externally but not internally,** since even if it is widely known that the corporation's executives use titles outside their organization, this knowledge does not by itself inhibit communication within the corporation.

In the consultant's reasoning, the two portions in **boldface** play which of the following roles?

(A) The first describes a strategy that has been adopted to avoid a certain problem; the second expresses the consultant's assessment of the significance of that problem.

(B) The first describes a strategy that has been adopted to avoid a certain problem; the second is a judgment that the consultant uses to argue that the strategy is ineffective.

(C) The first describes a strategy that has a drawback that the consultant points out; the second presents a strategy that, according to the consultant, would achieve the same end while avoiding that drawback.

(D) The first describes a practice for which the consultant seeks to provide a justification; the second is a consideration offered as part of that justification.

(E) The first describes a policy that the consultant concludes is misguided; the second is introduced to explain why that policy was adopted.

Argument Construction

Situation   A business consultant presents the possible concern that the use of executive titles may impede vertical communication within a company; the drawback to simply dropping such titles, as some companies have done, is that such titles are useful in dealing with external businesses. The consultant proposes a solution: Use such executive titles with outsiders, but not with fellow employees of the company. The consultant asserts that awareness of such externally used titles does not have an inhibiting effect on company communications.

Reasoning   *What role do the two **boldfaced** portions play in the consultant's discussion of the best way to use executive titles?* The first portion states that some companies shun the use of executive titles; the surrounding context suggests that this is a strategy to avoid inhibiting communication, but the consultant points out that giving up titles has a drawback: such titles are useful with outsiders. The second portion advances the consultant's preferred strategy for preventing such inhibited communication without that drawback: keep the titles, but use them only with outsiders.

A   While the first portion does describe a strategy that has been used to avoid the problem of inhibited communications, the second portion is not in any way an assessment of that problem's significance.

B   The first portion describes a strategy used to avoid the problem of poor communications within a company, but the second portion describes an alternative strategy rather than suggesting that the first strategy is ineffective.

C   **Correct.** The first portion describes a strategy, dropping executive titles, that the consultant considers flawed because such titles are useful in dealing with outsiders; the second portion presents the consultant's preferred strategy of keeping the titles but using them only with outsiders, which clearly avoids the drawback of losing useful titles. The surrounding context contains the consultant's assertion that this alternative strategy will achieve the same goal: avoiding the inhibition of communication.

D   The first portion does describe a practice, dropping executive titles, and the consultant does describe the justification for that practice; however, the second portion describes an alternative practice rather than justifying the practice referred to in the first portion.

E   The first portion does describe a policy that the consultant considers misguided; however, the second portion does not say anything regarding why that policy was adopted.

The correct answer is C.

187. For new restaurant managers, a number of organizations offer food-safety certification courses. Although people can manage a restaurant without having taken such a course, the courses are effective in promoting safe food-handling practices. Their effectiveness is demonstrated by the fact that about a third of restaurant managers have taken such a course; only eight percent of restaurants cited for serious health-code violations are managed by someone who has done so.

Which of the following, if true, most strengthens the force of the support offered for the effectiveness of the courses?

(A) It is more difficult to maintain food safety in large restaurants than in small ones.

(B) New restaurant managers who are most likely to take a food-safety course are those who already have several years of experience working in restaurants.

(C) The various food-safety courses that are available differ considerably in both the material they cover and the amount of hands-on training they require.

(D) Most serious health-code violations involve improper food storage rather than poor cooking techniques.

(E) In terms of hours worked per week and number of meals served annually, managers who have taken a food-safety course are no different from those who have not.

Argument Evaluation

Situation   Food-safety certification courses are offered to new restaurant managers and are claimed to be effective in promoting safe food-handling practices. The evidence supporting this claim is that although about one-third of all restaurant managers have taken such a course, only eight percent of restaurants cited for serious health-code violations are managed by someone who has taken the course. The argument infers that taking a food-safety course reduces the likelihood of serious violations.

Reasoning   To most strengthen the support for this conclusion, additional information must rule out *alternative explanations* for why course-takers are underrepresented among managers of restaurants with serious violations. Evidence showing that managers who have taken the course are exposed to *similar work conditions and opportunities for violations* as those who have not would reinforce the idea that the difference in violation rates is attributable to the course itself rather than to differences in workload or restaurant activity.

A   This option does not strengthen the argument because it introduces a new variable—restaurant size—without connecting it to whether managers took the course. Unless we know that course-takers and nontakers manage restaurants of similar sizes, this information does not help explain the difference in violation rates.

B   This option actually weakens the argument by suggesting an alternative explanation for the observed effect. If course-takers are already more experienced, their lower violation rates may be due to prior experience rather than the course itself. This undermines the claim that the course is what makes the difference.

C   This option is irrelevant to the argument's strength. While it describes variability among courses, it does not indicate whether the courses are effective overall or explain the difference in violation rates between managers who took a course and those who did not.

D   This option does not strengthen the argument because it merely describes the types of violations that occur. It does not show that the food-safety courses specifically reduce these violations or explain why course-takers are underrepresented among cited restaurants.

E   **Correct.** This option most strengthens the argument because it rules out an important alternative explanation. If managers who took the course worked fewer hours or served fewer meals, they might simply have had fewer opportunities to incur health-code violations. By stating that both groups have similar workloads and exposure, this choice supports the conclusion that the lower rate of violations is due to the course itself, not differences in job demands.

The correct answer is E.

188. Ms. Rayner found that her ten-year-old son, Mitchell, often failed to complete his homework even though she responded by giving him brief time-outs. She decided to try calmly explaining to him why completing homework was important instead of using time-outs. After three months of this approach, Mitchell still sometimes failed to complete his homework. Ms. Rayner concluded that explaining the importance of homework to Mitchell was no more effective than using time-outs in reducing his failure to complete homework.

Which of the following, if true by the end of the three months, would most call into question Ms. Rayner's conclusion?

(A) Mitchell was more likely to fail to complete his homework in public settings, such as after-school programs, than he had been before.

(B) Ms. Rayner decided to investigate the effectiveness of systematically rewarding Mitchell whenever he completed his homework, as an alternative to using time-outs or explanations.

(C) Ms. Rayner herself had rarely been given time-outs when she failed to complete assignments as a child.

(D) Mitchell was failing to complete his homework less often than he had been when his mother had used time-outs.

(E) Mitchell reacted negatively after explanations just as often as he had after time-outs.

Argument Evaluation

Situation Ms. Rayner is comparing two methods—*giving brief time-outs* and *calmly explaining the importance of completing homework*—to reduce her son Mitchell's failure to complete homework. After switching from time-outs to explanations and observing that Mitchell still sometimes failed to complete his homework, she concludes that explanations are *no more effective* than time-outs.

Reasoning To call Ms. Rayner's conclusion into question, new information must show that the explanation-based approach was actually *more effective than time-outs*, even if it did not completely eliminate the problem. Evidence that Mitchell failed to complete his homework *less frequently* under the explanation approach would undermine the conclusion because Ms. Rayner's reasoning mistakenly treats continued failure as proof of equal effectiveness rather than comparing *relative improvement*.

A This option does not weaken the conclusion because it focuses on where Mitchell fails to complete his homework, not on whether explanations are more or less effective than time-outs overall. It provides no basis for comparing the two methods.

B This choice is irrelevant to the conclusion. The fact that Ms. Rayner is considering or testing another approach does not affect whether explanations were more effective than time-outs during the three-month period in question.

C This option is irrelevant because Ms. Rayner's childhood experiences do not affect the effectiveness of either method on Mitchell. It provides no information about the comparative outcomes of time-outs versus explanations.

D **Correct.** This option most directly undermines Ms. Rayner's conclusion. If Mitchell failed to complete his homework less frequently under the explanation approach than under time-outs, then explanations were more effective, even if they were not completely successful. Ms. Rayner's conclusion incorrectly treats "not eliminating the problem" as "no improvement," making her comparison flawed.

E This choice does not undermine the conclusion because it addresses Mitchell's emotional reactions, not his homework completion behavior, which is the outcome Ms. Rayner is evaluating. Similar reactions do not imply similar effectiveness.

The correct answer is D.

189. A lack of a particular nutrient in the soil during the earliest stage of plant growth has been identified as the cause of a certain crop defect. In order to help reduce the occurrence of this defect, the government has proposed that this nutrient—normally found in such materials as organic compost and untreated topsoil—be added to commercially sold fertilizer used for a wide range of crops.

Which of the following, if true, most strongly supports the claim that the government's proposal, if implemented, will achieve its goal?

(A) The nutrient is an important component of soil health for many types of plants.

(B) Many farmers begin planting before soil testing can identify nutrient deficiencies in the earliest stages of growth.

(C) Both organic compost and untreated topsoil contain a wide variety of beneficial substances.

(D) Small quantities of the nutrient are already present in some fertilizers that are widely used.

(E) The nutrient plays an important role in the development of plant root systems.

Argument Evaluation

Situation   A specific crop defect has been traced to a deficiency of a particular nutrient *during the earliest stage of plant growth.* To reduce the occurrence of this defect, the government proposes adding the nutrient *to commercially sold fertilizer,* which is widely used at the start of planting. The argument claims that this proposal, if implemented, will successfully reduce the defect.

Reasoning   To support this claim, the correct answer must show that adding the nutrient to fertilizer would *effectively deliver the nutrient at the critical early stage* when the deficiency causes the defect. Evidence that the fertilizer is applied before deficiencies are typically identified, or that it reliably reaches crops at that early stage, strengthens the argument by demonstrating that the proposal directly addresses the cause of the problem.

A   While this shows the nutrient is generally beneficial, it does not specifically support the claim that adding it to fertilizer will reduce this particular defect. Importance alone does not demonstrate that the proposed method addresses the identified cause in the relevant timeframe.

B   **Correct.** This option strongly supports the proposal by showing why adding the nutrient directly to fertilizer would be effective: It ensures plants receive the nutrient before any deficiency can be detected and remedied through other means. The fertilizer acts as a preventive measure at exactly the stage when the nutrient is needed, making it likely the proposal will achieve its goal.

C   This option is irrelevant to the proposal. The argument concerns whether adding the nutrient to fertilizer will reduce the defect, not whether natural materials are beneficial. This choice does not explain why the proposal would succeed.

D   This choice weakens or, at best, fails to support the claim. If the nutrient is already present in widely used fertilizers and the defect still occurs, that fact suggests that simply adding the nutrient may not be sufficient to solve the problem.

E   Although this explains *why* the nutrient matters, it does not show that adding it to fertilizer will successfully reduce the defect. The question is about the effectiveness of the proposal, not the nutrient's general role.

The correct answer is B.

190. Historian: Frobisher, a sixteenth-century English explorer, had soil samples from an island in Canada assessed for gold content. **The assessments found high gold content**, and Elizabeth I consequently funded two mining expeditions, which were both unsuccessful. **Modern analysis of the island's soil indicates much lower gold content** than Frobisher's reports indicated, and some scholars have therefore hypothesized that the methods used to assess the gold content of Frobisher's samples were inaccurate. This conclusion would be reasonable only if one could be sure that neither Frobisher nor anyone else had added gold to the samples before they were assessed.

In the historian's argument, the two **boldfaced** portions play which of the following roles?

(A) The first provides evidence in favor of the historian's position; the second presents evidence that has been used to support an opposing position.

(B) The first provides evidence in favor of a hypothesis that the historian critiques; the second provides evidence against that hypothesis.

(C) The first provides evidence that has been used to support one of two alternative courses of action; the second is a reason given for abandoning that course of action.

(D) The first and the second are both pieces of evidence that the argument characterizes as discredited by the circumstances in which they were obtained.

(E) The first and the second are two pieces of evidence that point to a discrepancy, the explanation of which is the issue that the argument addresses.

Argument Construction

Situation   A historian discusses an Elizabethan explorer named Frobisher: Frobisher had soil from a Canadian island analyzed, and that analysis identified significant amounts of gold, prompting Elizabeth I to sponsor unsuccessful mining efforts there. Modern analysis has found far lower quantities of gold in the island's soil; one possible explanation of this difference is that the original analysis of Frobisher's samples was flawed. The argument points out that, to conclude the original analysis was flawed, another explanation would have to be excluded: the possibility that someone had tampered with Frobisher's samples by adding gold.

Reasoning   *What functions do the two **boldfaced** portions play in the argument?* The first **boldfaced** portion refers to the original analysis of soil samples provided by Frobisher: It states that there was a high gold content identified in the soil. The second portion refers to a modern analysis of the island's soil, which found far lower gold content. These two portions taken together point to a discrepancy, and two possible explanations for that discrepancy are discussed in the remainder of the argument: There was either faulty analysis of the first samples or deliberate tampering with those samples.

A   The assessment that there was high gold content would support the historian's position only if that position relied on the presence of gold in the soil, just as the second portion would undermine their position only in a similar case; however, the historian's position concerns the reason for the discrepancy, not the gold content itself.

B   The historian is concerned with the explanation for the data that *led* to the hypothesis, long since disproved, that the island's soil is rich in gold, and not with critiquing the hypothesis itself; so while the second portion *does* present evidence against the gold-rich hypothesis, this is not the correct answer.

C   The assessment finding high levels of gold did indeed support a course of action, namely Elizabeth I choosing to send mining expeditions; however, that effort was likely abandoned because the expeditions failed to find much gold, and certainly not because of the assessment referred to in the second portion, which occurred hundreds of years after the queen's death.

D   The argument does not characterize the evidence presented in either portion as having been discredited, specifically, by the circumstances in which it was obtained; the evidence in the first portion was discredited, rather, by subsequent and more conclusive contrary evidence.

E   **Correct.** The two portions, taken together, point to a discrepancy: One analysis finds high gold content, the other finds low gold content. The reasons behind that discrepancy are at issue in the remainder of the argument: Either the analysis finding high gold content in the soil was flawed, or perhaps the soil itself had been tampered with.

The correct answer is E.

191. A particular accounting error frequently occurs in large corporations when financial reports are prepared using a certain spreadsheet template. Although small businesses often use the same type of spreadsheet template, this accounting error is only rarely detected in small businesses. This fact, however, does not indicate that most small businesses are less susceptible to the error, since __________.

(A)   large corporations and small businesses are not the only organizations that use the type of spreadsheet template associated with the error

(B)   the accounting error has been identified in organizations that did not use the spreadsheet template typically associated with the error

(C)   familiarity with spreadsheet software can reduce the likelihood of certain accounting errors

(D)   both large corporations and small businesses typically require more than a year of financial reporting before the error becomes evident, and small businesses, unlike large corporations, often change their accounting systems within the first year

(E)   the spreadsheet template associated with the error generally constitutes a larger proportion of the reporting tools used by small businesses than by large corporations

Argument Construction

Situation   An accounting error frequently occurs in large corporations when financial reports are prepared using a particular spreadsheet template. Small businesses also commonly use this same template, yet the error is only rarely detected in small businesses. The argument cautions that this rarity should not be taken to mean that small businesses are less susceptible to the error.

Reasoning   To complete the argument logically, the correct answer must explain *why the error might be rarely detected in small businesses, even if they are just as susceptible as large corporations.* Information showing that the error typically becomes apparent only after an extended period, and that small businesses often change systems before that period elapses, would account for the lower detection rate without implying greater resistance.

A   This option is irrelevant to the argument. The conclusion concerns differences between large corporations and small businesses, and information about other organizations does not explain why the error is rarely detected in small businesses.

B   This choice weakens the premise that the spreadsheet template is the primary cause of the error but does not explain why the error is rarely detected in small businesses. It fails to address the comparison at issue.

C   This option suggests that experience may reduce susceptibility, which actually undermines the argument's claim. If small businesses are more familiar with the software, they may genuinely be less susceptible, contradicting the argument's assertion.

D   **Correct.** This option provides a clear alternative explanation for the lower detection rate in small businesses. If the error takes a long time to surface and small businesses replace their systems before that time, the error would simply go undetected, not be absent. This fully supports the claim that rarity of detection does not imply reduced susceptibility.

E   This option works against the argument. If small businesses use the template more extensively, the error should be more common among them, not rarer. It fails to explain the observed difference.

The correct answer is D.

192. In the past, most children who went sledding in the winter in Verland used wooden sleds with runners and steering bars. Ten years ago, smooth plastic sleds became popular; they go faster than wooden sleds but are harder to steer. The concern that plastic sleds are more dangerous is clearly borne out by the fact that the number of children injured while sledding was much higher last winter than it was ten years ago.

Which of the following, if true in Verland, most seriously undermines the force of the evidence cited?

(A) A few children still use traditional wooden sleds.

(B) Most sledding injuries occur when a sled collides with a tree, a rock, or another sled.

(C) Very few children wear any kind of protective gear, such as helmets, while sledding.

(D) Because plastic sleds are less expensive than wooden sleds, many more children own a sled now than did ten years ago.

(E) Because the traditional wooden sleds can carry more than one rider, an accident involving a wooden sled can result in several children being injured.

Argument Evaluation

Situation   Children in Verland have been switching from traditional wooden sleds to faster, less controllable plastic sleds, introduced ten years ago. Many more children were injured while sledding last winter than were injured before the plastic sleds were introduced; the argument concludes from this evidence that plastic sleds are more dangerous than wooden sleds.

Reasoning   *What would undermine the argument that the higher total number of injuries is evidence for the plastic sleds' greater dangerousness?* The argument mentions only that the total *number* of injured children is higher. If, therefore, there was evidence that the *rate* of injuries is not necessarily higher— because more children are sledding now than were sledding ten years ago—then that evidence would undermine the claim that the higher absolute number of injuries indicates that the plastic sleds are more dangerous.

A   The fact that some children still use wooden sleds does not undermine the evidence for the claim that plastic sleds are more dangerous.

B   Because the information states that the plastic sleds are harder to steer, the fact that most injuries occur due to collisions would tend to support, not undermine, claims that the plastic sleds are more dangerous.

C   The lack of protective gear is not relevant to the question of whether plastic sleds are more dangerous.

D   Correct. If many more children own sleds now than did ten years ago, then it seems reasonable to think that more children go sledding now; that in turn would suggest that a greater absolute *number* of injuries might not imply a greater *rate* of injuries and therefore undermine the claim that the greater number of injuries means that the plastic sleds are more dangerous than the wooden ones.

E   The fact that wooden sleds can carry multiple riders does not undercut the claim that a greater number of injuries now than formerly must mean plastic sleds are more dangerous.

The correct answer is D.

193. A particular software malfunction has been observed frequently in large enterprise systems but only rarely in personal computers. Both enterprise systems and personal computers often use the type of third-party application identified as the source of the malfunction. Systems affected by the malfunction typically take more than a year of continuous use before the problem becomes apparent; however, personal computers, unlike enterprise systems, are generally replaced or upgraded within their first year of use.

Which of the following is most strongly supported by the information provided?

(A) The malfunction cannot be transmitted to mobile devices by personal computers.

(B) There is no way to determine whether a personal computer is affected by the malfunction before the problem becomes apparent.

(C) A failure to observe the malfunction in personal computer populations is not good evidence that personal computers are resistant to the malfunction.

(D) A system affected by the malfunction but not yet exhibiting problems cannot cause the malfunction in another system using the same application.

(E) The third-party application is probably not the only source of the malfunction.

Argument Evaluation

Situation   A particular software malfunction is frequently observed in large enterprise systems but rarely in personal computers, even though both types of systems commonly use the same third-party application associated with the malfunction. The malfunction typically does not become apparent until a system has been in use for more than a year. However, personal computers are generally replaced or upgraded within their first year of use, whereas enterprise systems remain in use much longer.

Reasoning   The information suggests that the *absence of observed malfunctions in personal computers does not indicate resistance* to the malfunction. Because personal computers are often replaced before the malfunction has time to appear, the problem may simply go undetected. Therefore, the rarity of observed cases in personal computers is explained by differences in duration of use rather than by any inherent immunity.

A   This option is unsupported. The passage does not discuss mobile devices or transmission between different device types, so no conclusion about transmission can be drawn.

B   This option goes beyond the evidence. While the passage states that the malfunction takes time to become apparent, it does not say that early detection is impossible.

C   **Correct.** This conclusion follows directly from the information provided. Since the malfunction requires more than a year to become apparent and personal computers are usually replaced before that time, the malfunction may exist but remain undetected. Therefore, the lack of observed cases does not show that personal computers are resistant.

D   This choice introduces claims about causation and transmission that are not discussed. The passage provides no information about whether systems can affect one another.

E   This option is not supported. The passage identifies the application as a source but does not suggest the existence of additional sources.

The correct answer is C.

194. Last year a record number of new manufacturing jobs were created. Will this year bring another record? Well, any new manufacturing job is created either within an existing company or by the start-up of a new company. **Within existing firms, new jobs have been created this year at well below last year's record pace.** At the same time, there is considerable evidence that the number of new companies starting up will be no higher this year than it was last year, and there is no reason to think that **the new companies starting up this year will create more jobs per company than did last year's start-ups.** So clearly, the number of new jobs created this year will fall short of last year's record.

In the argument given, the two portions in **boldface** play which of the following roles?

(A) The first is a claim that the argument challenges; the second presents an explicit assumption that has served as the basis for that claim.

(B) The first is a claim that the argument challenges; the second is a claim that has been advanced in order to challenge the main conclusion of the argument.

(C) The first provides evidence to support the main conclusion of the argument; the second is a judgment advanced in support of that main conclusion.

(D) The first provides evidence to support the main conclusion of the argument; the second presents a possible objection that the argument discounts.

(E) The first is a claim that has been advanced in support of a position that the argument opposes; the second is a possible objection to that claim.

Argument Construction

Situation   A record number of manufacturing jobs were created in the year previous. For this year to set a new record, manufacturing jobs must be created in greater numbers by the two sources of such jobs taken together: established companies and start-up companies. Established companies are creating fewer manufacturing jobs than they did the year previous; moreover, because companies are starting up at the same, or lower, rate than they did the year previous, and because there is no evidence that these start-ups will create manufacturing jobs at a higher rate per company than did companies that started up the year previous, the author concludes that the total of new manufacturing jobs will be fewer this year than last year.

Reasoning   *How do the two* **boldface** *portions relate to the argument that fewer manufacturing jobs will be created this year?* The first **boldface** portion presents the evidence that existing companies are hiring at a lower rate than in the year previous. That leaves only one other possible source of new manufacturing jobs that could exceed last year's jobs, namely start-up companies. Because start-up companies are forming at a rate no greater than last year's, the only way there could be more jobs created this year would be if these start-ups created more manufacturing jobs per company; this potential objection is presented in the second **boldfaced** statement. However, the author discounts this possibility by stating that there is "no reason" to believe it is true.

A   The first portion provides direct evidence for the author's argument and is not challenged anywhere in the text; the second portion does refer to an assumption, namely the assumption that start-ups will not create jobs at a higher rate than in the past, but that assumption relates to a separate claim.

B   The first portion is a claim the argument relies on rather than challenges; the second is a claim that could possibly be advanced to challenge the main conclusion, but that the author dismisses as lacking support.

C   The first portion is indeed support for the conclusion; however, the second portion includes only the potential claim that the new start-ups could create more jobs per company than start-ups did the previous year. The author's judgment that this higher job creation is unlikely falls outside the bounds of the **boldfaced** portion, so this option is incorrect.

D   **Correct.** The first portion, which states that existing companies are creating new jobs at a lower rate than they did last year, is direct support for the author's conclusion that fewer new jobs will be created this year; the second portion presents a possible avenue by which more jobs *could* in theory be created, namely if new start-ups created jobs at a higher rate than start-ups did in the past. However, the argument discounts that potential objection with the statement that there is "no reason" to expect such a higher rate.

E   The first portion is support for the author's position and not for an opposed position; the second portion relates to a different claim, not to the claim presented in the first portion.

The correct answer is D.

195. Astronomer: **Observations of the Shoemaker–Levi comet on its collision course with Jupiter showed that the comet broke into fragments before entering Jupiter's atmosphere in 1994, but they did not show how big those fragments were.** In hopes of gaining some indication of the fragments' size, astronomers studied spectrographic analyses of Jupiter's outer atmosphere. After the fragments' entry, these analyses revealed unprecedented traces of sulfur. **The fragments themselves almost certainly contained no sulfur**, but many astronomers believe that the cloud layer below Jupiter's outer atmosphere does contain sulfur. Since sulfur would have seeped into the outer atmosphere if comet fragments had penetrated this cloud layer, it is likely that some of the fragments were at least large enough to have passed through Jupiter's outer atmosphere without being burned up.

In the astronomer's argument, the two portions in **boldface** play which of the following roles?

(A) The first is a claim that the astronomer seeks to show is true; the second acknowledges a consideration that weighs against the truth of that claim.

(B) The first is a claim that the astronomer seeks to show is false; the second acknowledges a consideration that weighs in favor of the truth of that claim.

(C) The first reports observations that the astronomer argues have certain implications; the second is one of those implications.

(D) The first introduces the issue that the argument addresses; the second is a judgment advanced in support of the conclusion of the argument.

(E) The first provides evidence in support of the conclusion of the argument; the second acknowledges a consideration that weighs against that conclusion.

Argument Construction

Situation   An astronomer states that the Shoemaker–Levi comet shattered before it entered Jupiter's atmosphere, but there was no indication regarding the size of the comet's pieces. In an attempt to determine the size of the pieces, scientists used spectrographic analysis of Jupiter's outer atmosphere and found evidence of sulfur following entry of the comet's fragments. The astronomer states that the comet's fragments were highly unlikely to contain sulfur, but that the inner layers of Jupiter's atmosphere may contain sulfur. The argument concludes that the presence of sulfur was probably due to fragments of the comet striking the clouds of the inner atmosphere, and therefore that those fragments were large enough to reach that layer without burning away.

Reasoning   *How do the two **boldface** portions function in relation to the argument that the sulfur is evidence for the size of the fragments?* The first portion states that the Shoemaker–Levi comet shattered outside Jupiter's atmosphere, but that the size of the comet's fragments were not observed. This introduces the question at issue in the argument: how big were the fragments? The second portion states the judgment that the comet's fragments almost certainly did not contain sulfur; since the sulfur observed by the scientists must have come from somewhere, ruling out the comet itself as the source of the sulfur supports the conclusion: the fragments were probably big enough to release traces of sulfur from Jupiter's inner atmosphere.

A   The first portion is merely a statement about the limits of the initial observations, and the astronomer accepts that information as a given rather than attempting to demonstrate its truth; the second portion in no way weighs against the first portion, but rather advances the judgment that the sulfur was not from the comet.

B   The first portion is information the astronomer takes as a given and does not contest; the second portion, the statement that the fragments were unlikely to contain sulfur, has no bearing on the truth of the first claim: that scientists observed the comet's fragmentation but not the size of the fragments.

C   The astronomer is not concerned with the *implications* of the observations described in the first portion, but rather with their *limitations*; the second portion is not an implication of those observations, but rather a distinct judgment.

D   **Correct.** The first portion introduces the central issue under discussion: if the size of the comet's fragments could not be directly observed, then can that size be determined by other means? The second portion, the implicit claim that the presence of sulfur probably did not arise from the fragments themselves, is a judgment in support of the conclusion: if the sulfur did not come from the fragments, then it likely came from Jupiter's inner atmosphere, which in turn suggests that the fragments were big enough to release matter from that inner atmosphere.

E   The first portion introduces the argument rather than providing evidence for it, and the second portion supports the conclusion rather than weighing against it.

The correct answer is D.

196. Historian: In the Drindian Empire, censuses were conducted annually to determine the population of each village. **Village census records for the last half of the 1600s are remarkably complete.** This very completeness makes one point stand out: In five different years, villages overwhelmingly reported significant population declines. Tellingly, each of those five years immediately followed an increase in a certain Drindian tax. **This tax, which was assessed on villages, was computed by the central government using the annual census figures.** Obviously, whenever the tax went up, villages had an especially powerful economic incentive to minimize the number of people they recorded, and concealing the size of a village's population from government census takers would have been easy. Therefore, the reported declines probably did not happen.

In the historian's argument, the two portions in **boldface** play which of the following roles?

(A) The first provides evidence to support the main conclusion of the historian's argument; the second presents that conclusion.

(B) The first is a claim which the historian seeks to evaluate; the second presents evidence in order to call that claim into question.

(C) The first is a consideration that is advanced to counter evidence that weighs against the historian's conclusion; the second provides evidence to support that conclusion.

(D) The first provides a context for certain evidence that supports the position that the historian seeks to establish; the second provides evidence to support the main conclusion of the argument.

(E) The first provides a context for certain evidence that supports the position that the historian seeks to establish; the second is the main conclusion of the argument.

Argument Construction

Situation
: A historian states that the Drindian Empire conducted annual censuses, and the resulting records of village populations from the second half of the seventeenth century are comprehensive. Five specific years show widespread drops in population; the historian points out that those years followed an increase in a tax that was determined by the census figures. The historian concludes that the apparent population declines were probably the result of villages hiding people as a method of evading taxes, not actual declines.

Reasoning
: *What role do the two **boldface** portions play in the argument that the recorded population declines were not genuine?* The first portion provides context for the evidence that follows by stating that the census records under discussion are complete. The second portion, which states that those census results determined the amount of tax villages paid, provides evidence for the historian's conclusion: that *recorded* population declines probably did not reflect *actual* population declines, but rather resulted from villages' efforts to limit their tax liability.

A   The first portion establishes context for the evidence rather than being evidence in itself; the second portion is evidence and not a conclusion.

B   The historian advances the claim, in the first portion, that the records are complete, but does not evaluate that claim, and the second portion is in no way evidence that the records are *not* complete and so does not call the claim into question.

C   The first portion merely provides a context for evidence rather than *countering* any evidence; however, the second portion is indeed evidence for the historian's conclusion.

D   **Correct.** The first portion provides context for evidence the historian draws from the census records by stating that those records are complete; the second portion, which states that census results determined villages' tax liabilities, provides evidence for the conclusion: that the recorded population declines probably did not reflect real declines, but rather resulted from villages' efforts to avoid paying heavy taxes.

E   While the first portion does provide context for evidence used in the historian's argument, the second portion is not the main conclusion but rather is evidence for that conclusion.

The correct answer is D.

Questions 197 to 253 — Difficulty: **Hard**

197. Twenty-five years ago, 2,000 married people were asked to rank four categories—spouses, friends, jobs, and housework—according to the amount of time each category demanded. A recent follow-up survey indicates that a majority of those same people rank housework higher on the list now than they did twenty-five years ago. Yet most of the respondents also claim that housework has become less demanding of their time over the last twenty-five years.

Which of the following, if true, helps to explain the apparent discrepancy?

(A)   Some of the people surveyed were married to other people in the survey.

(B)   Many of the most time-consuming aspects of people's lives do not appear as categories on either survey.

(C)   Most of those who responded to the follow-up survey have retired in the last twenty-five years.

(D)   At the time of the follow-up survey, some of the people surveyed did no housework.

(E)   Many of the respondents to the follow-up survey claim that they now spend much more time with their friends than they did twenty-five years ago.

Argument Construction

Situation   Twenty-five years ago, 2,000 married people were asked in a survey to rank four categories—spouse, friends, jobs, and housework—with respect to the average amount of time demanded by activities in each category. In a recent survey, most of the same people were asked to rank those activities again. Many ranked housework higher than they had ranked it in the first survey. Yet most claimed that housework had become less demanding of their time over the past twenty-five years. In light of the higher ranking of housework, this claim is initially puzzling.

Reasoning   *Which answer choice provides the best explanation for the apparent inconsistency between the two findings cited from the recent survey?* A rise in the ranking of housework could occur either because the amount of time taken by housework increased or because the amount of time taken by one or more of the other categories declined over the twenty-five years. For example, suppose housework ranked fourth, i.e., lowest, in the first survey. If most of those surveyed had been fulltime employees twenty-five years ago, the category *jobs* would probably have ranked much higher than the category *housework*. But if those people were retired twenty-five years later, then the time demanded by jobs would be much less or even zero. Housework might then rank higher than jobs in the second survey even if it did not demand as many hours as it did previously.

A   The information that some people surveyed were spouses of others surveyed would not, by itself, indicate statistical error in the survey. Single people in the surveys would obviously have ranked the category *spouse* lower than did married people. We are given no information as to how many of those people who were single when first surveyed had since married. But even if we had such information, a rise in the ranking for the category *spouse* would not, without further information, explain the rise in the ranking for *housework*.

B   The surveys asked only for a ranking of activities in the four categories. Each ranking reflects the proportion of total time spent on those four categories, not including other kinds of activity.

C   **Correct.** Housework could move up in the ranking if the category *jobs*, for example, had drastically declined in the ranking below even housework. As explained above, this could occur if many or most of those surveyed had been employed fulltime twenty-five years ago but had retired in the meantime; this would be consistent with a rise in the ranking of housework as well as a reduction in the proportion of total time spent on housework.

D   This information is nonspecific about how many people did no housework. It is also nonspecific about how many of those who were surveyed ranked housework lowest or reported doing no housework. It does not help explain the apparent inconsistency in the overall survey results.

E   In the absence of further information about the ranking of the categories *housework* and *friends* in the two surveys, this new information does little to explain the apparent inconsistency. In fact, without some indication that many respondents do housework with their friends, this suggests that the ranking for the category *housework* should have declined if it changed at all.

The correct answer is C.

198. In Cecropia, inspections of fishing boats that estimate the number of fish they are carrying are typically conducted upon their return to port. The high numbers so obtained have led the government to conclude that the coastal waters are being overfished. To allow commercial fishing stocks to recover, the government is considering introducing annual quotas on the number of fish that each fishing boat can catch. Compliance with the quotas would be determined by the established system of inspections.

Which of the following, if true, raises the most serious doubts about whether the government's proposed plan would succeed?

(A) Some commercial fishing boats in Cecropia are large enough to catch their entire annual quota in only a few months of fishing.

(B) The quotas would have to be reduced if more boats began fishing in Cecropia's coastal waters.

(C) Because fish prices will rise if the quotas go into effect, it is unlikely that the quotas will significantly change the number of boats fishing Cecropia's coastal waters.

(D) The procedure that inspectors use to estimate the number of fish a boat is carrying often results in a slight overcount.

(E) Quotas encourage fishers to bring only the most commercially valuable fish into port and to discard less valuable fish, most of them dead or dying.

Evaluation of a Plan

Situation   The government of Cecropia is considering introducing annual catch quotas for fishing boats in order to allow commercial fishing stocks in coastal waters to recover. The quotas would be enforced by inspectors who will estimate the number of fish brought into port by each boat.

Reasoning   *What new information raises the most serious doubts about whether the plan would succeed if it is implemented?* The quota restrictions could raise problems associated with enforcement, economic viability, and acceptance by those whose livelihood depends, directly or indirectly, on the fishing industry. The restrictions would be pointless and would not attain the goal of protecting fishing stocks unless they could be effectively enforced. Other issues would have to be resolved for the proposed quotas to pass into law.

A   For large commercial fishing boats, the quota system could pose difficulties. Large capital investment would likely be tied up in such boats, and such boats might have to supplement their catches by fishing in waters not controlled by any nation. But large boats could presumably do so.

B   We are given no information as to whether possible reduction of fishing quotas is envisaged in the government's proposed plan—or whether quota reduction would count as a different proposal superseding the one under discussion.

C   This is a consideration in favor of the proposal. It suggests that the proposed quota system would succeed and that the viability of commercial fishing boats and the livelihoods of fishers would not be negatively affected.

D   This information does not suggest that the quota system is likely to fail. If fish counts are adjusted using a reasonable margin of error and there are appeal procedures to resolve disputes about fish counts, such disputes, by themselves, would then be unlikely to cause the quota system to fail.

E   **Correct.** The information about the proposed quota system indicates that the fish catch of each boat is monitored only in port. Boats could circumvent the quota system by indiscriminately catching and letting die all available fish but discarding the least valuable fish out at sea before submitting to the inspections in port. The non-survival of this part of the catch could, over time, impair the recovery of the coastal fish populations.

The correct answer is E.

199. Consultant: **A significant number of complex repair jobs carried out by Ace Repairs have to be redone under the company's warranty, but when those repairs are redone they are invariably successful.** Since we have definitely established that **there is no systematic difference between the mechanics who are assigned to do the initial repairs and those who are assigned to redo unsatisfactory jobs**, it is clear that inadequacies in the initial repairs cannot be attributed to the mechanics' lack of competence. Rather, it is likely that complex repairs require a level of focused attention that the company's mechanics apply consistently only to repair jobs that have been inadequately done on the first try.

In the consultant's reasoning, the two portions in **boldface** play which of the following roles?

(A) The first is a claim that the consultant rejects as false; the second is evidence that forms the basis for that rejection.

(B) The first is part of an explanation that the consultant offers for a certain finding; the second is that finding.

(C) The first presents a pattern whose explanation is at issue in the reasoning; the second provides evidence to rule out one possible explanation of that pattern.

(D) The first presents a pattern whose explanation is at issue in the reasoning; the second is evidence that has been used to challenge the explanation presented by the consultant.

(E) The first is the position the consultant seeks to establish; the second is offered as evidence for that position.

Argument Evaluation

Situation   The following information is attributed to a consultant. Some complex repair jobs done by Ace Repairs have to be redone under warranty and the repairs, when redone, are usually successful. But the mechanics who do the initial repairs and those who redo them are, overall, equally competent to do the repairs successfully.

Reasoning   *What role in the consultant's reasoning do the **boldfaced** statements play?* The first sentence describes a situation that is puzzling and needs explanation. One might be inclined to argue that the mechanics who redo the repairs are more competent that those who did the initial repairs. But the second **boldfaced** statement rebuts this explanation by telling us that it has been *definitely established* that there are no systematic differences in competence. The final sentence of the consultant's reasoning offers another explanation: that the redoing of a repair elicits from mechanics a higher level of focused attention than did the performance of the initial repair.

A   The first is an assertion made by the consultant concerning a puzzling phenomenon. It does not attribute a denial of any claim to the consultant; so the second does not provide a reason for a denial made by the consultant in the first **boldfaced** portion.

B   The first is not an explanation, or even part of one, for a finding, but rather, a description of a puzzling finding concerning a difference between success rates of initial repairs and those of repairs that are redone. The first, not the second, describes the finding itself.

C   **Correct.** The first is a statement of a puzzling fact that the consultant seems to have found and that needs explanation. The second provides evidence to exclude the hypothesis that the higher success rates in redoing repairs than in the initial doing of the repairs is explainable by reference to different levels of competence in the mechanics in each case.

D   The first is a statement of a puzzling fact that the consultant seems to believe needs explanation. Regarding the second, first note that the explanation that the consultant offers is to be found in the final sentence of the passage. The second **boldfaced** portion is part of the reasoning on which the consultant bases the explanation, not a claim that someone else has made in opposition to the consultant's explanation.

E   The first is an assertion by the consultant; the consultant presents it as established fact, not as a position that the consultant seeks to establish (i.e., provide evidence for). The second does not give evidence that helps establish the consultant's initial assertion.

The correct answer is C.

200. A library currently has only coin-operated photocopy machines, which cost 10 cents per copy. Library administrators are planning to refit most of those machines with card readers. The library will sell prepaid copy cards that allow users to make 50 copies at 9 cents per copy. Administrators believe that, despite the convenience of copy cards and their lower per-copy cost, the number of copies made in the library will be essentially unchanged after the refit.

On the assumption that administrators' assessment is correct, which of the following predictions about the effect of the refit is most strongly supported by the information given?

(A) Library patrons will only purchase a copy card on days when they need to make 50 or more copies.

(B) No library patrons will increase their usage of the library's photocopy machines once the refit has been made.

(C) If most of the copy cards sold in the library are used to their full capacity, the number of people using the library's photocopy machines over a given period will fall.

(D) Revenues from photocopying will decrease unless most library patrons choose to use the remaining coin-operated machines in preference to the card-reader equipped ones.

(E) Revenues from photocopying will increase if copy cards that are purchased are, on average, used to significantly less than 90 percent of their capacity.

Evaluation of a Plan

Situation   A library's photocopiers are coin-operated; a copy costs 10 cents. The library's management plans to refit most of the photocopiers to accept copy cards that allow 50 copies to be made at 9 cents each. The administrators believe that the refit will not result in fewer copies being made.

Reasoning   *Assuming that the administrators are right, which of the five predictions about the effect of the refit is most strongly supported by the information provided?* Suppose that only one card were sold and only 45 copies were made with that card. Then the amount that the user paid per copy would be 10 cents. Whatever the number of cards sold, provided the number of copies made per card averages less than 45, then the average revenue per copy would be more than 10 cents. This would produce an increase in total revenue if the total number of photocopy uses were no less than in previous years. The greater the number of cards sold, the greater the increase in total revenues, provided that the usage per card averages less than 45 copies. The lower the average usage per card, the greater the increase in photocopy revenue. The information provided suggests that the number of cards sold will be considerable, given that *most of the machines* are being refitted with card readers (and may be usable only with card readers).

A   The information provides no reason to suppose that library patrons would buy cards only for use on the same day they buy them. Furthermore, the claim that the number of copies made will not change suggests that this might be false; if, after the refit, patrons almost never make small numbers of copies and almost never make copies on impulse, one might expect a decrease in the number of copies made.

B   This is not supported by the information provided. For example, some library patrons could increase their usage while others make a compensating reduction in their usage.

C   If 51 percent of the cards sold *are used to their full capacity*, it could still be the case that average utilization per card would be substantially less than 50 copies. So it is possible that the total number of photocopy users would increase or remain constant over a given period even if there is no change in the number of copies made and most cards are used to their full capacity.

D   The given information suggests otherwise. If some but not most library patrons choose to use the card-operated machines, revenues will increase if utilization per card averages less than 45 copies.

E   **Correct.** Each card has a capacity of 50 copies, so 90 percent of that is 45 copies. If the total number of copies made in the library remains at least as great as before and utilization of each card averages less than 45, revenues will increase; the lower the average utilization, the greater the increase in revenue.

The correct answer is E.

201. Harvester-ant colonies live for fifteen to twenty years, though individual worker ants live only a year. The way a colony behaves changes steadily in a predictable pattern as the colony grows older and larger. For the first few years, the foragers behave quite aggressively, searching out and vigorously defending new food sources, but once a colony has reached a certain size, its foragers become considerably less aggressive.

If the statements above are true, which of the following can most properly be concluded on the basis of them?

(A) As a result of pressure from neighbors, some colonies do not grow larger as they become older.

(B) Unpredictable changes in a colony's environment can cause changes in the tasks that the colony must perform if it is to continue to survive.

(C) The reason a mature colony goes out of existence is that younger, more aggressive colonies successfully outcompete it for food.

(D) The pattern of changing behavior that a colony displays does not arise from a change in the behavior of any individual worker ant or group of worker ants.

(E) A new colony comes into existence when a group of young, aggressive workers leaves a mature colony and sets up on its own.

Argument Construction

Situation   The given information contrasts the lifespan of harvester-ant colonies (twenty years) with that of individual foragers in the colonies (one year). When the colony is young and relatively small, its foragers aggressively seek and defend food resources. But when the colony grows older and reaches a certain size, its foragers become less aggressive.

Reasoning   *Which answer choice is most strongly supported by the given information?* Obviously, the survival of a colony can be jeopardized by encountering unusual environmental challenges. But the given information suggests that, provided no unusual threats to the colony's survival are encountered, a colony's life cycle is biologically determined by constraints of colony size and age. The behavior of the individual foragers is correlated with the age and size of the colony; how a forager behaves in a colony near its maximum limits of size and age is quite different from an individual forager's behavior in the colony's early years. The behaviors of individual foragers are highly coordinated; the patterns of behavior of the colony are not caused by individual behaviors of the worker ants.

A   Although this might be true, the given information suggests that the limits on colony size do not depend on competition from neighbors but are, rather, general constraints that are based in harvester-ant biology.

B   Although this is likely true, the given information does not address the issue of how colony dynamics might be affected by drastic and unusual environmental changes.

C   Obviously, the survival of a colony that fails over a period to secure the food resources it needs would be threatened. But the given information does not state or imply that such failures are generally due to more aggressive competition by ants in another colony. It suggests that, in general, a colony's demise is primarily dictated by the biological constraints on colony size and age.

D   **Correct.** As explained, the given information suggests that, provided no unusual threats to a colony's survival are encountered, its life cycle is biologically determined by constraints of colony size and age, not by the behavior of individual forager ants or groups of such ants. The given information suggests that the biological constraints on a colony's size and longevity also determine behaviors of individual worker ants, who live about one year.

E   Nothing in the given information suggests that worker ants are the founders of a harvester-ant colony.

The correct answer is D.

202. To improve customer relations, several big retailers have recently launched "smile initiatives," requiring their employees to smile whenever they have contact with customers. These retailers generally have low employee morale, which is why they have to enforce smiling. However, studies show that customers can tell fake smiles from genuine smiles and that fake smiles prompt negative feelings in customers. So the smile initiatives are unlikely to achieve their goal.

The argument relies on which of the following as an assumption?

(A) The smile initiatives have achieved nearly complete success in getting employees to smile while they are around customers.

(B) Customers' feelings about fake smiles are no better than their feelings about the other facial expressions employees with low morale are likely to have.

(C) The feelings that employees generate in retail customers are a principal determinant of the amount of money customers will spend at a retailer.

(D) At the retailers who have launched the smile initiatives, none of the employees gave genuine smiles to customers before the initiatives were launched.

(E) Customers rarely, if ever, have a negative reaction to a genuine smile from a retail employee.

Argument Construction

Situation   Several large retailers where employee morale is low are requiring their employees to smile when they interact with customers; these requirements are known as "smile initiatives." The author of the argument concludes that because fake smiles create negative feelings in customers, these initiatives are unlikely to achieve their goal of improving customer relations.

Reasoning   *What assumption is required by the argument?* Even if customers can tell fake smiles from real ones and have negative feelings about them, the fake smiles could nonetheless improve customer relations. How? Suppose customers' attitudes are less negative about the fake smiles than about other facial expressions that result from low morale. Therefore, the argument requires the assumption that customer feelings about fake smiles are no better than their feelings about other facial expressions resulting from low morale.

A   The argument does not require this assumption. The initiative could fail to achieve its goal simply by failing to get employees to smile.

B   **Correct.** As explained above, if customers' feelings about fake smiles are not as negative as their feelings about other facial expressions that result from low morale, the smile initiative might nonetheless help improve customer relations. As a result, the argument needs to assume that customers' feelings about fake smiles are no better than their feelings about these other facial expressions.

C   The argument does not need to assume that the feelings employees generate in customers are a principal determinant of the amount customers will spend. Such feelings merely must have some effect on customer relations.

D   The argument needs to assume that not all employees at these retailers will give customers genuine smiles as a result of the smile initiatives. The argument does not, however, need to make any assumption about how many employees gave customers genuine smiles before the initiatives (though, presumably, many did not).

E   If this claim were false, then the argument would be even stronger. Therefore, the argument does not need to assume this claim.

The correct answer is B.

203. Many economists hold that keeping taxes low helps to spur economic growth, and that low taxes thus lead to greater national prosperity. But Country X, which has unusually high taxes, has greater per-capita income than the neighboring Country Y, which has much lower taxes. Some politicians have concluded from this that high taxes do not hinder national prosperity.

The politicians' reasoning is most vulnerable to criticism on which of the following grounds?

(A) It overlooks the possibility that even if Country X reduced its taxes, it would not experience greater national prosperity in the long term.

(B) It confuses a claim that a factor does not hinder a given development with the claim that the same factor promotes that development.

(C) It fails to adequately address the possibility that Country X and Country Y differ in relevant respects other than taxation.

(D) It fails to take into account that the per-capita income of a country does not determine its rate of economic growth.

(E) It assumes that the economists' thesis must be correct despite a clear counterexample to that thesis.

Argument Evaluation

Situation   Many economists hold that keeping taxes low helps increase economic growth and national prosperity. But a high-tax country, Country X, has greater per-capita income than Country Y, which has lower taxes. Some politicians have concluded from this that high taxes do not hinder national prosperity.

Reasoning   *What is a significant weakness in the politicians' reasoning?* Many factors besides level of taxation are likely to affect economic growth and national prosperity—factors such as having a highly skilled labor force, being rich in a valuable natural resource, and having effective and efficient government. So it is likely that more than one such factor is needed to sufficiently explain any country's level of economic growth or prosperity. A combination of such factors may be sufficient to outweigh any negative impact of high taxes on economic growth or national prosperity.

A   This possibility is quite consistent with the politicians' reasoning that higher taxes do not necessarily impede economic growth.

B   Nothing in the politicians' reasoning indicates that they believe that higher taxes contribute to economic growth or prosperity. They claim that higher taxes do not preclude economic growth and prosperity. Nothing suggests that the politicians conflate these two views in their reasoning.

C   Correct. Even though Country X, with unusually high taxes, has greater per-capita income than Country Y, which has much lower taxes, Country X's high-tax regime may contribute to making the country's per-capita income and national prosperity less than it would be with a low-tax regime. As explained earlier, many different factors can affect a country's national prosperity; some non-tax factors, absent in Country Y, may be boosting Country X's prosperity and compensating for some negative effects of its high-tax regime.

D   The politicians' reasoning suggests that high per-capita income may indicate, or result from, a high level of national prosperity or a favorable rate of economic growth. It need not—and does not—address the question of whether a country's per-capita income could decisively affect the country's rate of economic growth.

E   The politicians' reasoning indicates their disagreement with the economists' thesis; it cites as a counterexample to that thesis the fact that a high-tax country, Country X, has a higher per-capita income than a low-tax country, Country Y.

The correct answer is C.

204. Mayor: The financial livelihood of our downtown businesses is in jeopardy. There are few available parking spaces close to the downtown shopping area, so if we are to spur economic growth in our city, we must build a large parking ramp no more than two blocks from downtown.

Which of the following, if true, most seriously weakens the mayor's reasoning?

(A) The city budget is not currently large enough to finance the construction of a new parking ramp.

(B) There are other more significant reasons for the financial woes of downtown businesses in addition to a lack of nearby parking spaces.

(C) Building a parking ramp as much as four blocks from downtown would be sufficient to greatly increase the number of shoppers to downtown businesses.

(D) Explosive growth is most often associated with large suburban shopping malls, not small businesses.

(E) Some additional parking spaces could be added to the downtown area without the construction of a parking ramp.

Evaluation of a Plan

Situation   A mayor argues that to help spur economic growth in the city and sustain business in the city's downtown, a large parking ramp should be constructed no more than two blocks from downtown to alleviate a parking shortage for business customers.

Reasoning   *Which answer choice provides the information that most seriously weakens the mayor's reasoning?* It is reasonable to assume that constructing a large parking ramp within two blocks of downtown will involve a large capital investment, made even larger by the high cost of land so near to downtown. If a ramp slightly farther from downtown could equally well serve downtown shoppers, and given that people are also likely to need nonresidential parking in another location, building a ramp in the specific location mentioned by the mayor would not be necessary. Note also that even if providing significantly more parking for business customers were necessary for the survival of downtown businesses, it might not be sufficient.

A   This information addresses a problem that would need to be overcome in order to have a parking ramp constructed. For example, taxes may need to be raised or a bond issued to fund the construction. It does not directly address the question whether the parking ramp would be necessary. If it were necessary but could not be financed, the result would be that the goal would not be met.

B   This information indicates that the construction of the parking ramp would likely not be sufficient to ensure the survival of downtown businesses and that other measures would also be needed. This does not weaken the mayor's argument that the ramp would be necessary.

C   **Correct.** If this were true, a parking ramp four blocks from downtown would suffice to solve the downtown parking shortage. Therefore, the construction of a ramp exactly two blocks from downtown would not be necessary.

D   This provides a superficial reason for wondering whether economic growth in the mayor's city could be spurred without the measure that the mayor advocates. However, the information provides no reason to suppose that this city has not already achieved all the growth that it can achieve from large suburban shopping malls. Furthermore, the contrast between large malls and small businesses is not clearly relevant; the downtown businesses whose livelihood the mayor wants to save may be large ones.

E   This information does not significantly weaken the mayor's proposal, since it does not tell us whether the additional parking spaces would suffice for meeting the mayor's goal to spur economic growth in the city.

The correct answer is C.

205. Compact fluorescent light (CFL) bulbs are growing in market share as a replacement for the standard incandescent light bulb. However, an even newer technology is emerging: the light-emitting diode (LED) bulb. Like CFL bulbs, LED bulbs are energy efficient, and they can last around fifty thousand hours, about five times as long as most CFL bulbs. Yet, a single LED bulb costs much more than five CFL bulbs.

The information in the passage above most supports which of the following conclusions?

(A) LED bulbs are most likely to be used in locations where light bulbs would be difficult or costly to replace.

(B) CFL bulbs will need to come down further in price in order to compete with LED bulbs.

(C) LED bulbs are most likely to be used in locations where there is frequent accidental breakage of bulbs.

(D) CFL bulb designs are likely to advance to the point where they can last as long as LED bulbs.

(E) LED bulbs are likely to drop in price, to the point of being competitive with CFL bulbs.

Argument Construction

Situation   Both compact fluorescent light (CFL) bulbs and light-emitting diode (LED) bulbs are energy-efficient bulbs. LED bulbs can last around 50,000 hours, about five times as long as CFL bulbs, though (at the time the passage was written) they cost more than five times as much as CFL bulbs.

Reasoning   *What claim is most strongly supported by the given information?* The information in the passage gives only one reason not to prefer LED bulbs over CFL bulbs—which last five times as long as CFL bulbs—namely, that LED bulbs are more than five times costlier. Because of the greater cost of LED bulbs, it might make economic sense simply to change CFL bulbs numerous times rather than to use the longer-lasting LED bulbs. If, however, there were any practical reason that outweighed that particular economic reason—perhaps the repeated replacement of CFL bulbs would be particularly problematic—then it might be wise to choose LED bulbs over CFL bulbs.

A   **Correct.** In locations where replacing bulbs is particularly difficult and even costly, it would probably make sense to use LED bulbs rather than CFL bulbs. Assuming, then, that both types of bulbs are otherwise acceptable and that their users are rational, LED bulbs would be most likely to be used in such locations.

B   The given information indicates that LED bulbs at the time the passage was written cost more than five times as much as CFL bulbs, but LED bulbs last only about five times as long as CFL bulbs. That suggests that CFL bulbs were competitive at that price.

C   If there is frequent accidental breakage of bulbs in a certain location, then it is likely that the advantage of LED bulbs mentioned in the passage would not hold in such locations.

D   Nothing in the passage suggests that CFL bulbs can be made to be longer lasting.

E   Nothing in the passage indicates whether there was any evidence, at the time the passage was written, that manufacturers of LED bulbs would be able to bring down the cost of producing such bulbs.

The correct answer is A.

206. Colorless diamonds can command high prices as gemstones. A type of less valuable diamonds can be treated to remove all color. Only sophisticated tests can distinguish such treated diamonds from naturally colorless ones. However, only 2 percent of diamonds mined are of the colored type that can be successfully treated, and many of those are of insufficient quality to make the treatment worthwhile. Surely, therefore, the vast majority of colorless diamonds sold by jewelers are naturally colorless.

A serious flaw in the reasoning of the argument is that

(A) comparisons between the price diamonds command as gemstones and their value for other uses are omitted

(B) information about the rarity of treated diamonds is not combined with information about the rarity of naturally colorless, gemstone diamonds

(C) the possibility that colored diamonds might be used as gemstones, even without having been treated, is ignored

(D) the currently available method for making colorless diamonds from colored ones is treated as though it were the only possible method for doing so

(E) the difficulty that a customer of a jeweler would have in distinguishing a naturally colorless diamond from a treated one is not taken into account

Argument Evaluation

Situation   Colored diamonds of a type that comprises 2 percent of all mined diamonds can be treated so that they are not easily distinguishable from more valuable, naturally colorless diamonds, but many are too low in quality for the treatment to be worthwhile.

Reasoning   *Why do the argument's premises not justify the conclusion that the vast majority of colorless diamonds sold by jewelers are naturally colorless?* Since the type of colored diamonds that can be treated make up only 2 percent of all mined diamonds, and many diamonds of that type are too low in quality for treatment to be worthwhile, the vast majority of mined diamonds must not be treated to have their color removed. However, we are not told what proportion of all mined diamonds are naturally colorless. Naturally colorless diamonds may be far rarer even than the uncommon diamonds that have been treated to have their color removed. Thus, for all we can tell from the passage, it could well be that most colorless diamonds sold by jewelers have been treated to remove all color.

A   Even if some types of diamonds command higher prices for uses other than as gemstones, the types discussed in the passage evidently command high enough prices as gemstones to be sold as such by jewelers.

B   **Correct.** The argument does not work if naturally colorless diamonds are rarer than treated diamonds, as they may be for all we can tell from the information provided.

C   The argument's conclusion is only that jewelers sell more naturally colorless diamonds than diamonds treated to be colorless. Whether jewelers sell any colored diamonds or other gemstones is irrelevant.

D   The argument only concerns the types of colorless diamonds sold now, not the types that may be sold in the future if other treatment methods are discovered.

E   The argument does suggest this difficulty but implies that even so there are too few treated diamonds available for jewelers to sell in place of naturally colorless ones.

The correct answer is B.

207. The Sumpton town council recently voted to pay a prominent artist to create an abstract sculpture for the town square. Critics of this decision protested that town residents tend to dislike most abstract art, and any art in the town square should reflect their tastes. But a town council spokesperson dismissed this criticism, pointing out that other public abstract sculptures that the same sculptor has installed in other cities have been extremely popular with those cities' local residents.

The statements above most strongly suggest that the main point of disagreement between the critics and the spokesperson is whether

(A) it would have been reasonable to consult town residents on the decision

(B) most Sumpton residents will find the new sculpture to their taste

(C) abstract sculptures by the same sculptor have truly been popular in other cities

(D) a more traditional sculpture in the town square would be popular among local residents

(E) public art that the residents of Sumpton would find desirable would probably be found desirable by the residents of other cities

Argument Construction

Situation   After the Sumpton town council voted to pay a prominent sculptor to create an abstract sculpture for the town square, critics protested the decision. A town council spokesperson responded to the critics.

Reasoning   *What do the critics and the spokesperson mainly disagree about?* The critics argue that Sumpton residents dislike most abstract art and that art in the town square should reflect their taste. Since the critics are protesting the town council's decision, they are clearly inferring from the residents' general attitude toward abstract art that the residents will dislike the specific sculpture the prominent sculptor will create. The spokesperson replies by arguing that in other cities, sculptures by the same sculptor have been very popular with local residents. The spokesperson implicitly infers from this that the sculpture the prominent sculptor will create for Sumpton will be popular with Sumpton residents—and therefore that the critics are mistaken.

A   Neither the critics nor the spokesperson mentions consultation with the town residents on the decision.

B   **Correct.** As explained above, the critics raise points implicitly suggesting that the residents will dislike the sculpture, whereas the spokesperson responds with a point implicitly supporting the opposite conclusion.

C   The critics could concede that the sculptor's work has been popular in other cities, but nonetheless hold that Sumpton residents have different tastes from those of the other cities' residents.

D   The spokesperson gives no indication regarding the attitudes of Sumpton residents regarding traditional sculpture.

E   It may be that neither the critics nor the spokesperson holds this view. The spokesperson may hold that Sumpton residents are easier to please than residents of most other cities, whereas the critics may hold that Sumpton residents are far more traditional in their tastes than other cities' residents.

The correct answer is B.

208. Boreal owls range over a much larger area than do other owls of similar size. The reason for this behavior is probably that the small mammals on which owls feed are especially scarce in the forests where boreal owls live, and the relative scarcity of prey requires the owls to range more extensively to find sufficient food.

Which of the following, if true, most helps to confirm the explanation above?

(A) Some boreal owls range over an area eight times larger than the area over which any other owl of similar size ranges.

(B) Boreal owls range over larger areas in regions where food of the sort eaten by small mammals is sparse than they do in regions where such food is abundant.

(C) After their young hatch, boreal owls must hunt more often than before in order to feed both themselves and their newly hatched young.

(D) Sometimes individual boreal owls hunt near a single location for many weeks at a time and do not range farther than a few hundred yards.

(E) The boreal owl requires less food, relative to its weight, than is required by members of other owl species.

Argument Evaluation

Situation   The small mammals on which owls prey are relatively scarce in the forests where boreal owls live. That is why boreal owls range more extensively than do other, similarly sized owls in search of food.

Reasoning   *Which answer choice, if true, would most help confirm the proposed explanation?* One way to confirm an explanation is by finding further information that one would expect to be true *if* the explanation is valid. If the explanation in the passage is valid, then one would expect that variations in the population density of available small-animal prey for boreal owls would be accompanied by variations in the ranges of the boreal owls. Naturally the population density of available small-animal prey is likely to be affected by how plentiful food is for those small animals.

A   The comparison between different groups of boreal owls is not relevant to the comparison between boreal owls and other owls.

B   **Correct.** This indicates that abundance of food for the boreal owls' small-animal prey in an area (and therefore abundance of small animals in that area) correlates with a smaller range for the boreal owls there. This strengthens the proposed explanation.

C   This answer choice concerns a correlation between owls' need for food and the frequency with which owls hunt, whereas the phenomenon described in the passage and the proposed explanation have to do with the range over which owls hunt.

D   If one were to assume that boreal owls never hunt near a single location for weeks, that would in no way undermine the proposed explanation.

E   If anything, this answer choice tends to undermine the proposed explanation, because it suggests the possibility that boreal owls need not make up for the relative scarcity of prey in their habitats by ranging over larger areas.

The correct answer is B.

209. Microbiologist: A lethal strain of salmonella recently showed up in a European country, causing an outbreak of illness that killed two people and infected twenty-seven others. Investigators blame the severity of the outbreak on the overuse of antibiotics, since the salmonella bacteria tested were shown to be drug-resistant. But this is unlikely because patients in the country where the outbreak occurred cannot obtain antibiotics to treat illness without a prescription, and the country's doctors prescribe antibiotics less readily than do doctors in any other European country.

Which of the following, if true, would most weaken the microbiologist's reasoning?

(A) Physicians in the country where the outbreak occurred have become hesitant to prescribe antibiotics since they are frequently in short supply.

(B) People in the country where the outbreak occurred often consume foods produced from animals that eat antibiotics-laden livestock feed.

(C) Use of antibiotics in two countries that neighbor the country where the outbreak occurred has risen over the past decade.

(D) Drug-resistant strains of salmonella have not been found in countries in which antibiotics are not generally available.

(E) Salmonella has been shown to spread easily along the distribution chains of certain vegetables, such as raw tomatoes.

Argument Evaluation

Situation   Antibiotic-resistant salmonella caused an outbreak of illness in a European country where patients need prescriptions to obtain antibiotics and where doctors dispense such prescriptions less readily than in other European countries.

Reasoning   *What evidence would most strongly suggest that overuse of antibiotics was likely responsible for the outbreak, despite the cited facts?* The microbiologist reasons that because patients need prescriptions to obtain antibiotics in the country where the outbreak occurred, and the country's doctors dispense such prescriptions less readily than doctors in other European countries do, antibiotics are probably not being overused in the country—so antibiotic overuse was probably not responsible for the outbreak. Implicit in the microbiologist's reasoning is the assumption that overuse of antibiotics, if it had occurred, could probably have resulted only from overprescribing of antibiotics by physicians to treat illness in people in the country in question. Any evidence casting doubt on this complex assumption would suggest a weakness in the microbiologist's reasoning.

A   This strengthens the argument by providing additional evidence that antibiotics are not being overprescribed in the country.

B   **Correct.** This weakens the microbiologist's argument by indicating that an assumption implicit in the argument may be false: the salmonella outbreak could easily by explained by overuse of antibiotics in livestock feed (perhaps imported from other countries).

C   Even if antibiotic use has risen in the two neighboring countries, antibiotics still might be underused in both countries.

D   This suggests that antibiotic-resistant salmonella arises only in countries where antibiotics are used; even if this were true it would be quite compatible with the microbiologist's argument and does not weaken that argument.

E   This describes one mechanism by which salmonella can spread in a population; it says nothing about whether an outbreak of antibiotic-resistant strains of salmonella might have been caused by antibiotic overuse.

The correct answer is B.

210. Historian: Newton developed mathematical concepts and techniques that are fundamental to modern calculus. Leibniz developed closely analogous concepts and techniques. It has traditionally been thought that these discoveries were independent. Researchers have, however, recently discovered notes of Leibniz's that discuss one of Newton's books on mathematics. Several scholars have argued that since **the book includes a presentation of Newton's calculus concepts and techniques,** and since the notes were written before Leibniz's own development of calculus concepts and techniques, it is virtually certain **that the traditional view is false.** A more cautious conclusion than this is called for, however. Leibniz's notes are limited to early sections of Newton's book, sections that precede the ones in which Newton's calculus concepts and techniques are presented.

In the historian's reasoning, the two portions in **boldface** play which of the following roles?

(A)   The first is a claim that the historian rejects; the second is a position that that claim has been used to support.

(B)   The first is evidence that has been used to support a conclusion about which the historian expresses reservations; the second is that conclusion.

(C)   The first provides evidence in support of a position that the historian defends; the second is that position.

(D)   The first and the second each provide evidence in support of a position that the historian defends.

(E)   The first has been used in support of a position that the historian rejects; the second is a conclusion that the historian draws from that position.

Argument Construction

Situation   A historian discusses a controversy about whether or not Leibniz developed calculus concepts and techniques independently of Newton.

Reasoning   *What argumentative roles do the two portions in **boldface** play in the passage?* The first four sentences of the passage simply provide background information. Both **boldfaced** sections are within the fifth sentence, which reports an argument by *several scholars.* The key word *since* indicates that the first **boldfaced** section is a premise in the scholars' argument. A second premise preceded by another *since* follows in the next clause. The final clause of the fifth sentence reveals that the second **boldfaced** section is the conclusion of the scholars' argument. In the sixth sentence, the historian expresses misgivings about the scholars' conclusion, for reasons presented in the seventh and final sentence.

A   The historian does not reject the claim that Newton's book includes a presentation of Newton's calculus concepts and techniques. Instead, the historian merely points out that Leibniz's notes do not cover those sections of Newton's book.

B   **Correct.** The first **boldfaced** section is one of two premises in the scholars' argument, and the second **boldfaced** section is that argument's conclusion. In the following sentence the historian expresses reservations about that conclusion.

C   The historian does not defend the scholars' conclusion but rather expresses misgivings about it.

D   The second **boldfaced** section is the scholars' conclusion and does not present any evidence. Nor does it support the historian's position that a more cautious conclusion is called for.

E   The second **boldfaced** section presents not the historian's conclusion but rather the scholars' conclusion, about which the historian expresses misgivings.

The correct answer is B.

211. Images from ground-based telescopes are invariably distorted by the Earth's atmosphere. Orbiting space telescopes, however, operating above Earth's atmosphere, should provide superbly detailed images. Therefore, ground-based telescopes will soon become obsolete for advanced astronomical research purposes.

Which of the following statements, if true, would cast the most doubt on the conclusion drawn above?

(A) An orbiting space telescope due to be launched this year is far behind schedule and over budget, whereas the largest ground-based telescope was both within budget and on schedule.

(B) Ground-based telescopes located on mountain summits are not subject to the kinds of atmospheric distortion which, at low altitudes, make stars appear to twinkle.

(C) By careful choice of observatory location, it is possible for large-aperture telescopes to avoid most of the kind of wind turbulence that can distort image quality.

(D) When large-aperture telescopes are located at high altitudes near the equator, they permit the best Earth-based observations of the center of the Milky Way Galaxy, a prime target of astronomical research

(E) Detailed spectral analyses, upon which astronomers rely for determining the chemical composition and evolutionary history of stars, require telescopes with more light-gathering capacity than space telescopes can provide.

Argument Evaluation

Situation   Earth's atmosphere distorts images from ground-based telescopes, whereas space telescopes orbiting above the atmosphere should provide superbly detailed images.

Reasoning   *What evidence would undermine the claim that ground-based telescopes will soon become obsolete for advanced astronomical research?* The argument implicitly assumes that advanced astronomical research can be accomplished more effectively with the more detailed, less distorted images produced by space telescopes and that therefore almost all advanced astronomical research will soon be conducted with space telescopes. This reasoning would be undermined by evidence that ground-based telescopes have substantial advantages for advanced astronomical research despite their distorted images or by evidence that space telescopes will not soon become common or affordable enough to support most advanced astronomical research.

A   Even if this is true, there may be several orbiting space telescopes that will be, or have been, launched on schedule and within budget, so this answer choice does not cast doubt on the conclusion of the argument.

B   Ground-based telescopes on mountain summits are still subject to more atmospheric distortion than are space telescopes orbiting above the atmosphere.

C   Atmospheric distortion of telescopic images may result mainly from factors other than wind turbulence.

D   Even the best Earth-based observations of the center of the Milky Way Galaxy may be vastly inferior to space-based observations.

E   **Correct.** This indicates an inherent limitation of space-based telescopes: unlike Earth-based telescopes, they lack the light-gathering capacity that astronomers need to perform one of their primary tasks, i.e., detailed spectral analyses. So Earth-based telescopes are unlikely to soon become obsolete.

The correct answer is E.

212. Generally scientists enter their field with the goal of doing important new research and accept as their colleagues those with similar motivation. Therefore, when any scientist wins renown as an expounder of science to general audiences, most other scientists conclude that this popularizer should no longer be regarded as a true colleague.

The explanation offered above for the low esteem in which scientific popularizers are held by research scientists assumes that

(A)   serious scientific research is not a solitary activity, but relies on active cooperation among a group of colleagues

(B)   research scientists tend not to regard as colleagues those scientists whose renown they envy

(C)   a scientist can become a famous popularizer without having completed any important research

(D)   research scientists believe that those who are well known as popularizers of science are not motivated to do important new research

(E)   no important new research can be accessible to or accurately assessed by those who are not themselves scientists

Argument Construction

Situation   Research scientists desire to do important new research and treat as colleagues just those who have a similar desire. When a scientist becomes popular among a general audience for explaining principles of science, other scientists have less esteem for this popularizer, no longer regarding such a scientist as a serious colleague.

Reasoning   *What assumption do research scientists make about scientists who become popularizers?* The community of scientists shares a common goal: to do important new research. What would cause this community to disapprove of a popularizer and to cease to regard the popularizer as a colleague? It must be because many scientists believe that becoming a popularizer is incompatible with desiring to do important new research.

A   Many scientists make this assumption, of course—but it is not an assumption on which the explanation specifically depends. The explanation concerns the scientists' motivation, not their style of doing research.

B   This statement gives another reason that scientists may reject a popularizer, but because it is not the reason implied in the passage, it is not assumed.

C   Even if this is true, it does not address the core issue of the argument: what scientists believe about the *motivation* of popularizers.

D   Correct. This statement properly identifies an assumption on which the explanation for scientists' rejection of popularizers depends.

E   The passage is not concerned with whether nonscientists can understand new research, but rather with the beliefs and motivations of scientists who reject popularizers as colleagues.

The correct answer is D.

213. Urban planner: When a city loses population due to migration, property taxes in that city tend to rise. This is because there are then fewer residents paying to maintain an infrastructure that was designed to support more people. Rising property taxes, in turn, drive more residents away, compounding the problem. Since the city of Stonebridge is starting to lose population, the city government should therefore refrain from raising property taxes.

Which of the following, if true, would most weaken the urban planner's argument?

(A) If Stonebridge does not raise taxes on its residents to maintain its infrastructure, the city will become much less attractive to live in as that infrastructure decays.

(B) Stonebridge at present benefits from grants provided by the national government to help maintain certain parts of its infrastructure.

(C) If there is a small increase in property taxes in Stonebridge and a slightly larger proportion of total revenue than at present is allocated to infrastructure maintenance, the funding will be adequate for that purpose.

(D) Demographers project that the population of a region that includes Stonebridge will start to increase substantially within the next several years.

(E) The property taxes in Stonebridge are significantly lower than those in many larger cities.

Argument Evaluation

Situation   When a city loses population due to migration, fewer residents remain to pay to maintain the city's infrastructure, so property taxes tend to rise. These rising property taxes then drive even more residents away. The city of Stonebridge is starting to lose population, so Stonebridge's government should not raise property taxes.

Reasoning   *What would weaken the urban planner's justification for concluding that Stonebridge's government should refrain from raising property taxes?* The urban planner implicitly reasons that raising property taxes in Stonebridge in order to maintain the city's infrastructure would make the city lose even more residents, leaving even fewer paying to maintain the infrastructure, and that this would worsen the funding problem the tax increase would have been intended to solve. The urban planner's argument would be weakened by any evidence that raising property taxes in Stonebridge would not drive residents away or that refraining from raising property taxes would cause the same problems as raising them would cause, or worse.

A   **Correct.** This suggests that refraining from raising property taxes could drive more residents out of Stonebridge than raising them would, and thus would not help the city avoid the problem the urban planner describes.

B   This does slightly weaken the argument because the grants may still be provided to maintain certain parts of the infrastructure, even if increased property taxes drive more residents away. But losing more residents could still make it harder to raise enough funds to maintain the rest of the city's infrastructure, as the urban planner argues.

C   Even if this approach would address the immediate maintenance funding problem, the small increase in property taxes could still drive more residents away, forcing additional future tax increases on those who remain, just as the urban planner suggests.

D   This does slightly weaken the argument, but the residents who will move to the region might still avoid moving to Stonebridge if the property taxes there are too high, and those who live in Stonebridge might still move to other cities in the region.

E   Residents fleeing Stonebridge because of high property taxes would likely avoid moving to the many larger cities with even higher property taxes, but they might be happy to move to many other places with low property taxes.

The correct answer is A.

214. Which of the following most logically completes the argument?

Utrania was formerly a major petroleum exporter, but in recent decades economic stagnation and restrictive regulations inhibited investment in new oil fields. In consequence, Utranian oil exports dropped steadily as old fields became depleted. Utrania's currently improving economic situation, together with less-restrictive regulations, will undoubtedly result in the rapid development of new fields. However, it would be premature to conclude that the rapid development of new fields will result in higher oil exports, because __________.

(A) the price of oil is expected to remain relatively stable over the next several years

(B) the improvement in the economic situation in Utrania is expected to result in a dramatic increase in the proportion of Utranians who own automobiles

(C) most of the investment in new oil fields in Utrania is expected to come from foreign sources

(D) new technology is available to recover oil from old oil fields formerly regarded as depleted

(E) many of the new oil fields in Utrania are likely to be as productive as those that were developed during the period when Utrania was a major oil exporter

Argument Construction

Situation A country that had been a major oil exporter has seen its exports decline in recent decades due to economic stagnation, a failure to invest in new fields, and the steady depletion of its old fields. But looser regulations and an improving economy will bring rapid development of new oil fields in the country.

Reasoning *Which answer choice would most logically complete the argument?* The passage describes the conditions that led to Utrania's no longer being a major oil exporter: a lack of investment in new oil fields due to a stagnant economy and restrictive regulations. The passage then says that due to changed regulatory and economic conditions, there will now be rapid development of new oil fields. Nonetheless, this might not bring about an increase in Utrania's oil exports. To logically complete the argument, one must explain how oil exports might not increase even when the condition that led to decreased oil exports has been removed. Suppose there were an increase in domestic oil consumption. A dramatic increase in the rate of car ownership in Utrania could reasonably be expected to significantly increase domestic oil consumption, which could eat up the added oil production from the new fields.

A This answer choice is incorrect. There is no reason why stable oil prices should prevent Utrania's oil exports from increasing.

B **Correct.** An increase in car ownership would increase Utrania's oil consumption—and this supports the claim that oil exports might not increase.

C If anything, this suggests that oil exports should increase. So it would not be a good choice for completion of the argument.

D The advent of new technology allowing oil to be extracted from fields previously thought to be depleted would mean that there is even more reason to think that Utrania's oil exports will increase.

E This does not help to explain why exports would not increase. On the contrary, it suggests that the new fields will lead to increased exports.

The correct answer is B.

215. The use of growth-promoting antibiotics in hog farming can weaken their effectiveness in treating humans because such use can spread resistance to those antibiotics among microorganisms. But now the Smee Company, one of the largest pork marketers, may stop buying pork raised on feed containing these antibiotics. Smee has 60 percent of the pork market, and farmers who sell to Smee would certainly stop using antibiotics in order to avoid jeopardizing their sales. So if Smee makes this change, it will probably significantly slow the decline in antibiotics' effectiveness for humans.

Which of the following, if true, would most strengthen the argument above?

(A) Other major pork marketers will probably stop buying pork raised on feed containing growth-promoting antibiotics if Smee no longer buys such pork.

(B) The decline in hog growth due to discontinuation of antibiotics can be offset by improved hygiene.

(C) Authorities are promoting the use of antibiotics to which microorganisms have not yet developed resistance.

(D) A phaseout of use of antibiotics for hogs in one country reduced usage by over 50 percent over five years.

(E) If Smee stops buying pork raised with antibiotics, the firm's costs will probably increase.

Argument Evaluation

Situation   Using growth-promoting antibiotics in hog farming can produce widespread resistance to antibiotics among microorganisms, thereby making the antibiotics less effective in treating humans. The Smee Company, a pork marketer with 60 percent of the pork market, may stop buying pork raised on feed containing these antibiotics.

Reasoning   *What additional evidence would most help to support the conclusion that if Smee makes the change, it will significantly slow the decline in antibiotics' effectiveness for humans?* We are already informed that if Smee makes the change, it will eliminate the use of antibiotics in hog feed by farmers supplying at least 60 percent of the pork market. The argument would be strengthened by evidence that Smee's decision would indirectly cause use of the antibiotics to stop more broadly: for example in hog farms supplying significantly more than 60 percent of the total amount of pork marketed.

A   **Correct.** This suggests that if Smee makes the change, hog farmers supplying other major pork marketers will also have to stop using antibiotics in hog feed, making the change more widespread and thus probably more effective.

B   Even if the decline in hog growth from discontinuing the antibiotics cannot be offset, many hog farmers will still have to stop using the antibiotics as a result of Smee's decision. On the other hand, even if the decline can be offset with improved hygiene, that change might be too expensive or difficult to be worth its benefits for most hog farmers.

C   Whatever new antibiotics authorities are promoting, microorganisms may soon develop resistance to them as well. Smee may or may not refuse to buy pork raised on feed containing these new antibiotics.

D   This is evidence that Smee's decision may significantly reduce antibiotic use in hogs, but it provides no evidence of how this reduction may affect antibiotics' effectiveness for humans.

E   If anything, this provides reason to suspect that Smee will not stick with the change for long after the costs increase, so it weakens rather than strengthens the argument that the change will significantly slow the decline in antibiotics' effectiveness.

The correct answer is A.

216. In order to reduce dependence on imported oil, the government of Jalica has imposed minimum fuel-efficiency requirements on all new cars, beginning this year. The more fuel-efficient a car, the less pollution it produces per mile driven. As Jalicans replace their old cars with cars that meet the new requirements, annual pollution from car traffic is likely to decrease in Jalica.

Which of the following, if true, most seriously weakens the argument?

(A) In Jalica, domestically produced oil is more expensive than imported oil.

(B) The Jalican government did not intend the new fuel-efficiency requirement to be a pollution-reduction measure.

(C) Some pollution-control devices mandated in Jalica make cars less fuel-efficient than they would be without those devices.

(D) The new regulation requires no change in the chemical formulation of fuel for cars in Jalica.

(E) Jalicans who get cars that are more fuel-efficient tend to do more driving than before.

Argument Evaluation

Situation The Jalican government is requiring all new cars to meet minimum fuel-efficiency requirements starting this year. Cars that are more fuel efficient produce less pollution per mile driven.

Reasoning *What evidence would suggest that annual pollution from car traffic will not decrease in Jalica, despite the new policy?* Air pollution from car traffic is unlikely to decrease if the new standards will result in more cars on the road or more miles driven per car; or if air pollution from car traffic in Jalica is increasing because of unrelated factors such as growing numbers of Jalicans who can afford cars, construction of more roads, etc. Evidence that any of these factors is present would cast doubt on the argument's conclusion and thus weaken the argument.

A The question at issue is not whether the new policy will reduce dependence on imported oil as the government intends, but rather whether it will reduce air pollution from car traffic.

B A government policy may have consequences that the government did not intend it to have.

C Even if these pollution-control devices make cars less fuel efficient, the new fuel-efficiency standards may still improve cars' average fuel efficiency and thereby reduce air pollution.

D Even if the fuel is unchanged, the new fuel-efficiency standards may still result in cars using less fuel and may thereby reduce air pollution.

E **Correct.** If the new fuel-efficient cars are driven more miles per year than older cars are, they may produce as much or more pollution per year than older cars do even though they produce less pollution per mile driven.

The correct answer is E.

217. Plantings of cotton bioengineered to produce its own insecticide against bollworms, a major cause of crop failure, sustained little bollworm damage until this year. This year the plantings are being seriously damaged by bollworms. Bollworms, however, are not necessarily developing resistance to the cotton's insecticide. Bollworms breed on corn, and last year more corn than usual was planted throughout cotton-growing regions. So it is likely that the cotton is simply being overwhelmed by corn-bred bollworms.

In evaluating the argument, which of the following would it be most useful to establish?

(A) Whether corn could be bioengineered to produce the insecticide

(B) Whether plantings of cotton that does not produce the insecticide are suffering unusually extensive damage from bollworms this year

(C) Whether other crops that have been bioengineered to produce their own insecticide successfully resist the pests against which the insecticide was to protect them

(D) Whether plantings of bioengineered cotton are frequently damaged by insect pests other than bollworms

(E) Whether there are insecticides that can be used against bollworms that have developed resistance to the insecticide produced by the bioengineered cotton

Argument Evaluation

Situation   Although plantings of cotton bioengineered to produce an insecticide to combat bollworms were little damaged by the pests in previous years, they are being severely damaged this year. Since the bollworms breed on corn, and there has been more corn planted this year in cotton-growing areas, the cotton is probably being overwhelmed by the corn-bred bollworms.

Reasoning   *In evaluating the argument, which question would it be most useful to have answered?* The argument states that the bioengineered cotton crop failures this year (1) have likely been due to the increased corn plantings and (2) not due to the pests having developed a resistance to the insecticide. This also implies (3) that the failures are not due to some third factor.

It would be useful to know how the bioengineered cotton is faring in comparison to the rest of this year's cotton crop. If the bioengineered cotton is faring better against the bollworms, that fact would support the argument because it would suggest that the insecticide is still combating bollworms. If, on the other hand, the bioengineered cotton is being more severely ravaged by bollworms than is other cotton, that suggests that there is some third cause that is primarily at fault.

A   This would probably be useful information to those trying to alleviate the bollworm problem in bioengineered cotton. But whether such corn could be developed has no bearing on what is causing the bioengineered cotton to be damaged by bollworms this year.

B   **Correct.** If bollworm damage on non-bioengineered cotton is worse than usual this year, then bollworm infestation in general is simply worse than usual, so pesticide resistance does not need to be invoked to explain the bollworm attacks on the bioengineered cotton.

C   Even if other crops that have been bioengineered to resist pests have not successfully resisted them, that fact would not mean that the same is true of this cotton. Furthermore, the facts already suggest that the bioengineered cotton has resisted bollworms.

D   Whether other types of pests often damage bioengineered cotton has no bearing on why bollworms are damaging this type of cotton more this year than in the past.

E   This, too, might be useful information to those trying to alleviate the bollworm problem in bioengineered cotton, but it is not particularly useful in evaluating the argument. Even if there are pesticides that could be used against bollworms that have developed resistance to the insecticide of the bioengineered cotton, that does not mean that such pesticides are being used this year.

The correct answer is B.

218. Typically during thunderstorms most lightning strikes carry a negative electric charge; only a few carry a positive charge. Thunderstorms with unusually high proportions of positive-charge strikes tend to occur in smoky areas near forest fires. The fact that smoke carries positively charged smoke particles into the air above a fire suggests the hypothesis that the extra positive strikes occur because of the presence of such particles in the storm clouds.

Which of the following, if discovered to be true, most seriously undermines the hypothesis?

(A) Other kinds of rare lightning also occur with unusually high frequency in the vicinity of forest fires.

(B) The positive-charge strikes that occur near forest fires tend to be no more powerful than positive strikes normally are.

(C) A positive-charge strike is as likely to start a forest fire as a negative-charge strike is.

(D) Thunderstorms that occur in drifting clouds of smoke have extra positive-charge strikes weeks after the charge of the smoke particles has dissipated.

(E) The total number of lightning strikes during a thunderstorm is usually within the normal range in the vicinity of a forest fire.

Argument Evaluation

Situation Thunderstorms with unusually high proportions of positive-charge lightning strikes tend to occur in smoky areas near forest fires. Smoke carries positively charged particles into the air above fires, suggesting that smoke particles in storm clouds are responsible for the higher proportion of positive strikes.

Reasoning *What would cast doubt on the hypothesis that the extra positive-charge lightning strikes in thunderstorms near forest fires result from positively charged smoke particles carried into the storm clouds?* The hypothesis would be weakened by evidence that the positively charged smoke particles do not enter the storm clouds in the first place, or that they do not retain their charge in the clouds long enough to produce an effect, or that their positive charge cannot affect the charges of the storm's lightning strikes in any case, or that some other factor tends to make the lightning strikes above these storms positively charged.

A It could be that positively charged smoke particles cause these other kinds of rare lightning, too, so this does not seriously undermine the hypothesis.

B The hypothesis is not about the power of the positive-charge lightning strikes, only about why a high proportion of them occur in thunderstorms near forest fires.

C The hypothesis is about why positive-charge strikes tend to occur in smoky areas near forest fires that have already started before the strikes occur. Furthermore, an equal likelihood of positive-charge and negative-charge strikes starting fires cannot explain a correlation between fires and positive-charge strikes specifically.

D Correct. This means that even when drifting clouds of smoke persist for weeks after a fire, when the charge of their particles has already dissipated, the smoke somehow still makes the strikes positively charged in any thunderstorms arising within it. If so, some factor other than positively charged smoke particles must affect the strikes' charge.

E This information does not undermine the hypothesis. The hypothesis does not concern the possibility that there might be more lightning strikes in the vicinity of forest fires; rather it concerns the proportion of all such lightning strikes that are positively charged.

The correct answer is D.

219. Since 1990 the percentage of bacterial sinus infections in Aqadestan that are resistant to the antibiotic perxicillin has increased substantially. Bacteria can quickly develop resistance to an antibiotic when it is prescribed indiscriminately or when patients fail to take it as prescribed. Since perxicillin has not been indiscriminately prescribed, health officials hypothesize that the increase in perxicillin-resistant sinus infections is largely due to patients' failure to take this medication as prescribed.

Which of the following, if true of Aqadestan, provides most support for the health officials' hypothesis?

(A) Resistance to several other commonly prescribed antibiotics has not increased since 1990 in Aqadestan.

(B) A large number of Aqadestanis never seek medical help when they have a sinus infection.

(C) When it first became available, perxicillin was much more effective in treating bacterial sinus infections than any other antibiotic used for such infections at the time.

(D) Many patients who take perxicillin experience severe side effects within the first few days of their prescribed regimen.

(E) Aqadestani health clinics provide antibiotics to their patients at cost.

Argument Construction

Situation   In Aqadestan the percentage of bacterial sinus infections resistant to the antibiotic perxicillin has been increasing even though perxicillin has not been indiscriminately prescribed.

Reasoning   *What evidence most strongly suggests that the main reason perxicillin-resistant sinus infections are becoming more common is that patients are failing to take perxicillin as prescribed?* Any evidence suggesting that patients have in fact been failing to take perxicillin as prescribed would support the hypothesis, as would any evidence casting doubt on other possible explanations for the increasing proportion of perxicillin-resistant sinus infections.

A   This suggests that some factor specific to perxicillin is increasing bacterial resistance to it, but that could be true whether or not the factor is patients' failure to take perxicillin as prescribed.

B   If anything, this weakens the argument by suggesting that most people with sinus infections are never prescribed perxicillin, and that therefore relatively few people are getting prescriptions and then failing to follow them.

C   The relative effectiveness of perxicillin when it first became available does not suggest that the reason it is now becoming less effective is that many patients are failing to take it as prescribed.

D   **Correct.** These side effects would discourage patients from taking perxicillin as prescribed, so their existence provides evidence that many patients are not taking it as prescribed.

E   If the clinics do not charge extra for perxicillin, that would make it more affordable and hence easier for many patients to take as prescribed.

The correct answer is D.

220. Psychologist: In a study, researchers gave 100 volunteers a psychological questionnaire designed to measure their self-esteem. The researchers then asked each volunteer to rate the strength of his or her own social skills. The volunteers with the highest levels of self-esteem consistently rated themselves as having much better social skills than did the volunteers with moderate levels. This suggests that attaining an exceptionally high level of self-esteem greatly improves one's social skills.

The psychologist's argument is most vulnerable to criticism on which of the following grounds?

(A) It fails to adequately address the possibility that many of the volunteers may not have understood what the psychological questionnaire was designed to measure.

(B) It takes for granted that the volunteers with the highest levels of self-esteem had better social skills than did the other volunteers, even before the former volunteers had attained their high levels of self-esteem.

(C) It overlooks the possibility that people with very high levels of self-esteem may tend to have a less accurate perception of the strength of their own social skills than do people with moderate levels of self-esteem.

(D) It relies on evidence from a group of volunteers that is too small to provide any support for any inferences regarding people in general.

(E) It overlooks the possibility that factors other than level of self-esteem may be of much greater importance in determining the strength of one's social skills.

Argument Evaluation

Situation   In a psychological study of 100 volunteers, those found to have the highest self-esteem consistently rated themselves as having much better social skills than did those found to have moderate self-esteem.

Reasoning   *What is wrong with the psychologist citing the study's results to justify the conclusion that exceptionally high self-esteem greatly improves social skills?* The psychologist reasons that the study shows a correlation between very high self-esteem and how highly one rates one's social skills, and that this correlation in turn suggests that very high self-esteem improves social skills. This argument is vulnerable to at least two criticisms: First, the argument assumes that the volunteers' ratings of their own social skills are generally accurate. But very high self-esteem might in many cases result from a tendency to overestimate oneself and one's skills, including one's social skills. Second, the argument fails to address the possibility that good social skills promote high self-esteem rather than vice versa, as well as the possibility that some third factor (such as a sunny disposition or fortunate circumstances) promotes both high self-esteem and good social skills.

A   An experiment's subjects do not have to understand the experiment's design in order for the experimental results to be accurate.

B   To the contrary, the argument concludes that the volunteers with the highest self-esteem attained their enhanced social skills as a result of attaining such high self-esteem.

C   **Correct.** As explained above, very high self-esteem may often result from a tendency to overestimate oneself in general, and thus to overestimate one's social skills.

D   A group of 100 volunteers is large enough for an experiment to provide at least a little support for at least some inferences regarding people in general.

E   As explained above, the argument overlooks the possibility that some third factor may play a significant role in determining the strength of one's social skills. But even if some factor other than self-esteem is more important in determining the strength of social skills, that would still be compatible with very high self-esteem being of some importance in improving one's social skills.

The correct answer is C.

221. Political advertisement: Mayor Delmont's critics complain about the jobs that were lost in the city under Delmont's leadership. Yet the fact is that not only were more jobs created than were eliminated, but each year since Delmont took office the average pay for the new jobs created has been higher than that year's average pay for jobs citywide. So it stands to reason that throughout Delmont's tenure the average paycheck in this city has been getting steadily bigger.

Which of the following, if true, most seriously weakens the argument in the advertisement?

(A)   The unemployment rate in the city is higher today than it was when Mayor Delmont took office.

(B)   The average pay for jobs in the city was at a ten-year low when Mayor Delmont took office.

(C)   Each year during Mayor Delmont's tenure, the average pay for jobs that were eliminated has been higher than the average pay for jobs citywide.

(D)   Most of the jobs eliminated during Mayor Delmont's tenure were in declining industries.

(E)   The average pay for jobs in the city is currently lower than it is for jobs in the suburbs surrounding the city.

Argument Evaluation

Situation   Every year since Mayor Delmont took office, average pay for new jobs has exceeded average pay for jobs citywide. So, the average paycheck in the city has been increasing since Delmont took office.

Reasoning   *Which answer choice, if true, would most seriously weaken the argument?* If average pay for new jobs continually exceeds that for jobs generally, new jobs pay better (on average) than old jobs that still exist. But suppose the following occurred. Every year all of the highest paying jobs are eliminated and replaced with somewhat lower-paying jobs that still pay more than the average job. The result would be that every year the average pay for a new job would be greater than that for existing jobs, but the average pay for all jobs would nonetheless decrease. Thus, if every year during the mayor's tenure the jobs that were eliminated paid better on average than jobs citywide, that would seriously weaken the argument: the conclusion could be false even if the information on which it is based is true.

A   The percentage of people in the city who have a job has no direct bearing on whether the average pay for jobs citywide is increasing or decreasing.

B   Whether the average pay was low when the mayor took office in comparison to the ten preceding years is immaterial to the comparison addressed in the argument's conclusion.

C   **Correct.** This information weakens the argument because it opens up the possibility that the jobs eliminated had higher average pay than the jobs created during Mayor Delmont's tenure. This in turn would mean that the average pay was not increasing during Mayor Delmont's tenure.

D   This, too, has no bearing on the argument, because we have no information about the average pay for jobs in those declining industries.

E   This is also irrelevant. No comparison is made (or implied) in the argument between jobs in the city and jobs in the suburbs.

The correct answer is C.

222. To prevent a newly built dam on the Chiff River from blocking the route of fish migrating to breeding grounds upstream, the dam includes a fish pass, a mechanism designed to allow fish through the dam. Before the construction of the dam and fish pass, several thousand fish a day swam upriver during spawning season. But in the first season after the project's completion, only 300 per day made the journey. Clearly, the fish pass is defective.

Which of the following, if true, most seriously weakens the argument?

(A) Fish that have migrated to the upstream breeding grounds do not return down the Chiff River again.

(B) On other rivers in the region, the construction of dams with fish passes has led to only small decreases in the number of fish migrating upstream.

(C) The construction of the dam stirred up potentially toxic river sediments that were carried downstream.

(D) Populations of migratory fish in the Chiff River have been declining slightly over the last 20 years.

(E) During spawning season, the dam releases sufficient water for migratory fish below the dam to swim upstream.

Argument Evaluation

Situation   A new dam includes a mechanism called a fish pass designed to allow fish to migrate upstream past the dam to their breeding grounds. The number of migrating fish fell from several thousand per day before the dam was built to three hundred per day in the first season after it was built, indicating—according to the argument—that the fish pass is defective.

Reasoning   *What evidence would suggest that the fish pass is not defective?* The argument implicitly reasons that a defective fish pass would make it difficult for the fish to migrate, which would explain why the number of migrating fish fell when the dam was completed. Any evidence suggesting an alternative explanation for the reduced number of migrating fish, such as an environmental change that occurred when the dam was built, would cast doubt on the argument's reasoning.

A   A defective fish pass could prevent most of the fish from migrating upstream regardless of whether those that succeed ever return downstream.

B   This would suggest that dams with properly functioning fish passes do not greatly reduce the number of migrating fish, so it would provide further evidence that the fish pass in this particular dam is defective.

C   **Correct.** This suggests that the toxic sediments may have poisoned the fish and reduced their population. A smaller fish population could be sufficient to explain the reduced number of fish migrating, which casts doubt on the argument's assumption that the explanation for their declining numbers involves the fish pass.

D   A slight and gradual ongoing decline in migratory fish populations would not explain an abrupt and extreme decline right after the dam was built.

E   This supports the argument's proposed explanation for the declining fish population by ruling out the alternative explanation that the dam does not release enough water for the fish to migrate.

The correct answer is C.

223. People with a college degree are more likely than others to search for a new job while they are employed. There are proportionately more people with college degrees among managers and other professionals than among service and clerical workers. Surprisingly, however, 2009 figures indicate that people employed as managers and other professionals were no more likely than people employed as service and clerical workers to have searched for a new job.

Which of the following, if true, most helps to resolve the apparent paradox?

(A) People generally do not take a new job that is offered to them while they are employed unless the new job pays better.

(B) Some service and clerical jobs pay more than some managerial and professional jobs.

(C) People who felt they were overqualified for their current positions were more likely than others to search for a new job.

(D) The percentage of employed people who were engaged in job searches declined from 2005 to 2009.

(E) In 2009 employees with no college degree who retired were more likely to be replaced by people with a college degree if they retired from a managerial or professional job than from a service or clerical job.

Argument Construction

Situation   College graduates are more likely than others to search for another job while they are employed. A greater percentage of managers and other professionals are college graduates than of service and clerical workers. In 2009, however, managers and other professionals were no more likely than service and clerical workers to have searched for another job while employed.

Reasoning   *What additional piece of information would most help resolve the apparent paradox described?* The apparent paradox concerns a 2009 phenomenon that initially seems at odds with a general pattern in job-search behavior. However, the phenomenon seems less puzzling when one considers the following. Depending on the current state of the employment market, some college graduates may choose to take a job as a service or clerical worker, seeing it as a way of paying their expenses while aiming to transition to a job more suited to their medium- and long-term career aspirations.

A   This information provides one answer to the question, why do people choose to accept or decline a particular job? However, this has no clear relevance to the apparent paradox we are asked to resolve; the paradox concerns the proportions of people in different kinds of jobs who search for a new job even while employed.

B   This information is too vague to contribute to resolving the apparent paradox. It is little more than a truism that, given certain labor supply and demand conditions, pay rates for different jobs vary.

C   **Correct.** College graduates in clerical jobs might feel that they had more advanced skills than their jobs demanded. College graduates in managerial or professional jobs would be less likely to have a similar feeling.

D   This information regarding a decline in job searches from 2005 to 2009 has no clear relevance to the apparent paradox we are asked to resolve. For example, we are not told that this decline occurred predominantly among managerial or professional workers.

E   This information suggests that the supply of college graduates was larger in 2009 than it had been some decades before. If the supply were large enough in 2009, it could be the case that some college graduates accepted service or clerical jobs that, decades previously, would not have been filled by college graduates. But we lack enough specific information for this answer choice to help resolve the apparent paradox.

The correct answer is C.

224. To reduce traffic congestion, City X's transportation bureau plans to encourage people who work downtown to sign a form pledging to carpool or use public transportation for the next year. Everyone who signs the form will get a coupon for a free meal at any downtown restaurant.

For the transportation bureau's plan to succeed in reducing traffic congestion, which of the following must be true?

(A) Everyone who signs the pledge form will fully abide by the pledge for the next year.

(B) At least some people who work downtown prefer the restaurants downtown to those elsewhere.

(C) Most downtown traffic congestion in City X results from people who work downtown.

(D) The most effective way to reduce traffic congestion downtown would be to persuade more people who work there to carpool or use public transportation.

(E) At least some people who receive the coupon for a free meal will sometimes carpool or use public transportation during the next year.

Evaluation of a Plan

Situation   In City X, the transportation bureau's plan to reduce traffic congestion involves giving every downtown worker who signs a form pledging to carpool or use public transportation next year a coupon for a free meal at any downtown restaurant.

Reasoning   *What claim must be true for the transportation bureau's plan to reduce traffic congestion to succeed?* Obviously, if people sign the pledge just so they can get a coupon for a free meal, and if no one who signs the pledge actually carpools or uses public transportation, then the plan will not succeed. Therefore, for the plan to be successful, at least some of the people who receive the coupon must at least occasionally carpool or use public transportation during the next year.

A   If this were true, it would certainly help the plan succeed. But the question asks what *must* be true for the plan to succeed, and it is not necessary that anyone fully abide by the plan. The plan could well succeed, for instance, if no one fully abided by the pledge but a large number of people only partially abided by the pledge.

B   This is not necessary. Even if everyone prefers restaurants outside the downtown area, they may still want a free meal at a downtown restaurant.

C   It could be that a majority of the downtown traffic congestion in City X results not from people who work downtown, but from people who shop downtown or live downtown but work elsewhere. The plan could still work as long as there was a sufficient reduction in the congestion caused by the downtown workers.

D   The plan could work even if it is not the most effective way to reduce traffic congestion. If there is a more effective way to reduce traffic congestion, then it might be advisable to implement that plan instead of, or in addition to, this one. But second-best plans, for instance, can be successful.

E   **Correct.** Certainly, this is not sufficient for the plan to succeed; compliance would probably need to be well above the minimal level. But, as explained above, this is necessary for the plan to succeed. Suppose someone objected to the idea that this must be true for the plan to succeed by saying that, even if no one who received the coupon carpooled or used public transportation, congestion could still be reduced if enough *other* people carpooled or used public transportation. That is true, but in that case, it would not be the *plan* that succeeded. The goal would be accomplished, but it would have been accomplished without the plan itself being successful at accomplishing it.

The correct answer is E.

225. When new laws imposing strict penalties for misleading corporate disclosures were passed, they were hailed as initiating an era of corporate openness. As an additional benefit, given the increased amount and accuracy of information disclosed under the new laws, it was assumed that analysts' predictions of corporate performance would become more accurate. Since the passage of the laws, however, the number of inaccurate analysts' predictions has not in fact decreased.

Which of the following would, if true, best explain the discrepancy outlined above?

(A) The new laws' definition of "misleading information" can be interpreted in more than one way.

(B) The new laws require corporations in all industries to release information at specific times of the year.

(C) Even before the new laws were passed, the information most corporations released was true.

(D) Analysts base their predictions on information they gather from many sources, not just corporate disclosures.

(E) The more pieces of information corporations release, the more difficult it becomes for anyone to organize them in a manageable way.

Evaluation of a Plan

Situation   It was assumed that new laws, implemented to increase the amount and accuracy of information released by corporations, would increase the accuracy of analysts' predictions about corporate performance. This outcome has not occurred, however.

Reasoning   *What claim would best explain the new laws' failure to reduce the number of inaccurate analysts' predictions?* The new laws were intended to increase both the accuracy and the amount of information. If the amount of information increased to such a level that analysts became overwhelmed by it, this could help explain the laws' failure to reduce the number of inaccurate predictions.

A   Even if the new laws' definition of "misleading information" can be interpreted in multiple ways, it could be that the accuracy of corporate information has increased. This fact alone does little if anything to explain the discrepancy.

B   The fact that all industries are required to release information at specific times of the year is not helpful in explaining why the number of inaccurate analysts' predictions has not declined. Presumably analysts would wait for the information to be released to make predictions.

C   This might help somewhat in explaining the failure to bring about the desired outcome. It would do so by ruling out one scenario that would make the outcome more likely to occur: If past predictions had been inaccurate because they were based on false information, it would seem likely that the law would reduce the number of inaccurate predictions. But even if most of the information corporations released in the past was true, one would still expect some improvement in the accuracy of predictions if the information became universally accurate, and there was more of it available.

D   The fact that analysts base their predictions about corporate performance on information gathered from many sources in addition to corporate disclosures does not explain why, if corporate disclosures improved, there would not be at least some improvement in the accuracy of predictions about corporate performance.

E   **Correct.** If the amount of information corporations release becomes so great that organizing it in a manageable way becomes difficult or impossible, then it could become more difficult to interpret and understand. This could interfere with analysts' ability to make accurate predictions about performance, even if the information provided is 100 percent accurate.

The correct answer is E.

226. Economist: Even with energy conservation efforts, current technologies cannot support both a reduction in carbon dioxide emissions and an expanding global economy. Attempts to restrain emissions without new technology will stifle economic growth. Therefore, increases in governmental spending on research into energy technology will be necessary if we wish to reduce carbon dioxide emissions without stifling economic growth.

Which of the following is an assumption the economist's argument requires?

(A) If research into energy technology does not lead to a reduction in carbon dioxide emissions, then economic growth will be stifled.

(B) Increased governmental spending on research into energy technology will be more likely to reduce carbon dioxide emissions without stifling growth than will nongovernmental spending.

(C) An expanding global economy may require at least some governmental spending on research into energy technology.

(D) Attempts to restrain carbon dioxide emissions without new technology could ultimately cost more than the failure to reduce those emissions would cost.

(E) Restraining carbon dioxide emissions without stifling economic growth would require both new energy technology and energy conservation efforts.

Evaluation of a Plan

Situation An economist argues that without new technology, attempts to restrain carbon dioxide emissions will stifle economic growth. The economist concludes from this that if such emissions are to be reduced without stifling economic growth, there must be increases in governmental spending on research into energy technology.

Reasoning *What assumption is required by the economist's argument?* An obvious question to the economist's argument is why an increase in *governmental* spending is required. Could nongovernmental spending alone not be at least as effective? If it could be, then the economist's conclusion would not follow. Therefore, for the economist's argument to be a good one, it would need to be true that nongovernmental spending alone would not be as effective for the intended purpose as increased governmental spending would be.

A Nothing in the argument requires the assumption that only a reduction in carbon dioxide emissions can stifle economic growth. The argument is perfectly compatible, for instance, with the assumption that economic growth would be stifled if there were significant climate change—perhaps leading to severe crop shortages—as a result of increased carbon dioxide emissions.

B **Correct.** As explained above, a natural response to the economist's argument is to ask, "Why can we not just use nongovernmental spending to come up with new technologies that will allow us to restrain carbon dioxide emissions without stifling economic growth?" Without an answer to that question, the economist's argument cannot be a good one. If answer choice B were true, it would bridge the logical gap by providing a reason that increased governmental spending—and not just nongovernmental spending—would be needed.

C This does not have to be assumed. True, the argument assumes that *if* we try to reduce carbon dioxide emissions without increased governmental spending on research into energy technology, then the economy will be stifled. But the argument is compatible with the occurrence of economic growth despite a lack of governmental spending on research into energy technology, as long as carbon dioxide emissions are not reduced.

D The argument does not require this assumption. As explained in answer choice A, the argument is compatible with the idea that the economy could be stifled by climate change that results from a failure to reduce carbon emissions. This could result in great economic cost.

E The argument does not indicate that new energy technology alone cannot be sufficient for restraining carbon dioxide emissions without stifling economic growth.

The correct answer is B.

227. Researchers have developed a technology that uses sound as a means of converting heat into electrical energy. Converters based on this technology can be manufactured small enough to be integrated into consumer electronics, where they will absorb significant quantities of heat. A group of engineers is now designing converters to be sold to laptop computer manufacturers, who are expected to use the electrical output of the converters to conserve battery power in their computers.

Which of the following would, if true, provide the strongest evidence that the engineers' plan will be commercially successful for their group?

(A) The sound that is used by the converters is generated by the converters themselves.

(B) Most laptop computer manufacturers today receive fewer complaints than in previous years regarding shortness of operating time on a single battery charge.

(C) The overheating of microprocessors in laptop computers presents a major technological challenge that manufacturers are prepared to meet at significant expense.

(D) Although battery technology has improved significantly, the average capacity of laptop computer batteries has not.

(E) Electrical power generated by the converters can be used to power the fans installed to cool computers' components.

Evaluation of a Plan

Situation   A group of engineers is designing converters that absorb heat and then use sound to convert it into electrical energy. The engineers hope to sell the converters to laptop manufacturers for the purpose of using the electrical output of the converters to conserve battery power.

Reasoning   *Which claim provides the strongest evidence that the engineers' plan will be commercially successful?* A claim that reveals that there would be demand among laptop manufacturers for the converters would provide such evidence. If these manufacturers currently face a major challenge that they would be willing to meet at significant expense, they would provide a demand for this product if it could be shown to work well.

A   Whether the sound is generated by the converters or by something else would be irrelevant to whether the plan would be commercially successful, unless the sound production required a significant amount of electrical energy. If it did require a significant amount of electrical energy, this would tend to weaken the hypothesis that the plan would succeed.

B   This suggests that laptop manufacturers may not feel a great need to use these converters to conserve battery power.

C   **Correct.** If laptop manufacturers are prepared to meet the challenge of the overheating of microprocessors at significant expense, in a way that provides an additional benefit such as conserving battery power, they could very well be a receptive market for these converters.

D   This would not provide strong evidence that the plan will be commercially successful unless we had further evidence that laptop manufacturers see it as a challenge that they would be willing to meet at significant expense.

E   Presumably, the electricity generated by the converter should be able to contribute toward satisfying any of the energy needs of the computer. The passage provides no reason to think that the cooling fans are special in this regard. The converters generate electrical energy by absorbing heat so, in principle, there might even be circumstances in which the use described in this answer choice could undermine the converters' functionality.

The correct answer is C.

228. According to a widely held economic hypothesis, imposing strict environmental regulations reduces economic growth. This hypothesis is undermined by the fact that the states with the strictest environmental regulations also have the highest economic growth. This fact does not show that environmental regulations promote growth, however, since __________.

Which of the following, if true, provides evidence that most logically completes the argument above?

(A) those states with the strictest environmental regulations invest the most in education and job training

(B) even those states that have only moderately strict environmental regulations have higher growth than those with the least-strict regulations

(C) many states that are experiencing reduced economic growth are considering weakening their environmental regulations

(D) after introducing stricter environmental regulations, many states experienced increased economic growth

(E) even those states with very weak environmental regulations have experienced at least some growth

Argument Construction

Situation   Claims that strict environmental regulations inhibit economic growth are undermined by higher economic growth in states with such regulations. However, the passage infers (for a reason the argument omits) that the presence of higher growth in states with strong regulations does not prove that these regulations are the *cause* of the greater economic growth observed there.

Reasoning   *What would make it less likely that environmental regulations cause economic growth?* The argument notes that stricter environmental regulations correlate with higher economic growth, which undermines the hypothesis that such strict regulations reduce growth. The argument suggests, however, that environmental regulations may not actually cause growth. In that case, there should be other factors that contribute to the higher economic growth in states with strict environmental regulations.

A   **Correct.** If higher investment in education and job training promotes the higher economic growth observed in states with strict environmental regulations, then those regulations may not cause that growth.

B   Higher economic growth in states with moderately strict environmental regulations merely shows another correlation and implies nothing about the causes of that growth.

C   States with poor economic growth might consider reducing regulations, but no evidence has been provided that such a policy would cause economic growth.

D   Increased regulation directly preceding increased growth would tend to undermine the argument, not support it, especially if all other factors remained constant.

E   The presence of some economic growth in states with low environmental regulations implies nothing about the causes of higher growth.

The correct answer is A.

229. The prairie vole, a small North American grassland rodent, breeds year-round, and a group of voles living together consists primarily of an extended family, often including two or more litters. Voles commonly live in large groups from late autumn through winter; from spring through early autumn, however, most voles live in far smaller groups. The seasonal variation in group size can probably be explained by a seasonal variation in mortality among young voles.

Which of the following, if true, provides the strongest support for the explanation offered?

(A) It is in the spring and early summer that prairie vole communities generally contain the highest proportion of young voles.

(B) Prairie vole populations vary dramatically in size from year to year.

(C) The prairie vole subsists primarily on broad-leaved plants that are abundant only in spring.

(D) Winters in the prairie voles' habitat are often harsh, with temperatures that drop well below freezing.

(E) Snakes, a major predator of young prairie voles, are active only from spring through early autumn.

Argument Evaluation

Situation   Prairie voles live in groups made up of relatives. Because they breed year-round, there are generally young voles in each group. These groups are larger in late fall and winter, while group size decreases in spring, summer, and early fall, probably because of a seasonal difference in the mortality rate of young voles.

Reasoning   *What provides support for the claim that increased mortality among young voles causes the annual reduction in vole group size observed in spring?* If vole groups are large in late autumn and winter and much smaller during the rest of the year, then something must be causing the reduction in group size that occurs each spring through early autumn. The explanation states that increased mortality in young voles probably accounts for the decline in group size. Therefore, identifying a likely cause of such increased seasonal mortality would support the explanation.

A   A higher proportion of young voles in spring would undermine the suggestion that their increased mortality causes a decline in group size at the same time.

B   There is no evidence that annual variations in overall prairie vole populations are related to the seasonal reduction in vole group size each spring.

C   An abundance of food in spring would not contribute to increased mortality among young voles at the same time.

D   Harsh winters would not account for increased mortality among young voles in spring, given the information in the passage that vole familial groups are large through winter.

E   **Correct.** If snakes that eat young voles are active in spring through early autumn, then that would support the explanation that increased mortality among young voles during the same period causes the seasonal decline in vole group size.

The correct answer is E.

230. From 1980 to 1989, total consumption of fish in the country of Jurania increased by 4.5 percent, and total consumption of poultry products there increased by 9.0 percent. During the same period, the population of Jurania increased by 6 percent, in part due to immigration to Jurania from other countries in the region.

If the statements above are true, which of the following must also be true on the basis of them?

(A) During the 1980s in Jurania, profits of wholesale distributors of poultry products increased at a greater rate than did profits of wholesale distributors of fish.

(B) For people who immigrated to Jurania during the 1980s, fish was less likely to be a major part of their diet than was poultry.

(C) In 1989, Juranians consumed twice as much poultry as fish.

(D) For a significant proportion of Jurania's population, both fish and poultry products were a regular part of their diet during the 1980s.

(E) Per capita consumption of fish in Jurania was lower in 1989 than in 1980.

Argument Construction

Situation　　During a specific period—1980 to 1989—the population of Jurania increased by 6 percent, fish sales increased by 4.5 percent, and poultry sales increased by 9 percent. Some of Jurania's population growth was the result of immigration from nearby countries.

Reasoning　　*What would necessarily follow from increased sales rates of fish and poultry products in Jurania relative to increased population over the same period?* If the population of Jurania increased by 6 percent, sales of fish increased by 4.5 percent, and sales of poultry products increased by 9 percent, all during the same period from 1980 to 1989, then changes in the relationship between population size and sales of those food products necessarily follow.

A　Many factors can affect profits, so a greater increase in poultry sales relative to fish sales would not necessarily cause wholesale distributors of poultry to experience a faster growth in profits than wholesale distributors of fish do.

B　The diets of Jurania's new immigrants are a possible contributing factor to the relative changes in sales of fish and poultry, but other factors could account for the same changes.

C　The increase in poultry sales is twice the increase in fish sales, but that relationship implies nothing about the overall consumption of fish versus poultry.

D　The consumers of fish and the consumers of poultry might be separate groups, and both fish and poultry might be consumed occasionally rather than regularly.

E　**Correct.** Fish consumption grew at a lower rate than the population did from 1980 to 1989, so per capita consumption of fish must be lower at the end of that period than it was at the beginning.

The correct answer is E.

231. Junior biomedical researchers have long assumed that their hirings and promotions depend significantly on the amount of their published work. People responsible for making hiring and promotion decisions in the biomedical research field, however, are influenced much more by the overall impact that a candidate's scientific publications have on his or her field than by the number of those publications.

The information above, if accurate, argues most strongly AGAINST which of the following claims?

(A) Even biomedical researchers who are just beginning their careers are expected to already have published articles of major significance to the field.

(B) Contributions to the field of biomedical research are generally considered to be significant only if the work is published.

(C) The potential scientific importance of not-yet-published work is sometimes taken into account in decisions regarding the hiring or promotion of biomedical researchers.

(D) People responsible for hiring or promoting biomedical researchers can reasonably be expected to make a fair assessment of the overall impact of a candidate's publications on his or her field.

(E) Biomedical researchers can substantially increase their chances of promotion by fragmenting their research findings so that they are published in several journals instead of one.

Argument Construction

Situation   Junior biomedical researchers believe that the volume of their publications is a major determinant of their career success. However, the people in charge of hiring and promotions are more interested in the significance of a candidate's publications than in the number of those publications.

Reasoning   *What is likely to be untrue if the people responsible for hiring and promotions in the biomedical research field are significantly more impressed by the impact, rather than the quantity, of candidates' publications? If junior biomedical researchers are mistaken in their belief that the sheer quantity of their publications is a major determinant of their success, it would follow that focusing on quantity is not their best strategy.*

A   The claim that impact matters more than quantity of publications does not imply that early-career researchers would not be expected to have published significant articles.

B   The information presented has no bearing on whether or not contributions in the field have to be published to be considered significant.

C   The information presented has no bearing on the question of whether or not the value of unpublished work would be taken into account.

D   The information suggests that the people responsible for hiring and promotions assess the impact of a candidate's publications, but it implies nothing about whether or not such assessments are fair.

E   **Correct.** If the people responsible for hiring and promotion are favorably impressed by the impact more than by the quantity of publications, then fragmenting research findings in order to increase the sheer quantity of publications is unlikely to help researchers attain promotion.

The correct answer is E.

232. Rabbits were introduced to Tambor Island in the nineteenth century. Overgrazing by the enormous rabbit population now menaces the island's agriculture. The government proposes to reduce the population by using a virus that has caused devastating epidemics in rabbit populations elsewhere. There is, however, a small chance that the virus will infect the bilby, an endangered native herbivore. The government's plan, therefore, may serve the interests of agriculture but will clearly increase the threat to native wildlife.

The argument above assumes which of the following?

(A) There is less chance that the virus will infect domestic animals on Tambor than that it will infect wild animals of species native to the island.

(B) Overgrazing by rabbits does not pose the most significant current threat to the bilby.

(C) There is at least one alternative means of reducing the rabbit population that would not involve any threat to the bilby.

(D) There are no species of animals on the island that prey on the rabbits.

(E) The virus that the government proposes to use has been successfully used elsewhere to control populations of rabbits.

Argument Construction

Situation Invasive rabbits are a problem for Tambor Island's agriculture. The government wants to kill the rabbits by introducing a virus, but that virus may also attack the native bilby. The virus's introduction will increase the threat to native animals.

Reasoning *Since the argument claims that introducing the virus clearly increases the risk to native wildlife, in this case the bilby, on Tambor Island, what does it assume about other factors that might affect that claim? The claim that risk to the bilby would be clearly increased by the virus ignores other effects that could result from the virus. If the virus reduced other risks to the bilby, that might cause an overall reduction in risk to the bilby, even if the virus presents some risk.*

A The claim that the virus will clearly increase risk to wild species is not based on any assumption about its effect on domestic species.

B **Correct.** The argument assumes that the rabbits' overgrazing does not present a major risk that herbivorous bilby populations will starve, because that danger would suggest that a declining number of rabbits might reduce overall risk to the bilby, even once the direct risk posed by the virus is taken into account.

C Concern for the risk the virus poses to the bilby is not based on an assumption that the rabbit population could be sufficiently reduced by a safer method.

D The argument is not based on an assumption about whether or not Tambor Island has species that prey on the rabbits but only describes a possible risk from attempting to reduce rabbit populations by means of a virus.

E The argument states that the virus has caused epidemics among rabbits elsewhere but does not assume that those epidemics were started by governments rather than occurring naturally.

The correct answer is B.

233. Which of the following provides the most logical completion of the argument?

Many of Vebrol Corporation's department heads will retire this year. The number of junior employees with the qualifications Vebrol will require for promotion to department head is equal to only half the expected vacancies. Vebrol is not going to hire department heads from outside the company, have current department heads take over more than one department, or reduce the number of its departments. So some departments will be without department heads next year, since Vebrol will not __________.

(A)   promote more than one employee from any department to serve as heads of departments

(B)   promote any current department heads to higher-level managerial positions

(C)   have any managers who are currently senior to department heads serve as department heads

(D)   reduce the responsibilities of each department

(E)   reduce the average number of employees per department

Argument Construction

Situation   Vebrol's department heads are retiring in significant numbers. There are only about half as many qualified junior employees to fill the resulting vacancies. Vebrol will not hire department heads externally, have department heads lead multiple departments, or eliminate departments. For an unstated additional reason, some departments will lack department heads.

Reasoning   *If the total number of qualified junior employees is only half of Vebrol's projected need for department heads, and if Vebrol will not address that shortfall through external hiring, doubling department heads' responsibilities, or eliminating departments, what additional factor would guarantee that some departments will be without department heads?* If Vebrol will necessarily have departments without department heads, it follows that they are probably not using any means, including recruiting senior staff as department heads, to amend that projected shortfall.

A   The number of employees promoted per department would not affect the fact that the number of junior employees eligible for promotion is half the projected need.

B   Not promoting current department heads would be expected to limit the shortfall, not ensure it.

C   **Correct.** If Vebrol is ruling out an additional way to address the shortage of department heads—in this case, by not having senior employees serve as department heads—then that decision would logically ensure that some departments will not have heads.

D   Reducing the departments' responsibilities would not affect the availability of department heads.

E   Reducing the total number of employees per department would not affect the question of whether or not those departments have heads.

The correct answer is C.

234. Ecologist: The Scottish Highlands were once the site of extensive forests, but these forests have mostly disappeared and been replaced by peat bogs. The common view is that the Highlands' deforestation was caused by human activity, especially agriculture. However, **agriculture began in the Highlands less than 2,000 years ago.** Peat bogs, which consist of compressed decayed vegetable matter, build up by only about one foot per 1,000 years and, **throughout the Highlands, remains of trees in peat bogs are almost all at depths greater than four feet.** Since climate changes that occurred between 7,000 and 4,000 years ago favored the development of peat bogs rather than the survival of forests, the deforestation was more likely the result of natural processes than of human activity.

In the ecologist's argument, the two portions in **boldface** play which of the following roles?

(A)   The first is evidence that has been used in support of a position that the ecologist rejects; the second is a finding that the ecologist uses to counter that evidence.

(B)   The first is evidence that, in light of the evidence provided in the second, serves as grounds for the ecologist's rejection of a certain position.

(C)   The first is a position that the ecologist rejects; the second is evidence that has been used in support of that position.

(D)   The first is a position that the ecologist rejects; the second provides evidence in support of that rejection.

(E)   The first is a position for which the ecologist argues; the second provides evidence to support that position.

Argument Construction

Situation   An ecologist points out that the common position is that human activity—primarily agriculture—led to the replacement of the formerly extensive forests of the Scottish Highlands by peat bogs. The ecologist points out several factors that cast doubt on this explanation and instead point to natural processes as the cause. The ecologist points out that agriculture began in the Highlands less than 2,000 years ago, that peat bogs build up at only about a foot per 1,000 years, and that the peat bogs throughout the Highlands are at depths greater than four feet. Finally, in support of the alternative explanation, the ecologist points out that climate changes that occurred 7,000 to 4,000 years ago would have favored peat bog development over forest survival.

Reasoning   *What role do the two portions in* **boldface** *play in the ecologist's argument?* The ecologist rejects the common position that agriculture primarily accounts for the replacement of forests by peat bogs in the Scottish Highlands. The ecologist puts forward three main pieces of evidence as grounds for that rejection: that agriculture began in the Highlands 2,000 years ago (the first **boldfaced** portion), that peat bogs build up at one foot per 1,000 years, and that tree remnants in peat bogs throughout the Highlands occur at depths greater than four feet (the second **boldfaced** portion).

A   The first **boldfaced** portion is used in support of the ecologist's rejection of the common explanation; it has not been used to support that common explanation. The second **boldfaced** portion is compatible with the first and is not used to counter it.

B   **Correct.** The first **boldfaced** portion—which states that agriculture began in the Highlands less than 2,000 years ago—is used in the passage as grounds to reject the common explanation for the Highlands' deforestation. That **boldfaced** portion serves as grounds for such a rejection in light of two claims, one stating that peat bogs build up at only one foot per 1,000 years, and the other—the claim made in the second **boldfaced** portion—that the remains of trees almost all occur at a depth greater than four feet, which would indicate that the deforestation occurred well before agriculture.

C   The ecologist accepts, not rejects, what is expressed by the first **boldfaced** portion, and the second **boldfaced** portion has not been used to support what is expressed by the first **boldfaced** portion.

D   The ecologist accepts, not rejects, what is expressed by the first **boldfaced** portion, and the second **boldfaced** portion is compatible with what is expressed by the first **boldfaced** portion and so is not used to reject it.

E   The first **boldfaced** portion is simply asserted but not argued for; the second is compatible with the first but is not used to support the first.

The correct answer is B.

235. Beets and carrots are higher in sugar than many other vegetables. They are also high on the glycemic index, a scale that measures the rate at which a food increases blood sugar levels. But while nutritionists usually advise people to avoid high-sugar and high-glycemic-index foods, despite any nutritional benefits they may confer, they are not very concerned about the consumption of beets and carrots.

Which of the following, if true, would best explain the nutritionists' lack of concern?

(A) Foods with added sugar are much higher in sugar, and have a larger effect on blood sugar levels, than do beets and carrots.

(B) Most consumption of beets and carrots occurs in combination with higher-protein foods, which reduce blood sugar fluctuations.

(C) Beets and carrots contain many nutrients, such as folate, beta-carotene, and vitamin C, of which many people fail to consume optimal quantities.

(D) The glycemic index measures the extent to which a food increases blood sugar levels as compared to white bread, a food that is much less healthy than beets and carrots.

(E) Nutritionists have only recently come to understand that a food's effect on blood sugar levels is an important determinant of that food's impact on a person's health.

Argument Construction

Situation   Beets and carrots have high levels of sugar compared to most other vegetables, and also score high on the glycemic index, which measures the elevation of blood sugar produced by eating a particular food. Such sugary, high-glycemic foods are not recommended by nutritionists, even when the foods in question have other important nutrients. Despite their sugar content and glycemic effects, however, nutritionists do not tend to warn against beets and carrots.

Reasoning   *What factor would make nutritionists less concerned about the consumption of beets and carrots?* The information specifies that nutritionists warn against high-glycemic foods, even when those foods have significant nutritional value. If, however, some other factor moderated the blood-sugar effects of eating beets and carrots, that would help explain why nutritionists tend to be unconcerned about consumption of these two vegetables.

A   The fact that other foods have worse effects on blood sugar than do beets and carrots does not explain why nutritionists would not warn against the lesser, but still harmful, effects of these vegetables.

B   Correct. If beets and carrots are generally eaten in conjunction with higher-protein foods that moderate their impact on blood sugar levels, that would explain why nutritionists do not regard their high glycemic index as cause for concern.

C   The information specifies that nutritionists warn against high-glycemic foods even when those foods have other important nutrients, so the presence of such nutrients in beets and carrots would not explain nutritionists' lack of concern about their effect on blood sugar.

D   The fact that the glycemic index uses the effect of white bread as a baseline would not explain why nutritionists are unconcerned about the high glycemic index of beets and carrots.

E   Even if nutritionists only became concerned about the effect foods have on blood sugar recently, that would not explain why they are currently unconcerned about the effects of beets and carrots.

The correct answer is B.

236. Biologist: Species with broad geographic ranges probably tend to endure longer than species with narrow ranges. The broader a species' range, the more likely that species is to survive the extinction of populations in a few areas. Therefore, it is likely that the proportion of species with broad ranges tends to gradually increase with time.

The biologist's conclusion follows logically from the above if which of the following is assumed?

(A) There are now more species with broad geographic ranges than with narrow geographic ranges.

(B) Most species can survive extinctions of populations in a few areas as long as the species' geographic range is not very narrow.

(C) If a population of a species in a particular area dies out, that species generally does not repopulate that area.

(D) If a characteristic tends to help species endure longer, then the proportion of species with that characteristic tends to gradually increase with time.

(E) Any characteristic that makes a species tend to endure longer will make it easier for that species to survive the extinction of populations in a few areas.

Argument Construction

Situation   A biologist states that species spread across a large area are likely to outlast species confined to narrow areas, because their broad distribution gives them greater resilience when faced with localized extinctions. The biologist concludes that species with broad distributions will tend to make up an increasing percentage of total species over time.

Reasoning   *What additional assumption is necessary for the conclusion to follow logically?* The biologist's conclusion that the total of broadly ranged species will tend to increase in number relative to narrow-range species implies an assumption that greater endurance of species leads to a greater overall proportion of those species. This might not be the case if, for example, new species with narrow ranges tended to appear much more often than new species with broad ranges. Therefore, the biologist's argument holds only if the implied supposition—that characteristics which prolong a species' survival also promote a greater proportion of species with those characteristics overall—is true.

A   The current proportion of species with broad ranges compared to species with narrow ranges does not support the assumption that the proportion of broadly ranged species tends to increase over time.

B   The biologist's argument suggests that broad distribution helps many, though not necessarily most, species survive localized extinctions, but the argument does not assume that fact.

C   Whether or not species can repopulate areas after localized extinctions is not relevant to the biologist's argument that the total number of broadly distributed species will increase proportionally over time.

D   **Correct.** The biologist's argument relies on the assumption that a characteristic which promotes a species' longevity will also tend to promote the overall proportion of species with that characteristic; if additional factors prevented such an increasing overall proportion, the argument would not hold.

E   The statement that factors which promote greater longevity of a species will help that species survive is most often true, not an underlying assumption of the biologist's argument.

The correct answer is D.

237. In a certain rural area, people normally dispose of household garbage by burning it. Burning household garbage releases toxic chemicals known as dioxins. New conservation regulations will require a major reduction in packaging—specifically, paper and cardboard packaging—for products sold in the area. Since such packaging materials contain dioxins, one result of the implementation of the new regulations will surely be a reduction in dioxin pollution in the area.

Which of the following, if true, most seriously weakens the argument?

(A) Garbage containing large quantities of paper and cardboard can easily burn hot enough for some portion of the dioxins that it contains to be destroyed.

(B) Packaging materials typically make up only a small proportion of the weight of household garbage, but a relatively large proportion of its volume.

(C) Per-capita sales of products sold in paper and cardboard packaging are lower in rural areas than in urban areas.

(D) The new conservation regulations were motivated by a need to cut down on the consumption of paper products in order to bring the harvesting of timber into a healthier balance with its regrowth.

(E) It is not known whether the dioxins released by the burning of household garbage have been the cause of any serious health problems.

Argument Evaluation

Situation   People in a specific region burn household garbage, a practice which releases toxic dioxins. New regulations mandate a reduction in paper and cardboard packaging for products sold in that region. Because dioxins are found in paper and cardboard packaging, the argument concludes that these new regulations will necessarily lead to lower levels of dioxins in the region.

Reasoning   *What factor might prevent the regulations from reducing dioxins?* The argument anticipates that reduced burning of paper and cardboard packaging—as one component of burning household garbage—will *surely* reduce dioxin pollution. The argument would therefore be weakened if some additional consequence of burning garbage with a significant percentage of paper and cardboard offset the expected reduction in dioxin pollution.

A   **Correct.** If garbage containing a large percentage of paper and cardboard burns hot enough to destroy some dioxins, then reducing paper and cardboard as a percentage of garbage burned might have the unintended consequence of lowering the temperature of garbage fires and thereby releasing more of the total dioxins, rather than destroying them. There is not enough information to determine whether overall dioxin emissions would be lower, higher, or the same, but this fact does weaken the argument that such emissions would *surely* be lower.

B   The proportion of packaging materials in household garbage does not affect the question of whether burning less paper and cardboard will necessarily reduce dioxins.

C   The relative use of paper packaging in urban vs. rural areas has no bearing on the question of whether the regulations will reduce dioxins.

D   The motive for the new regulations has no bearing on any argument about their effects.

E   The argument concerns a reduction in dioxins, not in the health effects from dioxins, so this fact would not affect the argument.

The correct answer is A.

238. For individuals newly hired as data analysts, a number of organizations offer formal data-analysis training programs. Although individuals can work as data analysts without having completed such a program, the programs are purportedly effective in teaching sound data-analysis practices. Evidence for their effectiveness is provided by the following data: Whereas approximately one-third of employed data analysts have completed such a program, only eight percent of analysts whose work resulted in serious reporting errors have done so.

Which of the following, if true, most seriously weakens the conclusion drawn from the data above?

(A) Employers generally offer higher salaries to data analysts who have completed a formal data-analysis training program.

(B) Newly hired data analysts who are most likely to complete a training program are those who already have several years of experience working with data in related roles.

(C) Although formal data-analysis training programs are offered by a number of different organizations, they are generally similar in both content and instructional approach.

(D) Most serious reporting errors result from faulty data supplied to analysts rather than from mistakes made by the analysts themselves.

(E) In terms of workload and average number of reports produced annually, data analysts who have completed a training program do not differ from those who have not.

Argument Evaluation

Situation Organizations offer formal training programs to newly hired data analysts, and these programs are claimed to be effective in reducing serious reporting errors. The evidence cited compares two proportions: about one-third of all employed data analysts have completed such a program, while only eight percent of analysts whose work led to serious reporting errors have completed one. From this comparison, the argument concludes that the training programs are effective.

Reasoning To most seriously weaken this conclusion, new information must show that the lower proportion of trained analysts among those who made serious errors can be explained by a factor *other than the training itself*. Evidence that analysts who complete training already differ in relevant ways—such as having greater prior experience—would undermine the causal link between the training program and reduced errors by suggesting that the observed effect is due to preexisting differences rather than the training.

A This option does not weaken the argument because salary differences do not explain why trained analysts are less frequently involved in serious reporting errors. Higher pay could be a result of training, a reward for certification, or related to company policy, but it does not suggest that the training is ineffective or that the lower error rate has another cause.

B **Correct.** This choice most seriously weakens the conclusion by introducing a strong alternative explanation. If analysts who complete training programs already have significant prior experience, then their lower likelihood of being involved in serious reporting errors may be attributable to their prior experience, not to the training itself. The data cited in the argument, therefore, does not isolate the effect of the training program, undermining the claim that the program itself is effective.

C This choice is irrelevant to the argument. The conclusion concerns whether training programs are effective, not whether they differ from one another. Similarity among programs neither explains away the data nor challenges the claimed causal relationship.

D   This option partially weakens the argument by suggesting that serious errors may occur for reasons unrelated to analysts' skills. However, it does not show that trained analysts are more likely than untrained analysts to receive faulty data. Without that connection, this choice does not sufficiently undermine the inference that training reduces analysts' contribution to errors.

E   This option actually strengthens the argument rather than weakening it. By ruling out differences in workload or exposure as an explanation for the lower error rate among trained analysts, it makes it more plausible that the training itself accounts for the difference.

The correct answer is B.

239. Some farmers have recently begun planting cotton grown from genetically modified seed designed to increase resistance to insect pests. Compared with farmers using ordinary seed, those using the modified seed required only slightly less insecticide per acre to control pests. The modified seed, however, costs more per acre than ordinary seed. On the basis of these facts, some analysts conclude that switching to the modified seed would be unlikely to benefit most cotton farmers economically.

Which of the following, if true, would most seriously weaken the analysts' conclusion?

(A) Many of the farmers who tried the modified seed had previously grown other crops using genetically modified seed.

(B) The insecticides typically used on ordinary cotton are substantially more expensive per unit than those typically used on other crops.

(C) For most cotton farmers, cotton accounts for the largest share of their total farm revenue.

(D) Farmers who tried the modified seed planted approximately the same average acreage of cotton as farmers who used ordinary seed.

(E) Farmers who tried the modified seed had previously spent significantly more per acre on insecticides than most farmers using ordinary seed.

Argument Evaluation

Situation A group of farmers began planting cotton genetically engineered for insect resistance. These farmers still needed to use insecticide; indeed, they required only slightly less insecticide per acre than did farmers who planted ordinary cotton. Engineered cotton seeds are more expensive than ordinary seeds, and they produce cotton crops of no greater value, so the argument concludes that the engineered seeds are probably not cost-effective for most farmers.

Reasoning *What would suggest that the use of the genetically modified seeds might be cost-effective?* The argument concludes that, since the genetically modified seeds are more expensive and since they required only slightly less insecticide per acre than ordinary cotton, their use is probably not cost-effective. That conclusion, however, is based on the assumption that the two groups of farmers—planters of ordinary seed versus planters who switched to modified seed—began at the same level of insecticide use. If farmers who plant modified seed previously had a much higher level of insecticide use, then achieving a level of use slightly lower than that of farmers planting ordinary cotton might represent a dramatic savings. It would further suggest that the insect resistance of the modified cotton might be much better than the initial data appeared to suggest. That better resistance would then cast doubt on the argument that the use of the modified cotton seed is unlikely to be economically beneficial for most farmers.

A This option is irrelevant to the economic conclusion. Prior experience with genetically modified crops does not indicate whether the modified cotton seed is cost-effective or whether insecticide savings offset the higher seed cost.

B This choice does not weaken the argument because it does not compare costs between modified and ordinary cotton. The argument concerns relative costs *within cotton farming*, not between cotton and other crops.

C This statement is irrelevant. The proportion of revenue derived from cotton does not affect whether switching to modified seed reduces costs or increases profits per acre.

D   This option neither weakens nor strengthens the argument. Equal acreage ensures comparability but does not change the cost analysis regarding seed price and insecticide savings.

E   **Correct.** This choice most seriously weakens the argument by showing that the baseline costs for these farmers were higher. If farmers who switched to the modified seed historically used much more insecticide, then reducing to a level even slightly lower than that of farmers planting ordinary cotton might represent a dramatic savings, potentially outweighing the higher seed cost. This directly challenges the conclusion that switching is unlikely to be economically beneficial.

The correct answer is E.

240. Which of the following most logically completes the argument?

Ten years ago, the country of Benovia adopted new workplace safety regulations requiring protective equipment, improved training procedures, and upgraded machinery safeguards for all new manufacturing facilities. In the last few years, the annual number of factory workers hospitalized overnight or longer for injuries sustained on the job has been significantly lower than it was before the regulations went into effect. This evidence does not show that the regulations have made manufacturing work safer, however, since __________.

(A) over the last ten years, production quotas have increased at many of Benovia's largest manufacturing plants

(B) of the patients treated at hospitals in Benovia, the percentage being treated for workplace injuries has not decreased in the last few years

(C) five years ago, hospitals in Benovia adopted stricter criteria for determining when a patient needs to stay overnight

(D) most manufacturing facilities currently operating in Benovia were built or upgraded within the past ten years

(E) the proportion of factory workers who regularly bypass safety procedures has changed very little since the new regulations were adopted

Argument Construction

Situation Ten years ago, Benovia implemented new workplace safety regulations aimed at reducing injuries in manufacturing facilities. In recent years, the number of factory workers hospitalized overnight or longer for on-the-job injuries has declined compared with the period before the regulations were adopted. The argument questions whether this decline actually demonstrates that manufacturing work has become safer.

Reasoning To complete the argument logically, the correct answer must provide an *alternative explanation* for the decrease in overnight hospitalizations that does *not depend on improved workplace safety*. Information showing that fewer workers are hospitalized overnight because of *changes in hospital admission practices*, rather than because injuries are less frequent or less severe, would undermine the inference that the safety regulations caused the observed decline.

A This option does not weaken the evidence because increased production quotas might increase the risk of injury rather than explain a decrease in hospitalizations. It does not offer a reason why fewer workers are hospitalized overnight and therefore does not account for the data cited.

B This option might initially seem relevant, but it does not directly explain the decline in overnight hospitalizations. The argument concerns the severity of injuries, as measured by extended hospital stays, not the overall proportion of workplace injuries treated. Workers could still be injured at the same rate but hospitalized for shorter periods.

C **Correct.** This choice most logically completes the argument by providing a direct alternative explanation for the observed decline in overnight hospitalizations. If hospitals now require more severe injuries before admitting patients overnight, fewer workers would be hospitalized for extended stays even if the number or severity of injuries has not decreased.

D This option does not undermine the evidence because it actually suggests that the new regulations may be widespread and influential. If anything, this fact could support the claim that regulations improved safety, rather than casting doubt on it.

E This choice does not explain the reduction in hospitalizations. While it suggests that unsafe behavior persists, it does not show that the decrease in overnight hospital stays is unrelated to actual improvements in safety.

The correct answer is C.

241. People's television-viewing habits could be monitored by having television sets, when on, send out low-level electromagnetic waves that are reflected back to the television sets. The reflected waves could then be analyzed to determine how many people are within the viewing area of the television sets. Critics fear adverse health effects of such a monitoring system, but a proponent responds, "The average dose of radiation is less than one chest x-ray. As they watch, viewers won't feel a thing."

Which of the following, if true, is the most direct criticism of the proponent's response?

(A) The system cannot determine whether persons in the viewing area are paying attention to what is being broadcast.

(B) It is possible to gather reasonably useful data on who is watching programs by having selected families keep diaries of television watching.

(C) Some of those who would watch television sets with the monitoring device on are already ill with conditions that keep them at home.

(D) Even recipients of large, harmful doses of radiation do not sense the radiation as it strikes the body.

(E) Because it would invade privacy, acceptance of the monitoring device would have to be voluntary on the part of viewing families, and that restriction would skew the results.

Argument Evaluation

Situation   A proposal has been made to create television sets that emit electromagnetic waves in order to detect the number of people watching. This proposal has provoked concerns regarding possible damage to the health of those viewers subjected to electromagnetic monitoring. A proponent of the system dismisses such concerns with the claim that the radiation is less than that of a chest x-ray and, moreover, with the statement that the viewers will not feel the radiation.

Reasoning   *What fact would directly counter the proponent's dismissal?* The proponent's dismissal of the health concerns relies on the dubious implication that doses of radiation have a negligible effect on health if people can't feel those doses. Therefore, a direct and logical response would point out that being unable to feel radiation is not an accurate indicator that such radiation is harmless.

A   Inability to detect viewers' attention may be a drawback of the monitoring system, but the fact that the system has drawbacks is not a direct criticism of the proponent's implied claim that it has negligible effects on health.

B   The fact that there are valid alternatives to the monitoring system is not a direct criticism of the proponent's questionable implications regarding the system's safety.

C   The fact that already-sick people would be subjected to the radiation is not a direct counter to the proponent's implied claim that the system is harmless to people's health in general.

D   **Correct.** The proponent's dismissal of health concerns regarding the radiation emitted by the system is based on the implication that, if viewers can't feel the radiation, that radiation therefore has negligible negative health effects. It is therefore a direct and logical criticism to point out that simply *not feeling* radiation in no way demonstrates that the radiation is not harmful.

E   Privacy concerns are certainly an issue with the system, but since the proponent is dismissing health concerns specifically, a direct criticism would likewise have to address health concerns.

The correct answer is D.

242. Smithtown University's fundraisers succeeded in getting donations from 80 percent of the potential donors they contacted. This success rate, exceptionally high for university fundraisers, does not indicate that they were doing a good job. On the contrary, since the people most likely to donate are those who have donated in the past, good fundraisers constantly try less-likely prospects in an effort to expand the donor base. The high success rate shows insufficient canvassing effort.

Which of the following, if true, provides the most support for the argument?

(A) Smithtown University's fundraisers were successful in their contacts with potential donors who had never given before about as frequently as were fundraisers for other universities in their contacts with such people.

(B) This year the average size of the donations to Smithtown University from new donors whom the university's fundraisers had contacted was larger than the average size of donations from donors who had given to the university before.

(C) This year most of the donations that came to Smithtown University from people who had previously donated to it were made without the university's fundraisers having made any contact with the donors.

(D) The majority of the donations that fundraisers succeeded in getting for Smithtown University this year were from donors who had never given to the university before.

(E) More than half of the money raised by Smithtown University's fundraisers came from donors who had never previously donated to the university.

Argument Evaluation

Situation   Smithtown University's fundraisers have an unusually high rate of success, in that 80 percent of those they contact donate. The argument claims that this fact demonstrates inadequate effort on the fundraisers' part, not that these fundraisers are unusually effective, because people are more likely to donate if they have done so previously. The argument suggests that, therefore, a *lower* rate of success would suggest that *greater* efforts were being made to attract new donors by reaching out to those less likely to give.

Reasoning   *What would support the implied claim that the fundraisers have a high rate of success because they focus on easy, higher-likelihood contacts and neglect lower-likelihood contacts?* The conclusion—that the fundraisers owe their success rate to the low-effort approach of contacting mainly established, high-likelihood donors—lacks support from the information given. The argument infers, without evidence, that the fundraisers *must* have neglected less-likely contacts in order to maintain their high success rate. If, however, there was evidence that the fundraisers did in fact have an unusually high level of success with such less-likely contacts, then that fact would undermine the conclusion. If, on the other hand, there was evidence that they *weren't* especially effective at getting donations from less-likely prospects, then that fact would support the conclusion.

A   **Correct.** If the fundraisers at Smithtown had rates of success with less-likely donors comparable to those of other fundraisers, then that would support the contention that the Smithtown fundraisers keep their success rate high simply by keeping the proportion of such challenging contacts low.

B   If Smithtown's fundraisers secured large donations on average from new donors, then that fact would be neutral in regard to the conclusion and not support that conclusion. It would not actively *undermine* the conclusion, however, because the fundraisers could still be making inadequate efforts to reach such new donors, whose numbers might be very few.

C   The fact that the fundraisers received unsolicited donations has no bearing on the reason for their success rate with those they *did* contact.

D   If the majority of donations secured by the fundraisers came from less-likely donors, then that would tend to undermine, not support, the conclusion that the fundraisers owe their success to the neglect of such donors.

E   If a majority of the total funds secured by the fundraisers came from less-likely donors, then that would tend to slightly undermine, not support, the conclusion that the fundraisers owe their success to the neglect of such donors.

The correct answer is A.

243. Scientists typically do their most creative work before the age of forty. It is commonly thought that this happens because **aging by itself brings about a loss of creative capacity.** However, studies show that **a disproportionately large number of the scientists who produce highly creative work beyond the age of forty entered their field at an older age than is usual.** Since by the age of forty the large majority of scientists have been working in their field for at least fifteen years, the studies' finding strongly suggests that the real reason why scientists over forty rarely produce highly creative work is not that they have simply aged but rather that they generally have spent too long in a given field.

In the argument given, the two portions in **boldface** play which of the following roles?

(A) The first is the position that the argument as a whole opposes; the second is an objection that has been raised against a position defended in the argument.

(B) The first is a claim that has been advanced in support of a position that the argument opposes; the second is a finding that has been used in support of that position.

(C) The first is an explanation that the argument challenges; the second is a finding that has been used in support of that explanation.

(D) The first is an explanation that the argument challenges; the second is a finding on which that challenge is based.

(E) The first is an explanation that the argument defends; the second is a finding that has been used to challenge that explanation.

Argument Construction

Situation Scientists generally achieve their major creative breakthroughs before they turn forty. However, because most older scientists who achieve major creative breakthroughs became scientists later in life, the author argues that it is not age, but the amount of time spent in the field, that is probably the factor defining a scientist's period of greatest creativity, and further suggests that the fifteen years after becoming a scientist constitute that especially creative period.

Reasoning *How do the two **boldfaced** portions of the text relate to the argument that the reason scientists over forty produce fewer breakthroughs is not their age but rather the duration of their careers in science?* The first portion states the usual explanation for why most scientists who achieve breakthroughs are under forty: the assumption that creativity must diminish with age. The argument goes on to challenge this explanation. The second portion states the finding that a high proportion of scientists who achieve breakthroughs later in life also entered their fields unusually late; this finding provides a basis for that challenge by suggesting that the real constraint on creativity is not age but rather the amount of time spent in the field.

A The first portion is not so much a position as an assumption, though the argument does oppose it; the second portion supports the argument and is not an objection against its position.

B The first portion is indeed a claim, or at least an assumption, that the argument opposes, though it is not really advanced in support of anything but is rather a conclusion in itself; the second portion is a finding that supports the argument's position and not an opposing position.

C The first portion is indeed an explanation that the argument challenges, but the second portion is a finding that supports the argument's preferred explanation and not an opposing explanation.

D **Correct.** The first portion, the idea that creative breakthroughs' rarity among older scientists must result from creativity itself declining with age, is an explanation challenged by the argument; the second portion, the finding that especially creative older scientists quite often entered their fields late, provides a basis for the alternative explanation advanced as a challenge to the first: namely, that the real constraint on creativity is not age, but rather the amount of time spent in the field.

E The first portion is an explanation that the argument challenges rather than defends, though the second portion is indeed a finding used to challenge the first.

The correct answer is D.

244. Insect infestations in certain cotton-growing regions of the world have caused dramatic increases in the price of cotton on the world market. By contrast, the price of soybeans has long remained stable. Knowing that cotton plants mature quickly, many soybean growers in Ortovia plan to cease growing soybeans and begin raising cotton instead, thereby taking advantage of the high price of cotton to increase their income significantly, at least over the next several years.

Which of the following, if true, most seriously weakens the plan's chances for success?

(A) The cost of raising soybeans has increased significantly over the past several years and is expected to continue to climb.

(B) Tests of a newly developed, inexpensive pesticide have shown it to be both environmentally safe and effective against the insects that have infested cotton crops.

(C) In the past several years, there has been no sharp increase in the demand for cotton and for goods made out of cotton.

(D) Few consumers would be willing to pay significantly higher prices for cotton goods than they are now paying.

(E) The species of insect that has infested cotton plants has never been known to attack soybean plants.

Argument Evaluation

Situation   Insect infestations of cotton crops have led the price of cotton to grow sharply. Soybean prices, on the other hand, have stayed constant. Some soybean farmers in Ortovia intend to grow cotton instead of soybeans in order to benefit from inflated cotton prices.

Reasoning   *What additional factor would be likely to lower the price of cotton?* The information implies that cotton's price has climbed owing to limited supply: Insects have ruined cotton crops. If, therefore, there was evidence that this situation is likely to change and that cotton again will become more plentiful on the world market, then there would probably be a corresponding decline in cotton's price, and the farmers' plan to profit from high cotton prices would be much less likely to succeed.

A   The rising cost of growing soybeans might incentivize soybean farmers to switch to other crops but has no bearing on a plan to switch to cotton specifically.

B   **Correct.** If a safe, effective, and inexpensive pesticide has been developed to combat the insects that caused the cotton shortage in the first place, then the supply of cotton would be expected to increase, the price would be expected to fall, and the farmers' plan to take advantage of inflated prices for cotton would be much less likely to succeed.

C   Steady demand for cotton, combined with limited supply, would still be likely to maintain high cotton prices and therefore would not undermine the farmers' plan.

D   The farmers' plan does not depend on cotton prices continuing to climb, merely on those prices remaining at their current inflated level, so the reluctance of consumers to pay much more would not impact their chances of success.

E   The fact that a specific species of insect attacks cotton and not soybeans has no bearing on the farmers' plan.

The correct answer is B.

245. A particular logistics routing protocol used in large distribution networks often leads to shipment delays because packages that normally remain within local sorting hubs tend to be redirected into long-distance transit routes, eventually congesting regional distribution centers. When a routing override system, which counteracts certain effects of the protocol, is implemented along with the protocol, shipment delays occur far less frequently. Therefore, the routing override system probably disables the mechanism by which the protocol causes packages to be redirected into long-distance transit routes.

Which of the following is an assumption on which the argument depends?

(A) The routing override system does not directly remove packages once they have entered long-distance transit routes.

(B) Factors other than the redirection of packages into long-distance transit routes can cause shipment delays.

(C) The routing override system does not reduce overall delivery efficiency.

(D) For logistics networks, increased shipment delays are the most harmful effect of using the routing protocol.

(E) Distribution networks in which the routing override system but not the routing protocol is used are no more likely to experience shipment delays than networks in which neither system is used.

Argument Evaluation

Situation   A logistics routing protocol used in large distribution networks often causes shipment delays by redirecting packages that would normally remain within local sorting hubs into long-distance transit routes, which then congest regional distribution centers. When a routing override system is implemented along with the protocol, shipment delays occur far less frequently. Based on this reduction, the argument concludes that the routing override system disables the mechanism by which the routing protocol causes packages to be redirected into long-distance routes.

Reasoning   To justify this conclusion, the argument assumes that the routing override system *does not reduce shipment delays by some other means*, such as correcting delays after packages have already been misrouted. If the override system were simply removing or compensating for delays rather than preventing the redirection itself, the conclusion about the mechanism would not follow. Therefore, the reasoning depends on the assumption that the routing override system works by *blocking the protocol's tendency to misroute packages*, not by addressing the consequences after misrouting has occurred.

A   **Correct.** This is a necessary assumption. If the override system reduced delays by pulling packages back *after* they were misrouted, the observed reduction in delays would not show that the override system disables the *mechanism* that causes misrouting. The conclusion specifically attributes the effect to preventing redirection in the first place, so the argument depends on the assumption that the override system is not merely correcting the problem downstream.

B   This statement is not required by the argument. Even if other factors can cause delays, the argument concerns the mechanism responsible for delays in this case and how the override system affects it. The conclusion does not depend on whether other causes exist.

C   This option is irrelevant to the argument. The conclusion is about *how* delays are reduced, not about overall efficiency or side effects. The argument can stand even if the override system has negative effects elsewhere.

D   This option introduces a value judgment that the argument does not require. The conclusion does not rank harms; it only explains the cause of reduced delays. Whether delays are the most harmful effect is beside the point.

E   This option concerns the effect of the override system in isolation, which the argument does not address. The conclusion only depends on how the override system interacts with the routing protocol, not on what happens when the override system is used alone.

The correct answer is A.

246. A manufacturer of specialized computer workstations formerly made nearly all of its sales to corporate customers at prices well below the list price. Because surveys showed that other potential customers were being deterred by its relatively high list prices, the manufacturer, in an effort to increase its sales, reduced those prices to a level closer to what its customers had been paying. This move attracted some new customers, but overall the manufacturer's sales actually fell.

Which of the following, if true, most helps explain why the manufacturer's sales fell instead of rising?

(A) The manufacturer's new list prices were no lower than those of most of its competitors.

(B) Demand for specialized computer workstations has been increasing steadily for several years.

(C) Corporations rarely employ people who lack extensive knowledge about the prices of equipment as buyers of such equipment.

(D) Customers differ significantly in the proportions of their resources they are willing to devote to specialized equipment such as computer workstations.

(E) Buyers who purchase equipment such as computer workstations for their employers typically receive bonuses for negotiating large discounts from the list price.

Argument Evaluation

Situation   A computer workstation manufacturer routinely offered corporate customers large discounts off the list price. In order to become more competitive, the manufacturer then lowered its list prices nearer to the discounted level. Contrary to expectations, bringing list prices lower—and closer to the prices charged in practice—led to decreased sales.

Reasoning   *What additional factor would cause sales to fall despite lower prices?* Ordinarily, lower prices would be expected to lead to higher sales, so there is likely to be some additional factor that would explain why that correspondence does not hold in this case. The crucial point of the information provided is that, by bringing the list prices down closer to the prices that were charged in practice, the manufacturer was presumably no longer offering corporations *large discounts* off those list prices; that is, corporations no longer appeared to be benefitting from an impressive bargain.

A   If the manufacturer's list prices are no lower than that of its competitors, that factor would not explain why sales *fell*—though it might conceivably hinder *growth* of those sales.

B   A steady increase in demand for the manufacturer's products would not explain declining sales.

C   Corporations' preferences regarding whom they employ to buy such equipment would not explain why sales fell as prices fell.

D   Variations in customers' budgeting would not account for a drop in sales following lowered prices.

E   **Correct.** If buyers receive bonuses from their companies for negotiating large discounts off the list price, then that would incentivize those buyers to seek manufacturers with *high* list prices who offer dramatic discounts. This additional factor would then explain why *lowering* list prices—and presumably offering lower discounts to compensate for that reduction—might actually lower sales rather than increasing them.

The correct answer is E.

247. In countries where companies offer financial bonuses for employee suggestions that improve efficiency, reports of such suggestions are twice as frequent as they are in countries where no bonuses are offered. **At present, there is no reliable way to determine whether a reported suggestion would genuinely lead to improved efficiency**, so it is true that low-quality or insincere suggestions cannot be readily identified. Nevertheless, these facts do not warrant a conclusion that has been drawn by some commentators: **that in the countries with higher rates of reported suggestions, half of the reported suggestions are of little real value**. What these commentators are overlooking is that in countries where no bonuses are offered, employees often have little incentive to submit suggestions that could in fact improve efficiency.

In the argument given, the two **boldfaced** portions play which of the following roles?

(A) The first is a judgment advanced in support of the main conclusion of the argument; the second is that main conclusion.

(B) Each is a judgment advanced in support of the main conclusion of the argument.

(C) The first is an intermediate conclusion drawn in order to challenge a position opposed by the argument; the second is the position taken by the argument.

(D) The first is a position that the argument accepts as true; the second states a claim that the argument disputes.

(E) The first states the position taken by the argument; the second is a consideration presented in order to support that position.

Argument Construction

Situation   In some countries, companies offer financial bonuses for employee suggestions, and these countries report twice as many suggestions as countries where no such bonuses are offered. Because there is no reliable way to determine in advance whether a suggestion will genuinely improve efficiency, some commentators conclude that in countries with higher reporting rates, half of the suggestions must be of little real value. The argument challenges this conclusion by pointing out that employees in countries without bonuses have little incentive to report even genuinely useful suggestions.

Reasoning   The argument maintains that the higher number of reported suggestions in bonus-offering countries does *not* justify the claim that half of those suggestions are worthless. The overlooked consideration is that *underreporting* is likely in countries without incentives, meaning the comparison of raw reporting rates is misleading. Thus, the argument's reasoning hinges on explaining the disparity in reported suggestions by differences in incentives rather than by differences in the quality or sincerity of the suggestions themselves.

A   The second **boldfaced** statement is not the argument's main conclusion; it is the conclusion drawn by *other commentators*, which the author explicitly rejects. Therefore, this option mislabels the second statement.

B   The second **boldfaced** statement does not support the author's conclusion—it is the conclusion the author is arguing against. Thus, the two statements do not play the same supportive role.

C   The first **boldfaced** statement is not an intermediate conclusion; it is a factual concession. The second **boldfaced** statement is also not the position taken by the argument—it is explicitly identified as a conclusion drawn by others that the author disputes.

D   **Correct.** This option correctly captures the structure: The first **boldfaced** statement is a premise acknowledged as true. The second **boldfaced** statement is the flawed conclusion drawn by commentators, which the argument challenges.

E   The first **boldfaced** statement is accepted by the argument, but it is not the position the argument is trying to establish; it is background information. The second **boldfaced** statement does not support the argument's position—it is the opposing claim being criticized.

The correct answer is D.

248. Certainly, pesticides can on occasion adversely affect the environment in localities distant from where the pesticide has actually been used. Nevertheless, regulation of pesticide use should take place not at the national level but at the local level. It is in the areas where pesticides are actually applied that they have their most serious effects. **Just how serious these effects are depends on local conditions** such as climate, soil type, and water supply. And **local officials are much more likely than national legislators to be truly knowledgeable about such local conditions.**

In the argument given, the two **boldface** portions play which of the following roles?

(A) The first provides support for the conclusion of the argument; the second states that conclusion.

(B) The first states the conclusion of the argument; the second provides support for that conclusion.

(C) The first identifies grounds for a potential objection to the conclusion of the argument; the second states that conclusion.

(D) The first identifies grounds for a potential objection to the conclusion of the argument; the second provides support for that conclusion.

(E) Each provides support for the conclusion of the argument.

Argument Evaluation

Situation The argument addresses the proper level of government (national vs. local) for regulating pesticide use. The author argues against national-level regulation, conceding only that pesticides can cause problems far from the application site. The core of the argument rests on two premises: the most serious effects are local, and the severity of these local effects depends on local conditions.

Reasoning *What function is served by the two **boldfaced** portions?* The argument's prescriptive conclusion is that regulation should take place at the local level. The first **boldfaced** portion establishes the relevance and necessity of local knowledge for effective regulation. The second **boldfaced** portion states that local officials possess more of this necessary local knowledge than national legislators. Since the problem (local detrimental effects) requires local knowledge, which is addressed in the first **boldfaced** portion, and local officials have that knowledge, as stated in the second **boldfaced** portion, both statements provide direct support for the main conclusion that local regulation is preferable to national.

A The main conclusion is that regulation should be local, which is stated earlier in the passage. Both the first and second **boldfaced** portions provide support for that conclusion.

B Neither statement is the main conclusion. Both serve as support for the conclusion.

C The potential objection (that pesticides can affect distant localities) is stated *before* the main conclusion. Both excerpted portions are *support* for the conclusion, not objections.

D The first **boldfaced** portion establishes the *relevance* of local knowledge. It is not an objection. The second portion, however, does provide support for the conclusion.

E **Correct.** The first portion establishes what makes local knowledge necessary (the severity of effects depends on local conditions). The second portion establishes who possesses that necessary knowledge (local officials). Together, they support the argument's conclusion that regulation should be local.

The correct answer is E.

249. Cork stoppers for bottled wine can leak, crumble, or become moldy. As a result, winemakers are forced to discard what are often significant proportions of their inventory of bottled wine. **High-quality plastic stoppers cannot leak, crumble, or mold.** Plastic stoppers will also soon enjoy a price advantage. Prices for cork and plastic stoppers are now about even, but the price of cork is expected to rise sharply in the near future. Nevertheless, **most winemakers who have not already switched to plastic stoppers remain committed to cork stoppers.** It is clear, therefore, that those winemakers' business decisions are shaped primarily by considerations other than a commitment to keeping expenses low.

In the argument given, the two portions in **boldface** play which of the following roles?

(A) The first is evidence that has been used to support a position that the argument challenges; the second is that challenged position.

(B) The first is evidence that has been used to support a position that the argument challenges; the second is evidence on which that challenge is based.

(C) The first and the second each provide evidence in support of the main conclusion of the argument.

(D) The first provides evidence in support of the main conclusion of the argument; the second is an objection that has been raised against that main conclusion.

(E) The first provides evidence in support of the main conclusion of the argument; the second is a conclusion drawn in order to support that main conclusion.

Argument Construction

Situation Cork stoppers for wine bottles can lead to spoiled wine by leaking, crumbling, or growing mold, which causes lost inventory for winemakers. Plastic stoppers lack the problems that lead to spoilage; moreover, the price of cork is expected to increase soon, which will make plastic stoppers the less expensive option. However, winemakers who use cork stoppers have decided to continue their use. The argument concludes that winemakers who prefer cork are motivated by concerns other than cost.

Reasoning *What role do the two **boldfaced** portions play in the argument that winemakers who prefer cork are motivated by considerations other than costs?* The first portion states that quality plastic stoppers do not leak, crumble, or mold, and the context makes it clear that these advantages contrast with cork stoppers; therefore this is evidence that plastic stoppers can hold down costs related to wine spoilage. The second portion states that winemakers who prefer cork remain "committed" to its use, despite the evidence that using cork stoppers is the more costly choice. Both these portions, then, provide evidence for the conclusion: if the cork-preferring winemakers are not persuaded to use plastic by cost considerations, they must have other considerations that weigh more heavily.

A The first portion is evidence that plastic stoppers are more cost-effective than cork, which is not a position the argument challenges; furthermore the second portion's claim that winemakers who prefer cork intend to continue using it is not the same position.

B The first portion is evidence that plastic stoppers are more cost-effective than cork, which is not a position the argument challenges; nor can the second portion be evidence for a challenge that does not exist.

C **Correct.** The first portion provides evidence that plastic stoppers are more cost-effective than cork; the second portion provides evidence that such cost-effectiveness is not enough to persuade some winemakers to use plastic stoppers. Together, these pieces of evidence both support the conclusion: if the winemakers who prefer cork are not primarily motivated by lowering costs, they must be motivated by other considerations instead.

D The first portion does provide evidence for the conclusion, but the second portion is further evidence and not an objection.

E The first portion does provide evidence for the conclusion, but the second portion is further evidence—in the form of an assertion regarding winemakers' intentions—and not a preliminary conclusion drawn in support of the main conclusion.

The correct answer is C.

250. Historian: Newton developed mathematical concepts and techniques that are fundamental to modern calculus. Leibniz developed closely analogous concepts and techniques. It has traditionally been thought that these discoveries were independent. Researchers have, however, recently discovered notes of Leibniz's that discuss one of Newton's books on mathematics. Several scholars have argued that since **the book includes a presentation of Newton's calculus concepts and techniques**, and since the notes were written before Leibniz's own development of calculus concepts and techniques, **it is virtually certain that the traditional view is false**. A more cautious conclusion than this is called for, however. Leibniz's notes are limited to early sections of Newton's book, sections that precede the ones in which Newton's calculus concepts and techniques are presented.

In the historian's reasoning, the two **boldfaced** portions play which of the following roles?

(A) The first is a claim that has been advanced as a hypothesis in arguing for the position the historian rejects; the second is that position.

(B) The first is evidence that has been used to support a conclusion that the historian criticizes; the second is that conclusion.

(C) The first provides evidence in support of an intermediate conclusion drawn in order to support the position that the historian defends; the second is that intermediate conclusion.

(D) The first provides evidence in support of the position that the historian defends; the second provides evidence to support that position.

(E) The first is the position taken by the argument; the second is evidence that has been used to support that position.

Argument Construction

Situation   A historian is discussing the origin of calculus concepts developed by Newton and Leibniz. The traditional view is that their discoveries were made independently. Recent evidence (Leibniz's notes on Newton's book) has led "several scholars" to argue that the traditional view is false. But the historian offers counter-evidence to argue that this conclusion is too strong.

Reasoning   *What roles do the two **boldfaced** portions play in the argument?* The first **boldfaced** portion is a premise or piece of evidence cited by the scholars. It establishes the content of the book Leibniz read, which is necessary to link Leibniz's work to Newton's. The second portion is the conclusion reached by "Several scholars," based on the first portion taken together with the additional premise regarding the timing of the notes. This is the specific conclusion that the historian then challenges and argues against by saying "A more cautious conclusion than this is called for." Therefore, the first portion is evidence used to support a conclusion, and the second portion is that conclusion, which the historian's entire argument aims to criticize.

A   The first portion is presented as an undisputed fact, not a hypothesis. The second portion is indeed the position the historian rejects.

B   **Correct.** The first portion ("the book includes . . .") is evidence used by the scholars to argue that the traditional view is false. The second portion ("it is virtually certain . . .") is the conclusion drawn by those scholars, and this is the conclusion that the historian then criticizes by introducing the counter-evidence about the notes' limited scope.

C   The historian is arguing *against* the conclusion presented in the second portion. Neither portion is part of the argument the historian uses to defend their own position; they are part of the *opposing* argument.

D   The first portion supports the position that the traditional view is *false*; this is the view the historian *criticizes*, and not the cautious position the historian defends. The second portion is a view the historian criticizes rather than defending.

E   The first portion is used to dispute the traditional view (which the historian ultimately supports), but the second portion is a *conclusion*, not a hypothesis.

The correct answer is B.

251. Business Consultant: **Some corporations shun the use of executive titles** because they fear that the use of titles indicating position in the corporation tends to inhibit communication up and down the corporate hierarchy. Since an executive who uses a title is treated with more respect by outsiders, however, use of a title can facilitate an executive's dealings with external businesses. Clearly, **corporations should adopt the compromise of encouraging their executives to use their corporate titles externally but not internally**, since even if it is widely known that the corporation's executives use titles outside the organization, this knowledge does not by itself inhibit communication within the corporation.

In the consultant's reasoning, the two portions in **boldface** play which of the following roles?

(A) The first describes a strategy that has been adopted to avoid a certain problem; the second expresses the consultant's assessment of the significance of that problem.

(B) The first describes a strategy that has been adopted to avoid a certain problem; the second is a judgment that the consultant uses to argue that the strategy is ineffective.

(C) The first describes a strategy that has a drawback that the consultant points out; the second presents a strategy that, according to the consultant, would achieve the same end while avoiding that drawback.

(D) The first describes a practice for which the consultant seeks to provide a justification; the second is a consideration offered as part of that justification.

(E) The first describes a policy that the consultant concludes is misguided; the second is introduced to explain why that policy was adopted.

Argument Construction

Situation   A business consultant presents the possible concern that the use of executive titles may impede vertical communication within a company; the drawback to simply dropping such titles, as some companies have done, is that such titles are useful in dealing with external businesses. The consultant proposes a solution: use such executive titles with outsiders, but not with fellow employees of the company. The consultant asserts that awareness of such externally-used titles does not have an inhibiting effect on company communications.

Reasoning   *What role do the two **boldfaced** portions play in the consultant's discussion of the best way to use executive titles?* The first portion states that some companies shun the use of executive titles; the surrounding context suggests that this is a strategy to avoid inhibiting communication, but the consultant points out that giving up titles has a drawback: such titles are useful with outsiders. The second portion advances the consultant's preferred strategy for preventing such inhibited communication without that drawback: keep the titles, but use them only with outsiders.

A   While the first portion does describe a strategy that has been used to avoid the problem of inhibited communications, the second portion is not in any way an assessment of that problem's significance.

B   The first portion describes a strategy used to avoid the problem of poor communications within a company, but the second portion describes an alternative strategy rather than suggesting that the first strategy is ineffective.

C   **Correct.** The first portion describes a strategy, dropping executive titles, that the consultant considers flawed because such titles are useful in dealing with outsiders; the second portion presents the consultant's preferred strategy of keeping the titles but using them only with outsiders, which clearly avoids the drawback of losing useful titles. The surrounding context contains the consultant's assertion that this alternative strategy will achieve the same goal: avoiding the inhibition of communication.

D   The first portion does describe a practice, dropping executive titles, and the consultant does describe the justification for that practice; however, the second portion describes an alternative practice rather than justifying the verbal practice referred to in the first portion.

E   The first portion does describe a policy that the consultant considers misguided; however, the second portion does not say anything regarding why that policy was adopted.

The correct answer is C.

252. Since it has become known that several of a bank's top executives have been buying shares in their own bank, the bank's depositors, who had been worried by rumors that the bank faced impending financial collapse, have been greatly relieved. They reason that since **top executives evidently have faith in the bank's financial soundness**, those worrisome rumors must be false. **They might well be overoptimistic**, however, since corporate executives have sometimes bought shares in their own company in a calculated attempt to dispel negative rumors about the company's health.

In the argument given, the two **boldfaced** portions play which of the following roles?

(A) The first summarizes the evidence used in the reasoning called into question by the argument; the second states the counterevidence on which the argument relies.

(B) The first summarizes the evidence used in the reasoning called into question by the argument; the second is an intermediate conclusion supported by that evidence.

(C) The first is an intermediate conclusion that forms part of the reasoning called into question by the argument; the second is evidence that undermines the support for this intermediate conclusion.

(D) The first is an intermediate conclusion that forms part of the reasoning called into question by the argument; the second is the main conclusion of the argument.

(E) The first is an intermediate conclusion that forms part of the reasoning called into question by the argument; the second states a further conclusion supported by this intermediate conclusion.

Argument Construction

Situation Bank depositors were worried by rumors of impending financial collapse. Their fear was relieved after learning that the bank's top executives were buying shares in the bank. The depositors concluded that the rumors must be false because the executives showed faith in the bank. The argument then challenges this optimism.

Reasoning *What role is played in the argument by the two **boldfaced** portions?* The overall argument critiques the depositors' optimistic conclusion by offering an alternative explanation for the executives' actions. The key evidence in the argument is that the executives bought shares. The first **boldfaced** portion is the intermediate conclusion the depositors draw from that evidence. The second **boldfaced** portion is the main conclusion—the central point the author is trying to establish—that the depositors' conclusion that the rumors are false is unwarranted. The argument justifies its main conclusion by providing an alternative possibility: executives sometimes buy shares merely to dispel negative rumors. Therefore, the first portion is an intermediate step in the reasoning the argument is calling into question, and the second portion is the main conclusion of the argument itself.

A The first portion summarizes an *intermediate conclusion* that the executives have faith, not the evidence for that faith, namely that the executives bought shares. The second portion is the *main conclusion*, not the counterevidence.

B The first portion summarizes the *intermediate conclusion*, not the evidence. The second portion is the *main* conclusion of the entire argument, not an intermediate one.

C The first portion is correctly identified as an intermediate conclusion in the criticized reasoning. However, the second portion is the *main conclusion* of the argument, not the evidence used to undermine the depositors' reasoning.

D **Correct.** The first portion is the intermediate conclusion drawn by the depositors (that executives have faith), which is a key part of the reasoning the main argument then calls into question. The second portion ("They might well be overoptimistic") is the main conclusion of the entire argument.

E The second portion is the argument's main conclusion, which *challenges* the preceding reasoning, rather than being supported by the intermediate conclusion in the first portion.

The correct answer is D.

253. **In countries where automobile insurance includes compensation for whiplash injuries sustained in automobile accidents, reports of having suffered such injuries are twice as frequent as they are in countries where whiplash is not covered.** Some commentators have argued, correctly, that since there is presently no objective test for whiplash, **spurious reports of whiplash injuries cannot be readily identified.** These commentators are, however, wrong to draw the further conclusion that in the countries with the higher rates of reported whiplash injuries, half of the reported cases are spurious: clearly, in countries where automobile insurance does not include compensation for whiplash, people often have little incentive to report whiplash injuries that they actually have suffered.

In the argument given, the two **boldfaced** portions play which of the following roles?

(A) The first is a finding whose accuracy is evaluated in the argument; the second is an intermediate conclusion drawn to support the judgment reached by the argument on the accuracy of that finding.

(B) The first is a finding whose accuracy is evaluated in the argument; the second is evidence that has been used to challenge the accuracy of that finding.

(C) The first is a finding whose implications are at issue in the argument; the second is an intermediate conclusion that has been used to support a conclusion that the argument criticizes.

(D) The first is a claim that the argument disputes; the second is a narrower claim that the argument accepts.

(E) The first is a claim that has been used to support a conclusion that the argument accepts; the second is that conclusion.

Argument Construction

Situation   The argument begins with an observed correlation: in countries that compensate for whiplash injuries, people report them twice as frequently as in countries that do not compensate. This finding, combined with the difficulty of objectively testing for whiplash, has led "some commentators" to conclude that half the reported cases in compensating countries must be spurious. The overall purpose of the argument is to reject this specific conclusion drawn by the commentators.

Reasoning   *What roles do the two **boldfaced** portions play in the argument?* The first portion presents the central piece of statistical evidence or finding that the entire discussion is based upon. The proper interpretation of this finding is the central issue debated in the argument: Are the comparatively greater number of reports due to fraud, or due to a lack of incentive to report in non-compensating countries?

The second **boldfaced** statement is an intermediate conclusion drawn from the fact that *there is presently no objective test for whiplash.* This intermediate conclusion is then used, in conjunction with the first **boldfaced** portion, to support the ultimate conclusion drawn by the commentators that half of the reported cases are spurious. The final conclusion of the passage, however, criticizes these commentators' conclusion. Therefore, the second portion is a key premise that supports the conclusion the argument criticizes.

A   The argument evaluates the implications of the finding presented in the first portion, not its accuracy. The second portion supports the conclusion the argument rejects, not the one it reaches.

B   Again, the argument accepts the finding's accuracy as it is presented in the first portion. The second portion is not used to challenge the finding; instead, it's used to support the *fraud* explanation for the finding.

C   **Correct.** The first portion is a finding whose meaning (implications) is debated. The second portion is an intermediate conclusion that false reports are hard to identify; that intermediate conclusion is necessary to support the commentators' final conclusion, namely that half of whiplash reports are spurious. This is a conclusion which the overall argument explicitly criticizes.

D   The argument accepts the claim in the first portion rather than disputing it; it disputes the *implication* of the claim. The second portion does not present a narrower claim, but a distinct one.

E   The first portion is a claim used to support a conclusion that the argument rejects, not that it accepts. Neither portion states the argument's final conclusion.

The correct answer is C.

5.0 GMAT™ Official Guide Verbal Review Question Index

5.0 GMAT™ Official Guide Verbal Review Question Index

The Verbal Review Question Index is organized by the section, difficulty level, and then by verbal concept. The question number, page number, and answer explanation page number are listed so that questions within the book can be quickly located.

Reading Comprehension Practice Questions—Chapter 4 Verbal Reasoning—Page 52

Difficulty	Concept	Question #	Question ID #	Page	Answer Explanation Page
Easy	Application	2	500175	52	98
Easy	Evaluation	12	500206	57	104
Easy	Evaluation	17	500193	58	107
Easy	Evaluation	19	500195	59	108
Easy	Evaluation	21	500138	60	109
Easy	Evaluation	23	500140	61	111
Easy	Evaluation	31	500360	64	116
Easy	Evaluation	35	500364	66	118
Easy	Inference	7	500506	55	101
Easy	Inference	8	500202	56	102
Easy	Inference	10	500204	57	103
Easy	Inference	11	500205	57	104
Easy	Inference	13	500207	57	105
Easy	Inference	14	500208	57	105
Easy	Inference	15	500191	58	106
Easy	Inference	22	500139	60	110
Easy	Inference	24	500141	61	112
Easy	Inference	26	500143	61	113
Easy	Inference	28	500357	63	114
Easy	Main Idea	4	500177	53	99
Easy	Main Idea	5	500504	54	100
Easy	Main Idea	20	500137	60	109
Easy	Supporting Idea	1	500174	52	98
Easy	Supporting Idea	3	500176	53	99

(Continued)

Difficulty	Concept	Question #	Question ID #	Page	Answer Explanation Page
Easy	Supporting Idea	6	500505	54	101
Easy	Supporting Idea	9	500203	56	103
Easy	Supporting Idea	16	500192	58	107
Easy	Supporting Idea	18	500194	59	108
Easy	Supporting Idea	25	500142	61	112
Easy	Supporting Idea	27	500144	62	114
Easy	Supporting Idea	29	500358	63	115
Easy	Supporting Idea	30	500359	64	116
Easy	Supporting Idea	32	500361	65	117
Easy	Supporting Idea	33	500362	65	117
Easy	Supporting Idea	34	500363	66	118
Medium	Application	49	500200	72	127
Medium	Application	50	500201	72	127
Medium	Application	54	500149	74	130
Medium	Application	69	500149	78	138
Medium	Application	76	500510	82	142
Medium	Application	81	500515	84	145
Medium	Evaluation	38	500198	68	120
Medium	Evaluation	41	500184	70	122
Medium	Evaluation	42	500185	70	123
Medium	Evaluation	52	500344	73	128
Medium	Evaluation	58	500350	75	132
Medium	Evaluation	60	500352	76	133
Medium	Evaluation	62	500354	76	134
Medium	Evaluation	66	500372	77	136
Medium	Evaluation	67	500147	78	137
Medium	Evaluation	72	500370	80	140
Medium	Evaluation	75	500376	81	141
Medium	Evaluation	77	500511	82	143
Medium	Inference	37	500197	67	119

Difficulty	Concept	Question #	Question ID #	Page	Answer Explanation Page
Medium	Inference	40	500183	69	121
Medium	Inference	43	500186	70	123
Medium	Inference	44	500187	70	124
Medium	Inference	45	500188	70	124
Medium	Inference	46	500189	71	125
Medium	Inference	47	500190	71	126
Medium	Inference	55	500347	74	130
Medium	Inference	56	500348	74	131
Medium	Inference	59	500351	75	133
Medium	Inference	63	500355	76	135
Medium	Inference	68	500148	78	138
Medium	Inference	80	500514	83	144
Medium	Main Idea	36	500196	67	119
Medium	Main Idea	48	500199	72	126
Medium	Main Idea	57	500349	74	132
Medium	Main Idea	61	500353	76	134
Medium	Main Idea	78	500512	82	143
Medium	Main Idea	79	500513	83	144
Medium	Supporting Idea	39	500182	69	121
Medium	Supporting Idea	51	500343	73	128
Medium	Supporting Idea	53	500345	73	129
Medium	Supporting Idea	64	500356	76	135
Medium	Supporting Idea	65	500145	77	136
Medium	Supporting Idea	70	500368	79	139
Medium	Supporting Idea	71	500369	79	139
Medium	Supporting Idea	73	500374	81	140
Medium	Supporting Idea	74	500375	81	141
Hard	Evaluation	86	500134	86	148
Hard	Evaluation	99	500227	91	156

(Continued)

Difficulty	Concept	Question #	Question ID #	Page	Answer Explanation Page
Hard	Inference	83	500131	85	146
Hard	Inference	84	500132	85	147
Hard	Inference	85	500133	86	147
Hard	Inference	87	500135	86	149
Hard	Inference	89	500213	87	150
Hard	Inference	91	500215	88	151
Hard	Inference	93	500221	89	152
Hard	Inference	94	500222	90	153
Hard	Inference	95	500223	90	153
Hard	Inference	96	500224	90	154
Hard	Inference	97	500225	90	155
Hard	Inference	101	500378	92	157
Hard	Inference	102	500379	93	158
Hard	Inference	103	500380	93	158
Hard	Inference	106	500383	95	160
Hard	Inference	108	500012	96	162
Hard	Inference	109	500027	96	162
Hard	Main Idea	88	500136	86	149
Hard	Main Idea	98	500226	91	155
Hard	Main Idea	107	500384	95	161
Hard	Supporting Idea	82	500338	85	146
Hard	Supporting Idea	90	500214	87	150
Hard	Supporting Idea	92	500220	89	152
Hard	Supporting Idea	100	500377	92	157
Hard	Supporting Idea	104	500381	94	159
Hard	Supporting Idea	105	500382	94	160
Hard	Supporting Idea	110	500034	96	163

Critical Reasoning Practice Questions—Chapter 4 Verbal Reasoning—Page 165

Difficulty	Concept	Question #	Question ID #	Page	Answer Explanation Page
Easy	Argument Construction	116	500518	166	237
Easy	Argument Construction	121	500294	169	242
Easy	Argument Construction	123	500306	170	245
Easy	Argument Construction	126	500266	171	248
Easy	Argument Construction	128	500252	172	251
Easy	Argument Construction	130	500321	173	253
Easy	Argument Construction	132	500120	174	255
Easy	Argument Construction	138	500387	176	261
Easy	Argument Construction	140	500389	177	263
Easy	Argument Construction	141	500390	177	264
Easy	Argument Construction	142	500391	178	265
Easy	Argument Evaluation	111	500106	165	231
Easy	Argument Evaluation	112	500516	165	233
Easy	Argument Evaluation	113	500110	166	234
Easy	Argument Evaluation	115	500517	166	236
Easy	Argument Evaluation	119	500519	168	240
Easy	Argument Evaluation	120	500113	168	241
Easy	Argument Evaluation	122	500112	169	243
Easy	Argument Evaluation	124	500317	170	246
Easy	Argument Evaluation	129	500250	173	252
Easy	Argument Evaluation	131	500119	174	254
Easy	Argument Evaluation	133	500122	174	256
Easy	Argument Evaluation	134	500123	174	257
Easy	Argument Evaluation	135	500126	175	258
Easy	Argument Evaluation	136	500385	175	259
Easy	Argument Evaluation	139	500388	176	262
Easy	Argument Evaluation	144	500104	179	267
Easy	Argument Evaluation	145	500207	179	268

(Continued)

Difficulty	Concept	Question #	Question ID #	Page	Answer Explanation Page
Easy	Argument Evaluation	146	500257	179	269
Easy	Argument Evaluation	147	500268	180	270
Easy	Argument Evaluation	148	500304	180	271
Easy	Evaluation of a Plan	114	500314	166	235
Easy	Evaluation of a Plan	117	500114	167	238
Easy	Evaluation of a Plan	118	500235	167	239
Easy	Evaluation of a Plan	125	500262	171	247
Easy	Evaluation of a Plan	127	500269	172	250
Easy	Evaluation of a Plan	137	500386	175	260
Easy	Evaluation of a Plan	143	500393	178	266
Medium	Argument Construction	154	500300	183	277
Medium	Argument Construction	155	500253	183	278
Medium	Argument Construction	156	500230	183	279
Medium	Argument Construction	157	500304	184	280
Medium	Argument Construction	158	500102	184	281
Medium	Argument Construction	161	500107	186	284
Medium	Argument Construction	163	500265	186	286
Medium	Argument Construction	164	500286	187	287
Medium	Argument Construction	165	500228	187	288
Medium	Argument Construction	168	500285	188	291
Medium	Argument Construction	170	500237	189	293
Medium	Argument Construction	173	500295	191	296
Medium	Argument Construction	175	500520	192	298
Medium	Argument Construction	176	500521	192	299
Medium	Argument Construction	177	500522	193	300
Medium	Argument Construction	178	500395	193	301
Medium	Argument Construction	179	500396	194	302
Medium	Argument Construction	186	500091	197	309
Medium	Argument Construction	190	500184	199	314
Medium	Argument Construction	191	500215	200	316

Difficulty	Concept	Question #	Question ID #	Page	Answer Explanation Page
Medium	Argument Construction	194	500276	201	319
Medium	Argument Construction	195	500297	202	321
Medium	Argument Construction	196	500358	202	323
Medium	Argument Evaluation	160	500234	185	283
Medium	Argument Evaluation	162	500281	186	285
Medium	Argument Evaluation	166	500229	188	289
Medium	Argument Evaluation	167	500232	188	290
Medium	Argument Evaluation	169	500292	189	292
Medium	Argument Evaluation	171	500111	190	294
Medium	Argument Evaluation	172	500282	190	295
Medium	Argument Evaluation	174	500322	191	297
Medium	Argument Evaluation	183	500401	196	306
Medium	Argument Evaluation	184	500402	196	307
Medium	Argument Evaluation	187	500118	198	311
Medium	Argument Evaluation	188	500126	198	312
Medium	Argument Evaluation	189	500173	199	313
Medium	Argument Evaluation	192	500228	200	317
Medium	Argument Evaluation	193	500236	201	318
Medium	Evaluation of a Plan	149	500121	181	272
Medium	Evaluation of a Plan	150	500124	181	273
Medium	Evaluation of a Plan	151	500125	181	274
Medium	Evaluation of a Plan	152	500127	182	275
Medium	Evaluation of a Plan	153	500129	182	276
Medium	Evaluation of a Plan	159	500244	185	282
Medium	Evaluation of a Plan	180	500397	194	303
Medium	Evaluation of a Plan	181	500399	195	304
Medium	Evaluation of a Plan	182	500400	195	305
Medium	Evaluation of a Plan	185	500403	197	308
Hard	Argument Construction	197	500236	203	324

(Continued)

Difficulty	Concept	Question #	Question ID #	Page	Answer Explanation Page
Hard	Argument Construction	201	500275	205	329
Hard	Argument Construction	202	500280	205	330
Hard	Argument Construction	205	500100	206	333
Hard	Argument Construction	207	500118	207	335
Hard	Argument Construction	210	500261	209	338
Hard	Argument Construction	212	500309	210	340
Hard	Argument Construction	214	500241	211	342
Hard	Argument Construction	219	500297	213	347
Hard	Argument Construction	223	500293	215	351
Hard	Argument Construction	228	500404	218	356
Hard	Argument Construction	230	500406	218	358
Hard	Argument Construction	231	500407	219	359
Hard	Argument Construction	232	500408	219	360
Hard	Argument Construction	233	500411	219	361
Hard	Argument Construction	234	500412	220	362
Hard	Argument Construction	235	500527	220	363
Hard	Argument Construction	236	500528	221	364
Hard	Argument Construction	240	500158	223	370
Hard	Argument Construction	243	500249	224	374
Hard	Argument Construction	247	500347	226	378
Hard	Argument Construction	249	500251	227	380
Hard	Argument Construction	250	500078	228	381
Hard	Argument Construction	251	500326	228	382
Hard	Argument Construction	252	500085	229	383
Hard	Argument Construction	253	500063	229	384
Hard	Argument Evaluation	199	500257	204	327
Hard	Argument Evaluation	203	500327	206	331
Hard	Argument Evaluation	206	500279	207	334
Hard	Argument Evaluation	208	500246	208	336
Hard	Argument Evaluation	209	500109	208	337

Difficulty	Concept	Question #	Question ID #	Page	Answer Explanation Page
Hard	Argument Evaluation	211	500248	209	339
Hard	Argument Evaluation	213	500316	210	341
Hard	Argument Evaluation	215	500328	211	343
Hard	Argument Evaluation	216	500291	212	344
Hard	Argument Evaluation	217	500239	212	345
Hard	Argument Evaluation	218	500260	213	346
Hard	Argument Evaluation	220	500318	214	348
Hard	Argument Evaluation	221	500289	214	349
Hard	Argument Evaluation	222	500276	215	350
Hard	Argument Evaluation	229	500405	218	357
Hard	Argument Evaluation	237	500530	221	365
Hard	Argument Evaluation	238	500139	222	366
Hard	Argument Evaluation	239	500147	222	368
Hard	Argument Evaluation	241	500166	223	371
Hard	Argument Evaluation	242	500192	224	372
Hard	Argument Evaluation	244	500289	225	375
Hard	Argument Evaluation	245	500318	225	376
Hard	Argument Evaluation	246	500339	226	377
Hard	Argument Evaluation	248	500049	227	379
Hard	Evaluation of a Plan	198	500255	203	326
Hard	Evaluation of a Plan	200	500273	204	328
Hard	Evaluation of a Plan	204	500320	206	332
Hard	Evaluation of a Plan	224	500325	216	352
Hard	Evaluation of a Plan	225	500104	216	353
Hard	Evaluation of a Plan	226	500108	217	354
Hard	Evaluation of a Plan	227	500101	217	355

To register for the GMAT™ exam, go to www.mba.com/register

Appendix A   Answer Sheets

Reading Comprehension Answer Sheet

1.	23.	45.	67.	89.
2.	24.	46.	68.	90.
3.	25.	47.	69.	91.
4.	26.	48.	70.	92.
5.	27.	49.	71.	93.
6.	28.	50.	72.	94.
7.	29.	51.	73.	95.
8.	30.	52.	74.	96.
9.	31.	53.	75.	97.
10.	32.	54.	76.	98.
11.	33.	55.	77.	99.
12.	34.	56.	78.	100.
13.	35.	57.	79.	101.
14.	36.	58.	80.	102.
15.	37.	59.	81.	103.
16.	38.	60.	82.	104.
17.	39.	61.	83.	105.
18.	40.	62.	84.	106.
19.	41.	63.	85.	107.
20.	42.	64.	86.	108.
21.	43.	65.	87.	109.
22.	44.	66.	88.	110.

Critical Reasoning Answer Sheet

111.	140.	169.	198.	227.
112.	141.	170.	199.	228.
113.	142.	171.	200.	229.
114.	143.	172.	201.	230.
115.	144.	173.	202.	231.
116.	145.	174.	203.	232.
117.	146.	175.	204.	233.
118.	147.	176.	205.	234.
119.	148.	177.	206.	235.
120.	149.	178.	207.	236.
121.	150.	179.	208.	237.
122.	151.	180.	209.	238.
123.	152.	181.	210.	239.
124.	153.	182.	211.	240.
125.	154.	183.	212.	241.
126.	155.	184.	213.	242.
127.	156.	185.	214.	243.
128.	157.	186.	215.	244.
129.	158.	187.	216.	245.
130.	159.	188.	217.	246.
131.	160.	189.	218.	247.
132.	161.	190.	219.	248.
133.	162.	191.	220.	249.
134.	163.	192.	221.	250.
135.	164.	193.	222.	251.
136.	165.	194.	223.	252.
137.	166.	195.	224.	253.
138.	167.	196.	225.	
139.	168.	197.	226.	

Notes

Notes

Notes

Notes

Notes

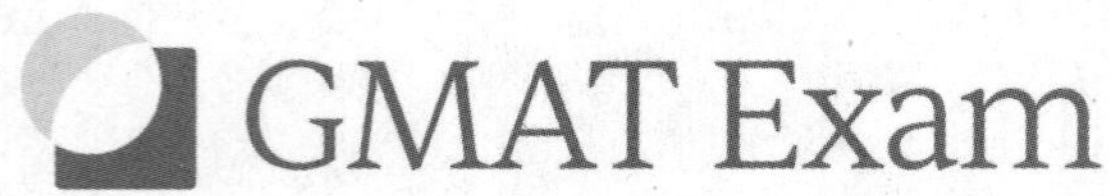

Elevate your prep with our free resources

GMAT Official Starter Kit

Sample 70+ real GMAT questions, a guided review, and Official Practice Exams 1 & 2, which simulate the real exam format and test-taking experience.

GMAT 6-Week Study Planner

Gain exclusive insights and strategies directly from the creators of the GMAT Exam. Utilize this guide to maintain a structured schedule, inform your activities, and monitor your progress.

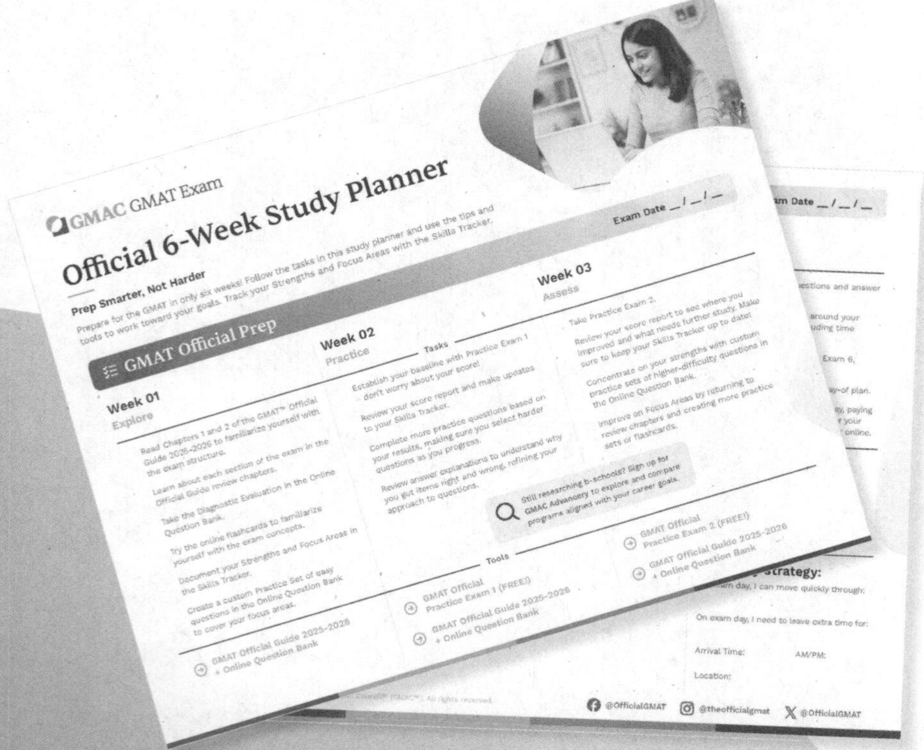

GMAT Official Starter Kit

GMAT 6-Week Study Planner